THE ADMINISTRATIVE FACTOR

THE ADMINISTRATIVE FACTOR

Papers in Organization, Politics and Development

BERNARD SCHAFFER

Fellow in Political Science and Public Administration
Institute of Development Studies
University of Sussex

and

Professorial Fellow
University of Sussex

FRANK CASS : LONDON

This collection first published 1973 in Great Britain by
FRANK CASS AND COMPANY LIMITED
67 Great Russell Street, London WC1B 3BT

and in the United States of America by
FRANK CASS AND COMPANY LIMITED
c/o International Scholarly Books Services, Inc.
P.O. Box 4347, Portland, Oregon 97208

ISBN 0 7146 2979 0

Library of Congress Catalog Card No. 72–92978

74. 2106
Printed in Great Britain by
Northumberland Press Limited,
Gateshead

To S. and S. J.

CONTENTS

CONTENTS

PREFACE

These papers were written over some twenty years, based on work done in British, Australian and American universities. They cover topics as apparently diverse as defence and development, the history of ideas, and politics and management. However, there are certain continuing themes. They are fairly consistently concerned with two aspects of the emergence of the administrative state during the past and present centuries. One aspect is the increasing impact of relations with authorities on the lives of groups and individuals. These facts of experience had a profound effect on the substance of political debate and education. A second aspect has been the particular experiments of political development.

There were underlying paradoxes here. Politics became increasingly devoted to questions of management, bureaucracy and reorganization. At the same time, the actual study of administration moved its ground, for many reasons, from early if borrowed confidence to later if more sensitive uncertainties, just as administrative training, a very different thing, was being rapidly expanded and institutionalized. Men used formal organizations more, while the independent, autonomous continuity of these institutions showed, despite the mid-Victorian development of responsibility, how little they could be trusted as neutral instruments. The more sophisticated the associated study of organization became, the less happy could the student of public administration be with the reification of the organization, the goal or the decision. A less metaphorical study of situations was being hindered by the vocabulary of many of their observers as well as their participants. Unsatisfactory as they were, familiar models of the institutions of the administrative state and the language of western management were used in the establishment of new states and development administration. The transferability of institutions is doubtless limited, but it became all too easy to blame apparent failures on pecularities of recipient societies rather than the harsh facts of poverty.

Two balancing themes emerge in some of the later papers. It becomes important to work out satisfactory concepts of organization, policy and decision. In particular, the outcomes of organizational situations have to be explained. Here the institutional impact seems to be a major factor. Institutionalization is a great decisional force. But political statement and ideology, policies and programmes are not the only aspects of organized situations which matter. There is also the rank and file official, the particular client, the discrete item of service. These face to face relationships also have to be explained. This should be the test of the administrative state, and a way of comparing one situation with another. The last paper suggests one way of making the comparison.

The papers are arranged in rough chronological order in each of the three sections. Wherever it seemed to make for clarity I have departed from that rule, as in the first section where the papers fell into three groups: nineteenth-century ideas, administrative education and the machinery of government. There are moments when the papers, inevitable in the discussion of politics and administration, express opinions, comment and forecasts which hindsight might well wish revised. Some favourite themes and texts come up more than once. I trust the reader to exercise his amused tolerance. Where the authors cited have later changed their style or status, like the late Lord Bridges or the many academic promotions, I have thought it right to leave them as they were at the time the papers were written. Other references, for example to works described as 'recent', should also be understood in terms of the dates given.

Some of the debt of gratitude due to many friends and colleagues is indicated here and there. I should particularly like to mention my former colleagues at Queensland University, Professor S. R. Davis, Dr. R. E. Dowling, Professor C. A. Hughes, and Professor K. W. Knight; Mr. K. E. Robinson and Professor Dennis Austin, formerly of the Institute of Commonwealth Studies, London; Professor R. S. Parker and Professor David Corbett; past or present colleagues at Sussex or the Institute of Development Studies, like Professors F. G. Bailey, B. D. Graham and C. T. Leys; and at least one of many Cornell friends, Professor Douglas Ashford.

Few of these papers could have been written without the patient and long-suffering help of pre-occupied and conscientious officials in many agencies and several countries. Many of them are close friends, but it seems that they must, as a later paper discusses, remain anonymous. The relation between the academic student of administration and the practitioner is delicate and can be difficult: much more so than with some other social sciences less centrally concerned with a critique of the institutional impact itself. I am the more grateful for the understanding and support I have received. I am indebted to the following for permission to reproduce papers contained in this volume:

The University of Queensland Press, for Chapter 1, published in the *Australian Journal of Politics and History*, Vol. III No. 1.

The Royal Institute of Public Administration, for Chapter 2, published in *Public Administration* (London), Vol. XXXVIII.

Public Administration (Sydney), for Chapters 3, 4, 6, 7 and 10, published in Vol. XXI No. 4, Vol. XVII No. 4, Vol. XVII No. 2, Vol. XIX No. 1, and Vol. XXIII No. 4 respectively.

The New Zealand Institute of Public Administration, for Chapter 5, published in the *New Zealand Journal of Public Administration*, Vol. XXV, No. 1.

The Public Administration Committee of the Joint University Council for Social and Public Administration, for Chapter 8, published in the *Public Administration Committee Bulletin*, No. 5.

Princeton University Press, for Chapters 9 and 11, published in *World Politics*, Vol. XV No. 2 and Vol. XVIII No. 1 respectively.

Leicester University Press for Chapter 12, published in the *Journal of Commonwealth Political Studies*, Vol. IV No. 1.

The Clarendon Press, for Chapter 15, published in *Political Studies*, Vol. XIX No. 3.

BERNARD SCHAFFER
Sussex

I

ADMINISTRATION AND ORGANIZATION

Modern politics is about the administrative state. What we can do in groups and even as individuals depends on relations with authorities. Hence political debate liked to assume that public organizations would work: fabianism assumed public administration; planning assumed implementation. But as the modern state was experienced, the assumptions seemed less easy and so the nature of the debate changed.

From the origins of modern conditions in the last century we can see early discussions about what administration actually was and how it should be done, and about how the organizations should be arranged. From this emerged too certain ideas about the relations between politics and administration and about how administration could be prepared for, studied and taught.

The first group of papers deals with those questions. A second group deals with the actual problems and experience of organizational change. For part of the last century the belief in the discovery of responsibility was such that public organizational change scarcely seemed a question for political debate. Later in the century, questions of reorganization (structure change) were distinguished from reform (personnel matters). Through this century there has been a continuing and partly political debate about what is now called major administrative reform: with bureaux of municipal reform in the U.S. early in the century; with major reorganization inquiries in America, in Britain with the Haldane report, and then with all their successors. How should reorganization be organized?

1

THE IDEA OF THE MINISTERIAL DEPARTMENT

Bentham, Mill and Bagehot

The ministerial department is a peculiar form of public organization which had to be invented. It emerged specifically in the mid-Victorian years. Before and since then, and elsewhere, the central machinery of government has had very different forms, and will go on doing so. In particular, the ministerial department is the ideal type for the function of responsibility. Such an exclusive emphasis may not always be possible. What, then, did responsibility mean and how could it be organized? Many of the erstwhile conditions have now gone, but the problem remains and what Bentham said about the trustees of his day has its severe contemporary applications.

THE DEPARTMENT

There were three major inventions in British governmental machinery in the nineteenth century. One was the classified civil service recruited by open, academic, competitive examination. The second was the elected, multi-purpose local authority. The third was the ministerial department. None of these was a sudden or independent invention, but their importance cannot be questioned. They have received unequal study. The history of the ministerial department has received least attention of all. The outlines are therefore unfamiliar and its peculiarity unappreciated. The purpose of this article is to summarize one aspect of the history of the ministerial department: the debate about notions of responsibility and organization from Bentham to Bagehot which went along with actual developments in central government practice.

The ministerial department came to have certain specific features. It was to be headed by a single political person, at once exclusively responsible, the most powerful and yet the most temporary element in the organization. Underneath the Minister would be certain senior officers reporting directly to the Permanent Head and appointed, like him, in consultation with the Prime Minister and the Permanent Secretary to the Treasury. The Minister would be responsible for these appointments. The Permanent Head would be at once the chief adviser to the Minister and the general manager of the department. As the general manager he would also be the accounting officer. Thence downwards there would be a continuing hierarchy. The patterning of departmental top organization on the grading of the civil service administrative class would create a type of organization characterized by filtering and therefore by strain. What would appear at the top was what Sir John Henry Woods called a super-bottleneck. This sort of organization was quite different in its shape and methods from what can be called the norm of executive organization. A comparison of the organization of the Treasury with that of the Board of Inland Revenue would show the distinction clearly. At the head of the pyramid would be an assistant not in any sense a deputy or jointly responsible person. The organization of this 'normal' department would reflect civil service classification and a distinction between administrative and other work and its dominance over such other work. The top of the pyramid would tend to consist only of the top grades of the administrative class.[1]

This was an organization of a peculiar type, dependent on parliamentary scrutiny and financial control, a reformed civil service and a restriction of departmental functions. If the organization was peculiar, it was still more peculiar that it should be held to be the best, and even the only, form of organization for central government. The nineteenth-century invention was precisely the belief that ministerial responsibility demanded departmental organization of this and only of this type, and that ministerial responsibility and departmental organization should be applied throughout central government.[2] One side of this was the actual development of the preconditions, for example the reform of public finance beginning with Graham's work at the Admiralty in the 1830s. This was gradual not sudden. So until the 1850s, that is for a generation after the Reform Bill, central government still freely used organizations other than ministerial departments and new non-ministerial organizations were set up. Thereafter this ceased to be true. Irresponsible and variegated eighteenth century and earlier forms were abolished or absorbed by ministerial departments. Nineteenth-century experiments in non-ministerial organization were replaced. No new non-ministerial organizations were created. New and major ministerial departments—for agriculture and for education, for example—appeared. This was a striking tendency. It continued until in this century a further transition occurred.

These developments have recently been discussed elsewhere.[3] Some aspects (like the failure of the first Poor Law Board) are familiar; others (debates about the Office of Woods and Works, for example) are less so. But the ideological side has scarcely been discussed at all. When it has, the assumption has been that Bentham was the first to enunciate the idea of a responsible ministerial department; that at the height of its acceptance, the doctrine was reiterated by Mill; and that there you have the main outlines. This is misleading about Bentham and Mill and indeed represents an inadequate statement of the whole development. Today, when there are anxious questions about the future of the ministerial department and about the whole problem of providing for responsibility in government, it may be worthwhile to re-examine the matter.

BENTHAM

What had Bentham to say about responsibility? For Bentham responsibility was a matter of being open to punishment. It was a liability rather for things done than for a failure to do anything. Public offices were places where such misdeeds were especially likely to occur. Some types of office made this the more likely. Bentham's contribution therefore began as an attack on one particular existing system. He was attacking the remnants of eighteenth-century administration in what he saw: the non-ministerial organization of the system before 1832. The ministerial offices of the years before 1832 were themselves specifically free from some of the later conditions of the ministerial norm: Lord Palmerston, for example, regarded a permanent civil service as a danger to, not a condition of, ministerial responsibility.[4] The fifty years of economical reform before 1832 did not blunt Bentham's attack. He was concerned with the actual corruption and influence that seemed to him to be consciously hidden by abstract nonsense about independence.

> The country justices are all gentlemen; their mess, like the member of parliament's, is all sweet without bitter, all power without obligation. What they vouchsafe to do, the country is to think itself obliged to them for: they do just as much as they like, and as they like it, and when they like it.[5]

What was wanted, Bentham thought, was officials in precisely the opposite position to that of the country justices: officials who would do as much as the country liked as and when the country liked it, and do it as their obligation. This was the object of concern, not abstract qualities like independence.[6]

The second thing about Bentham, however, was that the solution he recommended was not the responsible Minister of nineteenth-century Parliaments and Cabinets at all, but something much more like the American version. He was all in favour of 'single-seated functionaries' and dependence on the 'public opinion tribunal' as a way of securing 'appropriate moral aptitude'. The Minister was the person in a position of highly concentrated and public accountability. His reputation was the result of his own actions. This included an undertaking of responsibility for his subordinates lest they do evil on his behalf.[7] But Bentham did not want Ministers elected to or voting in the Parliament, though they would have certain rights of speaking and initiative there: thus would their influence be honest not dishonest. He acknowledged the similarity to American government.[8] The beliefs that led him against boards led him against parliamentary Ministers.

Certainly Bentham's views of the society around him did lead to an attack on boards, commissions and trusts, to some sort of design for pyramidal departments and to a number of interestingly specific prescriptions. The gravamen of his case was that answerability for results was weakened by the aggregation of positions constituting a board. A board was a screen behind which power could be abused and punishment miscarry. A multiplicity of members meant greater influence, greater protection and greater indifference to shame. The fellowship of the board would provide applause for a member or compensation elsewhere for disgrace. Closed methods failed to apportion public disgrace according to desert or public approval according to merit. Emulation or exertion were submerged under lassitude and neglect.

The evil went beyond the members of a board. The more deeply you penetrated subordinate levels the worse the abuses and the less the performance.

A Board, my Lord, is a screen. The lustre of good desert is obscured by it—ill desert, shrinking behind, eludes the eye of censure—wrong is covered by it with a presumption of right, stronger and stronger in proportion to the number of folds: and each member having his own circle of friends, wrong, in proportion again to the number, multiplies its protectors.[9]

This was so, as he said elsewhere in a less familiar passage,

not so much on the part of the members of the board itself, which by the prominence of its situation engages in some measure the public eye, as on the part of the subordinate functionaries; whose functions while they have little to attract the eye of the public have much to repel it, and who are the less looked after by the public in proportion as they are supposed to be well looked after by their superiors at the board.[10]

Here Bentham is indeed concentrating on the effects of the board on subordinates and is almost prepared to weaken his attack on board members to do this.

From his limited views of the motivation of conduct and of the functions of government Bentham devised a picture of the sort of organization he wanted. It would be one in which the 'exclusion of delay, vexation and expense' would be achieved with the appropriate 'aptitudes' at various levels. The necessary conditions were responsibility, the 'responsible location principle' and the fear of consequences. These conditions, which should replace independence, differed. Responsibility, indeed, depended partly on fear. It would be created by 'subordinateness' and 'accountableness'. Subordinateness was a result of certain powers—of direction, 'suspension', 'dislocation', 'suppletion' and punishment. So, if there was to be responsibility, the subordinate must be frightened of his 'superordinate' because of these suspensive and other powers. He must also be subject to directions. The directive power itself was insufficient. Further, it was only efficacious when the subordinate was accountable. By accountability was meant the necessity to report on the performance of operations undertaken 'in consequence of, and compliance with', the superordinate's directions. All these conditions of responsibility were to be distinguished. Subordinateness and accountability were the main conditions, though not the same thing: other departments were accountable but not subordinate to the Finance Department.[11]

Responsibility meant subordination and accounting for results. Fear was the ultimate sanction. This took Bentham to certain conclusions about pay, tenure and promotion. 'The military functionary is paid for being shot at. The civil functionary is paid for being spoken and written at.' Thus he argued that confusion about responsibility, reward and punishment had maximized official expense in English government. Officials ought to be rewarded for taking on their obligations; but they would carry them out for fear of punishment. This precept, accepted generally, was not applied in the English administration, in which functionaries professed responsibility in proportion to their rewards, present or expected. 'Note that only by the expectation of eventual evil (punishment included) can responsibility be established: neither by expectation of eventual good or by possession of good (reward included) can it be established.'[12] Bentham's most significant conclusion was about organizational structure: the need for a pyramidal hierarchy with one

individual at the top. Here he recommended a departmental form
and anticipated something of the Northcote-Trevelyan principles
for civil service classification; the association of the two things was
important. He wrote that a division between levels of control on
the one hand and lower levels of information on the other hand
would provide a better distribution of work than would many-
membered boards. He discussed the allocation of functions at the
top and bottom of 'the official climax'. He distinguished between
situations as they demanded talent, simple trust or trust and talent.[13]

His general recommendations contained specific criticisms and
further recommendations. For example, he said that people were
confused about arbitrariness.

> That which in the exercise of official functions constitutes arbitrary
> power is—not the unity of the functionary but his exemption from
> control, including the obligation, contemporary or eventual, of
> assigning reasons for his acts.

A second example was his argument that the practice of staggering appointments and limiting conditions of eligibility tended to
make boards self-perpetuating: retiring members would be re-
appointed and would later do the same for their beneficent colleagues; the board would degenerate into 'imbecility, corruption or
ineptitude'. He instanced the Bank of England and the East India
Company. The solution was 'the here-proposed all-comprehensive
temporary non-relocability system'. Of all those enjoying independence, trustees were the worst, and of all trustees, unpaid ones
were the worst. 'The more confidence a man is likely to meet with
the less he is likely to deserve. Jealousy is the life and soul of
government.' Individual and if possible contractual management
was the answer: this was how Panopticon was to be managed. He
observed that the branches of service most essential to the comfort
and luxury of the monarch were not put into the hands of boards.
Here a necessary exception was made to the normal use of boards
in a corrupt government,

> for were it in the hands of a board, each member in reality, as
> well as in name and pretence, becoming a part in the business, what
> is sufficiently understood is—that there never would be a house fit
> for service.

What was required for the monarch's house was also required for
Bentham's ideal penal house, Panopticon. Boards would be as unsuitable for that as they were—Russian experience, he said had
shown this throughout the eighteenth century—for effecting great
schemes of codification or improvement.[14]

Bentham did approach the general design and some of the details of the normal, ministerial, civil service department. But he was attracted to the American model. He ignored the reforms that had already taken place. Furthermore, despite his general attitude to boards and to departments, his inventive genius and his honest and ample parentheses provided a good deal of possible assistance to those who favoured non-ministerial organization itself. To take one instance: he suggested the use of annual and other reports as a link between the legislature and organizations otherwise limited in responsibility. His doctrine about annual reports was reflected in some of Chadwick's opposition to ministerial control and, in particular, in the Kennedy case in the 1850s. Kennedy, who at the time was one of the official Commissioners of Woods, objected to the Treasury's exerting any control over him and specifically over his annual report: this was to be a full and independent preparation linking his administration directly to Parliament and, if possible, to a special parliamentary committee.[15] Bentham saw the ways in which a board's decision could be fortified against outside opinion. There were suggestions about the use of powers of direction, 'dislocation' and inspection as controls over less responsible organizations. His distinctions between subordinateness, accountability and responsibility elucidate the variety of relations that may exist between one official and another. If one applies his argument to relations between one organization and another (as Bentham did with his example of the Finance Department) one can see that they may be linked by certain degrees of responsibility and subordination without being united. Here is an approach to an understanding and a classification of relations between a ministerial department and a non-ministerial organization.[16]

In the main stream of his argument, Bentham himself assumed 'a form of government of which corruption is the main instrument'[17] swarming with boards that were merely screens for abuse, multipliers of office and defences against punishment. But his footnotes did allow for boards in certain cases. At one point he said quite clearly and gave a list which suggested[18] that they could be used for very routine or very open work. He also implied that board members could be useful watches on each other. This tallied, not with what he himself had said elsewhere, but with an argument sometimes used later in the nineteenth century. 'It would be an error if ... a conclusion were formed that there exists not any case in which government by bodies corporate or boards can be conducive to the legitimate ends of government.' His possible examples included, 'where neither extraordinary talent nor extraordinary exertion is necessary, ... giving out money by others' direction, ... where misapplication would be manifest or easily detected, ... and insofar as division of power is necessary to good government'.[19] In his *Principles of Penal Law* he said that plurality in administrative councils might be some form of precaution against abuse of authority, though unity was *prima facie* desirable for responsibility. He thought that the advantages of plurality and unity might be combined if there were a single head and a subordinate council of associates and voting were avoided.[20] This bore an interesting resemblance to the top organization of the East India Company of which Bentham was thinking as well as to later arrangements for Indian government and other later institutions like Sir Horace Plunkett's Irish Department of Agriculture and Technical Instruction.

Altogether Bentham's list is an interesting contrast and sometimes a parallel with later non-ministerial forms. One would say that he was nearer to ideas of 'hiving off executive work'—as in the old German departments—than to such of our own contemporary uses as are the opposite of that. Indeed, some of his statements now provide a starting point for that understanding of the difference between administrative and executive posts that is of importance to any appreciation of the significance of non-ministerial organization. He said that precedent was of limited use as a basis for action. He provided a careful analysis of 'executive power'. His words about high and low level posts are enlightening:

> ... At the top and at the bottom of the official climax the greatest scope for the union of functions exists: at the top because there the functions are chiefly of the directive kind: and to the directive function, exercise may, in minute proportions of time, be given to the operations of functionaries, in indefinite number; at the bottom, because for the performance of the functions, though of the executive kind, the demand for performance will generally be so infrequent.[21]

Bentham did at times admit that the normal conditions of responsibility would not always be sufficient for enforcing 'appropriate aptitude' in officials and organizations. The public opinion tribunal could secure moral aptitude by its enforcement of responsibility through the single-seated functionary as Minister. But certain situations required more than moral aptitude. The normal conditions would not necessarily be sufficient where intellectual and active abilities were required. Here additional powers—administrative ones, for example—would be needed. And there would be a problem of finding evidence in case of official transgression.[22]

He saw that there were problems and indeed limitations in ministerial responsibility and organization. He was prepared to admit that the Minister's responsibility was limited by the possible ex-

tent of his vigilance, and that his responsibility depended on directive and dislocative powers which could not usefully apply to
subordinates so distant that an 'exercise' was effected before it could
be 'excluded'. These may have appeared marginal admissions to
Bentham; however illegitimate it may be, it is impossible for us
now to read him without feeling that these admissions go almost
too far.[23]

AFTER BENTHAM

Bentham contributed a very great deal to the theory of the normal
ministerial department of the later nineteenth century. He did not
have that precisely in his mind, and he did not only say that. If one
adds later experience to what he said one could sometimes almost
get an explanation of the amount of deviation from the normal
department to be found in the present machinery of government.
Chadwick was his disciple. Nor was the discussion of responsibility
and organization in central government after Bentham simply a
matter of a swelling chorus of philosophical radical praise for the
ministerial department. If Bentham had mainly been concerned to
criticize the boards and trusts of eighteenth-century administration
and its aftermath, there were those who were prepared to criticize
Bentham. Thus in *The Statesman*, 1836, Sir Henry Taylor's statement that boards and commissions were in fact useful and no longer
irresponsible was put in words which so clearly echo Bentham's
that they read as a conscious refutation.

> Formerly it might be objected to boards that the sense of responsi-
> bility was weakened by division. But in these days responsibility
> is brought to bear with an excessive and intimidating force, and in
> many cases the plural is the preferable responsibility.

Taylor approved of commissions as a means by which the statesman
could get his work done out of doors. He certainly preferred commissions to parliamentary committees for their greater degree of
permanence and suggested that they should decide and draft necessary bills and instructions: they should see the business through.
He also gave some characteristic advice on their organization.[24]

His corrective is sharper than his defence of boards and commissions. It is instructive to read his account of a Minister's office.
The office was not yet a department and responsibility in such an
office was not at all the problem with which we are faced. Even
within those terms, Taylor thought that there were inevitable limits
on political responsibility and control. 'The far greater proportion
of duties which are performed in the office of a Minister are and

must be performed under no effective responsibility.' That was, where no question of politics, party or individual injustice was involved. There was an echo here of Palmerston's view in the 1830s that responsibility existed as long as you did not have, or allow too much to, permanent officials. Taylor added that the statesman had no time for the 'inventive and suggestive' portions of his functions. It was the job of the executive agents to work towards legislation on the topics whose execution was provided for by legislature: the chain of functionaries should be suggestive as well as executive. Parliamentary interposition in administrative business should be restricted to certain types of case and certain conditions.[25] Taylor developed this later. In a letter to Earl Grey in 1855 and in another letter of 1852[26] he suggested the type of speaking but non-voting Minister which Bentham had suggested and O'Higgins was later to suggest in Ireland as a compromise with the full ministerial type. Perhaps the most suggestive of Taylor's points were the emphasis on the ability to work through others, the dangers of popularity and accessibility and the need 'in high and important spheres of action' for a frequent setting aside of general administrative rules.[27]

Taylor wrote when the flow of reform which had in fact begun in Bentham's day was fuller and more obvious. His concern was practical not constitutional. Hence his specific marginalia in the thesis of ministerial government picked out, for example, the uses of commissions and the translation of them into something more than bodies of enquiry only.

Then there is the position of Chadwick to be taken into account. Chadwick was a major Benthamite of the second generation. He was also a major propagator of boards and commissions. It is possible to explain away his support for non-ministerial organization. He soon enough ceased to be happy with his boards and commissions at the phase of enquiry. He had grasped the case against administration by commissions of technical experts: expert officials were another matter. He was much happier in the General Board of Health under Lord Morpeth than he had been in the first Poor Law Board.[28] Sympathetic Ministers and civil service status might have provided a better screen for the independence he was searching for than did the relatively public position of a board. But the fact is that Chadwick never understood that. A faithful disciple of Bentham, he was, like his master, never able to appreciate the advantages that would flow from an amateur, responsible, parliamentary Minister in charge of an official permanent machine. Nor could he distinguish clearly between the two. The contemporary ministerial office described by Taylor or by Palmerston did not encourage any assumption that it was with such vehicles that the Benthamite objectives would be reached.

In any case opposition to boards and non-ministerial organizations was not at all confined to philosophical radicals. It included angry Tories like Praed and perturbed Whigs like Sydney Smith.[29] The line of thought that has been called Gothic constitutionalism —the application of the spirit of early Victorian Gothic revivalism, of neo-romanticism in the field of government—was, like Taylor's, very different from the Benthamite. But it was sometimes, as in local government, indirectly sympathetic to some part of the Benthamite programme. The major figure in this line was Toulmin Smith.

It was, not surprisingly, Taylor's commissions which especially angered Toulmin Smith. He was indeed a spokesman of a widespread reaction in the 1830s and 1840s against radical commissions of enquiry, as in his *Government by Commission Illegal and Pernicious*, published in 1849. His case was that administration by Crown-appointed commissions, as well as the use of commissions of enquiry, was part of a contemporary centralization. He saw in this a threat to the natural rights expressed in the constitution according to Coke, in its principles of taxation and in its principles of local self-government. His first thesis was that particular legislation and, still more, administrative action or extra-parliamentary legislation were, irrespective of their content, things which lessened confidence in the existence of fundamental law. His second thesis was that the use of commissions was something which made encroachment particularly easy. Here he was attacking radical— generally Benthamite—experiments 'of which the beginning is always a Commission of Inquiry and the end a General Board of paid Commissioners'. In theory the use of commissioners was inevitably bad. In practice government nomination led to a packed commission of enquiry whose interest it would be to recommend the creation of a permanent body.[30] He referred back for support to Sydney Smith who, though a radical of a sort, had in the 1830s indulged his gift of irony at the expense of the commissioners of that decade. Toulmin Smith was right to see that some of the legislation of his time would make new demands on administrative organization. The ultimate outcome was often to be a ministerial department; but the immediate outcome then was often a non-ministerial board.

Furthermore, it was precisely the Benthamite first Poor Law Board itself that was particularly influential in the formulation of the nineteenth-century case against non-ministerial organization. It was nicely put in 1847 by Sir George Grey, as Home Secretary, in moving a bill to amend the Act of 1834.[31] He (unlike Toulmin Smith) was not against central supervision or even against delegated legislation. He was pleading against imperfect and indirect responsibility, against the lack of a check and the lack of opportunity for self-defence, against the position in which the House, the Minister and the commissioners were all placed. Grey perceived two features of responsibility. As with Bentham, there was a desire for culpability, or at least for a check. This would be secured by the competence, the power in the Minister: the one feature depended on the other. Grey also assumed that ministerial competence demanded departmental organization. Such departments would need Ministers who would in the end take the blame because they did possess the power to set things aright. In the growth of this sort of attitude a role was played by the debates in the 1850s on the reform of Indian government and especially on the arrangements for transferring responsibility from the Company and the Board of Control to Ministers. Evidence of the influence of those debates on this matter is found in Mill, Bagehot and Helps. Indeed, Bagehot said that the new India Office was the only case in which 'the real constitution of a permanent office to be ruled by a permanent chief' —the form of the normal, homogeneous, ministerial department— was discussed. He implied that James Wilson, his predecessor at the *Economist* and a former Financial Secretary, was the only protagonist who then had understood the matter.[32]

By the 1860s there was not merely an opposition to the use of boards; there was a separate emphasis on the use of responsible Ministers at the head of homogeneous departments. Such Ministers were to be answerable, accountable or culpable, and in positions of what Bentham could have called competent super-ordination. But this could be expressed for reasons completely independent of Bentham's. One can think by then of such textbook writers as Alpheus Todd or Earl Grey.[33] Todd gave in 1866 a remarkably explicit formulation of the relationship of direct and universal ministerial responsibility to the established constitutional doctrines of the Cabinet and collective responsibility. He had, apparently, started his book before Erskine May's work was first available in 1854.[34] Secondly, Todd quoted Earl Grey on this matter of direct and universal responsibility.

> It is no arbitrary rule which requires that all holders of permanent offices must be subordinate to some Minister responsible to Parliament, since it is obvious that without it, the first principles of our system of government—the control of all branches of the administration by Parliament—would be abandoned.

The one meaning of responsibility (he thought of it as parliamentary control of Ministers) demanded the other. He assumed departmental organization.

Todd's treatment of some details is interesting: for example his discussion of such a tool of responsibility as parliamentary questions, whose origins he dated to Pitt but whose formal recognition to May's work of 1854.[35] Commissions—'Royal, statutory and departmental'—he restricted to enquiry. They were permissible only because of ministerial responsibility and only so long as they were not issued

> with a view to evade the responsibility of Ministers in any matter; or to do the work of existing departments of state, which possess all needed facilities for obtaining information upon questions of detail, and which are directly responsible to Parliament.[36]

Parliament, Ministers and departments made irresponsible bodies intolerable. They made them unnecessary, too: this was not quite what Bentham had been saying. For Todd and Grey the abolition of sinecures had led to the clear division between supreme and political offices on the one hand and subordinate non-political offices on the other hand.[37] For them responsibility existed not merely to provide punishment but as a part of the architecture of the constitution and therefore as an accepted end in itself. It was expressed in a combination of parliamentary Ministers, departments and permanent civil service with the royal prerogative. Bentham had not exactly foreseen this and might not have particularly liked it. The completion of financial and service reforms in 1866 and 1870 was to strengthen this arrangement of responsibility.

MILL AND BAGEHOT

By the 1860s there was a wide acceptance of responsibility and the ministerial department. This was not at all an exclusively Benthamite creation. The results had not been what Bentham had had in mind. One usually thinks of Mill and Bagehot as the main exponents in the 1860s of responsible organization for central government. But were they, was Mill even, merely reiterating in 1861 just what Bentham had said? Did Mill, more or less than Bentham, fully state a conception of the ministerial department itself? Was not Bagehot a better exponent than either of those two? When one comes to Bagehot one doubts whether he at any rate thought that ministerial responsibility and the ministerial department were generally accepted.

Mill had, long before the 1860s, edited, augmented and completed

Bentham's *Rationale of Judicial Evidence.* Some of the strongest of
Bentham's argument lay there. It was necessarily of more importance for the development of contemporary opinion than was,
say, the *Constitutional Code*.[38] However, like Bentham, Mill was
prepared to accept boards in certain practical instances. He had
supported Chadwick and the early administration of the Poor Law
Board. He later supported the idea of using a government commission to supervise London's water supply. Here was a specific
instance where the development of local government would make
the use of non-ministerial organization less necessary, for Mill
thought that such a commission should exist only until London
had its own single Council. Similarly one finds him like others of
his time forced to contemplate some deviation from the normal
ministerial situation in Irish and Indian government. In the 1860s he
mooted for Ireland a body something like the Land Commission
which was later to be created.[39]

The Indian situation was the more important. Bentham had seen
certain possibilities in a translation of the East India Company
into some sort of advisory council. Mill went further. Indeed, he
devoted much more space in the relevant section of his *Considerations on Representative Government* to the case for using such
conciliar forms in departmental organization than he did to the
attack on boards. Naturally he had defended the East India Company, his employers, but this was much more than a matter of
defence. He thought he saw something generally useful in such a
form. If there were to be political Ministers, should they not have
boards of advisers like the Court of Directors associated with them
and appointed by the government? This was relevant not merely to
India but also to naval and military affairs and indeed wherever
'it is not sufficient that the Minister should consult some one competent person'.[40] This was an admission into which as into many
of Bentham's one can read a great deal. It certainly suggested that
Mill did not think that pyramidal departments always necessarily
provided ministerial competence. Elsewhere he explained how the
necessity for special experience for handling affairs intelligently
demanded a council to check the Minister, to whom the Minister
should present all important measures and by whose suggestions
he would have to be affected. The council that had been provided
in the 1858 Act did not, he thought, go far enough at all. Such
councils should be strong. They would be alternatives to the purely
pyramidal department.

The utility of such special and, in a sense, responsible councils
—able, experienced, professional and consultative (but by no means
merely ciphers)—was something in which Mill obviously and deeply

believed as one of the good results and lessons of Company rule. It was not at all something which he merely expressed as an official. Nor was it an idea which he would have restricted to Indian government. It was something he thought that ministerial government would require.[41] This is an outstanding example of the influence of the Indian debates of the 1850s on the formation of opinion on responsibility and departmental organization.

Mill's main thesis was concerned with a rational democracy, the paradox of representative and responsible government. This required a distinction between the legislature and the Minister and between the Minister and the official. A chain of responsibility would run from the official to the legislature through the Minister. Boards would prevent this. His opposition to bureaucracy was unambiguous. He did not equivocate about the need for responsibility. Much of this he had expressed as early as 1835.[42] It was more fully put in 1861 in his *Considerations on Representative Government*. However much of Bentham Mill may by then have discarded, it is true that in this matter he came at times near to repeating what Bentham had already said. Bentham is duly quoted. With an individual head—with a council if necessary—there was complete responsibility; with a concurrence of more than one functionary in a decision responsibility did exist but penalties were diminished by being shared; with a board and secret decisions by majorities there was no responsibility. Mill's opening paragraph on this topic in *Representative Government* states a belief very similar to what was to be stated in the Haldane Report nearly eighty years later: that responsibility is best provided and the work best done if all functions of similar subject be allocated to single departments.

It is, however, just as true that here (as elsewhere) Mill saw a vital defect in the Benthamite inheritance: how, for example, to provide for competence as well as liability: as so often he saw both sides but could not make them meet. Further, as one can read significance into Bentham's exceptions, so one can into Mill's. He wrote that 'boards ... are only admissible in [executive government] when, for other reasons, to give full discretionary power to a single Minister would be worse'. No examples are given to elucidate this tautology. Some exception to Bentham was presumably intended there as when Mill added that if a spirit existed which made the individual member identify himself with the board, the suffering and so the responsibility of the board would be his also. Mill did not admit that this very non-Benthamite situation ever occurred; but the admission was there. We may find extra meaning in his discussion of conciliar forms. In this distinction between legislative, ministerial and official phases and in his attitudes to decentralization, to knowledge and power in public administration, to public administration as a skilled business, to the limitations which are therefore necessary to parliamentary interference in detail —in all these things we may detect starting points. From them would much later emerge such a belief in the division between phases of the governmental process as would in fact justify non-ministerial organization itself. This was to occur when the responsibility of a Minister for officials in a vast department became a problem and when other forms of responsibility seemed necessary.[43]

One does not always see the same things in Mill as in Bentham. Mill drew different conclusions than Bentham from the two sides of responsibility. His distinction between politics and administration was different from Bentham's distinction between high-level and lower or executive official functions. Mill was not merely concerned to abolish boards as apt devices for corruption: he was concerned to design a lofty structure for government and society. Too much had happened and been changed and discussed between Bentham's day and 1861 for Mill merely to repeat Bentham. Mill was much more interested in the differences between Ministers and officials and much more concerned with the problem of supplying Ministers with expert assistance. Bentham, it has been stressed, did not envisage departments like those that were the later Victorian norm however much he contributed to some points of the theory on which the departments were based. Though Mill's concern did enable him to stress some things with which Bentham had not been so concerned—notably the difference between Ministers and officials—he did not always get nearer than Bentham did to the actual type of responsible ministerial pyramidal department. And in some ways Bentham is nearer to us. At least Bentham and we ourselves look out on an untidy machinery of government. Mill's contemporary machinery was much nearer his ideal and it was effectively no nearer to ours than was Bentham's in the vital matter of scale.

If Mill was the first, Bagehot was the second of the two main exponents. There are two things to be noted about his position in this matter: he was a more definite proponent of the ministerial department than Mill (or Bentham); and he wrote as though on the defensive. In 1867—six years after Mill's *Considerations* and a year after Todd's *Parliamentary Government*—Bagehot published *The English Constitution*. He began with a quotation from Mill. Though he was analysing rather than prescribing, what he had to say about non-ministerial organization was broadly what had been said by Mill and the others before. Certain differences were important. For example, Bentham and Mill had been attracted to conciliar forms in departmental organization but Bagehot was specifically opposed to them. Mill thought that the Indian Government Acts had not gone far enough in providing them for the Indian Office. Bagehot specifically said they had gone all too far.[44]

Bagehot emphasized two main points which had not been so emphasized before. The first and more familiar was the need for any department in its own interest to be represented by a party political Cabinet Minister in the House. The point had begun to emerge from, for example, the first Poor Law Board and had been implied by Sir George Grey. It was Bagehot who elucidated the party aspect. The second—and this was new and very important if at first difficult to see—was the peculiar advantages such an essentially temporary Minister brought to the internal office organization of the department. It was, for instance, only the amateur Minister—the 'extrinsic' chief—who could bring 'the rubbish of office to the burning glass of common sense'.[45] The first point dominated his superb chapter 'On Changes of Ministry'. Having stated all the disadvantages of a situation in which all the heads of government are likely to be swept away together, he went on to justify it. He specifically dealt with the weakness of the alternative to which Bentham had been attracted—a defender who was the more expert in the affairs of the department because he was not a member of the House though he could attend and speak. He too drew on the experience with the old Poor Law Board in this matter of political defence.[46]

Bagehot's parliamentary argument was quite unequivocal. In some ways his second point was the more important because it was the more original. From them both he drew a picture that was much more than Bentham's or Mill's the normal ministerial, civil service, pyramidal department. This picture included a place for the permanent, official head. Further, Bagehot would have allowed no exception at all. Not merely did he not want boards and so forth, he did explicitly want all departments to have this and precisely this one form. This emphasis was a new and a very important part of the theory of the ministerial department. Here Bagehot had gone beyond analysis to prescription and here his statement was more rigid and more complete than that of Mill, Bentham or anyone else. One might add that Bagehot's view would seem to have been based on an assumption of relatively small offices and relatively similar functions in each of them.[47]

The second thing to be said about Bagehot is that if here he went beyond analysis it was because he did not see anything like a general acceptance of the complete norm in the contemporary machinery of government. His words are evidence of the discussion of this

norm in the 1860s. But they suggest both that it was not yet necessarily established and that to Bagehot at least agreement about it
did not look at all inevitable. He wrote, in this matter, as one
on the defensive. Thirty years before Bagehot wrote Palmerston
had thought of a civil service based on political patronage as a
defence against bureaucracy. Todd and others had explained that on
the contrary, it was the existence of a permanent civil service and
the division between it and politics that was an essential part of the
responsible system. Now Bagehot saw a threat to that system and
in particular to the sort of departmental organization which should
complete it, coming from a contemporary 'seizure of partiality'
towards bureaucracy.[48]

AFTER BAGEHOT

Was there any evidence in the contemporary machinery of
government or in the development of opinion in and after 1867 to
suggest that Bagehot was right to be on the defensive? Insofar as
the influence of German thought and the administration of the
Prussian state was then becoming fashionable he did have cause
for concern. Among other things one may recall that it was German
administration that specifically developed non-ministerial organisation and hived off executive work as an alternative to the use of
comprehensive ministerial departments. The contemporary writing
of, for example, Arthur Helps, Fitzjames Stephen and others showed
such a partiality in highly relevant matters as, two decades later,
did the early Fabians.[49] In practice, however tidy the central
machinery of government of that time may look to us, it did still
contain a good deal of deviation in non-ministerial organization
within departmental organization. In particular we should note that
Bagehot's idea of the departmental virtues of the amateur Minister
were not all widely understood then or for some time. An outstanding example of this can be found in the contemporary discussions
about the creation of a ministry of education. The Select Committee on Education of 1883-4 was bogged down in a discussion
of the wholly irrelevant and hypothetical question of whether the
sort of person appointed to a Lord Presidency or a Vice Presidency,
a separate ministry or a parliamentary commissionership and so
forth would have the more knowledge of education, museums, etc.[50]
Early and Mid-Victorian government was rich with experiment in
political posts that were not simply for departmental Ministers.

But Helps and the others were not prepared to go very far with
their criticisms. This is the more striking when one considers who
these critics were. Helps, for example, was a distinguished civil

servant very much after the model of Sir Henry Taylor in his
literary ambitions and writings, in his attitude to his subject and in
other ways. His general approach came from a belief in paternalism and governmental patronage. He thought this more not less
necessary as civilization advanced. A serene confidence breathes
through the work: the British people were easy to govern under a
constitutional monarchy; there were no grounds for fearing a
bureaucracy since officials were too lazy to be ambitious for power
Indeed he thought that the limits of interference, which included
ridicule as one of the most potent, meant that the danger was too
little not too much government. Now this was a very forward-look-
ing attitude in some ways and doubtless different from Bagehot's,
but it did not take him to a defence of non-ministerial organization.
There his approach was not unlike that of Mill. The legislative and
administrative functions were distinct and done by different bodies.
The legislature should interfere as little as possible in administration. 'Trust your agents' should be the note in public as well as in
private business. But, at the same time, 'fear of responsibility was
the great fear of modern times'. He had an idea for having 'coun-
cillors' attached to a department, who would be neither permanent
civil servants, nor permanent commissioners, nor the same as members of advisory bodies or legislative committees, but he had not
approved of the conciliar idea that had been discussed in the 1850s
for the India Department, or of the Board of Health of that time.[51]
Nor would Fitzjames Stephen—a Utilitarian still more concerned
with doubts about democratic implications than J. S. Mill and a
vigorous controversialist if ever there was one—state a stronger
attack than did Helps.[52] Such was the state of opinion in the 1870s.

The fact was that by the mid-Victorian period one would not have
found any important general statement, as against particular exceptions,[53] opposed to ministerial responsibility and the emerging
department. There was the long history of a demand for a ministry
of health. In 1852 Kay-Shuttleworth was prepared to propose the
administration of charities with education under the same Ministers.[54] Early in the Crimean campaign *The Times* was calling for
the unification of all army departments under a Secretary of State
for War no longer responsible for the Colonies.[55] That did not
mean that there was a clear understanding of the ministerial department in the 1850s—Kay-Shuttleworth and *The Times* were, apparently, speaking of ministerial boards. But it did mean a movement
to responsibility and single political heads. By the 1880s even
such a work as the Duke of Somerset's *Monarchy and Democracy*
was concerned to deprecate the effects of party solidarity and the

Cabinet on ministerial responsibility and not to belittle the latter. What a writer like Helps wanted (and the same would be true for Chadwick) was not non-ministerial organization at all. It was a recognition of public administration, of the role of the permanent, efficient and in that sense independent officials. And by the 1870s most realized that all this depended on having, not on avoiding, a ministerial system: these were not (as Bentham might have thought of boards and responsibility) alternatives; they were conditions of each other. This was a great step forward in theoretical understanding. One may, perhaps, now believe that non-ministerial organization itself can depend on and assist the ministerial system: but that was another step still and at that time had not been taken and was not, generally, needed in the processes and scale of work then being done.

There may still have been some preference for the ministerial board. There was still much confusion about what the Minister would do. The word Minister was itself avoided except by radicals: but reformers tended to think always in terms of ministerial departments. Would it be an over-simplification to say that while radicals of, say, the 1930s and 1940s were excited by the idea of public corporations, radicals of the 1870s were equally excited by the idea of ministries—for health, education, agriculture and so on? Critics like Stephen, Maine or Lecky were not prepared to say what would be said elsewhere and later by Faguet or Mosca.[56] There was no reflection of the reaction that in Canada or Australia, for example, was already leading to a demand for official independence from Ministers.[57]

In general nothing came to disturb the acceptance of the ministerial department until after the turn of the century. Popular descriptions and accepted textbooks almost entirely neglected non-ministerial organizations. For Traill the central executive so completely meant responsible ministerial departments that he could hardly think of the first Poor Law Board as a branch of the central executive at all. Nor did he find any non-ministerial organizations of his own time worth mentioning. Similarly all the departments that Porritt dealt with were 'represented by a Minister in Parliament'. Courtney did devote a short chapter to commissions like that for statute law revision. He even devoted a somewhat larger chapter to what he called 'Parliamentary Commissions'; but these, with one or two exceptions, were also either investigating or judicial bodies and he stressed Parliament's jealousy of such forms. The fate of the Poor Law Board he thought to have been inevitable. But his exceptions—Ecclesiastical and Charity Commissions, and the Light Railway Commission—were not, we can see now, without significance.[58] Anson mentioned 'departments which may be described as non-political' and said that these were 'the outlying departments of the Treasury, the Ecclesiastical Commission and the Charity Commission'. This was not, in fact, a full and certainly not a helpful indication of what existed or of the characteristics of non-ministerial organization. What it did do was to indicate the way in which the Treasury was thought of as a convenient cloak for such inconvenient creatures. Dicey did not recognize the field at all. His discussion of the Minister was limited to a reiteration of the contrast between his position of legal responsibility and *droit administratif*.[59]

If the general attitude was one of acceptance, it had been Bagehot who had supplied the fullest statement. The distinction between Minister and official, the uses of the political Minister in the House and the amateur Minister in the department, the need for homogeneity in the machinery of government and the exclusion of all exceptions—in all these ways Bagehot thoroughly expounded the ministerial department and thoroughly opposed non-ministerial organization. Bagehot's understanding of the Minister was echoed in, for example, Trollope's contemporary Palliser novels. There was a popularization of the idea of a Minister. There was now to be no exception. Bentham's preference for a presidential system could be forgotten. Critics were not prepared to engage in a direct attack. The paradox of the ministerial department—the accountable, potent but temporary Minister and the permanent but obedient official—was to be universally applied in central government. Where it was apparent non-ministerial organization would be opposed. Broadly speaking it was either not to be recognized or not to be understood if it made an appearance. This was after all a thoroughly good mid-Victorian attitude to the exotic, the inconvenient or the deviant. Smiles were permissible. 'You are a Lord now—and you will be a President soon and then perhaps a Secretary. The order of promotion seems odd but I am told that it is very pleasant.'[60] You could afford a decorative cloak of odd titles as long as the basis was a solid homogeneous conformity. You could assume that the machinery of government was what it ought to be: a group of essentially similar responsible departments, no more and no less; the rest was mere delightful trappings. Like other contemporary compromises this hid large exceptions and tremendous strains. These have since triumphed. We can only look back from the present chaos with envy and admiration at the splendour of the Victorian attempt to establish such an exclusive invention for central government organization.

NOTES

1 *cf.* Sir J. H. Woods, *Public Administration*, Vol. 26, 1948, pp. 85-91. J. R. Simpson, 'Organising the Larger Units', *British Management Review* reprint, July 1949.

2 *cf.* J. Morley, *Life of Gladstone*, London, 1908 ed., Vol. II, pp. 51-4, for the Ayrton case when ministerial responsibility received a precise exposition and a supreme tribute.

3 F. M. G. Willson, *Public Administration*, Vol. 33, 1955, pp. 43-58. S. E. Finer, *ibid.*, Vol. 30, 1952, pp. 329-60.

4 A. C. Benson and Viscount Esher (eds.), *Letters of Queen Victoria 1837-1861*, London, 1908, Vol. I, pp. 106-8, letter of 25 Feb. 1838.

5 J. Bowring (ed.), *The Works of Jeremy Bentham*, Edinburgh, 1843, Vol. IV, p. 376.

6 *Ibid.*, p. 316.

7 *Ibid.*, Vol. IX, Constitutional Code, Book II, Ch. IX, S. III, Arts. 3 and 7 and S. XXV, Art. 26. For a very different view see W. Blackstone, *Commentaries*, London, 1803, Vol. II, p. 36, or L. V. Harcourt (ed.), *Diaries and Correspondence of the Rt. Hon. George Rose*, London, 1860, *passim*.

8 *Works of Bentham*, Vol. III, Plan of Parliamentary Reform, Catechism, S. IV; and Vol. IX, Constitutional Code, Book II, Ch. VIII, Arts. 3-6 and 10 and at p. 206.

9 *Ibid.*, Vol. V, Letters on Scotch Reform, Letter II.

10 *Ibid.*, Vol. VI, p. 558.

11 *Ibid.*, Vol. IX, Constitutional Code, Book II, Ch. IX, S. III, Art. 6; S. XXI, Art. 6; Ch. II, Art. 17; Ch. IX, S. V.

12 *Ibid.*, Ch. IX, Ss. XVIII and XIX; Ch. V, S. VI, Art. 3; Ch. II, Art. 16, Rule II, p. 151.

13 *Ibid.*, Ch. IX, S. III, Arts. 15 and 30; S. XVI, Arts. 11-14.

14 *Ibid.*, Book I, Ch. VI, p. 29; Book II, Ch. VI, S. XXV, Arts. 8 and 20; Vol. IV, Judicial Establishment, Ch. V, Tit. III, Obs., Ss. I and IV; Vol. IV, Panopticon, Postscript, Pt. I, 1791, S. II; Vol. IV, Papers Relative to Codification, etc., 1817, Pt. I, No. 12 and Letter II to the Emperor, July 1815, p. 524.

15 *Great Britain Parliamentary Papers*, 1854, Vol. X, Select Committee on Crown Forests, Question 882, etc.

16 *Works of Bentham*, Vol. IX, Constitutional Code, Book II, Ch. VI, S. XXVII, Art. 56; Ch. IX, S. XX, Art. 10; Book I, Ch. VIII; etc.

17 *Ibid.*, Book I, Ch. V, S. XIX, Art. 39.

18 *cf. ibid.*, Vol. IV, pp. 516-28.

19 *Ibid.*, Vol. VI, p. 558 n.

20 *Ibid.*, Vol. I, p. 571.

21 *Ibid.*, Vol. III, pp. 198-9. *cf.* H. A. Clegg, *Industrial Democracy and Nationalisation*, Oxford, 1951, pp. 107-8.

22 *Works of Bentham*, Vol. IX, Constitutional Code, Book II, Ch. IX, S. XXV, Arts. 20, 22, 24; Book I, Ch. VIII.

23　*Ibid.*, Book II, Ch. IX, S. XXV, Arts. 26, 27, 32, 35.

24　Sir H. Taylor, *Works*, London 1883 (1st ed. 1836), Vol. IV, pp. 352-5.

25　*Ibid.*, pp. 321, 324, 327, 330 n., 355-8. *cf.* Graham Wallas, *Men and Ideas*, London, 1940, pp. 115-20.

26　Taylor *op. cit.*, App. p. 403, letter dated 23 Nov. 1855. E. Dowden (ed.), *Correspondence of Sir Henry Taylor*, London, 1888, p. 196, letter dated 1 May 1852.

27　Sir H. Taylor, *The Statesman*, London, 1836, Chs. III and XIII and pp. 254, 279.

28　*cf.* S. E. Finer, *Life and Times of Sir Edwin Chadwick*, London, 1952, pp. 159-60.

29　*cf.* G. O. Trevelyan, *Life and Letters of Lord Macaulay*, London, 1890 ed., Ch. VIII, pp. 380-1.

30　J. Toulmin Smith, *Government by Commission Illegal and Pernicious*, London, 1849; see especially Book I, Chs. I-III, Book II, Chs. III-IV, and pp. 16, 17, 23-8.

31　*Great Britain Parliamentary Debates*, Third Series, Vol. XVII, p. 340, 4 May 1847. See contributions by Hume, Banks and Henley as well as those of Grey and Russell; *n.b.* the signs of opposition to the use of the word 'board' itself.

32　W. Bagehot, *The English Constitution*, World's Classics ed., 1928, pp. 191-2. E. A. Helps (ed.), *Correspondence of Sir Arthur Helps*, London, 1859, p. 204.

33　A. Todd, *Parliamentary Government in England*, London, 1867-9. Third Earl Grey, *Representative Government*, London, 1858. *cf.* also H. Coxe, *The British Commonwealth*, London, 1854. W. E. Hearn, *The Government of England*, London, 1867.

34　Todd, *op. cit.*, 1892 ed., preface by Spencer Walpole, p. iv.

35　It was the Irish MP's who were to make parliamentary questions take several steps forward in importance. It is surprising how far departmental organization went irrespective of the parliamentary question.

36　Todd, *op. cit.*, Book VII, p. 62; Book III, Ch. I; Book IV, Ch. III, S. 5, pp. 85-92, p. 95. *cf.* A. Helps, *Thoughts upon Government*, London, 1872, p. 169.

37　Todd, *op. cit.*, pp. 165-6.

38　J. Bentham, *Rationale of Judicial Evidence*, London, 1827 ed., preface, pp. v-xvi. *cf.* M. St. J. Packe, *Life of John Stuart Mill*, London, 1954, pp. 72-3.

39　See various articles by Mill, *e.g.* in the *Examiner*, 27 Oct. 1833, pp. 675-6; the *Sun*, 12 May 1834, p. 2; the *Morning Chronicle*, 2 Aug. 1834, p. 2; the *Globe*, 8 Sept. 1835, p. 4; the *Morning Chronicle*, 31 Oct. 1846, p. 4 (for a later opinion on the Poor Law Board); *Public Agency v. Trading Companies*, London, 1851, pp. 19-23; *England and Ireland*, London, 1868.

40　J. S. Mill, *Considerations on Representative Government*, World's Classics ed., p. 347.

41　See references in *Representative Government*; and various articles and reports, *e.g.* on the India Bill of 1853 in the *Morning Chronicle*, 5 and 7 July, p. 5 on each occasion; *Contention for Continuation of the East India Company: Report of the Debates at the East India House Relative to the Proposed Change in the Government of India*, London, 1858, pp. 6-8; *Review of Improvements Under the East India Company*, London, 1857-8, pp. 1-38; various pamphlets on the India Bills and Resolutions of 1858: *A Constitutional View of the India Question, Practical Observations on the First Two of the Proposed Resolutions on the Government of India, A President in Council the Best Government for India, The Moral of the India Debate.* This last pamphlet is especially interesting.

42 *London Review*, July and Oct. 1835 (reprinted as Appendix in J. S. Mill, *Dissertations and Discussions*, London, Routledge, 1859-70). *cf. Representative Government*, Ch. VI.

43 *Representative Government*, pp. 344-6; *n.b.* the significance of his words about 'the fluctuations of a modern official career'.

44 W. Bagehot, *The English Constitution*, World's Classics ed., pp. 191-2.

45 *Ibid.*, p. 176.

46 *Ibid.*, pp. 162, 164, 167-8.

47 *Ibid.*, pp. 170, 174, 180-1, 190-3.

48 *Ibid.*, p. 170.

49 A. Helps, *op. cit.*, Chs. II-IV and App. E. A. Helps, *op. cit.*, Intro, p. 9 and pp. 204, 209, 213. A. Helps, *Friends in Council*, London, 1859, Series II, Vol II, On Government, pp. 181-2, and Series I, Vol. II (new ed. 1869), Ch. V. Government. For Fitzjames Stephen see Leslie Stephen, *Life of Fitzjames Stephen*, London, 1895, pp. 350-1. Duke of Somerset, *Monarchy and Democracy*, London, 1880, Ch. XV, pp. 159, *ff.* The Duke was Chadwick's old enemy Seymour of the Board of Health.

50 *Gt. Brit. P.P.*, 1883, Vol. XIII and 1884, Vol. XIII.

51 *Thoughts Upon Government*, Chs. II-IV and App., especially pp. 6, 23, 27, 28, 38, 233, *ff. Friends in Council*, Series II, Vol. II, pp. 181-2. E. A. Helps, *op. cit.*, pp. 204, 213.

52 *cf.* Stephen, *loc. cit.*

53 *cf.* Sir C. Rivers Wilson, *My Official Life*, London, 1916, p. 63.

54 F. Smith, *Sir James Kay-Shuttleworth*, London, 1923, p. 301.

55 *The Times*, 8 Ap. 1854.

56 *cf.* E. Faguet, *The Cult of Incompetence*, English ed., 1911, p. 37, Ch. III etc. G. Mosca, *The Ruling Class*, English ed., 1939, Ch. 10, S. 8.

57 *cf.* G. McG. Dawson, *The Principle of Official Independence*, London, 1922, pp. 23, *ff.* F. E. Eggleston, *State Socialism in Victoria*, London, 1932, Ch. III.

58 H. D. Traill, *Central Government*, London, 1887, pp. 133-4. Edward Porritt, *The Englishman at Home*, London, 1893, Ch. VIII, pp. 227-8. Leonard Courtney (Lord Courtney of Penwith), *The Working Constitution of the United Kingdom*, London, 1905, pp. 152-5, 208, 210-18.

59 W. R. Anson, *Law and Custom of the Constitution*, London, 1892, Pt. II, The Crown. A. V. Dicey, *Law of the Constitution*, London (1st ed. 1885), Intro. to 8th ed. (1915) and Ch. XI. But *cf.* Sir Frederick Pollock, *Law Quarterly Review*, Vol. 25, 1909, p. 53, for a more interesting view.

60 A. Trollope, *Phineas Finn*, World's Classics ed., Pt. II, p. 66.

2

SIR ARTHUR HELPS AND THE ART OF

ADMINISTRATION

The Benthamite argument against boards and trustees and in favour of responsibility was refuted in the early Victorian years by Sir Henry Taylor in The Statesman. *Sir Arthur Helps followed Taylor in expressing the contrary case for official independence: discretion and initiative exercised by executive agents who would do the politician's 'inventive and suggestive' work. This was the starting point for the modern discovery of the separateness of administration. But the language for expressing the idea had to be created: there was as yet no word for administration, or civil service or, indeed, minister. Helps was one of the best examples of the highly significant nineteenth-century writers in the long tradition of reason of state and mirrors for princes. He turned his mind as far as the vocabulary would allow him not to politics (rising to public office and the extension of the state) but to its administrative agents.*

1959 was the centenary of the second series of *Friends in Council* by Sir Arthur Helps. These once-famous dialogues were amongst the many writings of this nineteenth-century civil servant, a post-Greville Clerk to the Privy Council. Is there any reason why students of public administration should now be interested in Helps's work?

We might note in the first place that the similar writing of Helps's contemporary Sir Henry Taylor, *The Statesman*, has, though this was not always so, received much more attention than Helps's work.[1] If there is a market for Taylor, there should at least be a stall for Helps. The similarities are striking. Mid-century public servants with literary pretensions, they both set out to express views on success in administrative life. This object put them in the long but delicate tradition of *Fürstenspiegel*, of advice to princes rather than sermons to the public, a tradition which, being Machiavellian, was presumably out of fashion in mid-Victorian times. Typical of a certain sort of Victorian career, they both composed series of short pieces of advice on the demands of administrative behaviour.

In so doing they expressed views about the arts of rising and the role of Parliament which were, perhaps, unacceptable at the time.

If we are now more interested in Taylor's work than were his contemporaries, we ought also to be interested in Helps. There has, inevitably, never been very much writing of this sort. It makes peculiar demands on career (achievement without involvement), ability (literary as well as practical) and tastes, and, before the era of the Organization Man, it could rarely have been widely acceptable. It is addressed, after all, to the success of the governors, who are few, not to the welfare of the governed. It is not preaching, and it is not, in the modern manner, science. We ought to cherish the little that we have. While *The Statesman* and Helps's later work *Thoughts upon Government* were failures, the earlier writings of Helps, the two series of *Friends in Council*, where dialogue enabled Helps to attribute his more dashing views to fictional characters, were in their time successful. Furthermore, we should begin to be more fair to the public service they were both writing about: the pre-reform service. This is one reason why we read Taylor now: it is a reason for reading Helps too.

To understand Taylor and Helps we must see how they fitted into their service, and, with Stephen, Chadwick, Trollope and their work, they themselves help to complete its picture. It is clear by now that they were working in a service which could provide a worthwhile career for men of considerable talent, and that had not been true a generation before Stephen. We are reminded of how much reform there had been before the actual reform years of 1855 or 1870. We can now distinguish at least four types of which this pre-reform service was composed, other than the lesser breeds who were the acquaintances of Trollope's Johnny Eames, or who were described in the pages of evidence taken by Trevelyan and Northcote or later in the 1860 report on the Civil Service. The first type would be the satisfied and competent mainly concerned with the social pleasures to be found after 4 p.m.: the young Algernon West[2] or, in fiction, Eames himself. There were those who saved their resources for an occasional but splendid flame of official genius, like Sir James Stephen in the 1830s. There were those who were called in by incipient crisis: the specialist, the expert, the campaigner; the Chadwicks, the Hills, the Kay-Shuttleworths, the Southwood Smiths. Then there were those like Taylor and Helps themselves, more or less competent than the Wests, who consumed their resources of energy in literary ambition: historical romance or biography for one, a mood of recreation and intellectual comment for another.

This was Helps's Civic Service. There is one particular verdict on his role in the reform of this Service which places him very high indeed. In his introduction to Smith's *Life of Kay-Shuttleworth*, Sir Michael Sadler wrote,[3] 'Edwin Chadwick, Arthur Helps and he (Kay-Shuttleworth) are characteristic figures at a time of readjustment of English social ideals.... All three were creators of a new Civil Service. The English race is not good at bureaucracy. But he, Helps and Chadwick, saw the need for an efficient, scientific and determined public service.... Helps had the safer place and the less turbulent duty. But his writings, more than Chadwick's or Kay-Shuttleworth's, disclose the fine motive which inspired the fighting members of the group.' Helps was not one of the fighters. It was his writing that earned him this praise.

CAREER AND WRITINGS

Bearing in mind the similarity to Taylor, the relative rarity and peculiar value of this sort of work and Sadler's opinion, we may be unwise to give all our attention to Taylor and none to Helps. Helps's career, without his writing, is the sort which (like Taylor's) may earn oblivion. Somewhat younger than Taylor (he was born in 1813, Taylor in 1800) his education was more orthodox: Eton and Trinity, Cambridge. His public service career was as smooth, though somewhat more varied: private secretary to Melbourne's Chancellor of the Exchequer, Spring-Rice (whose daughter Taylor married in 1839) and then, in 1839, to Lord Morpeth; Commissioner of Claims; and successor to W. L. Bathurst as Clerk to the Privy Council in 1860, where he remained until his death in 1875. His entry was not dissimilar from his predecessors, Greville and Bathurst, but he was much more truly politically neutral than the one, much abler than the second and much busier than either. Like Taylor he received no honours until late in life: C.B. in 1871 and K.C.B. in 1872. His widow was awarded a pension on the Civil List.

The apparent highlights of his career were all on paper, as his type and as Sadler's verdict may lead us to suppose. He was a sort of literary devil for Queen Victoria: he revised Albert's *Speeches* for the press in 1862 and prepared the Queen's own *Leaves from the Journal* for the press in 1868 and *Mountain, Loch and Glen* in 1869. His own writings, outside our immediate concern, covered history, biography, fiction and drama, and he achieved real success with the four volumes of his *Spanish Conquest in America* (reissued as separate biographies) and his *Life and Labours of Mr. Brassey*, 1872 (which ran to seven editions). None of this put him beyond the Victorian pale (though some work with Kingsley in 1848 was slightly less orthodox) and as an essayist for the journals he was more successful still: the Stephens remembered him as the most prolific writer of the influential 'middle' essays of the day.[4]

Such a literary career could be borne without any skimping of his duties, by an exercise of Victorian energy within the confines of his job. Helps was relatively well born, well educated, a friend of Palmerston, a fairly successful man. He was also popular with his subordinates. G. C. Boase described him in the D.N.B. as 'shrewd, singularly clear-headed, highly cultivated', and his subordinate, Preston-Thomas, gives a warm picture of his courage, tolerance and humour.[5] This sort of man does not keep his colleagues' respect unless he does his work, which was not, in fact, all that limited. It was the Office's accession to public health functions which, according to Preston-Thomas, had necessitated the bringing in of such an able man—one of the ablest of the century, according to Macaulay's recommendation—to replace Bathurst. He had already served as Commissioner for Relief in famine-stricken Ireland. The Office was not without its crises during Helps's tenure, and they were peculiarly varied: cattle plague, educational policy, public health and such a delicate matter as the Queen's continued retirement. Helps played his role in them all; one might have thought that his support for Lowe and Lingen's policy of payment by results for educational grants would not have endeared him to Sadler.[6] It was, appropriately enough for the author of the sort of writings we are interested in, precisely in the role of intermediary between the Queen and her Ministers that he was at his best.[7]

His contemporaries would expect us still to be reading his histories. Sadler indicates that we ought to read what he wrote about administration and one at any rate of Helps's contemporaries would agree: if Sadler's tribute is one of the surprises about Helps, Ruskin's opinion is surely the other. Ruskin carried a high admiration for Helps's style and type of work, and he expressed this, in more or less the same form, from *Stones of Venice* to *Fors Clavigera*. This interest led to a friendship between Ruskin and Helps, who dedicated some of the essays in the second series of *Friends in Council* to Ruskin. The height of Ruskin's admiration, like Sadler's, is striking. He said that if you read for use, not for show, you would know the proverbs of Solomon and 'by way of commentary, afford to buy, in convenient editions, Plato, Bacon, Wordsworth, Carlyle and Helps'.[8] This is not only an attitude to manner, to 'the beautiful quiet English of Helps' to which Ruskin acknowledged a debt of clarity and simplicity.[9] Ruskin saw a relationship between the lightness of Helps's touch and the provisional character of his thought. This permitted him, 'mingled with an exquisitely tender and loving satire', a certain 'playfulness'[10]; his wisdom was that he was satisfied to be helpful rather than decisive.

The charm of Helps's style depends, then, on the modesty of his practical purpose and in this very restraint his usefulness lies. What you can know and teach about administration is, from this point of view, a matter of limitation and of style. The administrator is concerned with the style of doing and with expression—hence Taylor's chapter on official style; and this curbing of ambition enables such a teacher (a Taylor or Helps) to write about his subject like, in Helps's own words, 'a happy combination of Machiavelli, Pascal and Dr. Watts'.[11] Taylor and Helps were both quite explicit about this. We can see how the approach is employed in *Thoughts Upon Government*, which was never well known, and in some of the essays in the once celebrated *Friends in Council*.

HIS GENERAL VIEWPOINT

The first series of *Friends in Council*, dedicated to Morpeth, was published in 1847, eleven years after *The Statesman*. The second series was published twelve years later. *Thoughts Upon Government*, dedicated to Lord Derby (so Helps had honoured both parties), was published late in Helps's life, in 1872. It is merely mentioned as tenth in the list of his 'other works' in the D.N.B. entry. A second series was intended[12] but never appeared. Two things immediately strike the reader of this first work. One is that the book is far more successful when Helps abides by his manner of giving discrete pieces of advice from office experience than when he attempts much wider abstractions on government. The second is that, beyond the aphorisms and the occasional pictures of the Service of his time, there is a general view which gives some coherence to the whole. This view, like Taylor's, is Burkean rather than utilitarian, but it is Burke with some difference. Helps wanted a degree of governmental intervention and he is wary of economy which may easily (in public salaries, abolition of offices and the supervision of financial detail) be false: the State should be the best employer. He was a paternalist. The danger was too little, not too much, government: lazy officials, the fear of ridicule and the operation of special interests all contributed to this. His belief in the limited possibility of successfully intended action at any one moment made him sceptical of planning reform beyond the point of specific improvements: he may not have been happy with things as they were but he did not expect much change; he was something less than a social engineer. Still he saw public administration as a force in opposition to what he called 'vulgarity', the representation of interests; if the extent of its schemes at any one time were limited, the possible fields of public action were many, and his enumeration of them was quite modern. He was probably nearer to a perception of the Fabian argument about social cost—the common sense of municipal trading—than he was to accepting the Victorian reliance on the doctrine of *caveat emptor*. Our difference may be that we think of special interests as applicants for governmental assistance, as much as the reverse, and we cannot be sure of the efficacy of ridicule which, he wrote,[13] 'will not allow governmental interference in small matters, even though it might be justified by very good reasons derived from general principles'.

His paternalism was not wholly conventional for its time. When he was conventional it was often in good company and to amusing ends. Like Disraeli, he thought that by the 1870s all the political problems had been solved. In a wonderful and only half-consciously typical picture of the individual citizen who, having read his newspaper, sits back in his railway carriage to discuss Army reform, he gives us a beautiful insight into what the conventional actually was.[14] But the fact is that his criticisms of individualism, in *Thoughts Upon Government* at any rate, came probably just a little too late after Mill and Stephen, or a little too soon before the 1880s to gain the attention they may have deserved.

Helps was, too, a stranger to his time in being prepared to criticize the responsible ministerial department. The important thing was his understanding of the fact that relations between officials and politicians constituted a full-scale problem, with the motives of the legislature, the costs of the full panoply of answerability, the paradoxical relations of officials to Ministers and the comparative advantages of the conditions of administration in private business. Dealing with the excesses of responsibility in his practical way, he begins, 'In the first place there is not time enough in the world for it. Wretched would be the pair above all names of wretchedness, as Dr. Johnson well says, "who should be doomed to adjust by reason every morning all the minute details of a domestic day".'[15] He illumines this problem from his own experience, as elsewhere he illumines from public health administration the problem of central-local relations with its balance of local familiarity and prejudice as against central knowledge.

Sometimes Helps ventures on a defence if not a criticism. He is better still in dealing out advice on how to come to terms successfully with the conditions of public administration as they were. Between these two points of observation and prescription his best work swings. Ministers, he thinks, tend to ignore office administration, but they suffer from want of time. This is worsened for them by the pressure not so much of great matters as of small business and by the growth, since Pitt's time, of parliamentary questions. They might then do well to use some neglect and they may do better to engage some counsellors in the departments. But departments were less able to employ good men than was, for instance, the press. The pressure was worsened by the ample and hasty publication of official papers and by the extent of Treasury control. The attractiveness of public employment could be increased against these disadvantages by keeping some cosy offices, a fifth seat on a Board for example, as a reward for good careers, as with superannuated private secretaries of long service.

Certain themes continually reappear. If the notion were not alien to Helps, one might say that he had a general theory of administration in which time was the great problem and the recruitment, use and reward of able men and the betterment of office methods were the great demands. But while these things provoke a hundred observations Helps does not extend his argument beyond particular observations and precepts. 'There is an absolute need for men.'[16] How to get them? Here Helps was in opposition to Macaulay: he did not like open competition and he did not like students in business. He has his own notions about recruitment. He is, for example, attracted to the idea of allowing a man to choose his own immediate subordinate in certain conditions.

Helps saw that it was a matter of getting the right man in, as well as keeping the wrong man out and that each office needed its few original minds. He saw, too, that recruitment was not the end of the matter: promotion, pay and honours needed attention too. 'When, by any process of selection, you are fortunate enough to have got good men to serve you, you must take care to keep them satisfied.'[17] He felt that, difficult as the whole question was and lacking any single solution, efforts must be made to give more or less satisfactory answers and that this depended, amongst other things, upon knowing what you were looking for. Rare as such an able man was, it was the more important to define the qualities of the great organizer, his mastery of detail for example, and his avidity for fact. Helps distinguishes the argumentative from the organizing powers. He is unsure about how much can be taught and examined.[18] But he agrees with Northcote and Trevelyan that the good man must not be ground down with early routine.

The provisional nature of Helps's observations allows him, often consciously, to contradict himself. One of the ways of providing thinking men in government is, he says, to use non-departmental Ministers. Elsewhere he says that non-departmental Ministers should be replaced by more departmental Ministers so as to relieve the bigger offices like Colonies and Home Affairs. The contradiction does not matter and in fact both courses have been followed. His inconsistency made him the better prophet, his empiricism the better adviser. He has, for example, a favourite story about the impact of the careful arrangement of public correspondence on a particular piece of legislation in taxation consolidation which obviously comes from his own experience. He gets a good deal out of this story by way of advice on the use of assistants and information and on the arrangement of papers.[19]

Helps takes details seriously, as Bacon did in his essay on Councils. The careful use of honours is one of these details. Indeed if honours are available they should be used. It is an inadequate treatment of the life of most public services to ignore this matter, and therefore a gap in public administration. Helps distinguishes two uses: for recognition and for encouragement. He argues that the expert will be able to tell which use has been implied in any particular instance. Not resting all his case on this one point he can write lightly enough about it, and he does so, telling one story and inventing, as he could do superbly, three fables and quoting another on the way.[20] There is no room here for the fables though they are beautifully pointed.

We may quote the story. 'In George III's time there was a man who had rendered some political service to the government (political service in those days not being a thing of the highest merit), and this man wished to be allowed to drive through the park. "No, no," said the King, "we cannot do that; but you may make him an Irish baron if you like"; and an Irish baron he was made.'

Getting and handling able men is one thing; office methods another. His chapter on the conduct of business, where he uses proverbs like Bacon and a whole imaginary case like some modern writers, has as many and as good maxims as Taylor's better known pages. He deals with the limitations of abstracts, the importance of dates, the patchwork effect of the habit in public administration of employing many hands in one letter, and the art of sub-division —'this supreme effort of division and classification'.[21] He appreciates the role of indirect results: 'nearly always the most important' of any course of action.[22] The superior must understand his subordinates' characters and in designing his schemes must allow for their indolence. 'The administrator can hardly ever make too much allowance for the indolence of mankind. Where his administration will fail, is in people omitting to do, from indolence, that which he supposes he has given them sufficient means and instructions for doing.'[23] One part of Helps's concern is to tell you what the rare able man can do to get by in his constraining situation. Another is to say something of what happens because of his rarity, for example 'that the action of government chiefly consists in a series of surprises'.[24] Another concern is to discuss the difficulty of doing much about this, the futility of universal cures and the variety of limited but useful remedies.

Helps's experience provided him with stories and his prejudices enabled him to draw from these some maxims and proverbs, but he knew that a proverb was not an argument. 'The worst, however, of proverbs is that, when you have a proverb embodying one phase of thought, you generally want an exactly opposite proverb to correct it.'[25] He employed the length and concreteness of the fable somewhat more brilliantly than the briefer and more generalized form of the aphorism. His maxims are not always exciting but they are sound. 'It must be borne in mind that the words "central authority" are "prave 'ords", as Fluellen would have said; but that, when you come to look at things closely, "central authority" means four or five able men, with a staff of secretaries and clerks.'[26] He gives another warning that 'occasion is not opportunity'.[27]

Warnings are at least as frequent as encouragement but wisdom is always present if sometimes somewhat chilling. 'The merits of the most eminent of the permanent civil servants are known to very few persons; which makes their position especially dependent upon the discriminating kindness of their chiefs.'[28] His concern for limitation is once again expressed: the official 'will generally find, that when he goes wrong in the expression of his views, or his decisions, it is because the form of expression used has been needlessly wide.'[29] He is not always so chilling: 'You will find, that almost every man who has been concerned in governing, is much more liberal as regards the payment, and the other rewards of agents, than the man who has had no experience in that direction.'[30]

His experiences and his concern to secure originating mind in organization prompted a deep interest in the problems of councils and committees. His assumptions about them are historically interesting. He speaks of the organization of a Board as of an actual committee meeting and of the Board members themselves as making up the essential working staff. Hence, he is against *ex officio* members. Like Bentham, he believes in payment for all members. He sees that when work is delegated it will be delegated to a few Board members and he thinks that this delegation should be moved about from time to time. He devises interesting standards for the classification of types of Board or Council, for selecting their uses and for managing their conduct. Since the general hostility to this sort of organization provoked by Bentham up to the modern studies of them, there have been few more useful discussions of Councils than Helps's chapter IX in the *Thoughts*. Helps is sure enough of his ground to allow himself a gloss on Machiavelli and Bacon. 'I doubt not that the effect of weariness is one of the main elements of decision in any assemblage of men.'[31] Or, as he says in *Friends in Council*, 'If we could know the number of resolutions which have been carried under the influence of mere fatigue and disgust, we should be astonished at the effect that weariness and fear of "damnable iteration", as Falstaff calls it, have produced'.[32] He also allows himself a comment on the Bible. 'The well-known passage in the Bible, "in a multitude of counsellors there is safety", has frequently been misconstrued. It does not allude to the safety of the counsel, but of the counsellors.'[33]

Helps speaks of the Privy Council, as Mill of the East India Company, out of experience, interest, affection and conviction. We gain some insight into its nineteenth-century administrative history as a nursing mother of future Ministries or, as Helps calls them, sub-departments, and we detect some anticipation by Helps of the later responsibilities for which the Council would come to be used as a potential reserve. Thinking of the Privy Council, Helps composes these conservative words of wide application, 'Doubtless its constitution was not designed to be what it is now; but the thing has grown up to be what it is, as indeed has happened in regard to several of the most important bodies in Great Britain'.[34]

FRIENDS IN COUNCIL

In *Friends in Council*, Helps had had similar interests to those later expressed in *Thoughts Upon Government*. The most relevant chapters are 'Government' in the first series, and 'On Government' and 'On the Arts of Self-advancement' in the second series. The layout of 'Government' is typical. It begins with a fable about a fable, i.e. a fable about an animal telling a fable about man. It continues with an essay by 'Milverton', a public man somewhat more responsible than the lawyer 'Ellesmere'. It concludes with a dialogue between 'Milverton' and the other characters about his essay. The essay has two brief sections on the form and the objects of government and a much longer and a much better section on the mode and means of government. It is this part of the chapter that will most interest us.

As elsewhere Helps is Burkean, paternalistic, moderate and optimistic about the British people. Milverton sees honesty as one of the conditions of official life. 'I do not mean merely the common honesty of not betraying secrets and not seeking after sinister purposes—that merit official people share with bankers' clerks and the mercantile community in general, whose honesty is something wonderful—but I mean the less obvious honesty of being careful that things should be fairly considered and that right should be done.'[35] The danger is simply that government does not play the role it ought to. 'It is the same in dealing with public as with private agents. If you look too sharply after them, they will endeavour to escape your blame rather than to do your business.'[36]

What is said about mode and means is also very much like what Helps said later. The emphasis is already on getting and using men: find them and reward them. This is not mere rough anticipation of his later writings, however. Helps's words here, about the recruitment of ability, seem to me to be his best statement and indeed one of the best statements that have been written on the whole problem. 'Incomparably the first means is the procurement of able men; not tools, but men. It is very hard to prophesy of any business or affair in the world, how it will turn out; but it cannot be a bad thing to have an able man to deal with it. ... But the difficulty is to find able men. To hear some persons talk, you would suppose that it was the simplest thing imaginable to make good appointments, and that it needed nothing but honesty on the part of the person appointing. But sound men of business are very rare, much more rare than anybody would be likely to conjecture who had not had considerable experience of life. And what makes the difficulty greater is, that the faculty for business is seldom to be ascertained by any *a priori* test. Formal examinations of all kinds fail.

'For look what it is that you demand in a man of business- Talents for the particular business, the art of bringing out those talents before the eyes of men, temper to deal with men, inventiveness together with prudence and, in addition to many other moral qualities, that of moral courage, which I have remarked to be the rarest gift of all.

'As it is, very many men fail from a want of proportion in their gifts. ... Many of these defects are not fully ascertained until the man is absolutely tried (*Capax imperii nisi imperasset*). ... On the other hand, there are men whose talents for governing are not developed until they are placed in power, like the palm branches which spring out only at the top of the tree. But still these considerations must not induce men in authority to say that since choice is so difficult, it must be left to chance or favour, but it only shows how wary statesmen should be in their choice, and that when they once do get hold of a good man, how much they should make of him.'[37]

He is very forthright, accordingly, about honours. 'Next to offices comes honours as means at the disposal of government. Cant, which is the creature of civilization, and must be expected to attain a great height as civilization advances, takes many forms; and one of the forms it has taken in modern times is the pretending to despise honours, calling them baubles, tinsel, toys, trappings and other hard names. This is all nonsense. They are very valuable things, and men of clear and open minds, who are after all less ignominiously swayed by such things than other men, will tell you so. Nelson's exclamation on going into action, "A Peerage or Westminster Abbey", will find response in the minds of many of the worthiest amongst us. In fact it is difficult for a government so to deteriorate and degrade its honours as to make them unacceptable.'[38] He is equally forthright about his preference for using paid men, 'for you cannot rely on work that is given'.[39]

Here, as later in *Thoughts Upon Government*, Helps stressed the use of committees and councils. But here he allowed himself also to emphasize what he called 'the difficulty of conjoint action'.[40] He has something to say of what would now be called machinery of government work. 'It is obvious that in every form of government considerable attention should be paid to the distribution of functions amongst the great officers of State.'[41] He makes some recommendations about particular changes. Some of his notions might not now be thought of as very original (as with certain types of advisory council) or very possible (as with the creation of 'a certain number of official seats in Parliament—say for the first and second office in each department').[42] But his reasons for his proposals are always interesting. 'There is still to my mind a want of something which I think may be noticed in all governments of modern times, and that is, a power of attracting from time to time fresh ability and fresh views, and putting the department in reasonable communication with the world about it.... What is wanted is to bring more intellectual power within command of the heads of departments, and moreover that this power should neither be elicited in a hostile manner, nor on the other hand that it should be too subservient. It should rather be attainable without the walls of an office than within. It should be at hand for a Minister; but it should not be too closely mixed up with ordinary official life.... It can hardly be doubted that it would often be an immense advantage to a Minister to be able to call in a man of known ability, conversant with the department and yet not much tied by it, to hear his opinion upon some difficult dispute (from the colonies for instance) in which both the Minister and his subordinates may be liable to err from their very knowledge of the parties.'[43]

The essay 'On Government' in the second series of *Friends in Council*,[44] which contains an approving note on Hare's *The Elec-*

tion of Representatives,[45] and on the less famous Craik,[46] is very similar to the first essay. After a short introduction the essay is again given by Milverton, who admits that he might be repeating himself,[47] and there is a concluding discourse. There are one or two historical references of some importance. Students of the development of government regulation in the nineteenth century will appreciate Helps's reference to the failure (then, after the Act of 1851, fairly fresh in his readers' minds) to solve the problems of controlling railway development and in particular to the work of Dalhousie.[48] In 1859 it was not beside the point to insist on the vast demands on intelligence made by public service. It was certainly not a conventional notion and it was important that it was Helps's very sense of these demands, not any suspicion of government as such, that made him limit his expectations of what could be done. 'There should be men in office who love the State as priests love the Church.'[49] But Parliament was making their position difficult. Apart from reforming the parliamentary system, what could be done about this? On the one hand you could strengthen the departments. Here Helps refers again to some of his favourite devices. On the other hand you could reform recruitment, but this should be an unfettering of the system rather than a reform on the Northcote-Trevelyan lines.

PROVERBS AND APHORISMS

We have noticed Helps's interest in proverbs and brief writings; this was a fashion of his times followed by Taylor. Helps could write aphorisms as well as quote them and he shows this better in *Friends in Council* than in *Thoughts Upon Government*. Now in the first volume of the second series he has two chapters on proverbs. Not without interest themselves, they also serve to introduce the chapter 'On the Arts of Self-Advancement'. Here his sources include Napier and Thiers as well as Guicciardini, and through his lawyer character Ellesmere he has some striking things to say about self-advancement, that important part of the administrator's life, or the art of rising, as it is described elsewhere.

All this is instinct with a sense both of urgency and also of the difficulty of the actual performance of business. It is 'through the interstices of ill-contrived arrangement'[50] that armies have sunk. 'At last,' Helps approvingly quotes Thiers 'my very dreams were administrative.'[51] How is the work to be done? Helps and his authorities agree in warnings against that current dogma, the man with the clean desk. 'Take almost anything that is offered to you.'[52] says Helps, or Ellesmere. You need be concerned not lest your agents are unfaithful, but lest they neglect your business.[53] The advancement of affairs and of your own career both demand that you must do much yourself. Do not then be too delicate. 'This earth is not for the refined. They cannot expect to get anything in the scuffle that is going on. You all remember the well-known story of Lord Thurlow; how, whenever a bishopric was vacant, he always said to the King, "Please, your Majesty, I have a brother", until at last George III (a man not without persistency himself) was tired of hearing this cuckoo exclamation from his Chancellor, and gave a bishopric to the brother. Again, in business it often happens that a man is too delicate to ask a question, which ought to be asked, which he longs to ask: and his not asking this question is forever a detriment to him—perhaps, his ruin.'[54] And do not lay your plans on too large a scale. There is another reason for this. Helps is well aware both of the limitations of foresight and of what is nowadays called the unanticipated consequences. 'Do not suppose that anything will turn out rightly. Never believe in estimates.... It is best to begin with a little aversion, not only in marriage, but in all other affairs that are to endure for a long time.'[55] 'Attempt little.... Avoid delicacy', and do not expect too much of others. 'When you have, therefore, to act with other men, calculate on their vanity being inordinate, on their weariness and forgetfulness being very great, and on their placability being excessive.'[56]

Through Ellesmere, Helps is ready to be at his least conventional and therefore at his most illuminating. 'Those who wish for self advancement should remember, that the art in life is not so much to do a thing well, as to get a thing that has been moderately well done largely talked about.'[57] 'Be modest in speech about your merits, but not in demands that may further your fortunes.'[58] He is prepared to say what Bagehot says about the administrator in his essay on Peel,[59] that he must be somewhat superficial and near sighted. Industry and promptness are required for success. One condition for such qualities is 'a certain limitation of view ... and a certain joyous superficiality of character.'[60] Bagehot and Helps are in the closest of agreement here. 'Human affairs are provided for from day to day. The man who sees too widely is nearly sure to be indecisive, or to appear so. Hence, also, comes an appearance, sometimes of shuffling, and sometimes of over-subtlety, which is very harmful to a man.... But the best reason for being limited in your views is that other people are limited, and that you do not act in harmony with them if you are farsighted. I would not, however, speak against farsightedness, if a man who possesses it would only know on what occasions to keep it to himself.'[61] A second condition of industry and promptness must be that you must know when not to use these qualities for 'it must be remembered that the man who studies self-advancement judiciously, must know how to wait. There are occasions and positions in life in which every move will be a bad one. It requires great self-command at such junctures to pause, and wait, especially for an energetic man who is used to action. But he must learn the wisdom of doing nothing.'[62]

Ellesmere comes close to a definition of the central issue in organization. 'But the difficulty of difficulties and the thing that requires an imaginative supervision, is the joining of different kinds of work together so that no time or substance be lost.'[63] Helps understands the burden of action. He sees this as creating demands for intelligence and for able men. This is a problem in the public life of a country. He has noticed that the over-enforcement of responsibility, as with a high degree of Parliamentary interference, enhances this problem by pressing on the limited time available and giving voice to the forces of vulgarity, ridicule and special interest.

This tension between rare men and limited time is part of the conditions of administrative life. It follows that within these conditions we must seek to get and keep able men as far as possible. It will not be very far and many devices will have to be used. 'Let the world think what it may, there are but few men who are endowed with great aptitude for managing public business, or indeed business of any kind. And the whole of my arguments merely tend to this, that every opportunity should be given for the chance even of finding such men.'[64] We must recognize just what we mean by the able man in administration, and we must perceive that an understanding of the delicate details of honours, for example, may be as productive as any attempt at single-minded reform of recruitment. How is the able man to conduct his career within these limiting conditions? Something can be done, Helps believes, to advise him about his predicament provided he is 'judicious' enough to realize that 'One maxim is good now, another maxim good then; and the "now" and the "then" come within the undescribed—perhaps undescribable—province of common sense'.[65] The man will have his talent. Ellesmere distinguishes the qualities of the man, the modes of action and the arts of self-advancement. He must, then, use his qualities in part in these modes of action (for example in the use of committees) and in part in the business of rising.

Helps does not expect any radical changes in the conditions themselves within which administration must occur. His observations about these conditions are not without sufficient institutional description to be of some interest in their own right. But, like Taylor, he does not attempt to formulate a science or a complete doctrine. He is not worried by contradiction. He is not preaching to the people. His role is advisory, not exhortatory. A man must know how to pick among his notes the appropriate precept for the moment. It is precisely to officials who have the qualities to do this that Help's writing is addressed.

NOTES

In the following notes the three works of Sir Arthur Helps are abbreviated as follows:

    F.C.1.—*Friends in Council* (First Series), 1847; F.C.2—*Friends in Council* (Second Series), 1859; T.G.—*Thoughts upon Government*, 1872.

1   *cf.* Wilfrid Harrison, *Sir Henry Taylor and The Statesman, Public Administration*, v. xxx, 1952, pp. 61-70; Leo Silberman, ed., *The Statesman*, by Henry Taylor, Cambridge, 1957.
2   Rt. Hon. Sir Algernon West, *Recollections*, London, 1899, 2 vols.
3   F. Smith, *Sir James Kay-Shuttleworth*, London, 1923, p. ix.
4   Leslie Stephen, *Life of Sir James Fitzjames Stephen*, London, 1895, pp. 100 and 175.
5   H. Preston-Thomas, *The Work and Play of a Government Inspector*, London, 1909, pp. 10, 12, 19, etc.
6   Lord Edmund Fitzmaurice, *The Life of Lord Granville*, London, 1905, vol. ii, pp. 426-7 and 428-9.
7   Preston-Thomas, *op. cit.*, p. 6.
8   John Ruskin, *Modern Painters*, Library Edition of Works, 1904, vol. v, p. 425.
9   *Stones of Venice, op. cit.*, vol. xi, p. 153.
10   *Modern Painters, loc. cit.*, pp. 427-8.
11   F.C.2, vol. ii, p. 97.
12   T.G., p. vi.
13   T.G., pp. 29-30.
14   T.G., pp. 143-4.
15   T.G., p. 37.
16   T.G., p. 61.
17   T.G., p. 79.
18   *cf.* Chapter xi and Chapters xiii-xiv.
19   T.G., pp. 148-151.
20   T.G., p. 83.
21   T.G., pp. 208-9.
22   T.G., p. 210.
23   T.G., p. 204.
24   T.G., p. 125.
25   T.G., p. 198.
26   T.G., p. 59.
27   T.G., p. 41.
28   T.G., p. 80.
29   T.G., p. 206.
30   T.G., p. 53.
31   T.G., p. 101.
32   F.C.1, vol. ii, p. 62.
33   T.G., p. 97.
34   T.G., p. 110.

35 F.C.1, vol. ii, p. 85.
36 F.C.1, p. 86.
37 F.C.1, pp. 63-5.
38 F.C.1, pp. 65-6.
39 F.C.1, p. 82.
40 F.C.1, p. 60.
41 F.C.1, p. 69.
42 F.C.1, pp. 77-8.
43 F.C.1, pp. 70-2.
44 F.C.2, vol. ii, c. ix.
45 F.C.2, pp. 200-1, n.
46 F.C.2, p. 183.
47 F.C.2, p. 175.
48 F.C.2, pp. 176-7.
49 F.C.2, p. 179.
50 F.C.2, vol. i, p. 242.
51 F.C.2, p. 241.
52 F.C.2, p. 232.
53 F.C.2, p. 240.
54 F.C.2, p. 238.
55 F.C.2, p. 232.
56 F.C.2, p. 237.
57 F.C.2, p. 243.
58 F.C.2, p. 249.
59 *Works*, ed. Forrest Morgan, Hartford, 1891, vol. iii, p. 22, esp., 'So the brain of the great administrator is naturally occupied with the details of the day, the passing dust, the granules of that day's life; and his unforeseeing temperament turns away uninterested from reaching speculations, from vague thought, and from extensive and far-off plans.' Bagehot's essay was first published in 1856.
60 F.C.2, *loc. cit.*, pp. 246 and 248.
61 F.C.2, pp. 246-7.
62 F.C.2, p. 248.
63 F.C.2, p. 241.
64 F.C.2, vol. ii, p. 190.
65 F.C.2, vol. i, p. 248.

3

PUBLIC ADMINISTRATION AND THE

POLITICAL EDUCATION

An earlier paper (Australian Journal of Politics and History, Vol. IV) contrasted American with other traditions in public administration and in the emergence of the discipline. This paper was written a few years later, after some years of teaching public administration and after organizational studies, the sociology of organization and decisions and behavioral politics had become much more familiar. In 1957 the separation of administration from politics had seemed the main point; by 1962 the question was what administrative study could do for a political education when this new material was taken into account. In particular, this demanded a reconsideration of the nature of administration, of the separation of politics and administration and of the collapse of the dichotomy. This related to political experience, the human relations of organization and the administrator and the politics of organization theory. Old problems about official independence and neutrality were still here; there was an anticipation of new concerns and other questions: the machinery of government; decision-making; implementation.

A great deal of recent theoretical literature in public administration has consisted of an extension of the criticisms of classical theories from psychological and sociological sources. Other studies have ignored the classical movement altogether, as with some of the more abstruse mathematical material, particularly in decision-making theory. Some of the best and bravest thought, however, has been an attempt to come to terms with these critical developments so as as to re-establish a general notion of rational organization. This is true both of the whole corpus of Herbert Simon's work,[1] and of R. S. Parker's recent paper.[2] However, as an article in the *International Review of Administrative Sciences* has pointed out, there have always been several points of concern in the public administration movement; political, as well as managerial; psychological and sociological. One of the best ways of disciplining the body of work that has been done in public administration over the last generation, that is to say since the 1930s, may be to reconsider the relationship between public administration and political questions: to reassess this particular dimension in public administration theory.

We should not be afraid from time to time of going back to the roots, which are, after all, rich and varied. There are many traditions in the study of public administration, some of them very ancient and very different from those which have been dominant in British, American and similar systems. The realism of the reason of state school, the ancient tradition of cameralism and the administrative law approach, are obvious cases in point. It is true that even the British tradition of study in public administration is relatively recent. There is a very striking story in Beatrice Webb's autobiographical volume, *Our Partnership*, in which she tells how difficult it was to establish the idea that the teaching of political science itself ought to include down-to-earth institutional material.

Grosvenor Road,
July 14th, 1896

'Advertised for Political Science Lecturer—and yesterday interviewed candidates—a nondescript set of University men. All hopeless from our point of view—all imagined that political science consisted of a knowledge of Aristotle and modern! writers such as De Tocqueville—wanted to put the students through a course of Utopias from More downwards. When Sidney suggested a course of lectures to be prepared on the different systems of municipal taxation ... the wretched candidates looked aghast and thought evidently that we were amusing ourselves at their expense ... Finally, we determined to do without our lecturer—to my mind a blessed consummation.'[3]

The Webbs's solution, of course, was to use two members of the interviewing committee themselves (Sidney Webb and Graham Wallas). From these appointments, and encouragement by the National Association of Local Government Officers, as it then was, flowed the British tradition in public administration. This is a tradition which still exists and has recently been notably defended by Mr. Hanson and Professor Robson.[4] But the outstanding tradition in this century has been the American. Despite the fact that it originated in an attempt to copy some part of the European, and despite its present and long-standing crisis, it is now more influential than ever, partly through such media as technical assistance programmes. Many characteristics could be claimed as central to this American school. In a way the most significant of them was the separation of administration from politics.

The movement towards administrative separation has many

sources, not all of them American. The difference, for example, between Palmerston and the Haldane Report marks the impact of nineteenth-century public service reform in establishing the separation. In 1837 Palmerston explained to the young Queen Victoria that what was meant by the word bureaucracy was a bad European system of government which was created by the use of permanent public officials, a system that did not, should not, and could not exist in England.[5] Eighty years later the Haldane Report could study the machinery of government and pay altogether more attention to the problem of bureaucracy than to the problem of politics. Public service reform meant the separation of administration from politics, at least in the appointment of administrators; it meant also (in the United Kingdom) the separation of the administrator from other types of public servant. It often meant in the United States (though not in the United Kingdom until this century) a desire to separate the actual processes of administration from political interference. This might mean less congressional intervention, the use of independent regulatory commissions, the invention of such a device as the city manager, the short ballot movement to secure fewer political elections and more official appointments, and so forth. But public service reform was not the only source of the separation of administration from politics. The rise of scientific management, and the prestige of the Prussian type of military organization and of business organization, enhanced the prestige of the manager and the administrator, and depressed that of the politician. The relatively open political system of the United States made clear the existence of distinct administrative processes.

The power of the notion of separation had already been expressed in the 1887 essay by Woodrow Wilson.[6] Wilson laid down that the way to solve administrative problems, not merely to reform public service personnel, but to improve organization and methods, was precisely to recognize the essential difference between administration and politics. Administration was to politics as the counting house was to society. Wilson's essay also contained the confusion, as well as the force, of the idea. It was never clear whether Wilson perceived the difference between saying that administration was a logically different entity from politics and that administration as a process ought to be separate from, and on the whole independent of politics. On the whole, we may suppose that Wilson's particular attitude to the problems of American government motivated him to move from the logical distinction to the institutional recommendation, since what he wished for was less congressional intervention and more presidential power. Whatever the confusion present in Wilson and the movement as a whole, by the 1920s the movement felt that it had fulfilled the programme laid down for it in the essay and had established a theory of who the administrator was, what he did, and what he knew, as a professional being distinct from politics altogether. In particular, he was someone who knew about organization; someone even who knew the whole answer to the problem of perfecting organization anywhere at all; someone whose job was planning, organizing, command, co-ordination and control, to use Fayol's words. Fayol himself laid down in 'the administrative theory' the distinction between administration and all the other processes that went on in any organization, and the distinction between administration and government. POSD-CORB was another mnemonic which symbolized at that time the distinctiveness of the administrator.

Clearly, there were many different sorts of separation that were in mind here, some real and some mythical. But the main point is that at the very moment when the public administration movement achieved its greatest influence, and at the very moment when the scale and independence of administration seemed to be larger and more significant than ever before, the intellectual respectability of the separation began to disappear. Our entire experience of public administration since the 1930s has contributed to this disintegration. A few points may be particularly emphasized.

First the New Deal brought into American public office many intellectuals who had been brought up in the way of assuming that administration, once the election was over, could be conducted independently of politics. All the material we now have on the New Deal shows how quickly they were disillusioned about this matter. Arthur Schlesinger's great history of the New Deal shows the gradual, but ultimately radical and extremely moving change in Harry Hopkins's position.

> 'The purity of the social worker was beginning to melt under new allurements. The first tempter, perhaps, was politics, "Politics", said Hopkins at the height of the Davey fight, "has no business in relief and wherever it gets in, we intend to get rid of it damned fast." Patronage was only one aspect of this problem. Another was the theory that relief was a means of purchasing elections ... In time the political pressure began to tell ... For a while he considered resignation; then, always the realist, he drew the inevitable conclusion. "I thought at first I could be completely non-political", he later said, "and they told me I had to be part non-political and part political. I found that was impossible at least for me. I finally realized that there was nothing for it but to be all political." '[7]

Secondly, the very logic of the distinction between politics and administration began to be questioned. For example, it began to become clear that organizations were not situations in which some made decisions, and others operated them. If all organizational members were making decisions, then some decisions were more important than others. All that could be meant by a policy decision was one which was particularly important to somebody or other making it; a decision which was a 'policy' one for somebody was not a policy decision for another. This was a relativist view of organizations as decision making complexes in which decisions were policy to some members (but not necessarily to all) in so far as they involved important, substantial or risky commitments. This did not destroy the logical difference between politics and administration, but it removed a substantial part of its coherence.

Thirdly, case after case, some of them dramatic, pathological or disastrous, showed the actual emergence of political matters themselves in the most low level and detailed decisions. This is part of the importance of the Crichel Down case or the debates about the defence of superior orders in the Nuremberg Trials. It is a matter of particular importance, as it happens, in the Cabinet system of government. The career of the cabinet minister may well be put at risk by the detailed decision taken low down in the organization without his knowledge, but which unexpectedly looms in political significance through a breakdown in that process of political evaluation of decision making which Appleby has laid down as one of the essential characteristics of public administration.[8] In some ways this is more likely than with decisions which in the very first place are taken at high level and hence involve the support and participation of cabinet colleagues and the party majority itself. The merest details of procedures of control can have the highest degree often of dysfunctional significance, for the actual policies of the organization; for what it is actually moving towards. This is revealed brilliantly in the studies of the *Dynamics of Bureaucracy* by Peter Blau.[9] Blau shows, for example, how the introduction of a simple statistical record of the number of cases handled changed altogether the directions in which a state employment agency moved, though this was not at all the intention of the statistical record, and the record was not, in fact, even intended as a control.

But perhaps the most important aspect of this disintegration is the questions which now have to be asked about the whole doctrine of official neutrality on which the separation, more than anything else, rests. Of course, some systems in fact (and the American was one) were never able to accept the doctrine of neutrality in its extreme form. Furthermore, it has long been a characteristic of radical movements when they first come into power to be suspicious of the bureaucratic instruments to hand. The ideologists of these movements have always anticipated this suspicion. This was part of the whole thesis of Laski's writings about parliamentary democracy in the 1930s. There are now at least three ways in which the problem of neutrality is extraordinarily relevant to administrative development. The first is the situation of the public services in newly independent territories. This may be regarded as the modern instance of the old problem of the coming into power of socialist or labour parties for the first time, in more highly developed states. Clearly, in this situation, the theory of the pure instrumentalism of administration is quite irrelevant to what can be in practice acceptable.

Secondly, there is the problem of excess of neutrality. It is one thing to say that officials must be neutral and anonymous but proficient instruments in the hands of political masters who may change from time to time. But this obligation on their part must impose some sort of obligation on their political masters not to act so as to make this neutrality too difficult to sustain. Alternatively, the professionalization of administration and conditions of high employment security in society as a whole may no longer make it so necessary to insist on the whole doctrine of instrumentality as the basis of a proficient public service. It may be easier for many types of senior public servants to resign from the public service now than it was in different conditions. (This may be a replacement of one possibility by another: some services—especially diplomatic and military—always did contain officials whose social situation made it likely and possible that they would limit their neutrality and be ready to go.) If it is easier it may be right for them to be more prepared to resign. If they are so prepared then they may set limitations on their neutrality which hitherto could not be expressed. We have, perhaps, already begun to see this with some outstanding military and scientific officials, and this may in fact have been the motive for some of the movement of senior officials into business, not merely in the United States, but (more interestingly) in the United Kingdom. The importance of thinking about this matter has already been indicated by Dr. D. C. Corbett[10] and by Mr. R. S. Parker in his recent discussion of the Bazeley Case.[11] Officials in fact are not as neutral as we used to pretend that they were, but at the same time there may be neither a possibility nor a need for them to be so.

Meanwhile, in some instances much more than mere neutrality is demanded. Shils's discussion of *The Torment of Secrecy*,[12] shows how publicity may now be forced to invade what were hitherto private realms of belief and behaviour, for some officials at any rate. If we do not have to worry so much about the neutrality of some officials, we have to worry about much more than the neutrality of others. Altogether the doctrine of neutrality itself is not nearly as useful as it used to be.

But the disintegration of the separation of administration from politics is only one part of the matter. On the other side is the impact of the human relations school on our view of organization and management. This school may still correctly be held to have begun with the Hawthorne experiments and the work of Elton Mayo and the Harvard Graduate School of Business Administration and still indeed to be dominated by that work and the debate about it. As Landsberger has shown,[13] there are many ways in which this contribution can be presented. There is the distinction, for example, between the empirical and the ideological work of the school. This is a distinction between what the Hawthorne and similar experiments actually revealed about the irrationality and group nature of behaviour in organization, and the ideological advocation of a new sort of management as the solution to what was seen as the pathological problems of an adaptive society. Again, there may be some debate about what the human relations school (after all the tremendous amount of research that has been done) has really contributed to our view of organization.[14] Clearly it has emphasized much more than before the significance of informality, small groups, conflict, apathy, and irrationality. There is also a debate about the role of social science as a mere revealing instrument, or as providing manipulative techniques (in the selection and assessment of men or through market or consumer research in the field of policy decisions, or the presentation and creation of images). Hence the rise of the Organization Man as someone who is a result of these manipulative techniques or who accepts them, wields them, or pretends to accept them.

But when one reconsiders the actual research report material in the great volume by Roethlisberger and Dickson,[15] what is borne in on one, more than anything else at all, is the error of the previous presentation of what the administrator particularly knew and was especially able to do. This was further buttressed by the gradual exposure of the ambiguity and usefulness of the classical principles of organizational theory. As a decision maker, then, the administrator is not after all so different from anybody else since all organizational members are decision makers. Nor is he so different from the politicians since his decisions, too, are part of the political process. On the other hand, as a manager, he knows incomparably less about what the organization is really like and what is going on in it than was once supposed. Still more important, he can affect it rationally, far less than classical theory ever supposed.

The whole contribution of recent work, then, has in no sense at all been to lessen one's sense of the strain and difficulty of the administrator's job. On the contrary, it is clearly seen as much more demanding and tense. But at the same time it is also clearly less homogeneous, less distinct, less of a separate entity than the assumptions either of nineteenth-century reform or the American public administration movement provided. Furthermore, the contribution of behaviourism to the study of organization has been to make it less possible to regard organizations solely from the dimension of goal achievement. They also have to be looked at as communities or societies existing to provide a greater or lesser degree of satisfaction for their membership. They continue to exist because they do in fact provide an equilibrium between inducements and contributions. The 'membership' includes both clients[16] and also co-opted agencies of the setting within which the organization operates.[17] The administrator, the person who sees to goal achievement, is altogether less masterful and central in a view of this sort.

This disintegration might then tempt us to say that we ought to leave the American contribution aside and return to the United Kingdom or to European traditions which, in any case, with the growth of state bureaucracy and of the significance of administrative law, might now be seen as more important than ever they were. However, I would argue that it is precisely the crisis in the American tradition which provides the clearest implications about the contribution of public administration to a general political education, much more clearly now than in its more secure past. The point could be put in many ways. Clearly the sorts of things that public administration continues to study are of political significance: the use of models, the study of public policy and decision making, bureaucracy (as significant for parties as for any other type of organization) and new types of contribution to the measurement of the gap between planning and execution. But the central point is precisely that the disintegration of the security with which administration could be separated from other questions, and particularly political questions, has now made the contemplation of the real problems of organization a much more liberalizing education than it had ever previously been. It is an introduction to a profound and passionate debate, and this debate, it seems to me, must be an essential part of a political education, now more than ever before. The point was well put recently by Professor Hodgetts and Dr. Corbett.[18]

'At its best this subject should be a means of liberal education leading to knowledge of oneself and others, broadening the sympathies and freeing the mind from prejudices engendered by familiar social circumstances ... Administrative organizations are human inventions. Their members and clients may sometimes think of them as mechanical, impersonal, inhuman, but that is only a figure of speech since human beings are the components of organizations and human beings create, use and change them for their own purposes. Many people lavish energy and care and even love on the creation and nurture of administrative organizations, that is the effects of relationships among people which constitute these organizations.'

It is precisely what has happened to the study of administration over the last generation or so which has made this debate more intense and more significant. The question for politics as it is approached through the study of organization is not at all the Leninist question of what is to be done but the more complicated and less certain question of what can be done. Organization is a network of decision making within which what is policy decision-making cannot be cut off from the rest, partly because this is a purely relative matter. The other side of this is that all public decision-making, including policy decision-making, occurs in organization. The question, then, is what difference, what limitations, and what influence does this impose, both in the sense of organization as a general phenomenon, and in the particular sense of the occurrence of decision-making in one organization, or type of organization, rather than another. The net effect of the recent work has been to make these questions more difficult (perhaps) but quite unavoidable.

From this point of view it is, in the first place, clear that each of the major contributions of the modern movement to the study of organization has tremendous political assumptions and political implications too. This can be seen in case after case. What, for example, is the most significant difference between the views on organization of Elton Mayo as against F. W. Taylor? On the one hand there is the person who regards organization from the point of view of the rabble hypothesis, that is to say, as consisting of a series of discrete individuals who may be operated upon on the assumption that they will react rationally to incentives. On the other hand, there is the point of view of Mayo who looks at social structures as consisting of powerful but purely emotive group membership. There is a similar degree of political significance in the difference between the Mayo ideology and its critics.[19] Do we want the 'traditional' society with conflict reduced to a minimum, social solidarity, and so forth, or do we want the pluralist society with limited group memberships and in general a state of dissensus? The debate and conflict in organizational theory between the Haldane, Buck and Brownlow tradition on the one hand, and the attitude developed by the Brookings Report on the other hand, is similarly rich in echoes of classic political controversy. On the one hand we have the rationalists who use sets of principles, consciously or unconsciously, to provide an atmosphere of confidence within which radical recommendations can be made and a tremendously simplified structure of government argued for. On the other hand, there are those who once again accept, as Burke accepted, that there is no reason at all why government should be simple or comprehensible at first or even second sight.

Striking echoes of this sort are found throughout the latest contributions to theory including much of the recent work on decision-making techniques and styles, and theories of influence. Should you allow for decision-making better by monocratic processes of hierarchy and sifting, relying on a simplified view of authority; or by a non-directive compromise in which the only influence comes from the possession of particular pieces of knowledge or information? Is it better to postpone decision until certainty is reached, or to impose some sort of decision sooner rather than later? Is it right or wrong to attempt to maximize agreement at the lowest possible level and thus allow the minimal amount of disagreement and decision-making to reach the top; or is it wrong to attempt to relieve the upper levels of organization from the burden of choice and from the chastening view of conflict? These are some of the current decision-making debates. They are all closely related to rival theories of political authority and responsibility.

Similarly, if you turn from how decision-making ought to be done to how it is done, you study the influences that operate on the official at the discretionary moment when he is about to take his decision. This takes you to the heart of the whole problem of the theories of influence and interests. In particular, we may now see that the organizational system itself has influence partly because of the patterns of communication and information supply which it sets up, and partly through what Selznick and others have called 'institutionalization';[20] that is to say, the identifications which develop in or towards the organization irrespective of the goals it is supposed, as a whole, to be serving. At this point Appleby, for example, wishes to distinguish between public and all other forms of administration, according to the notion of 'morality';[21] the greater degree of generality, inclusiveness and periodicity which public administration decision-making has to take into account at this moment of discretion. There is because of the recent debates a tremendous amount of political theory in administrative theory. This was always true. It is much more vivid and significant now precisely because of the disintegration of the single dominant school of the American movement. It is one thing simply to have Taylor's rationalism behind his scientific management; it is another to have the conflict between Mayo and Taylor and another thing again to have a conflict between Mayo and the critics of his ideology. It is one thing to have the Haldane or the Brownlow report; another thing to have a conflict between their reports and their critics.

From this disintegration and debate there emerges one issue of the very greatest significance to all students of politics. The point is that it can only emerge from a study of organization in the way in which these studies have developed over the last generation. It was always true that, to quote Herman Finer, 'Fabianism assumes public administration'. A large part of politics was always administration. Morant saw the public service as the very greatest instrument for social change and reform. Burke himself saw the point. 'Constitute government how you please, infinitely the greater part of it must depend upon the exercise of the powers which are left at large to the prudence and uprightness of ministers of state. Even all the use and potency of the law is dependent upon them. Without them your commonwealth is no better than a scheme upon paper; and not a living, acting effective constitution....'

The due arrangement of men in the action part of the state, far from being foreign to the purposes of the wise government, ought to be among its very highest and dearest objects.' Politics is decision-making in an organizational context and through organization. Morant saw the promise of that and Hopkins in the end came to see its limitations. The point is that recent study has shown the vast difficulties of the situation. There are problems like institutionalization, informal co-optation, the non-instrumentality of organization, unanticipated consequences, crucial decisions which would not seem to be crucial at the time, and so forth. Organization, that is to say, is the unavoidable instrument but it is not simply an instrument either. Looked at in this way, what public administration now shows us is not at all the distinct and masterly administrator, neutral from politics, effective in his management. On the contrary, we see the passionate aim and requirement of achieving at least something, against the whole series of difficulties which present themselves time and time again. This was Churchill's cry throughout the material in his war histories, the difficulty of getting a thing done.

The major significance of recent work is to show precisely the nature and unavoidability of this difficulty. The organization becomes settled and an end in itself, institutionalized. It establishes itself in its community or environment by processes of informal co-optation, by whole networks of commitment which alter altogether its original intentions. Its goals are not single or even harmonious, but undefined, many, changing, and generally competitive and conflicting. Within the organization some objectives or values are a matter of consensus beyond debate and must be accepted. Others are not perceived at all. Apathy is a major influence in what occurs within organization. For the rest there is conflict and competition. It is useless to suppose that simplification can be achieved within major organizations, still less within whole machineries of government. The machine will inevitably be a chaos of establishments. Perhaps this is as well. Attempts at simplification or control are likely to have dysfunctions. Detailed changes will have strange and unanticipated consequences, not all of them, of course, pathological or morbid.

But the point of all this difficulty is that we should not altogether desert Bentham for Burke but somehow or other compromise between them, as Mill himself attempted to compromise between Bentham and Coleridge. Organizations are not simply instrumental Yet, at the same time, it is more than ever through organization that things have to be done. It is no use ignoring the fact that decision-making occurs in this peculiar setting. Nor is it any use to pretend that these organizations are simply rational instruments, no more and no less. But this, of course, ought simply to increase one's sympathy and sense of excitement at the spectacle of some achievement in administration. The study of programmes and policies and of administrative invention has always been inspiriting. All the contribution of recent work in organization ought to make one much more sympathetic. If the administrator was a separate and more or less efficient manager of the rational machine, it was no doubt perfectly acceptable for the study of politics to ignore the study of the administrator once it had settled questions like public service reform and administrative control: once it was satisfied that proficiency had been provided and responsibility established. There may be doubts about proficiency and responsibility or the relevance of the ways in which proficiency and responsibility had been established in the past to present conditions. But, quite apart from that, if the administrator is not like the previous picture at all, surely the contemplation of his struggle becomes far more relevant and interesting for general political studies: relevant because the search for power and for particular programmes goes on continuously throughout the organization, and interesting because the rival views of what does and ought to happen in organisation are so similar to the rival views of what does and ought to happen in the political community as a whole. Furthermore, some recent work has sought ways for strengthening the possibilities both of manipulation and of rational decision-making within this peculiar setting. Other work has stressed organizational unreliability. The very coincidence of this advance of decision-making theory with the deepening understanding of the irrationality of organization is extraordinarily relevant to the current political science. Computers calculate routes just when the trustworthiness of the vehicles is brought into question. Administrative organizations are essential communities in the political process, inescapable but unreliable, factors as much as instruments. To be aware of organization in this sense seems more than ever before a vital part of a political education and, perhaps, any humane education, too.

NOTES

1 See esp., J. G. March and H. A. Simon, *Organisations*, N.Y., 1958.
2 R. S. Parker, 'New Concepts of Administration', *Public Administration* (Sydney), March 1962, pp. 21-32.
3 Beatrice Webb, *Our Partnership*. Ed. by B. Drake and M. I. Cole, London, 1948, p. 94.
4 W. A. Robson, 'The Present State of Teaching and Research in Public Administration', *Public Administration* (London), 1961, pp. 217-222.
5 Benson and Esher, eds. *The Letters of Queen Victoria*, 1837-1861, I, (1908), pp. 106-108.
6 'The Study of Administration', *Political Science Quarterly*, 2, June 1887, pp. 197-222.
7 A. M. Schlesinger, Jr. *The Age of Roosevelt*, III, Boston, 1960, pp. 353-5.
8 *Policy and Administration*, Alabama 1949, *passim. cf.* S. Encel, *Public Administration* (London) Autumn 1960, for some doubts on ministerial responsibility in Australia.
9 P. M. Blau, *Dynamics of Bureaucracy*, Chicago, 1955.
10 *Public Administration* (Sydney) June 1961, pp. 103-6.
11 *Public Administration* (Sydney) December 1961, pp. 291-304.
12 Glencoe, 1956.
13 H. A. Landsberger, *Hawthorne Revisited*, N.Y. 1958.
14 N. Grodzins, 'Public Administration and the Science of Human Relations', 11 *Public Administration Review*, 1951, pp. 88-102.
15 F. J. Roethlisberger and W. J. Dickson, *Management and the Worker*, Cambridge, Mass., 1939.
16 C. I. Barnard, *The Functions of the Executive*, Cambridge, Mass., 1938.
17 P. Selznick, *TVA and the Grassroots*, Berkeley, 1949.
18 *Canadian Public Administration*, Toronto, 1960, pp. v-vi.
19 *cf.* Landsberger, *op. cit.* For extreme criticisms see the well-known work by W. H. Whyte, *The Organisation of Man*, and also L. Baritz, *The Servants of Power*, Middletown, 1960.
20 *cf.* P. Selznick, *Leadership in Administration*, Evanston, 1957.
21 *cf. Morality and Administration in Democratic Government.*

4

THEORY AND PRACTICE IN THE MACHINERY

OF GOVERNMENT

The idea of administration and its disciplinary problems were discussed in some of the preceding chapters, and in other papers not here: Public Administration and the University (University of Queensland Gazette, *September 1957, pp. 8-13*), *Administrative Ideas and Local Government* (QIMA Journal, *December 1957, pp. 5-11*), *and Designing a Course in Public Administration* (APSA News, *March 1958, pp. 1-4*). *But as the distinction between politics and administration became more familiar and acceptable in the nineteenth century so it became all too easy to study bureaucracy and organization separately within the study of government. A comparison, for Britain, of the suspicious though knowing attitude of Palmerston to bureaucracy in 1837 with the Haldane report of 1918 is instructive, or, for the United States, of Presidents Jackson and Wilson.*

The Haldane report was, perhaps, the main example of an attempt to look at bureaucracy and the machinery of government as a wholly non-political problem. That contributed to its reiterated exemplary role. In the end, a growth of some scholarly criticism of it made it possible to see its faults and the limitations of this approach to reorganization: W. J. M. Mackenzie, The Structure of Central Government, in Campion and others, British Government since 1918, Allen and Unwin, 1950; D. N. Chester and F. M. G. Willson, The Organization of British Central Government, 1957; W. J. M. Mackenzie and J. W. Grove, Central Administration in Britain, 1957; and L. J. Hume, the Origins of the Haldane Report, in this number of Public Administration (Sydney) were all useful. My own first criticism was in The Machinery of Central Government, Local Government Officer and Student, Vol. I, No. 2, December 1953.

In fact alternative approaches to reorganization are possible, which do not rely on the big commission and principles of allocation and use standing machinery, a more conservative approach and more political sensitivity. They might look at the centre of the government machine and the possibilities of hiving off, as we are now, in fact, doing.

HALDANE

The Report of the 1918 Haldane Committee in the United Kingdom[1] must certainly be allowed some parental rights over the term 'machinery of government'. Its statement about the allocation of functions has been, perhaps, especially famous: 'Upon what principle are the functions of Departments to be determined and allocated? There appear to be only two alternatives, which may be briefly described as distribution according to the persons or classes to be dealt with, and distribution according to the services to be performed ... the one which we recommend for adoption is that of defining the field of activity in the case of each Department according to the particular service which it renders to the community as a whole.'[2] This was to be a way of describing work and for deciding upon its allocation. The consequences of each method were, the Report said, known; the two were the only ones available; the second—allocation by service—should always be used, the other always rejected.

The influence of this Report created a notion of a mystery to which there was one key. The benighted officials in the Castle were without this magic masterpiece. In fact this notion was wrong; worse, it was misleading. The status of the Report has been ill-deserved. Now that more work is proceeding about the machinery of government and the possibility of great improvements is being canvassed, it becomes more important to secure that this influence is ended and more possible to hope that this may be brought about. How far is this so? What sort of approach should replace it? It is the purpose of this paper to make some contribution to an investigation of these questions from the point of view of contemporary writing about the machinery of government, further study of the Haldane Report and its sources, and some experience of machinery of government work.

SOME CRITICISMS

We may begin here by looking at Professor Mackenzie's essay. In this assessment Mackenzie stressed the dominance over the whole Report of three members of the Committee (Haldane himself, Morant and Beatrice Webb) and of the particular ends with which these three remarkable persons had been or were concerned, such as a comprehensive Ministry of Health. The Report looked back to the old campaigns and interests of these reformers and its 'great principle' of allocation was simply a deduction from their special ambitions. Rightly enough they saw the bureaucracy and bureaucratic organization as a problem of independent significance. But their very zest imposed limitations. Perhaps this was most important, according to Mackenzie's account, in their famous definition of the three-fold functions of the Cabinet in which they totally ignored the fundamental fact about that institution: its parliamentary and national leadership of the majority political party. Responsibility and its provision is certainly one of the great factors in a governmental machine and the Haldane Committee's inadequate conception of the Cabinet coloured and flawed the whole of its picture.[3]

Mackenzie added other criticisms to this. The Report's ten-fold classification of governmental activities is not (now at any rate) the most useful. The contemporary five-fold one (defence, foreign affairs, social services, finance and law and order) is simpler and more complete. There are now functions unanticipated by the authors of the Report and their recommendations have had no relation to actual developments. In general, Mackenzie concluded, 'their conclusions were largely wrong, or at least irrelevant'.[4]

Mackenzie's own survey of the machinery of government indicated to him the role of politics and accident in what had happened, and this was, he thought, 'on the whole' outside administrative planning. He went on, however, to recommend that administrative planning about reorganization ought to take into account human relations including the interests of clients and of the staffs who were to be reorganized. This was a great step forward which, within the scope of the essay, Mackenzie could not fully illumine; nor did he attack nearly strongly enough the very citadel —the principle of allocation by service. He pointed out that we needed to know much more about the composition of the Report; we do now know more about this. We must now acknowledge, for example, that the ideas of the Report about the Cabinet owed a great deal to the evidence given by Hankey, not just to the predilections of Haldane, Morant and Webb. The influence of Montagu and, in relation to Treasury control, of Murray, counted too.[5]

Mackenzie also wanted to know more about what was then (1950) being done about the machinery of government. The work of Messrs. Chester and Willson and their collaborators does take us a good deal farther in this and other respects. Their chapter on 'The Handling of Administrative Change' is especially important, and may be compared with the revision of Mackenzie's views suggested in his recent volume with Mr. Grove.[6] The ostensible nature of Chester and Willson's discussion is primarily an elucidation of what the factors of change in the machinery of government have actually been. They explain that these factors have been concerned with (*a*) the number of Ministers and (*b*) the grouping of functions. About the first they note a balance between forces making for an increase and those making for a reduction in the number. They are certainly not prepared to allow that there has been any one factor that has determined or could be used to explain what has happened to the machine, though they are prepared to acknowledge the factors that have mattered and to move from this sort of description to some estimate of guides or solutions. They also discuss the sort of questions that can be called machinery of government questions, such as arrangements about the distribution of 'entirely new' functions or existing functions which need to be considered afresh or are not working as they should. They assess the machinery for taking thought about these questions, and the nature of the decisions taken.[7]

Three things stand out. First, Chester and Willson may accept most of the decisions, but, despite their evidence about the decision-making process here, they do not suggest that the creation of administrative machinery for machinery of government work is a waste of time. It has been improved. This implies notions of better rather than worse and it also implies an assumption of some sort of role for rationality in the decisions. The conservatism which, as Mr. Encel has said,[8] marks this volume is not a retreat from reason. This is welcome, of course; is it justified? The second thing is that Chester and Willson do not think the Haldane Report itself now matters. They show that various specific recommendations of the Report have been set aside, or, rather, that they have 'never been tried or even mooted',[9] or that their acceptance was due primarily to other bodies. But, of course, *this* very lack of effect of such a document is in itself a most important piece of evidence; is not a more deliberate assessment of the Report called for?

Thirdly the detailed material in this book also shows (this is not surprising) the involution of machinery of government decisions in politics, persons, policies and departmental traditions: what some people will call irrelevant considerations, but what Sir Horace Wilson more wisely referred to as 'apparently irrelevant factors'.[10] This can be seen with the Ministry of Housing and Local Government, the Ministry of Agriculture and Food, or with arguments about the organization of common services like the supply of defence material. The 1951 decision about the allocation of responsibilities for health, local government, housing and town and country planning, which led to the creation of the Ministry of

Housing and Local Government, was certainly the right one.[11] We may note that the Treasury's Machinery of Government Branch (which had by then been in the Organization and Methods Division for some time) had concerned itself with this matter.[12] The actual opportunity for change was a political and personal one. May we not also suppose that here was an instance where administrative planning was successful because it was prepared with a sound decision for which the occasion did arise? Very different was the decision to dump the remnant of the Ministry of Food into the Ministry of Agriculture and Fisheries. This decision was taken in 1955. By then the Machinery of Government Branch had all but disappeared, and the new procedure for machinery of government questions was therefore used.[13] Chester and Willson in effect defend the decision.[14] The alternatives they put (a rump Ministry of Food or an amalgamation with the Board of Trade) were unacceptable for important reasons: the need in the one case to restrict the number of Ministers and in the other not to over-burden the already toppling Trade department. But it is difficult to accept that the actual outcome was the only way left or that it was the solution that would have been produced by a M.G. Branch which was doing its job. If policy results were to be a factor in decisions about the machinery of government it would have to be remembered that the handling of consumer problems by a Ministry of Agriculture would certainly be different from their handling in any other organization. But in this case the political opportunity for a different solution did not arise.

The superficiality of the perennial debates about responsibility for defence supply is fully illustrated here. This could also be studied in the brilliant pages of Messrs. Scott and Hughes about War Production.[15] The deployment of terms like 'standard stores' or 'technical warlike stores' has always been talmudic in its nicety, but the real argument, despite the Haldane Committee or the Inchcape Committee or any of their successors, has been decided by factors quite external to this sort of discussion. Must M.G. work take these traditions into account too? The departmental philosophy of an Admiralty, or a supply department doctrine about the expertness of buying, do matter. Political occasions, policy results and departmental traditions must be factors in M.G. work if it is to be effective and sensible too.

MACHINERY OF GOVERNMENT WORK

An acceptance of Chester and Willson's work would commit one to a belief that M.G. work can and should be done and that there will be a role for officials to play in this. The Haldane way is not the appropriate method. The work should be conservative: the manner of what had been done indicates the possibilities and it can be shown that M.G. work itself must accept these limitations; good work is what is effective and, therefore, what is acceptable; the factors of actual change are the right guides to what ought to be changed. The knowledge needed for this is demanding, extensive, and empirical: what has been done and what has been said before. You must, then, bring senior officials into this work for their influence and for the sense of timing which Bridges has celebrated elsewhere.[16] M.G. work is an exercise in inter-departmental relations. Burke, it would seem, is the right philosopher for its practice. This is clearly in close sympathy with Professor Mackenzie's approach. It goes much farther than his essay did, and there is great wisdom in it. Certain questions must, however, be asked. Have the Haldane and other sets of principles really been disposed of? How, from this point of view, is M.G. work as an administrative and rational process to be conducted? What sort of knowledge and equipment can meet its demands?

First, then, have Chester and Willson been tough enough? Have they completely liberated the discussion of M.G. work from the influence of artificial principle and have they altogether disposed of the Haldane Report? It is true that they are at points unequivocal enough. They are convinced that there is thorough justification for scepticism about the existence of a single set of 'two or three rules or laws whose application would make it possible to decide at any moment, clearly and without room for controversy, how many departments there should be and which department should undertake this or that function'.[17] However, they do not elsewhere appear to have fully caught up with the notion that any statement of principles at all, in the old style, is as such, to quote Herbert Simon, 'essentially useless'.[18] Such statements can provide no basis for adjudication at all; they are inherently ambiguous. Willson and Chester are themselves kind to a previous attempt to set up a principle of 'homogeneity'.[19] This is certainly a highly generalized notion. It is fairly clear that it is either a tautology ('you should group together functions if they should be grouped together rather than apart') or wrong. Indeed Chester and Willson very properly show that sometimes functions should be kept apart precisely because they are 'similar'.[20] They quote the allocation of responsibility for the University Grants Committee to the Chancellor of the Exchequer rather than to the Minister for Education, recommendations against the allocation of the Crown Lands Commission to a Minister of Agriculture and the opposition to a Ministry of

Justice. The study of non-ministerial organizations like the U.G.C. or the Crown Lands Commission is full of examples like these cases. The allocation of the Children's Act to the Home Office may be quoted as another instance where a job was given to a department precisely because that department wanted to vary its work; the department wanted a 'beneficent' function to administer. Similarly the authors are much too kind to the 'dominant-subordinate' rule (which was the Haldane Report's offering as a device to solve those problems of allocation which even that Committee saw would survive the enunciation of its great principle) but their kindness breaks down as soon as they look round for a case where in practice the rule would be of any assistance.[21] This rule is, in fact, as 'essentially useless' as any of the others. It is the details and life of cases that provide the value of study in this field.

Mackenzie's original discussion of the Haldane principles (he has now modified his attitude)[22] was based on the assumption that the choice was between two clear methods, that it was a real choice and that it would have few, definite, recognizable and known consequences. What was wrong with the Haldane statement, it was implied, were two things: it did not take into account that the known consequences of using the clientele principle might in certain cases be more advantageous than those of the service principle; and both these principles were 'low-grade', that is, more applicable to the allocation of work within than between departments. Chester and Willson, like Mackenzie, see that the outcome will not always, as Haldane thought, be a foregone conclusion, but they are aware of four rivals (service, client, area, process) instead of Haldane's two. They bring other factors into account (the minimization of the number of Ministers and the clarification of responsibility) which can certainly be more helpful than the twofold or fourfold test, foregone or not. Unlike Mackenzie they see that the problem of allocation may be more difficult to solve and the range of choice become greater as you descend the scale of importance and function. But, whatever they say, elsewhere, they accept the 'four'. Why four? One could certainly think of other definitions of functional allocation which would be as useless as principles and as useful as diagnostic criteria as these are. They say that the source of the four is experience. Surely it is simply the literature of the subject? The experience they describe does not contain any decisions based on an attempt to carry out any one of these 'principles'; and one could use any piece of this experience as an example of almost any one of these generalizations in almost any way. Here is an example in the allocation of recruitment to the Ministry of Labour: area (they have the local offices); clientele (they are in touch with young civilian labour); service (manpower distribution); process (expertness in handling local individual applications and enforcements), and so forth.

Could these statements become diagnostic criteria? A great deal would have to be done before they could become useful parts of a comparative and consistent terminology. Chester and Willson do not seem concerned to carry over the quality of their descriptive work into an attempt to do this sort of work, that is to bridge the gap of theory and practice. For example while they say that there are indeed 'four general criteria' which are 'important tests',[23] at an earlier stage they attempt to dismiss one of them (class of persons or clientele) by showing that you could not organize the whole of government in this way. Of course, you could in fact describe the whole of government as organized in this way if you wanted to (farmers, Scotsmen, schoolchildren, foreigners) and here is one of the reasons for not bothering with that sort of discussion. Alternatively no one (except for Haldane) would want to argue that you ought to organize the whole of government in any one way or that all the problems of the machinery of government could be solved by using only one test. Do Willson and Chester feel that they now have exclusive definitions for these terms and knowledge of definite consequences from employing each method? Clearly this is not their usual position; but if these generalizations are merely to be used as 'tests' then they need, not the sort of treatment given to 'class of persons', but quite a different sort of discussion, which Chester and Willson do not provide at all.

The second problem is whether Chester and Willson have solved the difficulties of demonstrating that M.G. work, once you have given up the earlier hopes, can in fact be done as a rational administrative process at all and that it is worth the candle to try it; that it is not just another dogfight. We have already noted that we lack a comparative language for this work. The implications of this are very important. For one thing, if the approach to the sort of knowledge required for M.G. work (that is, the sort of knowledge which would put its possessor one up) is through 'the constant study of the factors influencing the structure' of a particular government then it would follow (*a*) that you will have a problem in staffing and siting the sort of unit that can devote itself to this and (*b*) that you may as well discard the Gulick-type notes on the theory of organization. No short cuts; the preparation for M.G. work in any system will depend on the existence of a Chester and Willson for that system, on their multiplication and on much more detailed applications of this method. There may be no reason for anyone to be dispirited by this, but he must see the problems it raises for the public service and for the student. For the practitioner it is a matter of the supply of information and the implications for his power of his devotion of time to his work. For the student it is a matter of the availability of material, unless he is prepared to accept the first verdict in particular cases, and official verdicts at that; and then of how he is going to communicate the contribution of one study to another case, or one system to another. Will patient virtue be rewarded?

Chester and Willson themselves give a study of the relations between a series of departments about responsibility for town and country planning.[24] This is a tantalizing sketch of the fuller study that could be done. The creation in the United Kingdom early in the last war of a Ministry of Works, and then a Ministry of Works and Building; its brief existence as a Ministry of Works and Planning; the birth and death of the Ministry of Town and Country Planning (how hard, one recalls, that its headquarters were built at last and its name engraved in stone just at the moment of its demise!) and the final emergence of a Ministry of Housing and Local Government (as a renaming of the Ministry of Local Government and Planning):—the whole sequence from 1940 to 1951, and the dimensions of the problems raised and of the personalities involved (Reith, Greenwood, Bevan, Dalton), is a first-class example of the sort of case which can provide research material at least and experience by proxy at best. This is no doubt the most important sort of M.G. knowledge. But the contribution is limited. The limitation of space is important, for it is the details that matter. The demands of conservatism should not provide an automatic acceptance of the official line or a wiping away of the memory of controversy. As Sir Horace Wilson comments on Chester and Willson, 'few general readers ... will have enough knowledge on the period covered ... to be able always to appreciate the significance of the factual statements made, many of which relate to events which, at the time, were felt to be of considerable importance'.[25]

Whether the M.G. man can transfer his knowledge he can at any rate transfer his questions. The attempt by Chester and Willson to suggest more useful questions, by a checklist, or by criteria more useful than client, service, etc., is a most important contribution. Again, the limitations must be seen. A recognition of the significance of size is one thing, for example; knowing the point at which to draw the line is another. These criteria are not very refined. The idea of giving the M.G. man the sort of checklist equipment his O and M colleague has is very sensible; it is certainly a possible key to the problems of this work to look for much more help to O and M. As a routine matter M.G. work is likely to be greatly assisted by the information produced by a series of O and M surveys over a field, where the surveys have in fact been done. But the questions on the checklist must be genuine, and not mere *petitio principii*, and, as has been argued elsewhere, the size and factors of M.G. decisions impose a strain which prevents O and M methods from being utterly reliable or relevant here.[26]

The M.G. man, then, would need to know a good deal of detail about cases, where to get his information and the questions to ask. He might also get to know about organizational devices, for example in the hiving off of executive work from Ministerial departments so as to relieve Ministers or reduce their numbers. But will all this be sufficient? For one thing, how can he use his cases without a language of comparison and transference? It has already been suggested that the use of diagnostic criteria as a basis for this language would demand a great deal of work that has not yet been done, and that their usefulness will remain limited. They are expositors, not censors; they indicate. The problems have still to be detected and then solved, and there will be problems of consequences, balance, selection and boundaries between similar or dissimilar arrangements. Nor is it sufficient to recognize that M.G. work is a result of politics and persons and to suppose that these may be left out of account in official level work on the one hand or theory on the other. What is the point of doing work that specifically excludes the most important determinants? These factors should be taken into account not only because they do matter but because they should matter. This, like terminology, is difficult: how to weight political opportunity, policy results, departmental politics: how to take all this into account but yet not convert M.G. into purely political (i.e. non-administrative) decision-making and so neither frustrate nor destroy the official machine for M.G. work; how to discover the very odd answers that must sometimes be given.

Chester and Willson are committed to two beliefs: (*a*) that the machinery of government is a result of these factors among others, and (*b*) that the procedure and machinery for doing M.G. work has gone through certain recognizable phases and is now (therefore?) better equipped than before. But why, unless it has learned how to take these factors in its stride? If this has been done it is a great achievement. We should be shown how and that it has happened, viz., that M.G. work has made an advantageous difference to the decisions taken. This is not done. Not everyone familiar with the 1948-51 period (when the M.G. Branch was at its peak of work) will agree with the estimate given here, and not everyone, presented with the decision about the Ministry of Food as evidence of the still better quality of the post-1951 systems, will accept that as good evidence of improvement.

It is difficult enough, when there are no short cuts, for the M.G. man to feel confident about himself (as against the actual parties involved) in knowledge of the particular case, or to be sure of the relevance or accuracy of his knowledge of other cases. He still has to demonstrate, indeed, that there is a case at all, that there is a need for re-arrangement or that existing arrangements should be defended against some proposal or agreed change. He still has to detect the problems. Where will he find the solutions, then, the devices and the formulae? How many factors is he (an official) to take into account, or how many may he ignore without destroying the viability of his recommendation? What sort of procedure and machinery for his work, what sort of O and M for M.G. work itself, so to speak, will solve these problems?

The Chester and Willson contribution therefore falls short at certain points: in its treatment of Haldane and in its discussion of the language and methods of M.G. work. This is scarcely surprising and scarcely a criticism, but some aspects of these two matters may be further considered here. What should we now say about Haldane Report? Secondly, granted that the way of empiricism is hard, the man who has followed the road can know it; can no more guides be given to those who have yet to travel?

THE ERRORS OF HALDANE

As a guide, a plan or a general theory, the Haldane Report, we can now see, suffers from a whole series of faults. Its notions of the functions of government and of the Cabinet institution were wrong. Its statement about the allocation of functions was meaningless and misleading. It has had no actual influence at all. Where developments have been in apparent sympathy with its recommendations, closer inspection reveals material differences or other causes. The Ministry of Health is an outstanding case in point. Often attributed to the Haldane recommendation, the decision was in fact taken independently of the Report and before it was finished.[27] In any case, the Report's recommendation was for a Ministry with housing policy only as a very minor and incidental adjunct, yet housing became the dominant creative function of the department set up. Many of the recommendations in the Report which were of deep importance to its members, like the creation of a Ministry of Justice or parliamentary standing committees on the U.S. or French model, have been completely ignored. This lack of result was not a misfortune but rather, as the Chester and Willson approach would suggest, a sign of the weakness of the Report itself.

This may be shown in other ways. It is most striking in connection with non-ministerial organizations especially for the running of nationalized industries. This has been, Lord Waverley said, 'Probably the most striking development in administrative technique of our generation,' (viz., of the 1920-1950 period).[28] It was to reverse the whole trends and doctrine of the Victorian period. At that precise moment what the Report did was to go out of its way to echo the old doctrine that such organization was unnecessary and improper. This is such a breathtaking misjudgment, it is so significant about the Report as a whole, and the way in which the Report attempts to justify its attitude is so peculiar, that this particular error deserves a degree of attention which it has not yet received.

The nature of the nineteenth-century opposition to any deviation from the ministerial department has been discussed elsewhere.[29] This, on the whole, continued as the conventional attitude in the first world war. It was, after all, only then that the usage of 'Ministry' was, so to speak, officially born. The Report was enveloped in this convention. The question was then important in relation to post-war reconstruction; to the replacement of wartime organization and of the weakening of normal controls; and to the legacy of the great Lloyd George experiments of the immediately pre-war regime. Those experiments had already initiated a new phase in the use of non-ministerial organization with the Road Board, Development Commission and National Health Insurance organization. This was the background. It was not that the Report by-passed the question. It was fully aware of the problem. Deliberately, carefully and seeking evidence where it could, it chose the wrong answer. Its answer was expressed in its recommendations about the organization of nationalized industry, about the Lloyd George experiments (none of the authors of the Report had any particular affection for Lloyd George) and in other cases. Its basic evidence lay in its famous use of certain words from the 1914 Report of the Royal Commission on the Civil Service—the MacDonnell Commission. We may briefly recall here what the Haldane Report said and suggest why it said it and how improper its use of the MacDonnell Commission was.

The Report said that 'where any great enterprise is nationalized' the administration should be done by a department. It saw nothing in the departmental organization for defence or postal services that could not apply to railways or coal (to quote its examples). In the general discussion of departmental organization it said it would have none of this deviation (viz., of the Lloyd George experiments) from Ministerial responsibility or the departmental norm. It did not accept that any non-ministerial organization would be better suited either to 'securing responsibility for official action and advice' or for 'certain functions of government which require for their exercise a judicial temper and a position of independence'. Scattered through the whole Report are recommendations which one way or another demonstrate its belief in the comprehensive ministerial department and its opposition to various forms of non-ministerial organization. The second part of the Report explains the importance of separating a ministry dealing with private enterprise from one 'responsible for the direct employment of large numbers of men and women', but this job would still be given to a 'minister'. Non-ministerial organizations as various as the Registry of Friendly Societies, the Stationery Office, the Development Commission, the Charity Commission, the Board of Control, should all be absorbed into ministerial departments. State functions in forestry should be allocated to a department. A Ministry of Intelligence and Research should ultimately replace the Privy Council Committees and the non-ministerial organizations stemming therefrom.[30]

Why was the Haldane Committee led in this direction? It was still the conventional opinion of the time. Chester and Willson mention the existence of a then general assumption that nationalization would be by departments.[31] But this, presumably, is an insufficient explanation. The further explanation depends on a realization that the motivation of the authors of the Report was not purely, as Mackenzie suggested, a set of particular interests, but, in addition, a desire encouraged by the wartime situation to reduce the number of separate departments. Thus it was sufficient to show that allocation by persons would lead to 'lilliputian' administration —an increase in the number of departments—to condemn that method as a bad thing.[32] Allocation by service was therefore the right method. There was nothing in this method, it was argued, that could not apply to nationalized services just as much as other services. The extraordinary thing is that this closed the eyes of the committee to a completely different matter: the actual growth of strain for ministerial departments in width of functions, number and variety of processes and staff, and the whole problem of scale and scatter. To this problem the argument about allocation was really irrelevant. Here the solution was to be found precisely in the use of non-ministerial organization to relieve departments. It would be non-ministerial organization, not this or that method of allocation, that would be in fact the outstanding device for keeping down the number of ministers and departments. The Committee's belief in its single talisman blinded it to the virtues of the device that would achieve just what it most wanted; indeed its faith led it to oppose that very device.

What makes this still more striking is the quality of the arguments the Report explicitly employed against non-ministerial organization. Its first argument was directed specifically against Lloyd George's Road Board and Development Commission. Here what it did was to make two assumptions. The first was that the argument for these boards had been that their functions had required for their exercise 'a judicial temper and a position of independence' and the second assumption was that this simply meant that the sponsorship of the boards had thought their functions to be especially important. This then enabled the Report to deny that the importance of a service was a sufficient argument for its exemption from the conditions of the normal ministerial department.[33] But this was a caricature of the actual arguments used for the creation of these two boards.

The second argument used by the Haldane Report was again based on an assumption. This was that there were only two reasons put forward for the creation of non-ministerial bodies. It had already dealt with one in the case of the Road Board and Development Commission. The other reason used, it said, was that boards might sometimes be better suited for 'securing responsibility for official action and advice'; and this had already been authoritatively demolished by the fourth report of the MacDonnell Commission. But, in the first place, the point in the MacDonnell Report[34] referred to by Haldane was not a general conclusion at all; it was a specific conclusion about certain Irish and, to a lesser extent, Scottish boards, and so to a very peculiar chapter of administrative history. The conclusion was to the effect that these boards worked in such a way as to confuse ministerial and administrative roles; and that they avoided civil service conditions, especially in their top staffing. In the second place, MacDonnel was in fact quite prepared to accept deviation from ministerial responsibility and the use of a board in the case of the Development Commission, for instance. Its criticism of the Development Commission and of the Road Board was simply of their failure to employ civil service conditions, a central topic for MacDonnell but not for Haldane at all. It could be demonstrated that the conclusion of the MacDonnell Commission about the Irish and Scottish Boards was not fully justified by its own evidence, which suggested a much more complex answer about the ways in which those boards had worked. It could also be shown that one of the two questions it put to all its

Irish and Scottish witnesses, why their boards did not employ any or many administrative civil servants (the other question was about board procedure and meetings), was not fully relevant to the special Irish and Scottish conditions then. It was still less relevant to new conditions elsewhere. But whatever faults may be attributed to the MacDonnell conclusion are much less than must be attributed to the Haldane Report for its wholly improper use of such a tentative, limited, doubtful and irrelevant conclusion.

A NEW APPROACH

A final attitude on the Haldane Report was one of the problems left over from the work of Chester and Willson. The other problem was whether any more guides can be given for the empirical practice of machinery of government work and its requirements and procedures. Chester and Willson attempt to derive from the straight description of what has happened some notions of the factors that have actually been at work. If you subsume the factors that ought to matter in the factors that have mattered, and if you proceed with further study along these lines, then you might well be able to amplify your conception of the forces at work and the devices employed. One could, for instance, add to the idea of the minimization of the number of Ministers several similar factors. Some such additions for British practice are suggested here, by way of example.

In the first place there has been at work the increasing importance of interdepartmental relations and, of what, in the U.K. context, may be called the centre of the government machine. This is a matter, firstly, of seeing the role of the Cabinet as a pinnacle of a machinery of interdepartmental relations and, secondly, of seeing that the Cabinet is a complex, not a single institution. The Cabinet now means a pyramid of committees, not a single meeting. It does not include all Ministers. Positions in the committee hierarchy are probably as important as formal membership of the Cabinet. Types of Minister, of committee and of joint staff are now more various than they once were, and as various as other types of organization in central government.

The current shape of the Cabinet is one thing. Secondly, the present methods of interdepartmental relations require a good deal of standing machinery. There are the committees and they have to be serviced. The thin divisions between servicing, central control and common services must be appreciated. There grow up a number of units performing functions ancillary not to any one department but to the whole machine. At the highest level one can detect a more or less permanent nucleus of such units which one might call the centre of the government machine. This would include the Prime Minister's Office, most sections of the Cabinet Office and certain sections of the Treasury. Round this nucleus is a varying constellation of other units depending on the personalities and problems of the Cabinet at the time. At one moment there may be found a small department like the former Ministry of Materials; at another moment one may find a Paymaster-General.

In the U.K., then, interdepartmental relations, or, rather, the creation and maintenance of this machinery and relations to and within it, have been a factor of increasing importance. A second factor has been the conception of the roles of departments and changes in these conceptions. These determine organizations and relationships. The history of town and country planning, again, would be an excellent example of this. What a Ministry of Town and Country Planning would look like, what its structure would be, what functions would be allocated to it and what its relationships would be like would depend on this conception: should its role be research or control, for example; should its planning relate to industrial location? One might add that rapid changes in role conceptions weaken the position of a department and this also is evidenced by this story. Decisions about the machinery of government emerge in this sense from decisions about roles; and this is as true as the notion that policy and programme will be changed by changes in organization.

A third factor has been the strain on the normal, pyramidal, administrative department imposed by technical work casework, interlinked topics and so forth. Other forces (public relations, consultation, the shedding of routine, government patronage, etc.) have also been at work. So the use of organizations ancillary to the ministerial department becomes one of the dominant features of the machinery of government. As the Cabinet is now a complex and as the official centre of the government is now a group of units, so the contemporary ministerial department must be seen as a nucleus for a variety of non-ministerial organizations. This, in turn, means that typical machinery of government problems are provoked by the relations of these bodies, decisions about their use and choices amongst the variety of devices and arrangements that is thus made available.

Changes in role and deviation from the norm may both be related to the impact on the governmental machine of new techniques of work. One is not referring here to the more obvious point about new or enlarged responsibilities and functions, but to actual techniques of work. These may arise from new functions: for example the need to develop new techniques of control in relation to government science. This has created new bodies (Atomic Energy Authority, the Research Councils etc.), new personnel systems (e.g. for the scientific civil service) and, also, new problems of administrative technique as between a responsible Minister (e.g., a Lord President of the Council) and a research council. A second example would be the handling of international relations by primarily home departments as well as by departments of defence, trade and foreign affairs.

Finally, in the British machine, one must expect to see a backyard with dustbins, a well-stocked museum and a no-man's land. There are departments like the Home Office where one can allocate the odds and ends which cannot go anywhere else. The dustbins are more important than the museum pieces, but these, too, are a specialty of the British machine and they are sometimes taken out to adorn new working machinery: the use of the Privy Council as a starting point for the organization of scientific research is an example. Despite the golden rule of administration, interests do overlap, work is duplicated and marginal difficulties do occur. Functions may be found in a no-man's-land, neglected or disputed. Sometimes this may not matter; sometimes it may be positively a good thing (another of the oddities of machinery of government work). In any case the area is there and we cannot hope to abolish it, though its frontiers may sometimes be changed.

You can get to know what will work from what has worked and what matters in any one system. You can also get to know what will not work. For example the idea of 'overlord' Ministers tried by the Churchill government in 1951 is now dead: the report of Lord Attlee's Committee to the Prime Minister may be taken as its recent funeral sermon.[35] Similarly one could become aware of the mythical elements in the doctrines of economy or co-ordination by amalgamation. Furthermore you can develop a sense of what sort of question is likely to come up: the selection of this rather than that type of organization; the choice between transferring a responsibility and using an agency arrangement; the importance, in any solution, of the department or the function or the section that did not look obviously important at first. You can also develop a grasp of the devices available or the formulae that might be acceptable.

If you surrender the hope for precision in this range of work some of its problems disappear. It still remains true, however, that the transfer of knowledge from case to case is a dangerous (not a useless) process. This is still more true, of course, for a transfer from system to system. How many of the factors suggested above for the recent experience of the British machine have been relevant for the Australian? Whole ranges of difference spring to mind: the centre of the government machine does not mean the same thing; the five-fold classification suggested by Mackenzie is of much less use in a federal system; in the allocation of functions between Australian Commonwealth departments differences in types of top staffing and Commonwealth-State relations will be factors quite foreign to the British experience. What can be transferred perhaps is a sense of scepticism and the sort of general questions suggested by Chester and Willson. The game itself may not be so different and some of the same rules may well, therefore, apply.

The rules, however, are not in a happy state. Chester and Willson allow themselves some criticism in this matter. Perhaps the single best rule is to use a report on the *prima facie* aspects of a case. It is easy enough in any instance to think, for example, of a number of possible reallocations of functions; the more difficult thing is to detect the real issues and the factors that will matter. This is primarily detecting what matters to the parties involved; it is the function of the *prima facie* report to reveal this essential information by some degree of provocation. Since decisions about machinery of government problems are decisions about human and more or less powerful interests and, as we have suggested, about policies and programmes themselves, these factors will be partly subjective and the possibility of affecting the issues as a result of M.G. work alone more or less restricted. The *prima facie* report and its handling will help to indicate the lie of the land. One of the things that might then appear is that the M.G. man is on the side if not of the angels at least of the big battalions, and he will often be defending the arrangements as they are. Indeed, if the best rule for the work is that the factors that have mattered are those that ought to have mattered (and we have not found a better) then this defensive function is likely to arise very often, at least when you are not dealing with arrangements for a new job. In any case, if useful M.G. work must take politics into account without itself becoming a purely political activity, then modesty about its role will be very appropriate. The limited is usually likely to be the more acceptable.

The other test of acceptability is whether your proposal can get through a top committee. This is both a test and a guarantee. One of the rules is, then, the deployment of committees. An awareness of what Philip Selznick has called the techniques of co-optation and commitment is likely to be of great use. This will be of relevance to Chester and Willson's recommendations for the employment of outsiders. Certainly there is also a sharp requirement for knowledge of the type we have discussed. This will constitute the special, extra-secretarial contribution of the M.G. man to these committees. He will remain aware of the limitations of this knowledge and of the limits of the game itself. His role will be strengthened by his knowledge, for example, of O and M and of the information it provides, but on the whole he had best avoid appearing as the protagonist. Let him be something between a diplomat, and an anthropologist of departmental rituals: he will know, respect and indeed appreciate them, but not treat them as sacrosanct.

Where does this leave the official who is to play his role as an M.G. man and so to participate in arguments about the machinery of government? It is the way of government to have arguments and these may well be about questions of this type; indeed these arguments are likely to be particularly sensitive for they are vital to that struggle for organizational survival which may be looked upon as the heart of the administrative role. There is no escape from this. A metaphor was invented for these questions—the machinery of government—and this metaphor once hardened into a myth. The myth of this machine had its deities, at whose shrines there were oracles to be consulted. The first deity extended two great arms, one pointing to clearly defined and presumably Elysian fields, the other to Lilliput and chaos. The worshippers here could have had no doubts into which of those vast hands all the parts of the machine must be placed; the oracles (Haldane, Webb, Morant) having sung their first song, they are needed, one supposes, no more. The rival being was not so hoary a monster. It was, after all, a transatlantic and somewhat jazzy importation without the classical associations of its rival. Its four arms waved wildly in all directions. Its devotees shifted about somewhat bemusedly, one thought. The myth may now be dismissed and the metaphor itself cannot solve anything. Worthwhile work about these matters will take the problems as they come. It will not attempt to derive from the deployment of the metaphor an indication of the questions, let alone the answers. Of course, it will be proper for there to be someone who will in fact take the problems or at least recognize that they are coming. This may well be his most important contribution. So, if we can, we may well choose to give him some help about the type of problem he is to anticipate and the words 'machinery of government' may be used to indicate a summary of what we mean. Perhaps this will improve his status. He may even be tempted to employ such respect as remains for the old religion in securing the acceptance of his proposals, and if he can get away with it this will not be foolish. He had best know just what he is about, and who is about him; perhaps he had best say something like what these people want him to say or what he can make them think they wanted him to say. This was the way of the wisest of the oracles.

NOTES

1 Ministry of Reconstruction: *Report of the Machinery of Government Committee*, Cd. 9230, 1918. On it, see also: W. J. M. Mackenzie, 'The Structure of Central Administration', in Campion *et al.*, *British Government since* 1918 (London, 1950), p. 57; B. B. Schaffer, 'The Machinery of Central Government', December, 1953, *Local Government Officer and Student*, p. 24; *The Organisation of British Central Government*, 1914-1956, D. N. Chester, written by F. M. G. Willson (London, 1957), pp. 293-4.
2 *Haldane Report*, Pt. I, para. 18-19.
3 Mackenzie, pp. 58-59, 79, 81-82.
4 Mackenzie, pp. 79, 61 *ff.*, 80-84.
5 *cf.* Lord Bridges, *Public Administration* (*London*), V. 35, p. 261.
6 W. J. M. Mackenzie and J. W. Grove, *Central Administration in Britain* (London, 1957).
7 Chester and Willson, pp. 333-8, 340, 342, 345, 348-9, 363.
8 *Public Administration* (*Sydney*), Vol. 16, p. 271.
9 Chester and Willson, pp. 250 and 292.
10 *Public Administration* (*London*), Vol. 35, p. 316.
11 Chester and Willson, p. 180.
12 *Ibid.*, p. 337.
13 *Ibid.*, p. 337.
14 *Ibid.*, pp. 113-4.
15 *Ibid.*, pp. 225-6.
16 'Administration: What is it?' in A. Dunsire, ed., *The Making of an Administrator* (Manchester, 1956), pp. 12-15.
17 Chester and Willson, pp. 341 and 366.
18 H. A. Simon, *Administrative Behavior* (New York, 1957), 2nd ed., p. xxxiv; *cf.* Chapter II, esp. pp. 30-35.
19 Chester and Willson, p. 349.
20 *Ibid.*, pp. 360-1.
21 Chester and Willson, p. 359.
22 Mackenzie, pp. 81 *ff*; *cf.* Mackenzie and Grove, pp. 363 *ff*.
23 Chester and Willson, p. 359.
24 *Ibid.*, pp. 162-8 and 176-80.
25 *Public Administration* (*London*), V. 35, p. 316-7.
26 Chester and Willson, pp. 344, 361-2; *cf.* Chapter 9 below.
27 Chester and Willson, pp. 151-2.
28 In Campion, *op. cit.*, p. 6.
29 See Chapter 1 above.
30 Haldane Report, Pt. 1, paras, 21-22, 30, 34, 37; Pt. II, C. V, para 17, 18, 27, 28, 34; C. VI, para. 9; C. VII, para. 10; C. IX; C. IV, para. 74.
31 Chester and Willson, p. 73.
32 *Ibid.*, p. 137; *Haldane Report*, Pt. I, para. 18.
33 *Haldane Report*, Pt. I, paras. 32 and 33.
34 *Ibid.*, Pt. I, para. 31 and n; *cf. Royal Commission on the Civil Service*, *4th Report*, Cd. 7388, 1914, c. ix, paras. 68, 69, 72.
35 *cf. The Economist* (London), 16th November, 1957, p. 577.

5

BROWNLOW OR BROOKINGS

Approaches to the Improvement of the Machinery of Government

The Brownlow Report of the President's Committee on Administrative Management in the U.S., 1937—significant year for administrative studies!—ranks with the Haldane report as the exemplar of the full-scale, ad hoc, principled, optimistic, rationalist, simplifying reorganization inquiry. The membership of the Brownlow committee, Brownlow himself, the role of Roosevelt (how different his actual working beliefs were was mentioned in the 1957 paper) and the evidence here about how a report is actually written and sold make Brownlow a case-study in major administrative reform. The contemporary but rival Brookings inquiry working for the Congress rather than the President, provides an instructive alternative discussion about what reorganization can and cannot do. The themes of Brownlow—too many agencies—are still favoured; the lessons of Brookings-reorganization should not be bureau shuffling—are still not learnt.

By now it is not necessary to explain at length what is meant by the term 'machinery of government'. In simple, it is the organization of those branches of government, and generally national as against local government, other than the primarily legislative and judicial sections: the structure of executive government.

In relation to this area there is a continually expressed demand for, and belief in, the great outside enquiry. There has been a strong traditional belief in the existence of independent decisions about the machine (e.g. reallocations of functions, or amalgamations of departments to secure economies) and how they should be taken (by major external investigations operating on sets of principles). Further, these enquiries have been expected to be able to re-design in some extensive or radical way what is, after all, the largest and the most complex section of the state. Such optimistic rationalism

is scarcely any longer the fashion with legislative and judicial reformers, but with the machinery of government it remains very
influential indeed. Its classic expression for the United Kingdom
was in the Haldane report; its classic expression for the United
States was in the Brownlow report.[1] These reports are not new but
their status has not by any means (in the case of the Brownlow
report scarcely at all) been destroyed. Thus a recent article has
suggested that[2] 'the real distinction and the real controversy, turns
on classification by service rendered as against people served. On
this matter the Haldane report has long been regarded as authoritative.' Further,[3] the article demanded 'a general inquiry', or 'a
full-scale investigation of the machinery of government', and this
is a recurrent and familiar request.

Fairly lengthy arguments have already been employed elsewhere[4]
to suggest that the Haldane report in particular was without influence, and rightly so. The lack of success, and the dishonesty of the
report, the inadequacy of its view of possible alternative arrangements, its disguise of policy ends in organizational recommendations, the tautology, the question begging and the naivete of much
of the original documents—all this had, one would think, been
sufficiently shown by now. But a general question remains. If we
set out to destroy this as a way of improving the machinery of
government (and where has that road ever led?), is there any
alternative to a reliance on mere accident? Other attacks on the
Haldane report and the recent publication of Brownlow's own
autobiography make it timely to reconsider these questions.

This paper will be especially concerned to use the publication of
Brownlow's autobiography, *A Passion for Anonymity*[5] and other
recent material as an occasion for a re-assessment of the debate
about his famous report and of the contemporary but neglected
work of the Brookings Institution.[6] It will thus attempt to provide
some estimate of what may, in fact, be done about enquiry and
recommendation in this field. In particular, the paper will say
something about the history of the Brownlow and the Brookings
reports and then something about the actual content of the Brownlow report. The contrasting position of the Brookings work will
be examined. The argument will be that this work provides an
alternative and preferable approach to the machinery of government, and that the Haldane-Brownlow method should once for all
be dispensed with.

I

Apart from their fame there are points in common between the

Haldane and the Brownlow reports. Both, for example, are suspicious of organization outside major departments, and both are in favour of consolidation of functions into a few large departments. But whatever has happened to the Haldane report, the Brownlow report, in complete contrast with the contemporary work of the Brookings Institution, has apparently had a glamorous fate. This report itself has suffered no recent wave of criticism, though the very movement of which it was part has had its ups and downs. Some of its pet phrases remain in use and some degree of actual implementation would certainly be claimed for it. How much could rightly be claimed is another matter, but it would seem that it was more successful than the Haldane report. Here, then, is clearly a more recent and a still more important example of one big effort at reorganization than the Haldane report itself. For those interested in the clash of approaches to the machinery of government the Brownlow case is clearly worth the closest examination. However, the decision to institute the Brownlow enquiry was gradually approached. The report was published in 1937. The Reorganization Act, which was supposed to enable it to be implemented, was passed in 1939. A thorough treatment of the report would accordingly be at least a full-scale history of the Roosevelt regime. Therefore only a few features can be mentioned.

THE CONTINUITY OF ORGANIZATIONAL CHANGE

The Brownlow report was not the first attempt at federal structural reorganization,[7] and the New Deal's was not the first (or last) decade to experience the conditions to which the enquiry's creation is most usually ascribed: a growing number of independent agencies and a diversity of subordinate organization. It is true that the reorganization movement before the 1930s concentrated on, and was most influential in, local and state government, but attempts at reorganizing federally also occurred. In the twenties, for example, executive orders transferred the Patent Office and the Bureau of Mines to Hoover's Department of Commerce from the Department of the Interior.[8] It is Hoover, indeed, in the twenties, in the 1928 election speeches, in 1932 and since, and not any of the true New Dealers, who has been most continually associated with reorganization of this type; that is, re-allocation of functions of agencies in the interests of economy. For example, it was Hoover's message of 17 February, 1932 which initiated (via the Appropriation Act)[9] the sort of legislation which has been the dominant method of reorganization. The executive orders issued by Hoover were (in 1932) inevitably defeated, but they were all pure examples of what we should call 'bureau shuffling'. One of his recommendations at any rate[10] (a proposal to transfer non-audit functions from the Accounting Office to the Bureau of the Budget) would have had Brownlow's approval.

It should also be recalled that a great deal of reorganization in this sense took place in the thirties, quite apart from the Brownlow report and its own results. The 1933 Act gave an authority to Roosevelt wider than anything given to Hoover, to Roosevelt himself again, or to any of his successors. Organizations were created and re-allocated (the Bureau of Mines, incidentally, back from Commerce to Interior) and powers expanded, and other reorganization executive orders were made under other Acts. In addition to the famous creation of organizations by the New Deal, then, there was in the 1930s a great deal of pure bureau shuffling and some of it with specific claims of economy attached.

HOW TO GET AN ENQUIRY

If reorganization means bureau shuffling in the interests of economy, it was not peculiar to Roosevelt as an aim and a great deal of action occurred irrespective of the Brownlow Committee. We must, therefore, ask why this classic example of the full-scale investigation was set up at all, and what in the end was especially significant about it. Was the point that it could achieve this sort of reorganization in some superior way, or that it could achieve some other sort of reorganization altogether?

Different accounts of its origin have, in fact, been given. It may be that after the Humphrey case[11] Roosevelt hoped to persuade Congress to place the members of many of the independent regulatory commissions in a 'purely executive' position:[12] or that it was purely a child of that peculiar complex, the National Resources Committee (chaired by Ickes) and its Advisory Committee (chaired by 'Uncle Fred' Delano).[13] Certainly that Board (successively the National Planning Board, the National Resources Board, the National Resources Committee and the National Resources Planning Board) was an appropriate symbol of the New Deal's palace conflicts, name changing and fertility of ideas. But what is now clear from Brownlow's own account is that he and a few others consistently yet vainly worked towards something like this end (that is, the grand enquiry) until that moment when Roosevelt himself decided that he had more to lose, in particular to congressional initiative, by disappointing than by using them.

How much of the credit should go to Brownlow? By then in his fifties, he was already a deeply experienced wire-puller, not to his own disadvantage. Out of a not wholly successful career in city management he had emerged as the first director of the Public Administration Clearing House, which his own influence with the Spelman Fund and others had created. A fairly complete chronology can be worked out from Brownlow's account, Meriam and Schmeckebier's study, other New Deal memoirs and the congressional documents.[14]

But four things stand out from the record. One is that the greater part of the final version of the Brownlow report was not dependent on the studies that accompanied it. It was already in the mind of Brownlow and his friends and, indeed, on paper and before Roosevelt before the Committee was appointed. The recommendations were known and in harmony with Brownlow's Jacksonian conception of the presidency. Brownlow's own account shows that he had organized his support (the Spelman, Rockefeller and Carnegie people, the N.R.C. or Uncle Fred and its Advisory Committee at any rate, and so forth: some part of the establishment in fact), well before the study was done.[15] It also shows that he had actually formed his conclusions of what the study was to show. Significantly Brownlow thought that it was very important to have the approval of ex-Governor Lowden, the man of the 1917 Illinois report; that is, the 1937 Federal document was to be a continuation of the 1917 State document,[16] the most celebrated chapter of the State phase of the reorganization movement. Furthermore, his visit to Europe in the summer of 1936 after the report was commissioned but before it was done confirmed his political attitude to the significance of strengthening the presidency,[17] as it also introduced him to Tom Jones's key phrase about Hankey—a 'passion for anonymity'—which his own report was to make so famous.

The second thing that stands out is that Roosevelt not merely knew what was coming—he did, when he wished, and much to the annoyance of such a genuine scholar as Lindsay Rogers, see that the report was altered.[18] The third thing is that despite the long period of preliminary talks officially referred to in the President's letter, the decision to institute the enquiry was in the end taken only after, and immediately after, the Senate had decided to set up its own enquiry under Senator Byrd. Until that moment Brownlow and his friends had been 'on tenterhooks' waiting for the green light.[19] Their own idea for an enquiry by the Public Administration Committee of the Social Science Research Council was never used. As late as 20 February 1936 Roosevelt displayed his opposition to the idea, a purely but wisely political opposition.[20] Within a few days Brownlow had put on paper what he thought an enquiry ought to achieve. Between 29 February and 4 March, Brownlow and

Byrd had discussed the Senate's plan and on the afternoon of the 4th (Brownlow having seen Byrd in the morning) Roosevelt had come round. Why was this? Partly because he now thought that he would be able to get out of Brownlow something better than ideas about bureau shuffling. The emergency organizations, the need for consolidation, the aim of economy, and so forth, were to be used merely as a 'spring-board'.[21] The job of bureau shuffling could really be left to the Senate Committee and to the Brookings Institution, which the Senate Committee was going to use. It was, then, Roosevelt himself who had first thought of two separate sets of studies, an idea about which Brownlow had not originally been very keen. What Brownlow was now to produce for Roosevelt was a plan concerned with 'administrative management', that is, with strengthening the presidential power.

Fourthly, it is clear that Roosevelt could not afford to leave the initiative to the Senate or to his Cabinet. He was out to capture the leadership of the movement personally, and in his letter to the Speaker and the Vice-President he gave a version of the history of the business up to the appointment of the Congressional and President's Committees which did, in fact, present things in the appropriate way.

In one sense these tactics were successful. Whatever Brownlow's work achieved in terms of actual reorganization it is certainly true that the work of the Byrd Committee and of the Brookings Institution has been all but forgotten. A brilliant set of reports has been consistently neglected and when it has been mentioned it has been misrepresented. It was indeed the President's Committee that achieved the fame. But this was not quite what Brownlow had intended. In a number of ways things did not go according to the planner's plans. Let us see firstly the content, and then the fate, of the Brownlow report.

HOW TO WRITE A REPORT:
THE RECOMMENDATIONS AND THE RATIONALIST MASK

The Brownlow report essentially consisted of six recommendations and these, in the final report, were just what Brownlow had anticipated in his hotel room before the Committee had been created. The first recommendation was for the appointment of a stronger White House staff, in particular for six administrative assistants.[22] The second recommendation was that a number of presidential staff organizations were to be created, and some organizations transferred to the President. These were concerned with budgeting, efficiency research, personnel and planning. This was later to be known as the Executive Office of the President, but the report itself did not use that title.[23] The third recommendation was for further reform of the civil service by the extension of the merit system, and more notably for the replacement of the bipartisan civil service commission with a single civil service administrator.[24]

The fourth recommendation was for an overhaul of what was described as 'the hundred' or 'over a hundred' 'independent' agencies which the report referred to and a concentration of them into 12 executive departments.[25] These 12 were to be the existing 10 departments, among which the Department of the Interior was to become a Department of Conservation, plus two new departments of Social Welfare and of Public Works. This recommendation included the destruction of the independent regulatory commissions. The fifth recommendation was for the replacement of the independent comptroller general with an auditor general to be appointed by Congress, responsible purely for an independent post audit.[26] There would be purely executive responsibility for accounting and current transactions. The comptroller general or his successor would thus not be an officer independent of the President controlling the settlement of claims, the determination of the use of appropriations, of the prescription of accounting systems. All this would disappear. The sixth recommendation was concerned with the procedures of the executive orders by which the power of reorganization was essentially to be placed in presidential hands.

The report was, then, in large part, a matter of bureau shuffling plus executive integration of the most extreme and arbitrary kind. For the rest, it referred to what was likely to happen anyway: for example, more assistance for the President and some degree of civil service and accounting reform. But the brunt of the report consisted of these notions of radical and sudden change, notions already in mind before the work of the Committee had begun. They were, apparently, to be justified and extracted from a confident statement of universals in the opening of the Report.[27] This statement is a breathtaking and characteristically confused piece of rationalism: '... the foundations of effective management ... are well-known. They have emerged universally wherever men have worked together for some common purpose....' And so on. Conveniently, these universal habits of work, articles of incorporation and the rest, all recognized that what was required (or was it what was inevitable?) was a 'responsible and effective chief executive as the center of energy, direction and administrative management', etc. The Congress might be unhappy about this, but the universe was, it seemed, against them.

Others might think that the problem of organization and the uses of enquiry were not quite what Brownlow was pretending they were. The role of the general statements on which the validity and conclusions of the enquiry were supposed to rest was partly, in truth, a matter of creating an atmosphere of belief in radical change: sure principles, confident recommendations; and change of a particular sort. In this atmosphere the investigations could proceed to their actual (in this case Jacksonian) programme: the highly political and quite specific objective of, e.g. abolishing the bi-partisan civil service commission. But the programme would be masked as an organizational one, a part of administrative betterment alone, and an unchallengeable part (however large its scale or sudden its appearance) since it was derived quite surely from pure and universal principle. Characteristically again this very confidence permitted a cavalier use of evidence and analogy. This was so with Haldane. It was precisely so with Brownlow too.

HOW TO SELL A REPORT: THE RECORD OF RATIONALISM

What happened to the Brownlow report? The administrative reorganization bills designed to carry out the proposals of the President's Committee became the subject and object of one of the most bitter controversies between the Congress and the President to occur at any time during the full tenure of Franklin D. Roosevelt.[28] How did this happen, was it wise and was it effective? Let us look at the emergence of the controversy, and at what was really achieved.

In the first place, the Brownlow report was done very swiftly—significantly so. The staff was not assembled until May 1936 and instructions sent to them only on 11 June 1936. Brownlow and Charles Merriam were away in Europe for the summer, and the third member of the Committee, Luther Gulick, was otherwise engaged. The report was drafted in November 1936, and presented by Roosevelt to his Cabinet on 8 January 1937, to congressional leaders on 10 January, and to press conference on 11 January.

Secondly, an examination of these various presentations by Roosevelt, as described by Brownlow, demonstrates the attractiveness of the report. To some it was presented as a matter of economy; to others as a matter of consolidation. What Brownlow himself really thought it mainly did was to strengthen the President. This gave the report considerable glamour, which it has retained. But precisely this presentation also provided it with many sources of opposition: officials suspicious of consolidation; congressional leaders suspicious of the extension of civil service; groups interested in maintaining the independence of regulatory commissions, and other bodies; the cynicism of the press about the 'selfless six', that is, the six presidential assistants who were to be selected according to their 'passion for anonymity'.

It was, then, fireworks from the start. This was all the more so, all authorities agreed, because the publication of the report happened to coincide with the fateful plan of Roosevelt for reforming the Supreme Court. 'It was that problem which within the next year determined the fate of the proposals of the report', Brownlow claims.[29] But that is quite unfair and very misleading. The report was bound to meet with opposition in any case. It was itself high politics.

The actual record runs like this. Congressional committees, and in particular a Statutory Joint Committee, were appointed to consider the report in January to February 1937. These included the Robinson (later Byrnes) Committees on Government Organization, distinct from the Byrd and Buchanan Committees to Investigate Executive Agencies of the Government.[30] The hearings proceeded through April. In June the Brookings Institution work was complete and the Byrd Committee conducted hearings on their reports from June to August. Meanwhile the Robinson-Byrnes Committee on Brownlow was at work from August onwards. The bills presented by Byrd on the basis of the Brookings work[31] dealt with the Farm Home Credit Administration, the abolition of the Reconstruction Finance Corporation, financial administration, and the appointment of a full-time director and assistant-director for the Budget Bureau. While none of these advanced after June 1937, the Senate and House legislation on the Brownlow report itself bogged down in the 75th Congress and only emerged again in 1939.

This legislation got stuck because of the evident clash with the Brookings report, the sources of opposition, and, in part, the backwash of the Court plan. Opposition grew: a bill passed the House of Representatives in August easily, another bill later got through the Senate but only by one vote. Then the House killed the Senate's bill altogether. Why, having been lost in that Congress, was the plan saved in 1939? This was simply because the Reorganization Bill of 1939 that succeeded was not, in fact, Brownlow's measure. Twenty-one organizations were now to be exempted from its operation. (Brownlow wanted no exemptions at all.) Altogether different procedures of subordinate legislation were to be employed.[32] Further, the plans that were prepared and carried under this legislation were few, and they were, Brownlow admits, prepared by the new Director of the Budget, Harold Smith, and not by the President's Committee. They were, in fact, only in small part related to the Brownlow report.

Later reorganization acts continued to carry (for example, in the three categories of exemption in the 1945 Act and in the provision for vetoes by either House in the 1949 Act) the inevitable mark of congressional intervention in the process of reorganization. The Brownlow claim, and its actual hope, for a virtually exclusive presidential power in this field were both doomed from the start.[33] The exemptions in 1939 included in the end all the independent regulatory commissions (except the Civil Aeronautics Administration), the Civil Service Commission, the Accounting Office, the United States Engineering Department and other key institutions. The United States Engineering Department had even been exempted from the 1938 bills: it was, at that time, the only such case and its whole experience in reorganization is the outstanding instance of the vanity of relying on the one big enquiry as a weapon against the toughened features of any existing machinery of government. Thus, the C.A.A. (under reorganization plans III and IV of 1940) became the only independent regulatory commission in which the Brownlow notion, of dividing administrative from judicial functions, operated. An Administrator of Aeronautics and a separate Civil Aeronautics Board were set up.[34] But this did not amount to consolidation. After the war the Hoover Commissions still had to complain of a weak or broken presidential line of command and of a superfluity of independent or subordinate agencies.[35] The bureau shuffling and the integration of the Brownlow plans either had not occurred or did not help.

The Accounting Office, then, was exempted from reorganization. The Civil Service Commission was not abolished. Instead, in 1939, McReynolds was appointed Presidential Liaison Officer for Personnel Management.[36] The stream of civil service reform (the Ramspeck Acts, the Hatch Acts, the Reed Committees) went on independently of this. Even the Liaison Officer for Personnel Management did not remain as a device. Eisenhower instead used the Chairman of the Commission as his personal adviser. Next the function was transferred back to a presidential special assistant.[37] These comings and goings with devices are themselves very instructive. The two new departments were not set up. This was indeed forbidden under the Reorganization Act. Three administrators of Federal Work, Federal Security (not welfare), and Federal Loans Administrations were created, and Brownlow admits that they never carried the necessary prestige of full cabinet members.[38]

The Executive Office of the President did appear, with an Office for Emergency Management added, and without the recommended contingent fund at the President's disposal. Has the tremendous growth and change of the X.O.P. since then been a tribute to the report? It is extending one's credulity to read into the report an anticipation of the twenty-fold increase that was to occur, or of the end of the N.R.P.C. and of the Office of Government Reports, the creation of the Council of Economic Advisers, of the National Security Council and its own associated bodies, of the General Services Administration and of the Office of Defence Mobilization. Why should we suppose that the report anticipated the vast increase in size, the increase in the number and variety of presidential assistants, the office filled by Sherman Adams and then by General Persons under Eisenhower, the change in the role of the Vice-President, the institution of a Cabinet Secretariat, the hundreds of clerical and staff employees in the White House alone? Still more important, this is not at all the small neat structure which was the essence of the report's recommendation, and it is consciously less neat under Kennedy. If the X.O.P. is the most important offspring of the Brownlow report (e.g. the appointment of assistants and the transfer of the Budget Bureau from the Treasury), the child was unnamed by its parents and it has grown astonishingly unlike its forebear.[39]

COMPETITIVE ADMINISTRATION AND STANDING MACHINERY: A CONTRAST WITH RATIONALISM

Contrast the Brownlow hope for consolidation and integration with the actual immediate increase in the number of agencies and inter-departmental conflicts, for example, with the ensuing wartime experience, or with the steady development of new forms of independence as in current contrasted devices. There is a similar contrast with what Roosevelt said in his actual wisdom to Brownlow himself as to Frances Perkins. Here we have the philosophy of competitive administration.

> This is the way I have always looked at it. We have new and complex problems. We do not really know what they are. Why not establish a new agency to take over the new duty rather than saddle it on an old institution? Of course, a great many mistakes are going to be made. They are bound to be made in anything so new and numerous as supplying our allies, training our army and navy, and recruiting the necessary industrial resources. Mistakes in military strategy are made. They just absorb them. There will be mistakes in domestic and supply strategy. We have to be prepared to abandon all practices that grow up out of ignorance. It seems to me it is easier to use a new agency which is not a permanent part of the structure of government. If it is not permanent we do not get bad precedents that will carry it over into the days of peace. We can do anything that needs to be done then—discard the agency when the

emergency is over. I think that there is something to be said for this. There is something to be said for having a little conflict between agencies. A little rivalry is stimulating, you know. It keeps everybody going to prove that he is a better fellow than the next man. It keeps them honest, too. An awful lot of money is being handled. The fact that there is somebody else in the field who knows what you are doing is a strong incentive to strict honesty.[40]

This amounts to a criticism of rationalism, the Brownlow report and its fame, but not of Brownlow himself. He did indeed provide some continuing influence and occasional advice about the use of particular devices; for example, there was his opposition to the Stettinius War Resources Board plan for war organization, and his advice about the O.E.M., the National Defence Advisory Commission and the bi-partisan appointments of Stimson and Knox. All this mattered much more than anything said in the report itself. Brownlow himself admits that the O.E.M. became the parent of dozens of separate defence and war agencies.[41]

Certainly advice and machinery were more important than the one report. Organization did not and could not develop as recommended. Brownlow's colleague, Gulick, has done a study of the wartime organization that followed hard on the report. The study is full of relevant evidence. What was the key to good organization? Clear statements of policy of purpose. If you concentrate functions you will ignore sections of the work. If you set up tzars (i.e. single powerful executives) the costs will be heavy. Dual supervision rather than unity of command is required. Conflict and change will inevitably continue to occur.[42]

Roosevelt never demonstrated in his practice of wartime organization that he had taken any of the Brownlow report seriously. Further, Brownlow actually admits that Roosevelt's very 'unorthodoxy' worked, e.g. with Hillman and Knudsen as joint chairmen of the wartime Office of Production Management, as earlier with his New Deal five-ring circus for works and relief appropriation administration.[43] Roosevelt was prepared to use Brownlow like hundreds of others as a source of occasional advice, as a guinea pig, or as the litmus paper for his own notions. He abided by the gospel according to Perkins, and a much better gospel too: his own, for his time and place.

What had the Brownlow report been in initiation, philosophy, recommendations and fate, but politics not science: part of a grand political design to swing the balance of the constitution and to move away from a 50 years' tradition of using regulatory commissions? The design partly succeeded and partly failed. The role and success of the report cannot be judged outside this context any more than can its recommendations. The error is to treat the report itself as an isolated, impartial, scientific study giving unchallengeable recommendations from first principles, and to treat it as a model for further studies of this sort. It is an error to suppose that it was as such successful. The report came, as Brownlow says, from the President's Committee. It was, as results in the machinery of government must be, borne out of a specific policy. It was successful only within the limits of the political requirements that gave it birth and these were very narrow and delicate indeed.

II

In the first part of this paper we saw that the fate of the Brownlow report in practice was not altogether happy: it was neither totally 'scientific' nor totally successful. Its actual failure was not unaffected by the contemporary and rival work of the Brookings Institution. But this grand dispute of the late 1930s and the Brookings studies themselves have since come to be neglected or misrepresented in accounts of the machinery of government. We are told, for example, that 'since 1936 there have been three major investigations of the machinery of the United States government',[44] that is, Brownlow and the two Hoover Commissions. What of the Brookings Institution? By length, detail, wisdom and strict relevance to these precise words, the Brookings studies deserve reference as least as much as the Brownlow report, but the standard United States textbooks also ignore both Brookings and also its successor studies, especially that by Meriam and Schmeckebier. Their book is occasionally mentioned in bibliographies whose authors seem not to have read it. For example, Pfiffner and Presthus continue to repeat the fable of 'upwards of 100 organizations' invented as an excuse and justification for their bureau shuffling by the President's Committee and long since exploded by Brookings, Meriam and Schmeckebier.[45]

There have only been two texts to give serious attention to the Brookings work,[46] but neither deals fully with the clash between the two reports: independently of differences about the constitution and of any overlap or disagreement about specific changes, there was here an argument about the whole role and method of organizational change. It is this that now matters to us, and it is on this, not on the details of the report, that we shall concentrate.

THE ERRORS OF RATIONALISM AND THE BROOKINGS ALTERNATIVE

We find in the Brookings reports both an attack on the Brownlow position, and a statement of an alternative. Here we shall look first at the attack, and then at the alternative. This position is developed more fully in the work of Meriam and Schmeckebier,[47] and that will be discussed. A later section will take up that work in more detail. The Brookings report devotes its first chapter to the problem of 'administrative organization'. Four or five key points are implied in this discussion. The first is that if the objective of reorganization is 'economy' (and efficiency in that sense) then it can be achieved by reorganization only if that means something quite different from structural change and functional reallocation, that is, quite different from bureau shuffling. Though Roosevelt himself from time to time apparently saw the point it was never seen by Brownlow. He indeed continued to believe (as in *The President and the Presidency*) in bureau shuffling as a source of economy.

Secondly, the Brookings report argued that it is not an adequate description of the machinery of government, or an adequate justification for reorganization, simply to employ terms like 'sprawling' or 'chaos of establishments'. A large and complicated array of organizations is quite inevitable in government and certainly in crisis government. In any case, the 'sprawl' or complexity may be more apparent than real. There are several problem areas in the machinery of government, especially where there are new functions, not one problem. Accordingly, several and piecemeal change is likely to be more effective than one solution or one big overhaul.

Thirdly, the complexity of the problem of choice between alternative decisions about reorganization is stressed, and the major 'Brownlow' assumptions are challenged. The Brookings approach perceives that simplicity is not always a characteristic of good organization, nor are overlapping, duplication and conflict characteristics of bad organization. Further, the statement remains one of the very few which manage to distinguish between overlapping as a matter of concern and duplication as a matter of activities 'Overlap' merely refers to a situation in which more than one agency is concerned with a particular field or topic, and this is usual and often inevitable. It is not at all the same as 'duplication', where more than one agency is performing the same function. There is a specific departmental theory assumed by both Haldane and Brownlow: unifunctionalism; concentration into a few large departments; opposition to the use of boards; staff and line; in general, the dominant theory of executive centralization and of hierarchy. This is criticised and challenged. Some of it is, in effect, untrue (e.g. that a few big departments are better than many smaller ones); the rest is misleading (e.g. that executive integration is the sole consideration). The Brookings report argued against the use of false analogies from industry, or from local or state reorganization experience, to the problems of the federal government. The President is not a city manager. This was especially important in the United States, and for Brownlow and Gulick themselves.

Leaving aside the problem of deduction then, the Brookings report criticises some of the dominant generalizations as false or fictitious and others as, at least, misleading. The effect of these generalizations had been to provide over-confident assumptions about the need, the possibility and the fruits of radical change. They have misdirected attention away from the causes of difficulty and the sorts of change that might be required.

Fourthly, if the Brookings Institution attacked one approach it substituted another. If consolidation was not the key to reorganization, the right way might be to use many small departments plus stronger presidential machinery (here was the point of agreement), and stronger congressional machinery (here was the point of constitutional difference). There remains the problem of allocation, that is, the structural changes on which other reorganization studies had concentrated. The core of the Brookings' position is the rejection of principles in favour of signposts (what Simon has since called 'diagnostic criteria'), the rejection of one or a few guides for many, and the relative readiness to take explanations as justifications: that is, the existing system shows what has happened and what is, therefore, likely to be workable.

History offers explanations and justifies arrangements. The objectives, working rules and policies of organizations must be considered. Some functions can never be consolidated. Day-to-day relationships, Federal-State systems, connections with special groups (to be encouraged or discouraged in different cases), the nature of the work load (constant, expandable, project, seasonal or emergency types, for example) may be considered. This is an unusually full, discerning, and at points quite original list of what has mattered, and, therefore, what must be sensibly considered in allocating and grouping work in that system.

Allocation is not, the Brookings volume stresses, the whole of reorganization. Changes here will probably not achieve what is often claimed for them, for example, economy. But if major re-allocations are to be considered, then this is something like the degree of complexity through which the decision must go. Clearly, the Brookings' attitude is one of the greatest significance quite independently of particular matters, of agreement or disagreement with the Brownlow recommendations, and apart from its attack on the Brownlow constitutional theory. It is worth looking at somewhat more closely.

Now, as Waldo suggested, the Brookings Institution had its own ideological tradition. The people working for it included F. F. Blachly, Millspaugh, Selko and others. They continued to produce material about reorganization that differed from the main stream, and in particular, to attack the Brownlow recommendations. For example, the work of Blachly and Oatman on administration, adjudication and the regulatory commissions marked the opposition to the abolition of the commissions in favour of subordination to executive departments. There was the work of Selko in defence of independent pre-audit, and Lewis Meriam's own work defending the bi-partisan Civil Service Commission.[48] Much the most important of these works is Meriam and Schmeckebier's *Reorganisation of the National Government. What does it Involve?* published in 1939. The first part of this is by Lewis Meriam and the second part, a history of reorganization efforts, is by Schmeckebier. As a whole it enables us to bring to a head the Brookings' attitude, the errors of the Brownlow approach and the lessons of the dispute.

To re-state the outlines of this as it had developed by 1939. Reorganization is not just bureau shuffling. (Meriam and Schmeckebier give the credit for this evocative term to William Hard.[49]) The guidance to that sort of reorganization is complex and conservative, and to be extracted not from universals but from particular histories and systems. Many of the existing dominant organizational assumptions were ill-founded. If the aim of reorganization was a reduction of expenditure, then bureau shuffling was not relevant at all. The essential means of economy is the curtailment of activities. The alternative to bureau shuffling and great enquiry is 'continuing reorganization', that is, better control of administration, including a continuing concern for organization. The exercise of this function requires machinery (or cabinet systems which they ruled out). In the constitutional opinion of Meriam and Schmeckebier and their friends this ought to mean congressional as well as the presidential machinery. The argument stands independently of that constitutional point, though the point is highly relevant to the fate of the first 1938 Roosevelt-Brownlow proposals about actual methods and form of reorganization legislation. In any case, Meriam and Schmeckebier draw their belief in continuous reorganization (including more assistance for President and Congress) from a notion of the irrelevance of the state organization movement. Even more telling than that (the point already made in the Brookings report) there was a critical examination of the evidence for the actual success of that movement itself. Nor did they believe that the political situation in the thirties made executive integration as against congressional control the sole requirement of good government.

THREE MAJOR ERRORS: CONSOLIDATION, BUREAU SHUFFLING AND THE CHAOS OF ESTABLISHMENTS

The notion of continuous reorganization, of standing machinery as against a single report and the single bill, of management as against external enquiry, is the key positive contribution of the Meriam and Schmeckebier study.[50] But in addition to that, the criticism of the Brownlow position is greatly strengthened. Of course, the Brookings reports specifically objected to many Brownlow recommendations. Brookings was specifically opposed to the creation of new departments of Conservation and Public Works. More significant was the Brookings opposition to the radical Brownlow recommendations, which sought to divide and destroy each of the independent regulatory commissions, the 'headless fourth arm', as they were somewhat oddly described; or to transfer independent pre-audit functions from an independent to a subservient body; or to abolish the Civil Service Commission. The Brookings reports were not wedded to executive integration as a panacea, or to the big departments as the sole proper type of executive organization. They could, accordingly, accept and, indeed, defend a variety of forms, limitations on executive power, multiplicity of agencies, the small-scale unit and, in general, the broad shape of things as they were. The Brookings school was not alone in some of this opposition. Wallace was later to be sympathetic.

There was, in addition, the great argument by J. M. Landis in *The Administrative Process*,[51] which contains a specific attack on the Brownlow report.[52] Clearly there was a case to be made for independence, for the processes and then for the organizations themselves in a field of regulation.

This was part of the importance of the Brookings work and its associated studies: there was no need to suppose that the Brownlow report was a scientific study, that its impartial evidence and recommendations were beyond question. Every point could be debated. We may add to the immediate work of Brookings and its school, of Wallace and of Landis on the regulatory commissions, the actual experience of Federal Government in the creation of balancing organization. Far from following any doctrine of consolidation, 'a deliberate administrative provision was then made for a counterplay of claims and of the analysis and argument to support them'.[53] Neatness meant firm commitments; it ought to be avoided. The explanation can be deduced from interest analysis; the Office of Small Business and its successors, for example. Justification can be deduced from the 'countervailing' theory of Galbraith. But Roosevelt had already put this argument to Frances Perkins

It has recently had its most up-to-date development in the criticisms of defence organization by Kissinger, Jackson and others. The central point is that organization should be shaped so as to express rather than conceal or minimize disagreement. This is a defensible position. It is very influential in the Kennedy administration. Its implications are shattering for much of the traditional organizational theory on which the Brownlow report was based.

One point, then, is that the sort of structure that Brownlow wanted is not beyond controversy at all. It is a pity that the lessons of this degree of argument and counter-experience have not been learned. In the case of defence organization, at any rate, it may have been very important indeed that the Eisenhower administration avoided them. But there are two other, and different, points where Meriam and Schmeckebier took the matter beyond controversy. Why this part of their book has been neglected is most difficult to understand, and the neglect even more difficult to forgive.

The first of these points is that significant reductions in expenditure cannot come from structural alterations and reallocations. This is mainly demonstrated by an analysis of Federal expenditure.[54] Anyone with budgeting experience would appreciate the little that can be controlled through estimates procedure. Similarly, Meriam and Schmeckebier show the small percentage of Federal government expenditure that could possibly be affected by bureau shuffling. Only 17.6 per cent of the Federal budget was for the operation of agencies and of that 88 per cent was for 'personal services'. Savings can come only from curtailment and beyond that, to a lesser extent from reductions in personnel; they cannot significantly come from structural change. When will this lesson be learned?

It is no answer to suggest that the aim of bureau shuffling is better control, not mere economy. The difficulties of effective executive control are created not by the number of organizations, but by crisis legislation, the lack of machinery for executive assistance (so more organizations, not fewer, are needed), the number of matters to be considered and the weight of responsibility: it is the range of attention, not the span of control, that is the problem. Nor is the answer that bureau shuffling will at any rate secure personnel savings. The increase in personnel is a result of political appointments, inefficient recruitment systems, poor qualifications, new services and very high 'installation' demands, as well as poor procedures. That is, politics, better personnel management, and organization and methods (as we would now say), not structural alterations, provide the answer.

The problem of curtailment of activities is to distinguish between functions and activities, and then to deal with the political strength of particular existing functions. Reorganization as curtailment is politics in the normal sense of the clash of interests. Congressional procedure, because it reveals the clash, has it uses in handling this phase of reorganization. As we have seen with Macmahon's doctrine of balance, it is foolish to suppose that organization is or should be exempt from the clash.[55] If, then, it is to curtailment that we must look for economies, and this is to be one of the objects of reorganization, the case for purely executive as against some congressional responsibility for reorganization disappears. In total, then, it would appear that curtailment, economy, efficiency and control are a result of many factors—pruning, policy changes, effective personnel practices, office procedures, machinery for executive control, and congressional procedures and machinery.

Furthermore, if we do engage on structural alterations it must be remembered what these will not achieve, and how these alterations should be arranged. That is to say you must recall the degree of complexity and the long list of possible criteria (as against a few principles) that have to be taken into account. It should be noted that the list of possible factors or criteria given here, as in the Brookings report, is, correctly, very extensive and that it includes some original notions, for example, the influence of models in organization; and furthermore, that the needs of executive control are only one factor to be considered among many. It is clear from the Brookings and the Meriam and Schmeckebier contributions to this point that you can derive a set of factors to be considered only by a consideration of the practices of the particular machinery of government involved in the possible changes. This would, of course, lead to the sort of problems of definition and weighting that Simon was later to discuss and which, indeed, Brookings and Meriam and Schmeckebier approached, even if they did not detect the problem of ambiguity itself. It also leads to the problems of interpretation and of boundaries between the application of rival models which have been discussed elsewhere.[56]

This is, in total, a decisive attack on the claims and the whole classical theory of bureau shuffling. The remaining part of the Brownlow case for bureau shuffling was that, at any rate, the New Deal system of the 1930s demanded consolidation. There was a 'chaos of establishments'. The second major point in the Brookings, Meriam and Schmeckebier contribution is the attack on this famous and still accepted myth. The whole support for this notion of chaos lay in the still more famous but varying number of agencies that were supposed to exist—'the hundred', 'over hundred', '130 odd', or '132' (to mention the various numbers used by the Brownlow report and its evidence). Appendix C of the Meriam and

Schmeckebier volume is a classic piece of criticism. The Brookings report had already argued that mere number did not justify reorganization. Brookings, Meriam and Schmeckebier had argued the case for control machinery plus multiplicity as an alternative to consolidation, and Meriam and Schmeckebier were now able to show that the famous number (and the list which was finally extracted by congressional insistence) was unclassified, insignificant and (to put no finer point upon it) not up to the highest standards of accuracy or truth. There were not 'one hundred and thirty-two agencies', in fact, in existence. Still less did those that did exist constitute a vast number of uncontrolled organizations employing masses of personnel.

The details of the criticism do not matter here. It does matter that carelessness has allowed Brownlow's phrase and number to stand, for on them rest an ideology of what the machinery of government should and should not mean, may but need not look like. It does matter in other ways too. The criticism provides some approach to the methods of classification and analysis of the non-departmental or, as we might say, the non-ministerial sections of the machine. Furthermore, five of all the Federal organizations employed 72 per cent of the total Federal personnel, and 30 of them employed 99.237 per cent.[57] Finally, the evidence of the time (and a careful reading of Brownlow's autobiography will show this) demonstrates that the organizational problem of the New Deal was due not to the number of organizations, but to the great rate of innovation and to disagreement about policy.

THE OBSTINACY OF RATIONALISM

The Brownlow report assumed given principles that had operated in a continuous movement of scientific management and reorganization which could sweep successfully through industry, local and state and now federal government. The notion of executive integration was the essence of this body of principle. Beyond that, the Brownlow case rested particularly on its assumption about a chaos of establishments: its principles (executive integration) would indicate what the machine ought to be like; and it had detected that the machine was not in fact like this at all: it was chaos. Some agencies were not fully controlled by the President: this, then, was a 'headless fourth arm'; it was, by axiom, a bad thing. There were too many agencies (and it gave an impressive number); fewer would mean an easier span of control (but the report forgot that this would not affect the President's range of attention, and that Roosevelt specifically preferred a multiplicity of sources of information);[58] it assumed that many organizations meant overlap and overlap meant duplication, and accordingly, that amalgamation would eliminate waste.

This was an easy belief (or pretence of belief) in deduction, analogy and axiom. A few hypotheses were treated as an exclusive and sufficient set of rules. It followed that many practical questions were begged. For example, 'the semi-autonomous status' of agencies within departments after 'consolidation',[59] or the status of the supervisory agencies precisely to be set up to be 'independent' where 'desirable' for business and federal governmental operations.[60] Many secondary assumptions were made; for example, that if boards were to be used for corporations they should always be of the board plus general-manager type. But, above all, executive integration was held to be the single key need and 'chaos' the key fault, of the government machine. From this the recommendations could obviously be deduced and, of course, accepted.

Meriam and Schmeckebier's work about bureau shuffling and about the 'chaos of establishments' amounts to a massive attack on this argument, and a massive contribution to the problem of machinery of government changes. But Brownlow believed then and restated later (in *The President and the Presidency*, and *A Passion for Anonymity*) much of the position attacked, and in some part essentially destroyed. He apparently continued to believe that the conflict between his committee and Brookings was on purely constitutional matters,[61] that bureau shuffling would achieve economy, that the 1917 Illinois reorganization and Gulick's work in Virginia were admirable models for Federal reorganization, that the whole machine could and should be grouped into a few departments,[62] that there could and should be exclusive presidential reorganization powers, without any exemption, and so forth.

It may have been natural for Brownlow to have ignored criticisms from the Brookings Institution. It is more surprising that he failed to note the significance of his own discussions with Roosevelt about his report's structural proposals,[63] or Roosevelt's own point that reorganization was relevant to control rather than to economy.[64] The Brownlow decisions between the rival evidence of Cabinet members about bureau shuffling were taken very blithely indeed. This, no doubt, was one of the reasons for their later lack of effect save where (as with the transfer of the Budget Bureau from the Treasury to the President) the recommendations were related to clear policy decisions which had effective support. One realizes the point of Roosevelt's sarcastic comment: 'The President said that he had puzzled a good deal over the proper dividing line between Agriculture and Interior which he said is an irrational zig-zag now;

and that Henry Wallace had suggested that organic and inorganic chemistry be the basis of allotment.' In fact the apparently organizational clashes between Interior and Agriculture, or Ickes's desire to turn Interior into a Department of Conservation, illustrate the delicacy and importance of the role of a department: that is, the compound of its functions, access to interests, traditions, policies and results. The role can even convert the man, as Ickes changed his attitude to some of the mythology of his department. But the Brownlow approach ignored all this; it was fatally attracted by the misleading status of scientific study and the will-o'-the-wisp of the one best way.[65] One is forced by the evidence and by Brownlow's own career and materials as much as by the Brooking work, to prefer the Meriam and Schmeckebier position.

Was this alternative position, in fact, not more successful? Of all the Brownlow proposals those that actually were most nearly adopted related to more assistance for the presidency. These were the things that most suited Roosevelt and these were in full accord with the Brookings' proposals too. If a distinction is made between executive integration, a transfer of excessive reorganization power to the President and so forth on one hand, and the recommendations for more machinery for presidential assistance on the other, it was the latter that counted, and it was that part of them that Brookings also proposed (for example, about the Budget Bureau) that were effective. It was the others that failed. If you take out of Brownlow's list of organizations those that did not really exist, or employed no staff at all, you end with a number around not one hundred but sixty; this was still the number of organizations reporting to the President and employing personnel that existed at the time of the Hoover Commissions.[66] The Brookings and the Meriam and Schmeckebier analyses did indeed give much more attention to the weakening of the Budget Bureau under Roosevelt himself,[67] and the need to strengthen the Bureau, than did the Brownlow report itself.

If one prefers the Brooking position, it would seem, then, that decisions about the machinery of government are partly devised and partly given. They are dependent on policy and likely to change. They are a matter of searching for some expedient way suggested by values, availability and experience. They are a matter of means to ends rather than an imposition of design on error. They are more likely to be fruitfully born out of continuous reorganization than occasional overall enquiry. This does not at all mean that decisions about the machinery of government should not be taken, but that they are very difficult decisions to make, they are not purely organizational, and their consequences are often not what is popularly claimed for them. Nor are these decisions concerned solely with structural alterations and functional re-allocations. Furthermore, they may well accept the inevitability of overlap, the need for balance or even some degree of conflict, and the advantages of numerous small departments. The best statement by Meriam and Schmeckebier against consolidation is a very subtle piece of argument indeed.[68] Granted that there is machinery for co-ordination, then the problems of contact, representation, friction and subordination are more likely to be dealt with, it is argued, in this sort of system (e.g. Roosevelt's competitive administration) than in the Haldane-Brownlow model.

The rationalist position about the machinery of government is influential and persistent because it is so attractive; its faults are twofold: on the one hand it sets up quite inaccurate models often about what the system is and, always, about what it can be; secondly it is quite misleading about the sources and processes of possible change either because of the genuineness of its rationalism or out of a desire to provide a cover for specific changes. Its record—even the Brownlow record, in fact; the Haldane record; the Hoover record—is dismal, but its myths retain their fascination. Both its faults are real and it is either foolish or dishonest to postulate a false image of what a government machine could and also should be like (simple, integrated, etc.). One of the reasons why the rationalist thinks change easy and necessary is precisely that he thinks the system ought to be tidy: it probably ought not; neatness may be a danger. And it is very dangerous to attempt a concentration on 'purely organizational' changes when alterations (political, etc.) may really be required.[69]

One's opposition, then, is, in part, to the record of the grand enquiries and to their rationalist mask. It is also an opposition to rationalism itself: that is to the deduction of changes from general statements. Some of these statements are useless (and this has been amply demonstrated by, e.g. Simon about principles of allocation), some are quite wrong (e.g. that overlap is one fault, that bureau shuffling will secure economies). They may come in handy as weapons in argument, but they will not always carry conviction, and they are a poor justification for the dangerous ground of major changes.

This is not the place to press this analysis further. But a positive conclusion emerges from the argument: a preference for the Brookings approach; the internal, the piecemeal and the avowedly political. Organizational changes are sought for what they produce, in policy, service, and so forth. Changing a whole machinery of government is, then, rather much: for who can say what is wanted of an organization of that scale? Yet it is a clear part of governmental experience, that, for these very reasons, decisions about organization are continually being made, and after severe struggle. It is part of the error of the rationalist position to think of change as an occasional crisis rather than a continuum. Advice about these decisions should therefore be constantly available. What follows, from one's view of the record of the great enquiries and the nature of organization, is that internal machinery—officials—must constitute a preferable source of advice. This is precisely because these decisions are matters of politics, not principle, of continual struggle, and, for the most part, of marginal (not total) change; their results uncertain; the guides peculiar not general. The continuity, the contingency, the organic nature of the assessment of organizational role demands help from sensitive, absorbed and modest weapons, more concerned with accuracy than with dogma.

I have said something elsewhere about the position of the official engaged in such advice about machinery of government matters.[70] Briefly, he does have special problems about status, knowledge and procedure, but, of course, he is not exceptional in having difficulties or in being engaged in advice about policy matters. What of the outside enquiry? Certainly enquiries may be used. But it is one thing to use them, another to rely on them. Again, it is one thing to use enquiries as arbitration between conflicting demands, an investigation of specified abuses or demands in policy or service (with consequential organizational recommendations), or as instruments of particular terms of reference (e.g. examine such and such a service and recommend economies); it is quite another thing to call into play that sort of outside enquiry which (like Haldane or Brownlow) assumes or pretends that it reconstructs a machinery of government by the use of purely organizational general principles. We may note that even the extension of O and M work from highly limited to wider jobs tends to weaken the bases of its success (time, freshness and the comparability of experience). The bigger the change sought the less likely that it can be justified or achieved on organizational grounds. The big, purely organizational enquiry must either fail or subvert its nature. This, indeed, is the record, and the subversion is likely to contaminate the type of recommendations it makes.

NOTES

1 S.D. 8, 75th Congress, 1st Session, 1937.
2 *Public Administration*, Sydney, 1958, p. 295.
3 *Ibid.*, p. 290.

4   *cf.* especially W. J. M. Mackenzie and J. W. Grove, *Central Administration in Britain*, London, 1957, esp. pp. 333 *ff.*

5   L. Brownlow, *A Passion for Anonymity*, Chicago, 1958. See also esp. A. Schlesinger, *The Age of Roosevelt*, H. Boston, 1959.

6   For the reports, see S.R. 1275, 75th Congress, 1st Session, 1937.

7   For earlier history, see W. Brook Graves, *Basic Information on the Reorganisation of the Executive Branch, 1912-1948*, Legislative Reference Service, Library of Congress, 1949; and, for still earlier material, O. Kraines, *Congress and the Challenge of Big Government*, New York, 1958.

8   Executive orders 4175 and 4239 of 1925.

9   Part II, Title IV, Sections 401-8.

10   Executive order 5959.

11   Humphrey *v.* U.S. 195 U.S. 602.

12   E. S. Corwin, *The President: Office and Powers, 1787-1957*, New York, 1957, p. 95.

13   A. Maas, *Muddy Waters*, Harvard, 1951, p. 277. *cf.* National Resources Planning Board, Progress Report, 1939.

14   Brownlow Report; Brookings Reports; Congressional Record, 74th Congress, 2nd session, v. 80, pt. IV, pp. 4146-4239; H.R. 460 74th Congress 2nd session and H.R. 4, 75th Congress, 1st session; Roosevelt, V Public Papers and Addresses: these are the main sources for the chronology of the events between 9 January 1936 (and section of Boyd Committee) to 16 August 1937 (presentation of the Brookings reports in one volume).

15   *A Passion for Anonymity*, pp. 299-300.

16   *Ibid.*, pp. 326 and 334-5.

17   *A Passion for Anonymity*, chapter 6.

18   Brownlow, *The President and the Presidency*, Chicago, 1949, p. 106.

19   *A Passion for Anonymity*, pp. 331-2.

20   *Ibid.*, pp. 333-4.

21   *Ibid.*, p. 337.

22   75th Congress, First Session, Senate Document 8, pp. 19-21.

23   *Ibid.*, pp. 33-40 and pp. 49 and 54.

24   *Ibid.*, p. 25.

25   *Ibid.*, p. 56.

26   *Ibid.*, pp. 33 and 42.

27   75th Congress, First Session, Senate Document 8, p. 16.

28   Maass, *op. cit.*, p. 95.

29   *A Passion for Anonymity*, p. 395.

30   See House resolution 60, 75th Congress, First Session, and Senate resolution 69, 75th Congress, First Session; the Joint Committee was set up by 50 Statute Law 7.

31   Senate 2350, 2529, 2530.

32   53 Statute Law 561. *A Passion for Anonymity*, pp. 413-4.

33   Maass, *op. cit.*, pp. 97 and 116-7.

34   W. Scott Payne, *The Latin American Proceeding*, I.C.P. Alabama, 1949, p. 4.

35   U.S. Senate, 84th Congress, Second Session, 16, 24 and 25 January, 1956. Hearings before the Sub-Committee on Reorganization, pp. 22-3.

36   Paul P. van Riper, *History of the United States Civil Service*, New York, 1953, p. 336.

37   *Public Administration Review*, 1959, p. 213.

38   *The President and the Presidency*, p. 96.

39 On the growth of the X.O.P. see the following: S. K. Bailey, *The President and his Political Executives*, September, 1956; *Annals of the American Academy of Political Science*, pp. 24-36; E. H. Hobbs, *Behind the President*, Washington, 1954; R. J. Donovan, *Eisenhower: The Inside Story*, New York, 1956; L. G. Seligman, 'Presidential Leadership', 10 *Journal of Politics*, 1956, R. H. Pear, 'American Presidency under Eisenhower', 20 *Political Quarterly*, 1957; R. E. Neustadt, 'The Presidency at Mid-Century', 21 *Law and Contemporary Problems*, 1956. For an earlier account, 1 *Public Administration Review*, 101-40.

40 *The Roosevelt I Knew*, p. 288. *cf.* 19 *Public Administration Review*, p. 219 and 20, p. 53; 1959 Public Policy; and 48 *Management Review*, on new types of independent organization.

41 *A Passion for Anonymity*, p. 425, and *The President and the Presidency*, p. 108.

42 L. Gulick, *Administrative Reflections from World War II*, Alabama, 1948, pp. 76, 91 to 96. *cf.* the apparently recidivous pathology of the independent regulatory commissions, or the defence establishment. 'Radical' new steps are continually taken, and always fail to solve them.

43 *A Passion for Anonymity*, p. 432.

44 *Public Administration*, Sydney, 1958, p. 209.

45 Pfiffner and Presthus, *Public Administration*, New York, 1953, p. 172.

46 *cf.* Brookings reports, at pp. 516, 167 *ff.*, 310-7, 650, 657 and 1066 *ff.*, for points of overlap, agreement or disagreement with the Brownlow works: e.g. in relation to the regulatory commissions, the fiscal system, the creation of new Departments of Conservation, Public Works and Welfare. D. Waldo, *The Administrative State*, N.Y., 1948, pp. 118 *ff.* treats the clash as one deduced purely from constitutional differences. S. C. Wallace, *Federal Departmentalisation*, Columbia, 1941, is the major work. Except in cap. V he is mainly interested in the Brookings defence of the regulatory bodies; though cap. V is a great advance it does accept that there are four and only four 'modes' of allocation p. 145). Nevertheless his respect for the 'revisionism' and eclecticism of Brookings was a major advance. See also R. Egger in 1 *Public Administration Review*, pp. 392 *ff.*

47 *Infra.*

48 Brookings report, chapters 3 and 13, and F. F. Blachly and M. E. Oatman, *Administration, Legislation and Adjudication*; F. F. Blachly, *Working Papers on Administrative Adjudication*; D. T. Selko, *The Administration of Federal Cabinets*; Lewis Meriam, *Federal Personnel Administration*, and Lewis Meriam, *Organisation for Public Personnel Administration*.

49 Meriam and Schmeckebier, p. 4.

50 *Ibid.*, Chapters 1 and 6.

51 Yale, 1938. *cf.* Corwin, *op. cit.*, p. 381, and G. McG. Dawson, *The Principle of Official Independence*, London, 1922.

52 Landis, *op. cit.*, pp. 15 and 16. *cf.* V. O. Key, 1 *Public Administration Review*, pp. 85 *ff.*, for a review of Blachly and Oatman (*supra*) and an outline of the debate about 'the headless fourth arm'. The debate has recently re-emerged.

53 Arthur Macmahon in *Democracy in Federal Administration*, edited by Conoway, Washington, 1955, p. 46. *cf.* Schlesinger, *op. cit.*

54 Meriam and Schmeckebier, *op. cit.*, Chapter 2 and Appendix A.

55 *cf.* F. E. Rourke, *The Politics of Administrative Reorganisation: A Case History*, 11 *Journal of Politics*, 1957, pp. 461 *ff*.
56 See pp. 63-6 above.
57 Meriam and Schmeckebier, p. 62.
58 Schlesinger, *passim. cf.* J. M. Ray, *Reflections of a Professor Turned Bureaucrat*, 1959 *Public Administration Review*, p. 238 *ff*.
59 Brownlow Report, p. 65.
60 *Ibid.*, p. 73, etc.
61 *A Passion for Anonymity*, p. 313.
62 *The President and the Presidency*, pp. 115-6.
63 See *A Passion for Anonymity*, pp. 380-1 for a memorandum on a discussion with Roosevelt, November, 1936.
64 *Ibid.*, p. 382.
65 Brownlow Report, p. 26. Schlesinger, *op. cit.*, pp. 341-9.
66 United States Senate, 84th Congress, Second Session, hearings cited above.
67 Meriam and Schmeckebier, pp. 152-3.
68 *Ibid.*, pp. 166-8.
69 *cf.* H. H. Ransom, 1959 *Public Administration Review*, p. 264. 'Danger exists of course that a preoccupation with reorganisation might blind us to basic policy issues.' He instances the U.S. defence reorganizations of 1947, 1949, 1953 and 1958.
70 Pp. 74-5 above.

II

MEN AND METHODS

The Fulton report, with which this section ends, was more concerned with personnel and management than with organization, with reform than with reorganization. The line is hard to draw, like others in administrative theory: line and staff, range of attention and span of control, task and function. The study of administration has barely achieved such consistency in terms and concepts as enables us to draw distinctions with much hope of understanding. Yet without this, the comparators which the discipline requires cannot be established and employed. Two of the following papers were concerned with some of these possible distinctions: executive and administrative; promotion and advancement.

6

THE DISTINCTION BETWEEN
EXECUTIVE AND ADMINISTRATIVE WORK

If terminology were cleared up, certain questions in public management would become more answerable. But the lack of clarity is itself important, as here the different usages of 'executive' and 'administrative' in British government and other situations. These differences become a useful comparative tool; nor are the differences merely opposites. Once some consistent meanings for the terms are established and the distinction between them, therefore, seen, other possibilities emerge. In particular the distinction suggested here indicated the possibility of hiving off executive work, which has now become, in fact, a dominant theme in the discussion of administrative reform. The definitions of 'administrative' and 'executive' are first steps to ways of recognizing the two sorts of work and hence their possible separation, insofar as they have different organizational requirements. This point was taken up in later discussions of development administration, elsewhere.

Terminology in Public Administration is imprecise. Its many sources of ideas and their different jargons, and growing attempts at an international exchange of administrative practices, tend to enhance this imprecision. Clarification is a major need.[1] The point of this note is to indicate one particular field of confusion and to suggest some of the questions about organization that emerge when more consistent terminology is employed.

The example of confusion is the use of the basic words 'executive' and 'administrative' themselves.[2] It is in American usage (perhaps influenced by the constitutional provision that the President 'take care that the laws be faithfully executed') that executive means (*a*) governmental work other than legislative or judicial; but also (*b*) those in charge of that work, as in the terms 'chief executive' and 'executive development'. British usage is normally quite different from this. Here the major influence is civil service classification instead of a written constitution. The executive is below the administrative class. The one is distinct from the other and it is the administrative that is the top level. 'Mere' is likely to be found qualifying the word executive but not the word administrative.

Thus the word executive can be used to describe a branch or section of government, a level in organization (which may be the top or the subsidiary level), a type of participant in organization (again, top or subordinate) and either a level or some distinct categories of work. Similarly, administrative is used to describe those exercising or the actual exercise of power in an organization, a branch of government, a particular Government, the top level officials or some other level or distinct category of officials: for example, the policy makers, the managers, those exercising overall control or, alternatively (as often in Australian practice), those performing relatively subsidiary clerical or supervisory tasks as distinct from technical or operational work.

With the word executive we may in particular note two special tendencies: to treat it as meaning primarily either the top level in organization or as that which is not legislative or judicial in government; and to use it (as in the United Kingdom civil service) as meaning non-administrative and hence subordinate, subsidiary, secondary, routine, specialized, operational etc.[3] These are not merely vague and different uses. Insofar as they are specific and consistent at all they are almost diametrically opposite.

This variety is doubtless not surprising, though we would do well to be aware of the vagaries of the practice. It is a little more than merely regrettable when we recall that a prime topic of administrative studies should be precisely the distinction between administrative and executive work. What may be meant by this distinction can scarcely be appreciated if the usage of the two key terms is itself so variegated.

For example, it was a major concern of the American writer, W. S. Willoughby, to distinguish between executive and administrative work. He wished to attack the interpretation of the United States constitution based on a three-fold separation of powers (which depended partly on an identification of executive and administrative) and deductions from that about the respective roles of Congress and President.[4] But Willoughby himself is most inconsistent in his use of the terms. At times 'executive' seems to be used to mean the carrying out as distinct from the 'direction, supervision and control' of a service; and other times it is specifically used to mean the 'distinctly political' function of decision-making, etc., or even 'as covering only the political duties of the titular head of the nation'. His use of 'administrative' is equally uncertain. This makes it difficult enough to follow Willoughby's theories. It is made more difficult when Professor Waldo, summarizing Willoughby's beliefs, seems to use executive and administrative as explicitly synonymous, one paragraph after he has said that a distinction between the two (but what?) is the important thing in both Willoughby and in Goodnow.[5]

The concern that lies behind these distinctions is primarily constitutional. In other writings, such as those of Milward and Brecht and Glaser, the concern is primarily organizational. Here confusion is rampant. Thus E. O. Stene[6] quotes A. E. Buck's third standard of re-organization: 'The undesirability of boards for purely administrative work.' This may seem to us to be orthodox enough, if not very specific: you should not use boards when there is work demanding the organization and qualities characteristic of the administrator. This is something like, we feel, some familiar MacDonnell recommendations. It has echoes of Bentham himself. But what are we to make of this when Stene goes on to define 'purely administrative work' as 'largely routine in character for which powers and objectives are precisely delimited'? This is not at all the definition we expected or the conclusion we were used to.

Usage is confused. Yet the distinction seems to be thought of great importance. The type of distinction being used itself varies. With each type our judgment of its validity, importance and results is made difficult by the looseness of the usage. Let us look here at the organization distinction and leave aside the constitutional. What can we make of this distinction? Does it suggest the possibility of a helpfully consistent usage for administrative and executive? What else does it suggest?

In British and Australian government one possibility for determining the usage of administrative and executive may already exist. We see that there clearly are in the central machineries of government broad distinctions between types of work and organization. In particular we are familiar with the distinction in cabinet government between the ministerial department and non-ministerial organization. The classic ministerial department that evolved in the United Kingdom after, say, 1860 with its Minister, its pyramidal organization, its hierarchy, its small administrative group at the top—this and its distinct characteristics could be called the norm of administrative organization.[7] Many forces have combined to enforce deviation from that norm: the desire to relieve the Ministers of responsibility; the desire to relieve Ministers and the administrators of sections of work; and the quite definite needs of some types of work for alternative forms of organization, management, and control. The Australian government machine has gone still further than the British in its deviation from the normal ministerial department.

If the ministerial department and its work were called administrative, what would follow from the use of administrative and executive to distinguish respectively the ministerial department and the non-ministerial organization as a deviant form? It would be of prime importance if there were ways of recognizing what types of work needed which type of organization: to use our terminology, to see what was in fact 'administrative work' that could be left to 'administrative organization'—the normal ministerial department; and what was 'executive work' that broadly required other types of organization. Equally clearly we do not yet have very precise tests or if we have we do not employ them. Non-ministerial organization is a chaotic field. The organization and methods of many nationalized industries in the United Kingdom have specifically been too much modelled on administrative organization and too little followed alternative executive patterns.[8] Administrative organization itself has often been left with much unsuitable work; hence the complaints about methods and structure—the departments are too big to be 'administrable businesses';[9] the structure of the administrative class has become swollen and inflated;[10] the Assistant Secretary's desk is clogged with case work, and so forth.

It is one thing to say that in broad terms one can recognize one type of organization in the ministerial department—and others that differ from it; or one type of work—the administrative work suitable to the department—and others that are not suitable to it; or to say that this recognition has not been fully enforced—the departments are doing unsuitable work, non-ministerial organization has not been fully liberated from the influence of administrative organization and so forth. It is another thing to establish precise tests by which administrative and executive work, in our sense of work suitable or unsuitable for the normal ministerial department, could be recognized. Much advice about relief for Ministers and departments simply consists of saying 'hive off executive work' without telling us how to recognize what may be hived off: that is, the advice does not provide tests for the recognition of executive work.

Do such tests exist? There have been two major approaches to providing them. The first is best represented in Brecht and Glaser's study of German administration.[11] But Brecht and Glaser were much better at describing the advantages that come from hiving off executive work from departments than at affording tests for what could in fact be hived off.[12] The 'technically well-defined field' and 'the considerable scope of business' are descriptions from which little can be deduced. Further, their discussion does not determine several organizational questions: for example whether the hiving off should be to a bureau in the department or to a more fully separate organization. The second approach is more fruitful. This is the distinction between the sort of controls, personnel and organization and methods employed by the administrative organization and the sort that the other, executive, organization employs. This approach is represented by writers like Milward and Clegg and in the results of inquiries like the Fleck Report and the old Bridgeman Report.[13]

These approaches do not always go very far. The discussion often consists of nothing more helpful than the similar distinctions between administrative and political. One notes that in that case all that is really left is that politics is what is done by politicians, that is people elected to office in certain conditions; and administration is done by appointed people. The definition of cabinet functions by the Haldane Committee and of administrative functions by the Treasury are very similar. But 'administrative' and 'executive' can clearly not be distinguished even in this way, since it is officials who perform both types of work. Secondly, many attempts at describing administrative work are merely derived from (a) formal definitions; or (b) a class of officials (so that they do not necessarily imply that these officials might not also be doing executive work or that that work might not also be done in their organizations). These definitions do not go on to provide a description of the difference between administrative and executive work. Thus the job analysis of the work of an administrator done by the Civil Service Selection Board includes several executive elements.[14] Thirdly, one may be tempted to say that executive simply means administrative work with the policy and discretionary elements taken away. But this would exclude too much, for policy and discretion enter at all levels of work. Other general definitions of executive work fail to provide criteria for deciding whether any particular piece of work is executive or not. Now what would in fact make the attempt at distinguishing between executive and administrative important would be the possibility of providing tests which could determine where work could be separated. One type of organization, personnel, control, responsibility and so forth could be suitably provided for one group of work and a different type for the other. The distinction between executive and administrative is worthwhile if it can suggest tests for organizational separation. The question therefore is simply what makes executive and administrative work separable.

One may suggest that administration is work that consists of arguments. This is a sort of work which cannot be self-contained. It involves external relations; with other branches and departments, with non-official persons, with subordinates and superiors and so forth. Its arguments lead towards decisions which require argument precisely because they are not self-contained, because they have an element of generality and because they have value elements. They depend significantly on non-measurable factors. This does not mean that the starting point of the argument may not in the first place be a draft of a letter as much as a big committee decision.

This sort of work is likely to require special qualities of structure, personnel and control. The function of organization is to minimize the amount of difficult thought by maximizing the use of standards. Administrative work arises where the use of standards instead of thought is very limited; executive where standards are appropriate. Administrative organization is therefore an organization simply of power. Executive decisions, self-contained, arrived at according to standards, are provided for in organization where specific sources of objective wisdom, financial, technical and so forth, are brought more or less automatically into play. Administrative organization is structurally characterized by long tiers of hierarchy; executive organization by the multiplication of parallel groups of specialized staff. In executive organization the work is measurable. It may be routine or it may be very complicated technical operations, but the procedure and results can be objectively gauged. It is with this sort of work that ideas about 'objective responsibility' may be appropriate; it is difficult to see that they can be appropriate with administrative work. With executive work management is measurement; whereas in administrative organization running the show means winning arguments and that includes the filtering process and selecting and rejecting the questions to be argued about. Executive organizations may be separated and granted autonomy simply because in executive work objective standards of management and control are effective. Control is inherent. The work is self-checking. Where such standards are not effective, control must still in the end be a matter of seeing that your arguments and not someone else's are the decisive ones, and your problems are the ones put on the agenda.

These differences between executive and administrative work therefore imply differences both within (for example structural differences) and outside (for example with responsibility and control) the organization. Organizations suitable for administrative work may be controlled by parliamentary scrutiny and debate but not by cost accounting or sampling. Administrative organization is subject to different ways of improvement from executive organization. It is improved by more conferences, quicker flows of the agenda, control of the hierarchical structure of the argumentative process. Filing is the key to improved administrative organization. The case files and series of forms of the executive organization are relatively simple to control. The subject files of administrative organization are certainly not simple.[15] Contrast that with the Fleck Report's discussion of executive organization: minimize the intermediate levels, that is to say change the shape from the administrative model as much as possible; employ modern managerial techniques of control in the organization; use standards of performance, progressing cost and source control and so forth.[16] These differences imply differences in the pathology of administrative and executive organizations. Indeed these may well be the best way to understand the differences. O. & M. studies of executive and administrative work may well provide the best evidence of the differences between the two. Successful examples of hiving off (for example the Export Credit Guarantees Department) may also be very helpful.

What this analysis suggests is, firstly, that it is possible to distinguish two very different categories of work done by organizations and that one may well be called administrative and one executive. The one type is essentially argumentative; the other measurable. These categories may be recognized not by the use of general definitions but by the use of certain specific tests. Such tests may include the types of control appropriate for a piece of work, its organizational structure, the ways in which its organization and methods may be improved and what characteristic faults are discovered. The point of the tests would be to discover whether work may be separated from other work, to discover where executive work may be separated from administrative work so that its different requirements (in organization, control and so forth) may be provided for. Thirdly, the significance of the difference is precisely that executive and administrative work do require different organization and can well be separated when they are differently and properly provided for.

It would follow that one should encourage a more consistent, more precise and more helpful use of the words administrative and executive. These definitions are not exclusive. That is, other uses of administrative and executive are obviously permissible, even if in any single piece of writing only one use were exercised. The word administrator will sometimes be used to mean other things than a person employed in the sort of argumentative work we have defined as administrative and suggested as suitable for the normal ministerial department. Still less can one hope that these tests of administrative and executive work will always be applied to decisions about organization. Administrative officials are never going to be free of case work; executive organizations are never going to be free of disputes. Decisions about hiving off a piece of work from a ministerial department to one that can employ different types of personnel, structure, methods and control, are never going to be automatic. But better terminology and more considered decisions must be helpful. In this case it is clear that the attempt at arriving at such a usage assists in the solution of a problem of great importance, namely, way of recognizing, organizing and separating different types of work. In general the results of striving for a more consistent and meaningful language in administration are likely to be very healthy.

NOTES

1   M. H. Bernstein, 'Research in Public Administration in the United States', at pp. 444-445, *Contemporary Political Science*, UNESCO, 1950.
2   R. S. Parker, 'Executive Development in the Commonwealth Public Service', 15 *Public Administration*, pp. 178-180.
3   For traditional British definitions of administrative and executive see C. K. Munro, *The Fountains in Trafalgar Square*, 1952, p. 45, and *Royal Commission on the Civil Service*, 1953, Introductory Factual Memorandum, H.M. Treasury, paragraphs 180 and 265.
4   Dwight Waldo, *The Administrative State*, 1948, pp. 111-114.
5   *Op. cit.*, p. 114.
6   *American Administrative Theory*, 1950, p. 8.
7   J. R. Simpson, 'Organizing the Larger Units' in *British Management Review*, reprint, July, 1949, p. 5.
8   H. A. Clegg, *Industrial Democracy and Nationalization*, 1951, pp. 107-8.
9   Sir John Henry Woods, 26 *Public Administration* (London), pp. 85-91.
10 Chorley Report on the Remuneration of the Higher Civil Service, 1948-9, p. 4.
11 A. Brecht and C. Glaser, *Art and Technique of Administration in German Ministries*, 1940.
12 A. Brecht, 'Three Topics in Comparative Administration', *Public Policy*, 1941, pp. 289-320.
13 Clegg, *op. cit.*; G. E. Milward, ed., *Organization of Large-Scale Enterprises*, 1950; Bridgeman Report on the Post Office, 1931-2; Fleck Report on the Organization of the National Coal Board, 1955.
14 *cf.* Parker, *loc. cit.*
15 I. Maclean, 'Trends in Organizing Modern Records', 1 Archives and Manuscripts, pp. 1-17.
16 *cf.* H. A. Simon, reported in 16 *Public Administration Review* at p. 124.

7

STAFF CONDITIONS AND CAREERS AS A
PROBLEM OF MANAGEMENT

*This chapter is based on a contribution to a conference on
Public Service Management: The Importance of Classification, Promotion and Arbitration. It was much concerned
to establish a distinction between the concepts of promotion
and advancement. This later became of some significance in
development administration, and was closely related to the
concept of career and hence to ideas in bureaucratic and
modernization theories. Any public service has to contain
aspects of promotion and advancement; the ways in which
these functions are structured will be of great importance
for it and for comparison with other services. The working
out of the distinction is also related to those problems of
classification first talked about by Ismar Baruch and discussed also by the Fulton report. There was some attempt
here to do something more about a comparative and prescriptive administrative theory and to enunciate the peculiar
significance for any public service of the way in which it
recognized and found people for its top administrative work.*

In 1935, when only eight of the American States had merit systems
in operation, the Commission on Public Service Personnel reported
in these words: 'The establishment of a career service is, in the
judgment of this Commission, the required next step in the history
of American government ... By career is meant a life work. It is
an honourable occupation which one normally takes up in youth
with the expectation of advancement and pursues until retirement.'
It is my thesis that the essential quality of a public service and the
key to the design of staff conditions is this concept of a career
service and the way in which it is handled.

The implications of the career concept in the public service go
well beyond the notions of merit or proficiency as against patronage.
Those notions are primarily concerned with the reform of recruitment, negatively in the first place (avoid getting people for the
wrong reason), or positively at a later stage (getting the people you
want). The career concept is related to this, but it also concerns

what is to happen beyond the first appointment.

At this stage the concept may lead us in two different directions. On the one hand we can have the public service that emphasizes *promotion*. This service will provide permanence and some degree of more or less guaranteed advancement. Promotion, however, as distinct from advancement, will come only for the best servant. The resultant problems of selection which this sort of service creates may lead you in a variety of directions, of which the distinction between promotion and advancement is one, and open or lateral recruitment may be others. This will be discussed more fully in due course.

On the other hand, there is the public service which emphasizes *advancement*. For this sort of service it is held that the promise of a permanent career can be fulfilled only by closing the service and by guaranteeing maximum advancement for all. Of course, this maximum might be a relatively low average, especially if the closing is within narrow compartments, programmes or specializations.

There is, then, a choice to be made and the forces arranged on either side are impressive. Let us understand the nature of the choice and these forces. The second kind of service is likely to demand relatively early recruitment, superannuation, good average levels of pay. It is likely to be, though is not necessarily associated with, in the American term, 'programme' or 'closed' careers. The promotional service, on the other hand, is likely to demand 'organization' or 'open' careers.

CLASSIFICATION

What is the relevance of classification practices to this choice? It would be generally agreed that by classification we mean some method of describing, and perhaps some method of actually organizing, the whole or parts of a public service into groups, scales, grades, classes, schedules or services. There are two different ways in which this may be done: the 'personal' or 'rank' method and the 'position' or 'job' method. Some would want to say that a public service must choose between these methods and that the choice is an important one. Some, indeed, particularly in the United States, would also want to say that a trend to the use of the job or position system was something to be warmly encouraged. We must ask ourselves what is the nature of this apparent choice between rank and position classification, and whether it is as important as is sometimes believed.

Here is a good definition of the personal or rank system: 'According to this principle, the rank or title of the individual gives him a right to the pay, prestige and perquisites of the rank or title and he carries with him the title and its rights whatever role in the organization he may play at a particular time.' Military services are often said to be the extreme version of this: a man is given a job because that is one of the vast variety of jobs to be done by persons of his seniority or rank. In fact, this is not true of military services in practice except in undeveloped or crisis situations.

The United Kingdom civil service is also said to provide an example of a service organized in this way. Again, one wonders about the validity of this. It might well be argued from the evidence that the original method the Northcote-Trevelyan Committee had in mind was job classification (if it is fair to impose this sort of concept on them at all), but that it was thought that there were in the main only two (later increased to three or four) types of job to be done; that is, apart from the jobs that could be hired out or done by special groups or by occasional organizations like royal commissions. One would not, however, want to go too far in this direction: if, say, a Higher Executive Officer in the National Assistance Board might think of himself as doing a particular job, for example, as an Area Officer, it is also true that he will think of himself and his career in terms of a movement from one rank or grade in his class to another, as much as from one job and job description to another. The tendency to group the whole non-industrial service into a relatively few classes and divide these classes into significant and service-wide grades is an important one. This is so even if there are far more such groupings than is sometimes thought, and some groupings that are so specialized in departmental or other terms as to be nearer to job than rank descriptions.

Clearly, there is something that matters very much at work here, the notion of the generality of certain types of work. This idea of uniformity has often been an important concept in civil service reform, as in France and the United Kingdom. It is part of the ethos of the administrative profession as painted by Lord Bridges, in his 'Portrait of a Profession'. The notion is important but problematical. The Northcote-Trevelyan report could believe in uniformity partly because it also had an over-simplified belief in the validity of one type of organizational structure, the ministerial department, in one type of work, one type of personnel, and one type of organization. Was this not in the end an illusion comparable with the contemporary Jacksonian belief in the essential simplicity of the work to be done by public officials, though the one attitude led to reform and the other to a relapse in standards? (In each case there was confidence in the personnel available, Democrats and Balliol men!)

Bridges can believe in uniformity for a reason different from

Northcote-Trevelyan. For him the unifying factor is a particular type of education and particular gates of entry. Both these reasons would now be difficult to sustain. Positive government has made the impact of ends greater and more significant for the administrative role, as we have been reminded by the most recent work of Dimock, Selznick, Kissinger and others. Administration is, therefore, more important and also more various. It is partly for this reason that since the 1930s we have seen a reaction in the United States away from the simple acceptance of the superiority of the United Kingdom administrative model.

What, then, would it now mean if we sought to place more emphasis on personal or rank classification in a public service? Let us suppose, for example, that you want a career service that will emphasize rapid opportunities of promotion for the best administrative talent. Will a rank system encourage this? Clearly, the question cannot be answered in that form. This is not because of what may be thought by the proponents of the position system to be a fault of the rank system. It is because the rank system has no inherent, inevitable faults or virtues as such. Suppose that the whole of the service is divided into a number of service-wide groups, ranked in some hierarchy of authority or seniority: one cannot begin to discuss the effects of this until one also knows at least (*a*) the criteria of grouping, (*b*) the number of groups (since rank alone need not reduce the number any more than job description need automatically multiply it), and (*c*) the usages about movement within and between groups.

Again, rank alone does not make promotion easier though it may be said often to clarify the distinction between promotion and advancement. Rank is not a system or a policy but a descriptive technique, good for some things but not for others. Again, no public service can, or ever has, allocated its persons to jobs purely by consideration of rank. There never has been a purely 'rank' public service, save in highly undeveloped states.

Is this not the case with position classification too? Certainly we could find public services which have been deeply influenced by this technique, and powerful arguments have been deployed by and against it. Let us look at a definition to begin with: 'Position classification emphasises the particular job performed at the time rather than the rank or title of the performer. In fact, the position is conceived as a structure of duties and responsibilities that exist apart from the performer just as a room exists whether or not it is occupied.'[2]

What is the bearing of this? We can see that a public service wishing to reform itself, but frightened of any general recognition of an administrative elite as such, may well want to enunciate the jobs to be done in some apparently concrete or earthy fashion. What could be more different from the deliberate aristocratic mistiness of an 'attaché' than, say, an 'economic plans preparation officer, Grade II'? This is encouraged by the notion that scientific management, since it can break down all jobs into their basic motions, can also be used to provide an analysis of all jobs, and a code for describing them. From therbligs to position classification, from Gilbreth to Ismar Baruch, was a tempting and apparently democratic step. A spirit of egalitarianism, considerable activity in collective bargaining or arbitration, and the general business of internal and external wage comparisons, might well encourage a tendency to describe public service jobs in this highly specific way, to build a seemingly rational relationship between pay, duties and qualifications.

Thus position classification might be said to conform to the Weberian model of a bureaucracy. Many forces were at work here. Bureaucratization, reform, egalitarianism, scientific management, pay research, O. & M., the growth of functions that could not be described by the old and simple nineteenth-century terminology. Treasury classes were all very well for the older functions of, say, a Home Office, but what of the frightening and strangely new jobs to be done in a Central Office of Information, to give a United Kingdom example? However, there are other things that we could also say about position classification: massive wage negotiations, for example, may well express themselves in a consolidation of a public service into fewer and broader classes rather than a series of particular jobs. These forces do not necessarily support position classification; and position classification alone does not, in fact, solve very many problems.

The problem of describing particular jobs and positions is certainly much more complex than was once supposed. Let us mention some of the difficulties, demonstrated in recent work by Jaques, March, Guetzkow and Simon. A position is not only a bundle of duties from which movements and qualifications can be deduced: it is also a network of methods, procedures and organizational relations that are significant insofar as they define a decisional role. This is a network that changes pretty constantly, for reasons that have long been discussed, like change in occupant, in policy, or in technique, and for other reasons too, like interactions and group susceptibilities within organization. Can certain jobs be described in this way if their major element is not duty but discretion? Can many jobs have particular descriptions that will be followed over fairly long periods of change?

In any case, a careful reading of Baruch himself shows that his argument justified not position classification as against rank classification, but some agreed code of description as against mere chaos. Thus he admits that the key phase of setting up a position classification system is not, in fact, the description of particular jobs but precisely the choice of method for grouping those jobs together. From there to the admission of rank is simply a matter of allowing that some groups of jobs will, in some sense (seniority, pay, authority, organizational hierarchy) be customarily superior to others. Even the most extreme technocrat would not want to argue against any such arrangement at all of groups in a public service. That is, as soon as you define a group you have to arrange some amount of increment within that group and prescribe some degree of movement between it and other groups. It is difficult to see that there can be a career service if this is not done and here you enter into a realm of problems with which rank attempts to deal. Nor is there, in fact, in Baruch's own four tests for a valid code anything which excludes a rank system of description (though he denied this).

The argument is not that it is not worthwhile attempting to develop methods of analysing jobs and hence describing them. Many such methods are possible and should be employed for different purposes: Baruch's method, Simon's decision-making schema, and so forth. Thus, one need not want to go all the way with, say, the Canadian Royal Commission of 1946 or with Wilmerding's old report[3] in laying the blame for so many faults of those public services at the door of position classification itself. There was certainly a great deal in these criticisms that should be remembered: the great value of simplicity in personnel arrangement and the need to take into account promotion and recruitment as well as salary fixing in setting a scheme of classification. The evils of any complex and fettering system which is based on the false analogy of the purchase of supplies ignores the major distinctions to be made in public personnel management, for example, between higher administration and other non-technical work. But the use of job description and position classification techniques does not inevitably lead to these characteristics. For example, position groups can be fitted into an overall grouping system even though there may well be a clash between the relative demands for incremental scales of a particular job on the one hand and the general grades on the other. This difficulty can presumably be overcome.

There is no need to pretend to describe what cannot be described; for example, you can avoid the extension of a very specific position classification to the highest levels of administration. There is no reason in logic why position classification should prevent you, for example, from clearly demarcating the lines of recruitment, development and role of an administrative corps within the service. Of course, empirically, it may well be true that public services which have given great attention to position classification have not made this vital distinction, while rank classified services have. In practice, the Canadian Royal Commission and Wilmerding may be justified.

Position and rank classification, then, are not policies but techniques, just as there are many other public personnel techniques like staff inspection, rating and so forth. They are techniques that can be used at either end of the same scale. It is sensible to say to a designer of a public service that he really must choose between an emphasis on promotion and an emphasis on advancement. It is not sensible to say that he must choose between these two techniques of description. Indeed, while public services do differ strongly about their policies on promotion and advancement, most public services, whatever the simple model of the textbooks may pretend, do, in fact, use both sets of classification techniques.

If a public service can, should, and normally does use both techniques, what is likely to be important about classification in relation to the sort of career service that it creates? Some matters here are quite obvious: for example, the change in the value of a position with changes in its personnel. We have already mentioned possible clashes in pay design between the needs of particular job definitions and the overall classification structure. What would seem to be clear is that the issues contained in these headings are partly objective and social: they are not, that is to say, open to free choice, and for the rest they will be determined not by inherent characteristics of particular classification techniques, but by the sort of career service that is wanted.

It is this question that can provide a criterion and a diagnosis for public personnel policy, an administrative typology, and some significant explanation of the important differences between public services. For example, it is clear that both the United Kingdom and the Australian public services use rank and job techniques of classification whatever the traditions may suggest, but that the differences between the services are, nonetheless, numerous. It means something quite important in the United Kingdom to say of an officer that he is, for example, a higher executive officer: there is no equivalently significant title that one could apply in Australia.

One can mention other Australian characteristics: the administrative elite is not clearly demarcated; there are a large number of short and overlapping salary bands (of course, the United Kingdom service uses overlapping salary bands too); recruitment is conducted at relatively early educational levels, and in fairly miscellaneous fashion. The description in salary terms of particular classes is a relatively peculiar Australian characteristic in which the role that the Public Service Arbitrator has exercised may be a subject for argument. We note, then, the impact of the Arbitrator and of the appeals system, the hunt for relatively frequent but small promotions, the time spent on comparatively small classification matters by departments and the Public Service Board, the difficulty that has met attempts at moving to wider and simpler classification bands. It is clear that the total of these characeristics is highly significant in terms of the choice between a service that emphasizes promotion and one that guarantees advancement. This is obviously a service of the second type. It is also apparent that these qualities are not explainable merely in terms of job-rank differences any more than they would be by, for example, what type of staff reporting was used. These are not fundamental determinants.

There would seem to be three key matters in classification from this point of view. Firstly, there is the question of designating and organizing the *authority responsible for classification*: the centralization of classification authority in the Commonwealth Public Service is an example of one type of solution. Secondly, there is the relative size of the groups of positions, the number of such groups in a service and the practices about movement between them: *the pattern and language of classification*. Thirdly, there is the *relationship between classification and other practices* like recruitment, training, promotion, pay, and so forth.

Take first the matter of the classification authority. This is often presented in Australia as though the only issue were the division of authority between the Board and the Arbitrator, as though many of the faults of classification could obviously be laid at the door of the Arbitrator, and as though this were a peculiarly Australian problem. Little or none of this seems to me to be completely justified. Two other matters are at least as important; first, the relation between personnel and financial controls, between public service board and treasury, and second the degree of decentralization of classification functions. Clearly, for example, the relative degree of centralization of authority in changing a classification structure, or a particular classification, is as likely to make at least as much difference to the way in which the administrative cadre is promoted, as the existence of a public service arbitrator.

In the United States, at any rate, under the 1949 Classification Act, the notion of decentralization has had a very powerful influence. The Civil Service Commission sets standards and performs some sort of post-audit and the individual department actually does the job within the general language of the G.S. section. In any case, why do we regard the Arbitrator as such a peculiar device when, say, 80 per cent of awards are merely registrations of agreement after negotiation and when in the United Kingdom, for example, there is a Civil Service Arbitration Tribunal, a Coleraine Committee, and so forth? Is the compulsory element of arbitration so peculiarly important in this context? It may well be a factor, but it is not by itself a total explanation.

No doubt public service authorities regard arbitrators as a nuisance, but some conflict is inevitable in any unstable price system, and final authority could not be given to a board as against a court, joint council, etc. The problem is not the lack of ultimate authority in the hands of the Board, but the sort of principles that are used to guide pay decisions. The debate about these principles before the Priestley Commission in the United Kingdom and the institution there of a civil service pay research unit under the authority of the National Whitley Council, could well be studied further. One might note, for example, that the Priestley Commission was specifically opposed to the giving of too much attention to the ironing out of all internal horizontal relativities of pay, just the sort of classification comparisons that take up so much time in Australia.

The second thing we should look at is what we call the pattern and language of classification. This is of the greatest importance. Let us repeat what we have said: neither the job nor the rank techniques of description can provide a complete language alone. The point of greatest difficulty is the building of some relationship between the overall code of the service, which it must have, and the particular jobs to be done, which must be defined at least for organizational if not also for personnel reasons. As you move through the overall code to the job, or vice versa, you encounter problems of definition of service, class, group, grade, position, and range; of length of range, of overlap; of enumeration and number. The complexity of this can be immense; for example, the 10,000 terms under the present Classification Act in the United States federal government service. The technical differences between each of these stages must be understood: for example, the status definition with the class, grade and range stages, the job definition with the service, group and position stages. Series of ranks and series of positions inevitably emerge.

Concious planning and policy are required, but we may well be tempted to go too far. The numerical weighting systems often employed in industry might be a will-o'-the-wisp for a whole public service. Yet as the processes of negotiation, the supply of talent and skills, the man in the post, and the values of mere pieces of work are constantly changing, we must seek for some stabilizing elements in the whole schedule. Certain types of instability are very unsettling indeed; there is little point in using a careful technique of position classification in processes of recruitment, testing, pay settlement and so forth, if the movement of men from post to post is extremely rapid. This is particularly true in posts where the impact of the occupant does matter. Accordingly, we must perhaps accept some degree of irrationality as the lines of relativity are pursued to their extremes.

Is some experiment called for? In relation to the problem of authority and machinery we suggested a glance at the pay research unit device. On the question of the techniques of classification we might look at such recent work as Jaques' *Measurement of Responsibility*, 1956. Jaques has worked out a 'time-span' analysis of discretion which may be capable of making two important contributions to the problem of classification. The first is that it could supplement job description and position classification. Those techniques take into account the complexity of the work and the sort of training required. They are relevant, we argued, to placing the service, group and position of a job. The Jaques measurement, being concerned with other factors like discretion and wastage power, amount to a definition of 'the size of the job', and hence to those definitions of relative status that are relevant to class, group and pay range. The second contribution this measurement might make is that it provides a pretty concrete test that can be applied irrespective of other differences. It is based on the sound discoveries that no job is without any element of discretion, and that the worry and effort of a piece of work must be analysed in terms of the decisions that have to be made during its course: that is to say, Jaques creates a common measure out of some of the most advanced theoretical and experimental work being done in his own field and by other workers like Simon and Lindblom.

Many techniques, therefore, are in fact used (and should be consciously and admittedly used) in the classification of a working public service: you may use job description, but you will then have to go on to other techniques to settle questions of pay. You will use some general code of rank, but this will not settle the question of whether salaries should overlap at any point. If you also want to mark off administrative talent and promote it fairly rapidly, you will probably have to have fairly few classes and large grades and provide for a variety of opportunities of movement between them. The unifying forces of a technique such as Jaques has worked out and the nature of what it sets out to measure may be highly relevant to the discovery and reward of administrative talent in the scattered jobs of a complex public service.

If the language and the rest of classification is important because of its impact on the nature of the public service, then classification must also be studied in the third way mentioned above, that is, in its relation to many other aspects of public personnel management. Indeed, classification does not make sense in any other way. The role and policy of the public service authority in recruitment and training, for example, must in part determine what is to be classified. We see that these personnel techniques are always seeking to affect the identification that the official accepts as he employs his discretion. Thus if classification as, amongst other things, a measurement of status is concerned with discretion, it is true that classification is a small part of the network that settles the way in which discretion will be employed.

The United Kingdom civil service tradition relied on a certain sort of recruitment, the French on a high degree of training, the Americans on open recruitment, as their major solutions to the problem of administrative talent in the public service. These traditional practices were little related to classification, and in post-war reform classification has not been the only field looked to. However, we should also note that the United States attempt at creating a senior civil service, the French grade of *administrateur civil* and the wider degree of promotion from the United Kingdom executive to the administrative class are, indeed, partly experiments in the field of classification. The United Kingdom administrative class has arguably been changed more by this movement than by educational or recruitment reform. It is in particular the relation between classification and selection that is most important here and it is the problem of promotion and selection that will be examined in the next section of this paper.

PROMOTION AND SELECTION

The career contract is a various instrument: compare, for example, what you can promise an engineering cadet with what you could promise an administrative cadet. Classification will only be one of the things that matter. In career planning, that is the decision of policy and methods as between the promotional or the advancement type of career service, the total of classification practices will certainly matter a great deal. The sheer number of positions and groups on the one hand, for example, must affect the problems of selection for promotion; the width of pay range and the number of grades, on the other hand, must affect the sort of guarantee of advancement that can be proffered. But, again, it will not only be classification that matters.

It is not easy to argue against the proposition that this range of problems in career interpretation is now the core of public personnel management. Perhaps, as Helps argued a hundred years ago, these were always the most difficult problems. Certainly, with all due respect to the terms of reference of the Recruitment Committee, public service nowadays may well have less discretion over what they can get than what they can do with what they have got.

In fact, the public service will have to make up its mind that the selection of administrative talent is a fundamental and inescapable issue; and see that there is a choice between emphasising promotion and emphasising advancement. This choice may be clarified if the distinction between promotion and advancement is kept clear. There are other practices which may help to hinder promotion in this respect: for example, the public service which relies overwhelmingly on early entry, fairly short initial automatic increment salary ranges, and numerous opportunities for comparatively insignificant advancement, fails to make clear the difference between this promise of advancement and the opportunity of promotion, and is certainly likely to maximize the problem of developing its talent and administrative selection. Promotion is simply internal selection, an alternative to other management succession practices such as the open service of lateral recruitment: a recruit has a right to advancement but not necessarily to promotion. Public personnel policy should not obscure, or prevent the operation of, this distinction

I would argue, in the first place, that the existence of an administrative elite with a developed public service is inevitable, like some other things around which debate occurs: staff reporting is another instance. The question is not whether, but how, such features should express themselves. A pretence, and it is no more than a pretence, that such an elite does not exist may lead to highly inefficient or accidental selection; or it may result in emergence of what Mr. Encel has recently demonstrated to be the significantly atypical elite (in terms of entry, qualifications and promotion) of the Commonwealth service. A study of the top levels of the public service outside those Mr. Encel has been looking at may complete the picture. A preliminary study of the Queensland service, shows, for example, something like 85 per cent of the present top having entered at an age below 17 years. It also shows the significance of certain positions like private secretaries, audit inspectors, state reporting bureau and parliamentary clerks as stepping stones to the upper reaches. Are these, in fact, satisfactory methods of providing administrative leadership?

Let us fully accept the difficulties of transference of administrative methods, and the profound ecological significance of the way in which a society does provide its administrative leadership. Let us accept, too, the significance of the debate between the administrative generalists and the programme specialists and the probable necessity of using many methods of administrative selection. Still one cannot see, in the light of current demands and of the impact of public authorities themselves on supply, any case in the modern world for the enforcement of the tradition of telegraph boy to permanent head. Indeed, what Australian experience tends to suggest is that such a tradition would now become merely a cloak for accident, for 'crisis' or makeshift arrangements, or in the end for radical change.

I am prepared to defend three assumptions. The first is that the way in which the public service selects its administrators is so significant that it should be conscious and apparent. The second is that the methods of public management should make it possible for the leadership of the service continually to select and maintain a promising administrative cadre, without being unduly bound by other practices in the provision of its succession. The third assumption is that where promotion is a means to this end, there must be some degree of stability. This is an essential condition. To quote Stahl:[4] 'Promotion policy is not something to be predicated on a high-powered sales technique. Employees should not be whipped into a continuous frenzy over promotional opportunity. No organization is so constructed that all can expect eventual promotion to the top few rungs of the ladder; in fact there is room for only a small minority to climb beyond the middle levels. Besides, many employees are perfectly content to stay in their existing positions and, if let alone, will continue a high order of efficiency.'

The key to this again is, evidently, distinction between promotion and advancement. The exemption of public service promotions from appeal is, of course, one of the practices that may contribute to this: it is certainly by itself insufficient. The practices have to extend through the whole of public management, through classification, through training, through staff reporting, through retirement policies: indeed, they must go beyond personnel management into questions of organizational structure. For example, one of the conditions of the promotion-advancement distinction within a career service may well be the use of relatively long salary grades, and especially a long initial grade. Some sort of advancement would thus be guaranteed. The actual amount of promotion would not be increased, but the opportunity of promotion could be given in pretty wide job and organizational terms. There would be a stable guarantee of some advancement, flexible opportunity of promotion, and hence a degree of incentive. Clearly, the installation of such a programme has a very wide range of implications in organizational as well as personnel terms.

What is it that a public service does when it promotes or when it advances a member of its staff? It may be said in the first place to be fulfilling the career contract. The career notion provides some definition of advancement: you must fulfil this promise and you must promise this minimum. Hence you are led into debates about the right length of the initial ('automatic', 'incremental') salary range, in which all the arguments are certainly not on one side. This also leads you into some of the basic debates about job classification: for example, does its use not weaken the advancement promise given as part of the career? But the career notions of permanence and advancement do not help with the problems of promotion: it is one thing (as both the United States federal civil service and the Commonwealth service have discovered) to recruit into a career service non-technical graduates; it is another thing to provide them with the sort of promotional opportunities they may want.

Fulfilment of career contract is one part of the matter, then, and an explanation of advancement. Another part is the provision of incentive. But incentives are a very tricky notion in personnel management, as all the work from Elton Mayo to Sargant Florence has shown. They are social, they are not fully susceptible to control, and different incentives are required for different objectives: for example, for effort, for punctuality, for improvement. Again, a distinction between promotion and advancement may be called for by this explanation. If advancement is not quite automatic it will be an incentive, but clearly in a very different way from the more limited but more exciting opportunity of promotion. Thus one argument for overlapping as against end-to-end salary structure between major classes of a service is that it enables you to guarantee long and fairly (though not completely) automatic advancement as one type of incentive, and an opportunity of relatively early promotion as quite another type.

The third thing the public service might be doing is simply to be using this sort of movement as an alternative to other sorts of movement which may be more difficult in general public service conditions (like firing) or in particular organizational circumstances (like transfers, secondments and reassignments). The relationship and the choice between these various forms of movement is another delicate section of public personnel management. On the one hand we must recognize that a career service cannot do without stairs up which it may need to kick people from time to time. On the other hand, we also recognize that careful planning of transfers and re-assignments, which may involve no increase in salary, can be part of an overall career planning programme of the greatest importance to successful promotion practices. Advancement, which means some increase in salary and seniority, stands quite to one side of this.

Fourthly, the public service may be using promotion itself as one way of dealing with the problem of management succession. Promotion in this sense is internal selection. Management succession, the continual re-creation of the administrative elite, it has been stressed, is a quite inevitable demand. It may not be expressed in a demand for promotion: it can be met in other ways, that is, by various forms of external selection. But if it is not met by promotion (and this would threaten the career concept itself) it will certainly be met in other ways, unless the public service is to collapse or be superseded. The one way in which it cannot be met effectively at all now is by advancement alone: this does not begin to measure up to the role—the senior clerk is not the junior administrator. Advancement does not provide acceptable answers to the questions of how, with whom, or by what authority the flow of vacancies in the administrative role is to be filled.

To look at some of the problems of method: there are, I take it, two standards in promotion—what a man has done and what a man might do. The second is doubtless the more relevant to the end we have in view, but are you sure that you can test it? You will be assisted if you know exactly what it is you require and, therefore, what you are looking for. Perhaps job classification will help here, but then there are two difficulties. Job classification at the administrative level is one. The second is that a service dominated by job classification techniques in its actual arrangement of classes and grades as well as groups, and its practices of movement between classes (that is in promotion itself), restricts the evidence of what a man might do as against what he has done. Of course, this can be qualified by a careful planning of interjob movement, of possible conditions for promotion, and by the use of additional tests. But these all have their own immense difficulties.

A second and connected problem is about seniority. Clearly, this is in part a qualification for advancement. It does not appear that it should be a qualification for promotion. Now, in the first place, this dichotomy would seem to be a powerful argument in favour of practices which distinguish between promotion and advancement; it would, for example, make it easier for a public service authority to bring something like Section 50 (4A) of the Commonwealth Public Service Act into play in cases of promotion. In the second place, if alternative tests to seniority are to be introduced, they must be thorough and relevant; seniority possesses comparative clarity and objectivity at any rate. It cannot be altogether avoided. To quote Champ Clark: 'No sane man would for one moment think of making a graduate from West Point a full general, or one from Annapolis an admiral, or one from any university or college chief of a great newspaper, magazine or business house. A priest or preacher who has just taken orders is not immediately made a bishop, archbishop or cardinal. In every walk of life "men must tarry at Jericho until their beards are grown".'[5]

We come back to the problem: how do you propose to judge potential capacity as against past record—by examinations, by tests, by staff reporting? Many methods could probably be used, but they must be introduced properly. The history of staff reporting, for example, shows not that formal systems fail but that they succeed only if certain conditions of control are established. The use of promotion examinations either as bars or in competitive form, is also full of difficulty except, of course, as tests of special knowledge: but they are employed, for example, in New South Wales, for limited (that is, internal) promotion in the United Kingdom, and in many United States local and state government merit systems. It is, indeed, arguable that certain complex types of examination are one of the most promising means of testing for internal selection.

A third problem of method is that the very argument for flexibility and openness in promotional opportunity tends to emphasize the role of the central public service authority. An instance of this is the Boyer recommendation for the placing of Administrative Officers in Training on the establishment of the Public Service Board itself. Clearly, centralization will have its own series of costs as, for example, the relative lack of opportunity for the senior departmental administrator independently to create his own 'cabinet'.

Fourthly, there are other potential and comparatively hidden but ultimately significant costs in promotion methods as they may be developed. Two may be mentioned: one is the impact on public service stability of an overdose of publicity in promotion business, though some degree of publicity is necessarily required. A second is that as tests search rightly into the potential qualities as against the evident record of a candidate, we may see at work one aspect of Whyte's 'organization man'. How far, in fact, is a public service or any other employer entitled to go in its examination of the less measurable qualities of its personnel? Shall we see the rise of departmental wives to compare with that terrible phenomenon the company wife? We must hope not.

What you are to test, how you are to test it and who the responsible authority will be form some of the problems of method. Then there is the problem of scope and area. Promotion is internal selection, but how widely is the 'internal' to be interpreted in terms of candidates on the one hand and jobs on the other? How far are you going to look for men and how freely are you going to move them? We have already suggested the variety of practices as between the open and closed, the organization and the programme services; between, for example, United States bureaus with one practice and their top departmental levels with another.

Certain points should be emphasized. One is that inbreeding would appear to be much more justified in the unifuctional specialized type of programme common to non-ministerial organizations, say, than to the traditional ministerial departments: policy departments, especially, should be exempted from it. The second point is that the very emphasis on merit and proficiency as a protection against the remnants of patronage leads to the narrowing of promotional scope and area. Any widening may, therefore, be suspect. This is part of a dilemma recently felt in the second Hoover Commission Personnel and Civil Service Task Force Reports. Thirdly, the rise of new pieces of work and new methods in departments may from time to time strongly affect their attitude to the matter; or, equally, it may be affected by the degree of centralization of personnel management in a public service as a whole. Fourthly, inter-agency promotion, the widening of scope and area to include the whole of an organization or a service must generally in the end be advantageous if the problems of methods can be solved: but if the agencies or organizations are very large the advantages may not be worth the problems and the cost. In Australia, however, the great majority of the public service organizations are not large enough to provide a satisfactory alternative to inter-departmental promotion: here the need for width of scope and area is very strong indeed.

CONCLUSION

I have argued that when the public service does move staff, does promote or advance them, it may be doing so for different reasons. Some of these demand advancement, some promotion. To fulfil one demand is not to fulfil another. The need for promotion, in the sense of the major career service method of selecting administrative talent, will not be met by providing general conditions of advancement. Promotion, internal selection is not the only way in which executive development may be provided, but it is a career technique, and the provision must be made somehow or other. If this is not openly recognized the means will tend to be accidental, and therefore to be irrational and inefficient, or submerged. Neither of these is satisfactory.

It must be remembered that, of all the effective forms of administrative selection, promotion is the one which fits most easily into the career concept. It is therefore in the interests of the career service to assist, not to hinder, the use of this form. The alternative would be to threaten the career service itself. Of all that hinders promotion sole emphasis on advancement and a blurring of the distinction between the two is the most likely and the most material. These practices, therefore, far from protecting, may actually weaken the career concept.

This is not an argument for any particular form of promotion. It is certain that the nature of the demand is indeed unlikely to be met by any one device. Furthermore, the problem as a whole is of such delicacy and significance that the possibility of transference of methods from one system to another must be severely restricted. But it is an argument for recognition of the need within the terms of a career service, and for the design of public personnel management around it. I have tried to suggest what some of the difficulties of promotion may be. In any case, this is what I would put forward as a major issue in the management of a career service. How do the Australian public services (perhaps we should ask the wider question about public employment as a whole) measure up to it?

NOTES

1 Waldo, *Ideas and Issues in Public Administration*, p. 254.
2 *Ibid.*, p. 255.
3 Commission of Enquiry on Public Service Personnel: *Government by Merit: An Analysis of the Problem of Government Personnel*, 1935.
4 *Public Personnel Administration*, 1956, p. 165.
5 *My Quarter Century in American Politics*, New York, 1920, Vol. I, p. 209.

8

THE CONDITIONS OF THE PUBLIC

ESTABLISHMENTS

Fulton in Winter

The report of the Fulton Committee on the Civil Service is doubtless one of the major public documents of our time. This not wholly serious paper examined some of its pre- suppositions: that there had been nothing so important since Northcote and Trevelyan in 1853; that nothing had happened to the civil service since then; that it could perceive and deal with the problems of its time (which it took, in part, to be an amateur and generalist administration) as well as its pre- decessors had done. Brownlow had concentrated on 'too many agencies' as the problem to be dealt with, Fulton on 'too many classes'. The report lacked a discipline of com- parison and costing. The paper ends with an attempt to anticipate the next in the line of the great civil service reports, this time on the post-Fulton civil service.

Within five months of the presentation of the Report of the Fulton Committee on the Civil Service it had become possible for Professor Max Beloff[1] to refer to 'The manifest failure of the Fulton Com- mittee on the Civil Service to produce a satisfactory general ap- preciation of the problems with which it was confronted', and to its 'somewhat inchoate set of solutions'. There is a somewhat opposite criticism that the Report endeavoured to start with the enunciation of a singularly clear, sharp note which was meant to shape it and to establish for it nothing less than a distinctive place in history. It began quite explicitly by aiming, indeed, at a very general appreciation. The position which the Fulton Report begins by adopting for itself is to look directly back to the one enquiry into the Civil Service which it acknowledges and with which it is prepared or, rather, seeks, to be compared: the Report of North- cote and Trevelyan of 1854 (as the Fulton Report says, though 1853 would have been more accurate) or alternatively, Macaulay's report which was, in fact, of 1854. It does not, incidentally, discuss Macaulay's occasion for his whole argument twenty-one years before that.

That opening was, in fact, unfortunate, for at least three reasons. The first is that the Report seems to misunderstand Macaulay's argument. What Macaulay had always said was not at all that it was meritorious of young men from Oxford and Cambridge that they had read nothing but subjects unrelated to their future careers, as the Fulton Report suggests. What he had argued, both before and again in his 1854 Report, was something quite else: that 'The youth who does best what all the ablest and most ambitious youths about him are trying to do well will generally prove a superior man'. If that happened to be 'skill in Greek and Latin classification', that then should be the skill that you should test and recruit. The difference between the two points is considerable. That Fulton fails to understand it is one of the reasons (though not, surely, the only one) why it assumes that a service based on Macaulay and Trevelyan is based on what it calls 'the tradition of the "all-rounder"'. Fulton, itself, introduces the notion of that tradition somewhat gently. But within twelve paragraphs it has become a much severer idée fixe, that 'the Service is still essentially based on the philosophy of the amateur (or "generalist" or "all-rounder")', or a 'cult of the generalist' which is, in fact, 'obsolete'. So, beginning with the explicit intention of making itself comparable with some very great predecessors indeed, the Report proceeds rapidly by way of sheer misunderstanding to an opening which was, to say the least, tactless.

The second observation is that by looking back to Trevelyan and Macaulay, the Report ignored a great deal of what has happened since then. It does not only seem to have ignored the well-known fact of Civil Service history that enquiries like itself have recurred, Playfair, Ridley, Macdonnell, Tomlin and so forth. It is not simply that it is unfair to ignore them, it is also unwise; many of them, like the Macdonnell Report, did, in fact, succeed in affecting the nature of the Service a great deal. There was, perhaps, something to learn from them, about successful Civil Service enquiries and about the Civil Service itself. The fact is that it is simply not true to say that the modern Civil Service is the Macaulay and Trevelyan Service. Perhaps by concentrating less on a search for a sufficiently striking predecessor, the Report could have concentrated more on some of the important changes which have recently happened, still are happening and are going to happen. One thinks at random of such an instance as the relocation of offices which is going to have tremendous implications for the recruitment, for the sex and age balance in the Service, for morale, for relative attitudes to clerical pay inside and outside the Service, and for flexibility.

In particular, the Civil Service has, in fact, changed a very great deal over the last generation. That happens to be true about recruitment and promotion into the highest reaches of the Service. It is also true of many other matters, despite what the Report says in para. 21. Mr. Douglas Houghton, who knows as much about these things as anybody, was surely very right to remind us of this.[2] He reminds us of sweeping changes in the grading of main departmental specialist classes. He goes on to list the establishment of new avenues of recruitment for scientists, technicians, and public relations staff, the breaking of completely new ground in training, recruitment, internal promotion and management. He claims particularly striking advances in training, O and M, welfare and the application of computers. He also refers to the Priestley Report of 1955, the setting up of the Pay Research Unit, the concept of 'fair comparability' and the settling of the long-standing controversy about the principles of fixing Civil Service pay and, finally, equal pay for women. It is an impressive record, and a fair comment that the Fulton Report seems to be quite unaware of this ground, to say nothing of those many other enquiries and changes between 1854 and the Second World War.

The third observation is that Macaulay and Trevelyan did seem to understand their times and the precise needs of the public service also. They did detect a genuine problem and they did design a specific and a workable solution for it. This is a question which any public service must meet: what sorts of men do you want at the top of the service? How might you best get them there? And how, in terms of the service as a whole, and the contemporary social, political and educational situation, can the methods be worked up? Has Fulton really answered this problem, not as brilliantly as Macaulay and Trevelyan did, for that would indeed be to ask a great deal, even though the Fulton Committee implies that we should ask it of them? Has the Report, rather, answered it at all usefully and meaningfully, or has it made a series of obeisances to some passing notions of the day or even yesterday?

The discussion which the Report has received has already made at least three points quite familiar: the first is that the emphasis the Report gave to the 'philosophy of the amateur' or 'cult of the generalist' was something more than tactless or inopportune. It did in fact imply a misunderstanding of the whole nature of professionalism as it can be built up and applied in great ranges of public service work and, in particular, ways of building up an achievement in administration and management, areas in which the Report, after all, is very interested. Secondly, the criticism of the 'amateur' administrator and of the combination of establishments and financial control and budgetary functions in a single department is certainly not something which comes at one with a sense of newness or revelation. The emphasis on institutionalized training is a little newer: it is merely as old as the Second World War. Whether these recommendations are going to be implemented or not, the reader of the Report gets from it an eerie feeling of déjà vu, a sort of kaleidoscope of the common parlance of recommendations of two whole generations: sometimes going back over 50 years and sometimes becoming almost up to date. Does it take us back to 1966, to 1964 or to some earlier date to be told that 'a century ago the tasks of government were mainly passive and regulatory. Now they amount to a much more active and positive engagement in our affairs'? To read once again about 'technological progress' and that there has been 'a complex intermingling of the public and private sectors'? The 'solutions to complex problems' do, one supposes, 'need long preparation', but it would, to say the least, be more enjoyable and provocative to read Bagehot even on why the administrator should not attempt to be too 'far-sighted'. Long preparations tend to be always a little too late, after all, as Ely Devons learnt so well. But this Report which expects to find 'great initiative' in precedent, that is, in the Service's 'accumulated knowledge and experience' does not read as though it is going to teach us very much about the arts of government.

The third point is that implementation is going to make a great deal of difference. It is coming to concern itself almost exclusively thus far with three recommendations. The first has already been applied in the setting up of the separate Civil Service Department; the second is the whole area of training and the Civil Service College in particular; the third is the replacement of the present Civil Service classification system with a unified grading structure. Leaving aside the Civil Service Department itself for the moment, there are two or three things which are already striking about the record. One is that the very powerful minority on the Fulton Committee opposed to its recommendation about the recruitment of graduates for (what one supposes can still be called) administrative work used the precise arguments which were Macaulay's, namely that you should look for your recruits according to where they happened to go and what they did for their education. Indeed, the brief for Mrs. Hart's speech in the House of Commons debate on Thursday, November 21st, incorporated the actual wording of the minority which was so close to Macaulay's thesis: that what was significant was not at all what degree was taken but that it was taken well; the Service would not be helping itself if it went clear against the pattern of educational distribution.

The second thing is that there does not seem to be any great disagreement between Mr. Wilson and Mr. Heath on the report. Mr. Heath, at any rate, is having some very judicious second thoughts, particularly about the recommendation for a senior policy adviser and planning unit separate from and equal to the Permanent Secretary. It is fairly clear that that idea is not going to be implemented in that form. The third point is that both Front Benches are worried about the quick and early identification of 'high fliers' in the new system and therefore the problem of recruitment. The fourth point, on the other hand, is that both Front Benches are still determined to give at least as much and if anything (see Wilson's speech) even more emphasis to training after selection; but what is actually going to happen about the Civil Service College is not as yet clear. To quote Wilson again, 'What would be needed by way of College facilities was not yet clear'.

The sifting, slow but sure, is already under way. What matters now is the Civil Service Department and Sir William Armstrong more than the Report. But reports do not die the death. Fulton will be read, taught from and used, perhaps, elsewhere. Some of its distinctive quality should be realized. Louis Brownlow's Report on presidential management in the 1930s said that the whole trouble with American Federal Government was that there were too many agencies: 'over 100', to be precise. Fulton is as precise and almost as reliant on the parallel notion that there are too many classes in the British Civil Service: '47 General classes ... and over 1,400 Departmental classes.' The 47 and 1,400 will no doubt become as famous at the 100. Are we not seeking here exactly the same will-'o-the-wisp argument above government, that the statement of a large number demonstrated complexity, that complexity is an evil and that government can and should be made simple? Certainly a great deal of evil is attributed to this statistic: 'The setting up of cumbersome organizational forms, it seriously hampers the service adapting itself to new tasks, prevents the best use of individual talent, contributes to the inequality of promotion prospects, causes frustration and resentment, and impedes the entry into wider management of those well fitted for it.' All this comes, apparently, from the Service's commitment to dividing work between higher and lower and between different skills, professions or disciplines, rather neatly one had always thought, and more or less inevitably? Is Fulton really going to make an end of all this? It appears, in fact, that the Report does recognize the need to distinguish between promotion and advancement and to promote some people quickly. It is, indeed, going to distinguish the higher, to be called the Senior Policy and Management Group, from the lower; and it is in favour of distinguishing 'families' (para. 242) and 'occupational groupings' (para. 223). What we are going to have, in fact, in addition to the fact recognized in the present Civil Service classification system, is a new top-to-bottom grading structure, broad-banded and overlapping salary levels. Is it to that familiar of personnel management that we are going to be indebted for a unique simplification and for a disappearance of all those dreadful evils? Has, in fact, anything really been invented here at all?

If something like the Brownlow doctrine of numbers rears its head here again, so too (even more astonishingly, perhaps, since it has been even more decisively criticized) does something like the Brownlow or the Haldane principles of allocation. The Committee did even consider 'whether we should recommend a grouping of departments on the basis of their main areas of activity'. It is true the Committee does not make that recommendation. That was not because it did not believe that such broad grouping was meaningful but because it preferred to recommend a conceptually similar grouping or twofold division, of the work of administrators themselves. Should one not be just as doubtful about an allocation of 'administrative jobs', which is done 'on the basis of their common subject matter' so as to form into a 'broad group' which is 'primarily economic and financial' and 'a second broad group of administrative jobs where the basis is essentially social?'

There was nothing very new there at any rate. The Committee was also going against the tide in recommending the breaking up rather than the unification of departments; these are the days of one big Ministry for all of Defence, all of Social Services and so forth. However, Labour government is also the days of multiplication of departments, at any rate in the economic field, and to split the public service away from the other functions of the Treasury is not, as we have said, a terribly startling notion. It has been implemented already, and perhaps it would have happened in any case. The fact is that there were always great advantages in the coincident flow of distinct aspects of information about integrated problems in a single controlling department. But the division, at least for the time being, has been established. Nothing that is said in paras 264-268 of the Report, and that is known of the way in which the division works in the many machineries of government where it has long been familiar, leads one to suppose that improvement will be axiomatic. On the contrary, the process of control may very well now be doubled. The Report does not even pretend to work out the detailed solutions. Perhaps that could not be expected; perhaps it is even a good thing. What is worrisome, however, is the Report's constant deployment of a general and normative discourse. The working procedures which will have to be devised, we read, 'should be flexible' while 'in many cases it would no doubt be desirable to set up joint teams for particular operations'. At the same time 'such arrangements should be based upon, and not allowed to blur, the closest possible distinction between the functions and responsibilities of each of the two central departments'. Similarly, we have elsewhere in the Report already been told that while an administrator 'must specialise' at the same time 'since modern administration requires men to have breadth as well as depth' we are reminded that 'such specialization should not be too narrowly conceived'. One always felt that administrative decisions were marginal choices between conflicting demands but one does wonder whether the particular demands are very helpfully stated or the choices indicated here.

Certainly sometimes the information quoted seems to be hard and quantified. 46 per cent of executive officers under the age of 40, a Treasury study shows, believe that 'their work does not fully use their capabilities to enable them to develop their potential' and 53 per cent of clerical officers under the age of 40 feel the same. Similarly, to quote another figure which is surely going to become famous, we find that administrators move on the average every 2·8 years. This yen for quantification would however be more impressive if it went with two other characteristics. The first is comparability. It is interesting, but sad, to know about the dissatisfied executive officers. It must be even less surprising (if no less sad), to know that rather more clerical officers are dissatisfied. But on the one hand we have here a general characteristic of modern life which one does not, with great respect, expect the Fulton recommendations to solve; on the other hand what would be much more striking would be to know the comparable percentages for similar employment outside the Service; that is precisely what the Fulton Report says it cannot tell us. Again and again it is comparability which is either lacking or, as we shall see, misused.

The second characteristic is a total lack of any effort to cost any of the recommendations whatsoever. In the circumstances of the time, and in a Report which makes the recommendations it does about the Treasury, or about 'accountable' management, or about the use of accountants, this is staggering. That includes the whole range of recommendations on training and the Civil Service College. Almost at the very end of the Report (in para. 298 of the 306 paragraphs) the Committee does come to admit that 'we are conscious that some of our own proposals call for increases in qualified staff'. The Committee goes on to list the proposals: planning units, the Civic Service College, the expansion of the training programme, more attention to personnel management and career development, expansion of departmental management services, the new Civil Service department which is to be larger than the present Pay and Management group of the Treasury, the new grading system, the comprehensive job-evaluation responsibilities: some increases indeed! What would have been a contribution both to the reception of the Report's general arguments, and to the reception of its particular arguments for analysis and quantification in government, would have been at least some effort at instances of the sort of costing which is a crying need here. The Civil Service College at least could have been a sample. Actually a comparative study of public services with top to bottom grading, broad banding, overlapping, salaries and job-evaluation (as an alternative to the personal or rank classification of the British Civil Service) would have been more difficult. But it would also have been worth-while effort at these techniques of comparison and quantification which the Committee talks so much about but seems so little either to understand or, in the end, believe in for its own part.

But this is only one of the severe inconsistencies which run right through the Report. It is the severest criticism of the Report, that the Committee, in bowing to many kinds of gods at once, has not in fact succeeded in working out the clear line of what it does believe in, what it is in the end prepared to recommend. There are at least four related points at which this does seem to be so. Macaulay and Trevelyan believed that you could use success at university work as the criterion for recruitment not because of the content but because of the fact of success. At any rate they believed in it. Fulton can never work out what the right position is about this; on the one hand it seems to be all against the vestiges of the old system; on the other hand it wants to relate, more than before, previous education to the grouping of administrative work and, indeed, to give a greater role to 'specialists', who are, presumably, defined precisely by previous education. Secondly, what is the Fulton attitude to mobility? It is apparently very bad for administrators. But they move, one would have thought, between some relatively common elements of work. At any rate Fulton should accept that, since it goes on to give great emphasis to the importance of common elements of administrative and management work and techniques. Yet it is opposed to mobility for administrators: that, apparently, is the great fault of the present Civil Service. On the other hand it seems to be in favour of mobility precisely between much more different sort of work; the work it itself describes as that of specialists and administrators; it is in favour of mobility again between jobs in the Service and jobs outside the Service. It is this sort of mobility which is going to do something about its concept of a 'gulf' between the Service and the rest of the community. Is there a good mobility and a bad mobility then? How are we to recognize it? Thirdly, when the British Civil Service employs a system which puts extremely intelligent and evidently well educated young men relatively quickly at the beginning of careers of promise into important work it is told that it is indulging in some obsolete cult. When the French public service does so, only even more completely and rigorously, it is apparently admirable. Perhaps indeed we should learn from the French Civil Service; Professors Chapman, Ridley and Blondel have been saying so for a long time. But if we do so it is unlikely to make our Executive and Clerical Officers happier.

The fact is, however, that the Fulton Committee knew more than a reader can sometimes believe about the Civil Service. At any rate it knew too what the Treasury (or those parts of it which were to become the Civil Service Department) wanted to happen. Is this why when one is apparently reading a criticism or a recommendation for change, one realizes, with a shock, that one is reading what is in fact a description of things as they are, or, at the most, things as the Treasury thought politic to have them re-entitled? In para. 185, for example, one reads that 'In some of the big technical departments there may well be a case for a further top post. For example, where a Department is engaged on large scale scientific research or on major building or engineering projects, it might be right to appoint a Chief Scientist of a Chief Engineer to be in charge of these operations. His job would be to take chief responsibility for the direction of the department's technical work.' War time departments, the old Ministry of Health and the Ministry of Public Works come readily to mind.

This shock of recognition is felt the more one reads what was surely meant as one of the major recommendations, the training grade itself. It must surely have been known that something like one half of promotion to the higher Civil Service does not come from 'normal' external direct recruitment to the administrative class; it comes also from those who have moved within the Service by limited internal competition or by promotion. The Fulton Report says that there should be direct entry from outside the Service for university graduates into a training grade; and there should also be every effort to promote bright young serving officers who are not necessarily graduates, into comparable positions in their midtwenties. It is in fact using radically different language certainly for describing something which is equally certainly, and has now for some time been, fully under way. No one who reads the Treasury evidence to the Committee could have failed to see that essentially the Report follows the Treasury mind.

It is not, of course, that the Report would make no difference at all. On the contrary, one feels at times it might make almost too much difference. In the House of Commons debate both Mr. Heath and Mrs. Hart were worried about 'high fliers'. The problem is in fact twofold: to succeed in promoting young people very quickly as a quite distinct need in any public service at all from processes of fairly guaranteed advancement; and at the same time that the brightest potential recruit should be able to appreciate that possibility of high-flying promotion. Just as there is an absolute need in any personnel system for advancement guarantees, so there is this very different need for evident promotion opportunity. The old system did at least provide that succinctly and patently. The new system may make no difference to the facts but it may appear to do so. Insofar as it does it will certainly lead to a deterioration in graduate recruitment. On the other hand, it is no use at all turning, with Mr. Heath, to the Foreign Service system as an alternative management. At the same time, it is smaller and therefore utterly simpler to operate.

An inconsistent report leaves one with an inconsistent attitude. Is the Committee being more subtle than one may suppose in pretending that it is arguing for more radical changes than is the case; or is it simply being less subtle than it ought to be in failing to anticipate likely consequences of changes which it is in fact advocating? Is it being less than helpful in simply stating a series of opposed arguments and needs without ever actually resolving them or indicating techniques of resolution? Or is it, again, being more than subtle in disguising a blatant series of proposals without actually having exercised any hard tests of comparison, quantification or costing? It is simple-minded or blatant to recommend such a heavy investment in training, and such a degree of reliance on training and on job evaluation (for, to quote Mr. Wilson, 'the modernization of the institution on whose efficiency and expertise, and indeed humanity, the success of almost every other effort in modernization depends to so great an extent') without deploying any evidence or testing at all the efficacy of training and job evaluation? We have elsewhere, the Canadian Report[3] which gave us a vivid picture of the 1919 legislation which led to what was the extreme instance of the application of job analysis to a public service. The Fulton Report does not seem to know about that. Yet surely it cannot suppose that top to bottom grading into a series of 20 broad salary bands in a modern public service of the size of the British could prevent, or would not indeed positively encourage, an emergence of manifold actual job classifications. No one who has looked at the work, for example, of the Australian Commonwealth Public Service Board, where there is such a system of classification and job evaluation reduced to a struggle over the particular definition and changes of specific job classifications.

Yet the fact is the Fulton Report does seem to be very simple-minded indeed from time to time. How innocent its words read on the insufficiency of contact between the Service and the rest of the community; the creation of a rival to the Permanent Head of the Department in the Senior Policy Adviser and his planning unit; or on Whitley Council machinery and the role of Staff Associations. But here again one feels that the Report is very difficult to judge. What is it in fact trying to recommend about anonymity for example? What it says there in the end is, 'On balance we think it best not to offer any specific precepts for the progressive relaxation of the convention of anonymity. It should be left to develop gradually and pragmatically.' Perhaps that sort of recommendation simply does not matter. What does seem to matter rather more is to estimate the full impact of the weight of a series of recommendations across the Report. Imagine a situation in which a specialist is recruited to a public department and given further training, both in his specialism and in management; he is also encouraged to discuss his work more openly outside the department; in consequence he becomes well known; other changes are going to make it more possible, and indeed admirable, for him to move during his career between the public service and, say, industry. Now one is not at all saying that such a series of changes is necessarily a bad thing. What one is saying is that the whole burden of them is not in fact brought together anywhere in the Report. What is brought together from time to time, as at the beginning, and the end, are quite other matters: the attack on the cult of the generalist, for example. Yet this is in total a much more important alteration than any specific thing in the Report, or than its overt comparisons with Macaulay or the 'obsolescence' of the Trevelyan-Northcote report.

That also applies to the implications of the Report for staff relations in the Civil Service and their organization. Save for some words on Whitleyism the actual trend of Trade Unions and Staff Associations in the Civil Service goes virtually without discussion; yet the fact is, in the first place, that, as Mr. Houghton implied, this is one of the greatest areas of change since the War; furthermore it exemplifies actual changes not only in the public service itself but also throughout the employment situation and Trade Union organization as a whole. It is utterly extraordinary that a

Report which sets out to pretend to be comparative should have looked not at all at the implications for Trade Union organization or its recommendations, particularly for classification and job evaluation. The point is, of course, that its view of what can be done in that way is utterly altered as soon as the fact of Trade Union organization is introduced. Is it that Fulton would prefer to imagine a world without the C.P.S.A. or the I.P.C.S. or the distant speck of the A.S.T.M.S.? But it included a number of members who at least knew and, in one or two cases presumably thought, differently. Perhaps the desire to compare itself with Macaulay and Trevelyan rather than with the 1955 Priestley Report simply seemed to make the point inappropriate. But its ignoring this dimension must surely be a severe limit to the perceptiveness of its predictions. What is a Report without recommendations? and what are recommendations but prediction? One wonders what the members of the committee really think about 'contact between the Service and the community it is there to serve', and the problems which the Home Civil Service faces in 'the second half of the 20th century' (which itself is now almost half over).

One of the ways of understanding a public service is to think of some exemplar who has followed its typical ways to the top. Can one apply this exercise to the Fulton Report Civil Service? Perhaps he will be a man with some scientific education who once thought he might make a man of science but instead made good with a spell in a planning unit, a smattering of management language and considerable success in timing his movement through training courses. He will be quite active in his community and not too careful about anonymity though not too dangerous either. A judicious movement out of the public service into industry will improve his availability for a top policy position so that he will be in due course the obvious man for the chairmanship of a Board. His experience may even be wide enough to earn him a membership (or indeed the chairmanship) of that committee which will in due course report on the Fulton Civil Service, and would indeed be doing so in five years time if the majority of the committee had its way.

But is will happen that the minority recommendation will be followed. Lord Post-Fulton will not be reporting in 5 year's time. Some excerpts from that Report (Comnd 3638) have fallen into our hands.

'The Service has been dominated by an hostility to all-round administration and flexibility in career movement, and to any rapid movement of young people into interesting and influential work. It has failed to develop amongst its personnel a general knowledge of the government machine and experience of different areas of government activity. It has perpetrated a cult of the specialist which is obsolete at all levels and in all parts of the Service. The cult has most damaging consequences, as the report of our Management Consultancy Group illustrates. It does not make for the efficient despatch of public business when one poor man has to stay in one job for year after year. The development of quantitative techniques for measuring personnel performance enables us to see a positive correlation of decision making time with a tenure of any one job for longer than three years. We estimate that the optimum period of tenure is 2·8 years. . . .

'The demands of detailed and constant work in the Civil Service department on job evaluation and re-evaluation and comparability has had two serious consequences; the first is the enormous inflation in the size and cost of the department; the second is its failure to give adequate attention to the other sides of its personnel responsibilities. At the same time the principles of broad banding and overlapping salary classifications, introduced as a consequence of our predecessor's report, exacerbated the critical importance of movement between classes in the Service. In response to powerful Staff Association demands there was, in consequence, over the last decade a great strengthening of the promotion appeals system, a subject to which our predecessor gave no attention. That has had two unfortunate consequences. The first is the enormously increased use of the criterion of seniority. The second is the effort by young officers to use all their spare time and cash acquiring extraneous collections of "objective" qualifications as their only hope of defeating that criterion. That has had in turn demonstrably deleterious effects of great severity on the health, material prosperity and marital well being of the younger members of the Service. . . .

'We found two difficulties with the employment of science, engineering and other specialists. One was that the development of the equipment to practise their own specialisms was severely frustrated by constant calls on their time to involve themselves in management; the second was that their apparent combination of craft with administration has tended to allow them to move easily out of public into private employment. The Civil Service has in fact become a training ground for private profit at public expense. . . .

'We have found two main difficulties with the institution of training grades for officers in their mid 20s and for the best graduate entrants. The first is that the notion of moving after successful graduation from university for an indeterminate but considerable number of years into what is explicitly called "training grades" is regarded as most uninviting by the best, most zestful and most ambitious products of academic education. At the same time, social and educational changes have made it impossible to recruit into the public service from nongraduates a significant and increasing number of young men who can by their mid 20s be put usefully side by side with young graduates in a training situation. We therefore suggest the invention of some more attractive title for training grades which will give a better description of their true function and their promise. Something which expresses the notion that the work is to be assistance to senior policy advisers would be opportune. . . .

'Our predecessor's report came at the end of a period during which the size of the Civil Service had indeed increased but when the absolute numbers of administrative and clerical workers had fallen and the whole proportion of professional, scientific and technical Civil Servants had risen. We are reporting at the end of a similar period in which we regret that there has been a severe absolute and proportionate increase in non-professional, scientific and technical jobs in the Civil Service. There is one single major reason for that. It is the enormous increase in personnel employed broadly in what could be called "pay and management" work. That is particularly the case in the following categories of work: training, personnel management, departmental management services, and job evaluation. We therefore recommend: (a) an enquiry into the costs and benefits of training in the Civil Service (b) a much simpler system for classifying the Service which will divide it into Senior and Junior levels and between different skills, professions or disciplines.'

NOTES

1   *The Times*, 12 November 1968, p. 9.
2   In a letter to *The Times*, 29 June 1968.
3   *Royal Commission on Administrative Classification in the Public Service*, Ottawa, 1946.

III

PUBLIC POLICY DECISIONS: THE INSTITUTIONAL IMPACT

Two themes are dominant in this section: civil-military relations, and development policy. On the civil-military question, the main concern is not with defence policy substantively but with the nature and conditions of the ways in which policy decisions in that area were being taken, and in particular with the matter touched in some preceding chapters: the relation between the shape of organization and policy outcomes. A second matter is the problem of dependency, which was one of the links with third world politics and development policies.

9

POLICY AND SYSTEM IN DEFENCE

The Australian Case

A previous paper, Military Affairs as a Field for Political Science in Australia, APSA News, Vol. VI, No. 2, May 1961, had discussed the bibliography and rise of a political science concern with defence policy, civil-military relations and the sociology of the military establishment. It had suggested that we follow, not critical policy work 'like Kissinger's' (p. 3) but an organizational approach.

Hence this paper took up the Australian example. The descriptive point was a financial ceiling which quickly became outdated through the influence of Kennedy and Vietnam involvement. But four points remain: the case-study of restriction and dependence; the organizational impact on policy outcomes, and the particular need for critical argument within the policy decision making process; the concept of a professional, absolute or objective contribution to the process; and the particular problems and disfunctions of the financial ceiling as a policy control. Restriction is a theme for smaller states, third parties and development politics. The way in which defence systems do and do not get argument is discussed. The higher defence organization expresses the degree of professional contribution. The financial ceiling is a much favoured but defective weapon.

DEFENCE POLICY

Defence policy and civil-military relations are now well established fields for political science. They raise problems that are important and exciting in their own right and as dramatic instances of general institutional problems of policy-making and control. Comparative and particular aspects of this field should be appreciated. What are the special characteristics of the Australian type of situation?

One characteristic is its sheer lack of dimension. Australian defence expenditure amounts to about £200 million per annum as against current United States expenditure of over £20,000 million. A second characteristic is its apparently high relative dependence on decisions elsewhere, through alliances and agreements about missions, bases, research, production, and weapons systems. The quickest study of the situation would also detect certain points at which the Australian was apparently similar to other systems: e.g., the pressure towards unification in the military establishment and in the organization of Defence Departments since the war, and also its relative lack of success. A quick study reveals other features as well, such as the notably poor parliamentary performances by the Australian legislature and by the Opposition in particular.

Such a degree of restriction and dependence raises the question of how far the Australian is just a repetition of the situation elsewhere on a smaller scale, or how far these conditions heighten the problems or even actually change them. We may say that a study of the Australian defence policy and system concerns something that is likely to be increasingly common: defence in countries that simply cannot afford to provide adequate expenditures for a worthwhile system on their own account, and yet are forced, in various ways, to provide some sort of show. The Australian system is merely a case in point. This article will indicate the main outlines of the policy, and the influences that operate.

The argument underlying the article is that defence policy urgently requires special sources of criticism and argument as a guarantee against rigidity. The relative lack of party questions and the overwhelming influence of the budgetary factor necessitate this, but, furthermore, the basic decisions in defence tend to be impulsive and traditional because they are so nearly immeasurable. Once taken, they are institutionalized as very few other policy decisions are. The traditions created, for example, around a separation of arms or even, indeed, a particular weapons system (a tank and its corps) are peculiarly binding. It is, then, fortunate that up to a point any defence organization does also have a series of natural irritants. It has a double look and therefore at least a double series of interests, motivations, and organizational participants, military and civilian, several departments, a high degree of line-staff and headquarter-field separation, a limitation of simple hierarchy and a use of joint interdepartmental committees, a peacetime system that includes techniques for wartime transition, regular and reserve forces, and so on. These are enhanced by traditions of exercise and training, by the participation of influential outside groups, like science, industry, and supply, and by the conflicting motivations of top military and top civilian personnel.

In particular, defence policy requires an absolute military contribution: that is, a contribution from military advisers from their own point of view, not one already dominated by non-military factors. An active conflict of ideas—military, financial, and political—is required at a very high level. The question for the Australian type of system is whether such entrenched sources of argument about policy are not undeveloped or vitiated to a dangerous degree. Two sources will be described, and their severe limitations indicated—i.e., the higher defence organization and the military profession. Other aspects of control and of the civil-military balance will be only very briefly mentioned. The article will conclude with a criticism and a suggestion for change.

CONSTRAINTS

Australian defence policy has emerged out of the situation dominated by the original Menzies policy for preparation for total war readiness within three years (that is to say, from 1949, when the Menzies government came into office, to 1952). The first statement of that policy virtually preceded the era of massive retaliation. It also preceded the famous confession by Sir Frederick Shedden (then Secretary to the Australian Defence Department) to the Public Accounts Committee that that three-year preparation had never been effective and, indeed, that by 1956, let alone 1952, preparation for a total conflict had not been achieved. For this and other reasons, the policy was surrendered and was replaced by a current policy that has been repeated in ministerial statement after statement in recent years.

Nominally, defence policy is reviewed once every three years, and the policy and the strategic philosophy that dominate it also dominate the programme over the ensuing three years. In fact, the ministerial statements that introduce these programmes and that review them from time to time have all, since the surrender of the previous policy, described very much the same unchanging structure, along the following lines. In the first place, Australia is not preparing for global or total conflict. That is to say, Australia has to assume either that nuclear war is unlikely or that Australia could not play a worthwhile role in such a conflict and could certainly not protect itself against nuclear attack. Hence expenditures on civil defence are dismally low. Furthermore, the assumption goes, non-nuclear attacks on the Australian territory itself are unlikely. Hence, the strategic role for which Australia prepares itself is a role in the Cold War and in limited wars.[1] It provides the type of forces that give it a voice in Cold War alliances and that can play a useful role in putting out brushfires (but not in defending Australia itself). The Australian forces in Malaya are the classic case in point. Indeed, while Malaya may not be really central to Australia's strategic position, the continuity of operations there and the degree to which they show the successful handling of a limited outbreak have so dominated Australian military thinking as to provide a parallel with, say, Britain and India in the last century. Other recent cases are the movement of token forces into Thailand (from Malaya) SEATO, and of instructors into Vietnam.

This situation might appear to provide a clear instance of a rational piece of policy-making, a determination of ends, a costing of these ends, and an allocation to these ends, in the most efficient way, of the many competing possible means. Unfortunately, there are some reasons to be concerned about the truth of this rational model. In the first place, the policy has presented us with a defence programme that has consistently spent close to the £200 million per annum figure. Do we really have here a policy that has to be met by an expenditure of £200 million, or do we have a compromise between a series of impulsive or instinctive decisions on the one hand (e.g., that Australia must have some sort of defence forces) and a purely extrinsic decision that the expenditure will be fixed at no more and no less than £200 million? It is possible that we have achieved the worst sort of compromise: a defence system that has stabilized at a particular level of expenditure, high enough to be a burden on the economy but not high enough to provide a worthwhile defence at all.

In the second place, the statements of the basis of this defence policy have been unusually unchanging at least since 1957. The three-year defence programme of 1957-1959 had the same basis as the 1959-1961 programme. We can now see that it is providing a similar basis again for the current 1961-1963 programme. It is clear that the defence policy is heavily influenced by one particular strategic philosophy, and there is little evidence of any effect in Australia over the last five years of the sort of critical reassessment that has been occurring elsewhere, notably in the United States. Nominally, any defence policy may be a result of particular national objectives. Historically, however, such policies have always been deeply influenced by the strategic philosophies of the time, such as command of the seas, say, or preparation for total war in three years. The recent debate has taken us away from a notion of preventive war via massive retaliation and brinkmanship to the current theories of counterforce strategy. This is going to have an effect on United Kingdom policy about the independent deterrent. It is probably going to have a radical effect in the United States and the United Kingdom on levels of civil defence expenditure. Should

Australia be exempt from this influence? Clearly not. Is there anything in the system to ensure that the effect will be rational and
speedy? This is to be doubted. A central concern of this article
is whether a dependent situation (in addition to a restricted situation) can provide not simply weapons, scientific resources, etc., but
the immediate sources of argument and change that are currently
required.

The whole problem may be seen clearly in relation to defence
science. In theory, this ought to be one of the most powerful influences making for radical change. Australia, however, has to buy
its defence science. But while there is one sense in which it can,
indeed, be bought, there is another in which it cannot. The Commonwealth Advisory Committee on Defence Science meets once
every two or three years.[2] There is a scientific adviser in Australia
and a Defence Research and Development Policy Committee apparently at or near the top of things. What is lacking is the activity
and the infrastructure to make the adviser and the committee effective. In their absence the sort of thing represented by the rare
meetings of the Commonwealth Advisory Committee is an inadequate way of providing what Australia itself cannot provide.

Another instance in which built-in rigidity can be seen is the
handling of the Moreshead Report, the confidential report of 1958
on the whole Australian defence structure.[3] Its handling suggests
not only that dependence and financial limitations produce rigidity,
but that rigidity once present reinforces itself. The handling of this
case showed that a report that attempted to be radical was ineffective; secondly, that many organizational possibilities (for instance,
the example of the United States Marines) were not considered at
all; and thirdly, that there was no force at work within the Australian defence structure that was a powerful influence for change
rather than against it. But the outstanding case is the recent reorganization of the Australian military forces themselves to a
pentropic system.[4]

This change was accompanied by a sacking of various senior
officers that aroused, in early 1960, a degree of parliamentary attention to defence matters quite unusual in Australia. It is true that
parliamentary information and performance throughout were notably poor. The idea was introduced to Parliament in two separate
stages, in 1959 and 1960. Parliamentary interest focused constantly
more on the generals to be sacrificed than the achievements to be
secured. As against this, the change showed that the Returned
Servicemen's League (R.S.L.), theoretically one of the most powerful pressure groups in Australia, could be virtually ignored when
the Government wished. The R.S.L. was and is deeply committed

to National Service training, but the Government was able to drop the policy very easily. Why was this? What gave the Government its peculiar strength and its peculiar incentive to change on this occasion was simply the enormous savings to be secured by the abolition of National Service training and the reliance on a large Citizen Military Force (C.M.F.) and a restricted regular (A.R.A.) element. One A.R.A. man costs £1,200, one C.M.F. man about £90 per annum. The economics of the change were extraordinarily tempting ones. It certainly was proper to get away from the situation in which, while there were only 4,100 A.R.A. men in the sole mobile brigade, there were 3,000 men directly employed on National Service training alone. But whether it is worthwhile pretending that two pentropic divisions, one of which consists purely of C.M.F. men and the other of a majority of C.M.F. men, are really a notable strengthening of Australian defence is another matter. What is sure is that they represent a considerable economy.

DEPENDENCE

Here we have, then, a restricted and dependent defence policy in which change appears to be difficult just because of those characteristics, save only where financial, rather than defence, reasons are effective.

Dependence means insulation from some things (e.g., defence science and strategic debate), delay (e.g., in re-equipment), and the acceptance of certain overseas doctrines (e.g., the United Kingdom assumption about the organizational faults of the old German high command). Delay is particularly notable. The Royal Australian Navy is to be re-equipped with two guided missile destroyers of the *Charles F. Adams* type with Tartar sea-to-air missiles.[5] This destroyer was long ago designed in the United States, it was first commissioned in the United States in September 1960, it was ordered by Australia in 1961, and first delivery is not due until the end of 1965 and the second until the end of 1966. This sort of dependence, particularly in equipment, research, and development, does lead to a great deal of debate and activity. An example is the interpretation of the United States-Australia Mutual Weapons Defence Programme Agreement about the inconvenient and tricky 'indigenous use' rule.[6] But the problems here are the availability of United States funds, the nature of the agreement, and its definitions. Furthermore, while Australia is involved in a series of overlapping and sometimes conflicting agreements and alliances that create particular pieces of machinery and devices for consultation, for many of her allies these arrangements are of marginal or secondary importance. They do not create a single hierarchy of defence policy nor do they take Australia to the central point of argument and decision-making with the key powers.

Dependence means that Australia is deprived both of certain types of decision-making and certain types of equipment and strategic change. Financial restriction means that it is priced out of weapons systems also. Furthermore, financial restriction is so tight that there is no point, high or low, at which finance is secondary in decision-making. Even in the original decision about ends or strategic philosophy, pricing out means that many weapons systems and activities have to be eliminated from consideration, and this in turn determines basic strategic policy as much as anything does. This has operated in relation to carriers, to aircraft, to nuclear submarines, to defence science, and ultimately to manpower and National Service training in particular.

There are certain definite implications of this situation. One is that the civilian (as against the miltary) element enters at all levels of decision-making and not merely at the very top. Secondly, the starting point for decisions about all the details of defence is finance: the total available; the financial implications of the apparently inescapable elements in the structure; and the financial interpretation of the 'absolute' military statements—that is, the statements from the military on particular policies, programmes, and requirements.

This is seen very clearly in the preparation of the annual estimates of the Army Department. This must begin with the annual finance available under the defence programme, which is pretty well fixed from programme to programme and from year to year. Secondly, once there are 21,000 A.R.A. plus a C.M.F. force plus a civilian element, there are inescapable costs of pay, feeding, accommodation, and so forth about which there can be very little debate. Particular branches then work out, on these and other bases (for instance, statements about training policy), actual requirements— e.g., ammunition, transport, and so forth. But these come after the previous elements. Clearly, then, the actual decisions are almost overwhelmingly a result of the original rigid financial restriction plus an equally rigid set of givens. There ought to be a clash between the military and civil elements—e.g., between a political determination of priorities and absolute military advice on priorities. But this potential clash is reduced in scale: the narrowness of the margin for manoeuvre is quite obvious to all participants. This in turn eliminates the proper military, and also the civil, roles to a considerable extent. Significant changes come as a result of external factors. From time to time, cuts might appear in the guise of military change, like the abolition of National Service training. For the most part they will be inevitably directed to the only part of the vote—i.e., in American terms, appropriation—where there is any room for manoeuvre—that is to say, 'Works and Equipment' and especially 'Capital Equipment'.[7] Here is where clashes and arguments about policy ought to take place; it is also the easiest place to cut. Changes here are, by definition, policy matters, but a policy that is the result of finance rather than military advice. Like the diet of the poor, a narrow military budget is much duller and more repetitive than a relatively rich one. Granted the original restrictive financial decision about defence policy (that you can spend £200 million per annum), the rest, apparently, follows. Of the whole Army Department vote, only 16·16 per cent is for new equipment.[8] That includes clothing and medical and dental stores and the like, as well as more warlike capital equipment. Is such rigidity alleviated in any way?

The key occasion for the central policy argument is the triennial review of the defence programme. The three-year period coincides with the parliamentary term; and the programmes became triennial after a quinquennial experiment. Changes can be introduced during the three years, as a result of external factors like the Korean crisis. Planning for the new programme will begin before the three-year period is up, as planning for the 1962 and ensuing programme was begun during 1961. There is not, however, a permanent, broad plan in operation, looking three years ahead. At the moment of formulating the plan, there should be the clearest clash of argument between finance and economy on the one hand, and the programme implied by purely strategic objectives on the other hand. But, as I have already indicated, the record of financial rigidity vitiates the statement of the strategic objects even before it comes to the crunch. A limited and rigid financial total aggravates the sheer difficulties of the size and costing of defence expenditure, in fields like science or development, or of a decision to purchase a new piece of equipment like the American destroyers. Costing in defence expenditure is notoriously tricky, especially in research, in development, in radically new projects where comparisons are unavailable, in overseas orders, and in joint projects. These are precisely the projects that are potentially of key importance to Australia but that the system makes it most difficult to achieve. The results may well be disastrous, in cuts of new capital equipment, but even more so in the avoidance of changes that will endanger the even annual total one year, or even one defence programme with another. This overwhelmingly financial approach applies most strongly in the matter of possible top political intervention. Formally, decisions go to the Cabinet when a major or a new type of equipment is involved, for works costing more than £200,000, for the annual defence works programme, and for the approval of the Annual Estimates. Virtually all these matters are presented for obviously financial and economic rather than defence reasons: they all appear in a financial guise.

The three main weaknesses here seem to be, first, the lack of a continual three-years-ahead plan, and therefore the severe reduction of the sheer number of occasions when the Cabinet can intervene; secondly, the vitiation of non-financial advice by financial considerations; and thirdly, the fact that changes have occurred only for financial or for extrinsic reasons. The machine itself does not appear to produce change. Financial crises, pressure from allies (as about Thailand), or actual conflicts (a.g., Korea) may.

It does not follow, at all, that the programme does not matter. Before the Defence Programme has been formulated by the Defence Committee and the Chiefs of Staff Committee to go to Cabinet, the Army Military Board, for example, will have prepared a series of alternative statements. Each will be a statement of needs, costs, and priorities, with the Budget Section influential in costing. A consideration of costs and priorities has therefore entered at a very early stage indeed in the formulation even of the particular parts of the programme by the particular departments. The key papers that emerge[9] are really statements of what the military advisers expect to get rather than what they think they ought to have.[10] The Defence Programme is of vast importance and influence throughout the defence structure. What it does is to impose a sense of financial rigidity year by year and triennium by triennium. In particular, as far as the Defence Department's role is concerned, its real effort, as a result, occurs in relation to the evenness and continuity of expenditures and the fulfillment of the Annual Estimates. For the last three months of the year, this is indeed a day-to-day function of the Finance Section of the Department.

Secondly, then, departments know that they have to phase their orders so as to meet expenditures that will fall into line with Annual Estimates, which are relatively unchanging year by year. The tradition of even and detailed Estimates, full expenditure of the Estimates within the year, and a minimal use of Treasurer's Advance and Additional Estimates, all tend to vitiate the potential role of the Defence Department and of financial control. Thirdly, the programme determines the relations between Service Departments and the Defence Department. Service Departments will go back to the Defence Department on questions that are likely to change or have a direct impact on the programme itself.

ORGANIZATION

Is there, then, anything in the organization and control, or in the structure of the military profession, that is going to produce in Australia itself the possibility of real argument and change in defence policy?

Let us first look at organization, and in particular at the higher defence organization. Certain brief comments may be made about the chart reproduced on the following page. First of all, it shows formally a high degree of international influence. Australia has to have a Chairman of the Chiefs of Staff Committee because its opposite numbers overseas have a similar appointment. Secondly, there is clearly a marked influence at the top by civilian officials. The position of the permanent head of the Defence Department, the Defence Committee, and the Assistant Secretaries serving the Secretary, Department of Defence, should be particularly noted. Thirdly, there is a complex interdepartmental infrastructure and a great variety of participants. One can distinguish, for instance, between the Department and the committees. The Department of Defence exists to administer the joint secretariat and the higher defence organization as a whole, to meet the function of apportionment and certain specific functions like the integration programme, to assist the phasing of annual expenditure, and so forth. With the committees there is a distinction between major committees (Defence Committee, Chiefs of Staff Committee), other committees, sub-committees working with the other committees, and the staffs, particularly the joint staffs of these committees. All this is usual in defence administration but relatively unusual in Australian administration as a whole. While other committees may formally appear on the same line as the Defence Committee and Chiefs of Staff Committee (Joint War Production Committee, Defence Administration Committee, and Defence Business Board), it is these first two committees that really matter, partly because they have beneath them a structure of other committees and the Joint Planning Committee in particular. The Joint Administrative Planning Committee, which handles logistics, also counts. The Principal Administrative Officers' Committees (Maintenance and Material, and Personnel) matter much less.

The history of this structure is not the same as the history of comparable structures in the United States or the United Kingdom. The Australian began with one Defence Department and has, so to speak, cast off other organizations from that nucleus from time to time. On the other hand, it has in recent years met problems that are similar to those of defence administration in general and

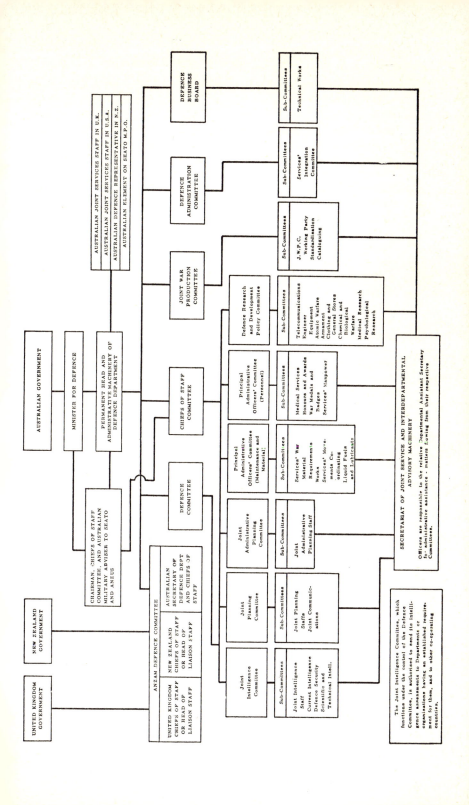

it has sought to copy the overseas model. But there are differences between the United Kingdom and Australian structures; moreover, there are other alternatives and some of them might have suited the Australian situation much better.

What seems particularly unfortunate in the Australian situation is that, while the model as a whole may appear to be similar to the United Kingdom's, it is in fact different in two important respects. One is the relative lack of specific political—that is, top-level Cabinet—machinery.[11] This is partly a result of the restriction of references to the Cabinet, already commented on. It has other aspects. The Opposition, for example, is one factor. The way in which it interprets its role affects both the Defence Department and the Cabinet itself, and thus Cabinet machinery, too. There is a political fear that, in the absence of a more instructed role, the Opposition would tend to concentrate on any apparently radical changes in expenditure from one year to another. Presumably this is the opposite of what the political critic should want, yet it is in fact all that his presence in the Australian system achieves.

The fact is that the Parliamentary system, unlike the Congressional, tends to weaken the role of a party Opposition in this field: there is both a lack of means of influence, and a lack of partisan questions. The present Opposition does nothing to amend this. From this point flow many of the limitations of the political contribution. Cabinet will deal with the questions that matter to it— that is, with questions that are policy ones in the sense that they substantially affect its fate. On the whole, Australian defence policy does not fall into this group. It may well be that the size of Australian defence expenditure urgently needs Cabinet discussion, but its very limitation plus the Opposition situation tend to remove precisely this decision from the Cabinet's agenda. Things are accordingly left to the Prime Minister and the Defence Minister, and mostly to one or the other of them. Political intervention occurs on marginal points, and on some few top appointments. So the Defence Committee is official, the Defence Council defunct.

The ministerial role, except for that of the Minister of Defence himself, is very limited, and one minister does not start arguments with his own decisions. This limitation, then, is a further part of the Cabinet problem. The difficulty is that some of the political points of view—for example, about overseas bases or about the placing of orders—can be handled by the Ministry of Defence. The other departmental ministers can merely express the extrinsic points of view that may occur on questions like the administration of military justice. If a minister intervenes in questions of allocation and priority, he will be endangering the absolute quality of the advice, presumably military, that the Government (or the Higher Defence Organization) receives; if he does not, little save a secondary role is left. This problem is enhanced in Australia by the organization and procedures of the Military Boards, and notably by the Australian tradition that establishes a wider gap between the minister and his department than occurs in the United Kingdom. The Service Departments are now in Canberra; even when the Army Department was in Melbourne, it tended never to have a 'Melbourne' minister. Ministers almost certainly do not and cannot attend sufficient Boards; they are inevitably uninformed, partly because of the weakness of the Parliamentary role and therefore a lack of respect for it (shown in the Defence Pay Regulations case, where the Departments simply neglected, over years, to secure the necessary Parliamentary approval for amended scales). Ultimately the departmental minister becomes a factor of rigidity rather than change. One result of this situation is that in practice this has meant no proper Cabinet consideration of defence, and so a transfer of the civilian function from the politicians to the officials. Furthermore, the top civilians somewhat outbalance the top military. This in turn has meant the rise of the Secretary of Defence Department and the Defence Committee to an extraordinary degree of influence. This is a second contrast with the situation in the United Kingdom, where the Secretary of the Defence Department recently retired from the Civil Service because he had insufficient to do. The Prime Minister's decision, on the occasion of the Moreshead report, not to unify but to increase the authority of the Ministry of Defence in the control of the joint services machinery and the application of defence votes has enhanced this influence

The Defence Department has created a civilian departmental hierarchy at an administrative level of Secretary, First Assistant Secretaries, and Assistant Secretaries. This partly reflects the tradition set by Shedden (for so long the Secretary) of bringing into the Department good, often graduate, staff with continuity in office. From the Chairmanship of the Defence Committee, at the top, down to Secretaryships of sub-committees, the civilian element has some control at all levels; and an Assistant Secretary serves on all the top committees other than the Chiefs of Staff Committee. The branches of the Assistant Secretaries prepare papers and provide expertise—for example, on such matters as who should be consulted and who co-opted (what is broadly meant by the administrative direction and control referred to above). A parallel between the civilian staffing hierarchy and the organizational hierarchy is carefully maintained. This is a stronger position than exists in the U.K. Department of Defence, and it is unusual for Australia.

Defence administration is still Australian, of course. Full details of civilian Commonwealth Public Service jobs will still be put in the *Commonwealth Gazette* so as to maintain the rights of appeal of all other Commonwealth servants against provisional promotions, even if this means revealing, as on occasions it has, the full details of the organization of scientific establishments of the Supply Department, or current intelligence activity under the Joint Intelligence Committee. An Assistant Secretary, as, say, a Joint Secretary is going to be a much more influential colleague than a lieutenant colonel, when that colonel has not been and will not be long in office. The officer profession in the A.R.A., partly because of tradition and partly because of size, cannot develop specialists, including the type of specialist in staff (or, as we might call it, Whitehall) work that is being developed in the United Kingdom. This continuity of the Defence Department officials has given them a sense of representing the real essence of defence policy (as against what is represented by the civilians of the Treasury Defence Division). This is an impressive but perhaps not altogether a proper thing.

These factors can be seen at work in the operation of the whole system of committees. Defence organization is never dominated by a simple hierarchy; the anti-linear factors operate in Australia, but not at all sufficiently. Committees proliferate in the Defence Department but not within the particular Service Departments. Relations between the Defence Department and the Service Departments are somewhat specialized. The Army Department has a policy opposed to permanent as against *ad hoc* committees or informal consultation. Formal committees (Estimates, Weapons Equipment Policy, Army Works Development) are relatively secondary and few. Furthermore, in the Higher Defence Organization as a whole there are only two dominant committees, the Defence Committee and the Chiefs of Staff Committee (as measured by the criteria of terms of reference, chairmanship, size of committee, sub-committees, structures underneath the committee, and staff). Some of the other committees possess much less influence and produce much less key decision-making than they ought to. The political element is altogether missing from this overall structure, with the exception of the Minister for Defence and, by implication, the Prime Minister himself. The one committee not mentioned here which does matter (Treasury Finance Committee) exists for 'consideration from the joint service aspect, of policy matters, conditions of service, personnel of the defence forces,'[12] and it matters perhaps much less than it should.

Even the Chiefs of Staff Committee is not as powerful as it might be. The normal model is for an external, political-civilian decision on the financial total and on broad ends of policy (Hart's grand strategy); while military thinking about the use of these resources (especially finance in peacetime, manpower in war) should be at some point 'absolute'—that is, independent. There are many reasons why this cannot operate in Australia, including the very small total itself. One way out of this is to attempt to separate financial and military advice altogether, but that would not make for very relevant military advice. Another is to provide top military advice with its own financial advisers. This is no doubt what is supposed to happen in Australia, and in the Departments themselves up to a point it is what happens, but at the top of the Higher Defence Organization this is not so. The chief civilian official, the chief financial adviser, has his own committee separate from the Chiefs of Staff Committee. Inevitably the influence of that committee, the Defence Committee, is very strong and the Chiefs of Staff are somewhat overwhelmed.

Overall, one doubts whether there are sufficient points of independent influence here; a clear enough source of absolute military thinking; sufficient impact from science or, now, from business (on central issues). The civil-military balance contains few powerful sources of change. The dominant element is one top official civilian group that operates, not through a unified department, but through the joint service machinery and the Defence Committee especially, and through the financial decisions, which include decisions about strategy, class of weapons, and so forth. This group is very small. The civilian role in the other Service Departments is unfortunately much narrower, the staffing standard poorer, the contribution, as in the Department of Army, continually eroded. Again, this aspect cannot be fully explored. It involves the role of the departmental permanent head,[13] and civilians generally, in the operation of financial control and the emphasis on continuity, for example; and the severe problems of adequate civilian staffing in these Service Departments. But it is a pity that in a situation where the whole requirement is a search for change, the essence of the civilian contribution in the Service Departments generally is, apart from financial control, continuity in its narrowest sense.[14]

Certain forces exist to establish a minimum below which the departmental civilian role cannot fall, such as financial control, the need to interpret the military style, and the need to conceal its more embarrassing absoluteness—for example, in a concern for safety in arranging exercises. But, for the rest, the role as it is filled in the Australian Service Departments at present is not very impressive. A vicious circle continually reduces the significance of the civilian contribution in the Service Departments. Against this a struggle is put up by the sheer quality of some few men at the top and by a few institutions like the Planning and Programme organizations in the Air Department. But in general there is a vast contrast between the high potential demand that the civilian contribution could meet and the minimal actualities that are provided. Except at the very top—notably, of course, in the Defence Department—military staffing is more impressive. If the general imbalance in the Australian defence system is seen partly in too great a Civilian control in the Defence Department, it is also seen in the underdevelopment of the civilian role in the Service Departments.

A further decisive organizational factor is the Australian acceptance of the United Kingdom doctrine against what is held to be the fundamental error of the German military machine in the two world wars: the separation of command from top staff functions. The fact is that both the United States and the United Kingdom have built up such vast top staff machines now that complete careers can develop within them. What Australia has is some of this machine without its men, its scale, or some of its detail. The domination by the Secretary and the Defence Committee and the lack of scale, of numbers, of the career staff men (whom doctrine would so condemn) and of points of countervailing power (like the American President's use of General Taylor as a special adviser on defence, or Churchill's use of Cherwell and his team as a counterbriefing unit whose search was for truth rather than agreement): all this makes the top organization in Australia altogether too simple and intimate a system to provide the sort of conflict that ought to be occurring.

Unification then is certainly not the answer. Australia, like other defence systems, has been subject to unification propaganda ever since the war. The arguments are the usual ones: that unification would provide economy; that the ultimate situation in weapons systems will impose unification; the model of the United States Marine Corps; the case for introducing sudden rather than gradual changes, and so forth. The record, here as elsewhere, of unification (as against greater authority for the Ministry of Defence and some integration of particular functions) is very limited. The amalgamation of the Departments of Supply and Defence Production is almost the only case in point; no other departments, no services, no particular fighting arms, and few civilian elements have been unified. There has been some integration (apprentice training in Navy and Army schools, canteen services, design inspection staffs) but integration is inherently difficult. The case against unification as such is not mainly the size of the vote, not that in war the departments might have to be split, not the political or even the constitutional difficulty in Australia of providing Assistant Ministers, but simply that unification is a simplistic solution to the difficulty of defence policy. The difficulty is that decisions on the overall defence effort and the grand strategy can be a military matter scarcely anywhere, still less so in Australia, where the factors are civil (financial) or extrinsic, and where the military themselves cannot have the know-how on the technical matters that do enter into Great Power strategy. If the Australian military is expert (that is, representative of measurable and verifiable judgment) at all, it is so only on very low-level questions. This may be a general phenomenon. It is at its extreme in the Australian type of situation. The military, then, are professional advisers, not 'experts'; accordingly, there is a need at the top for variety, division, balance, argument, not for unification.

This argument has emerged elsewhere since the war. The whole of defence organization is indeed a striking example of a struggle between common international patterns on the one hand, and indigenous influences and problems on the other. This is true both for organization itself and for the structure of the military establishment, which ought, of course, to operate as one of the most powerful of all the sources of argument and balance in the defence system. As far as organization itself is concerned, we have seen that there are differences and similarities between the Australian and the United Kingdom situations. The differences between the Australian and the American structures are also significant. The United States, particularly since the days of MacArthur, has had considerable influence on the actual Australian system (quite apart from policy). Equipment, SEATO, and ANZUS are now increasing this degree of influence. But the outstanding point about the organization of the Australian defence system is the absence from it of those very features of the American system that are so often criticized but in many ways so much to be admired: the manifold levels and points of argument and difference, and the deep political intervention into its structure. Australia may strive after this copy but cannot by itself adequately manage to follow the whole of it; following part of it might mean the worst of both worlds.

PROFESSION

The military establishment itself ought to act as a major force for criticism and change. Unfortunately, the officer profession in Australia (though individual members are of the very highest calibre) has certain inherent structural problems: it is virtually forced to base itself on a model that, apart from its dysfunctions elsewhere, cannot operate properly in the local conditions.

Basically the Australian system tries to copy the general military model. How does this work out? First, in the A.R.A., despite the variety of methods of entry, the overwhelming point is the conscious and increasing domination by the Royal Military College (R.M.C.) graduate. There is another form of entry through the Officer Candidate School at Portsea. Candidates for the O.C.S. are eligible either from the ranks on certain conditions, from university students or graduates, or from those between the ages of 18 and 23 with an intermediate (as against a leaving) certificate. But the R.M.C. graduate will be always somewhat, often very much, younger than the O.C.S. graduate, he will graduate a few days before to give him seniority, and it is prescribed that he will maintain that seniority until the rank of major.

These are the groups of A.R.A. officers with long service commissions, arranged according to avenues of entry: [15]

R.M.C.	631
O.C.S.	305
R.M.C. wings	423
Officers' qualifying courses	187
Other ranks' qualifying courses	86
Technical officers	42
Prescribed corps	276
Medical and dental officers	11

In addition there are 118 short-service officers, mainly in the prescribed corps as medical and dental officers and as chaplains. Of the current normal entry, 28 per cent are from the O.C.S. and 33 per cent from the R.M.C., but it is the R.M.C. graduate who in the end is going to head the profession. The R.M.C. has provided less than one-third of the entry in the past, it now provides approximately one-third, and it is recommended that it provide 50 per cent; but it gets 100 per cent of the top jobs. The O.C.S. has existed only since 1951, and there has been no 'normal' long-term situation. But other officers than R.M.C. graduates were and are available (for example, ex-militia officers). They have failed to get to the top. This is partly a problem of the age at which they reach certain ranks (as against the age at which the R.M.C. graduate will reach these ranks), but that is not, of course, the only factor.

Two points stand out from Tables 1 and 2. The first is that the A.R.A. has rather a large number of officers at the level of brigadier or above in proportion to the number of regular soldiers—1:600. If the C.M.F. figures are taken into account, the ratio works out as approximately 1:1000.[16] In the second place, R.M.C. men, though forming approximately one-fifth of the total number of

TABLE I. STRUCTURE OF OFFICER CORPS, JULY 26, 1961

Rank	No. in Rank	RMC	%	Others
Lieutenant General	2	2	100	—
Major General	11	9	81	2
Brigadier	25	21	82	4
Colonel	58	35	59	23
Lieutenant Colonel	208	84	42	124
Major	749	117	16	632
Captain	904	188	21	716
Lieutenant and 2nd Lieutenant	681	111	16·5	570
TOTAL	2,638	567		2,071

Note: above rank of major   RMC: 151   Others: 153

TABLE 2. PROMOTIONS IN 1958

	Total	RMC	%	Others
To Lieutenant General	1	1	100	
To Major General	1	1	100	
To Brigadier	1	1	100	
To Colonel	3	3	100	
To Lieutenant Colonel	24	21	85	3
To Major	52	26	50	26
To Captain	72	34	49	38
To Lieutenant	92	38	42	54

officers in the corps, provide all save six of the present officers at the brigadier level or above. Furthermore, the present promotion pattern is going to maintain this structure. While up to the career rank of major others do as well as the R.M.C. graduate, from lieutenant colonel and upwards the R.M.C. has a virtual monopoly. In future, O.C.S. men might do better, but it has to be noted that in the past war-experienced officers who were not normal R.M.C. graduates did not.

This is both an unusual type of profession for Australia (certainly as far as the Public Services are concerned) and also, despite the emphasis on traditions, a relatively new thing, for the history of the A.R.A. officer corps has been an extremely broken one. That is, we have had here a continual effort to introduce an overseas model that does not fit easily into Australia and has not so far found normal times in which it can operate.

The professional military model is based on early recruitment, notably in the R.A.N., but in the other services, too. The pressures towards this are very severe: the A.R.A. is introducing fifty scholar-ships per annum to allow future cadets to complete their matricula-tion. The cadet college, careful career planning, staff colleges, and postgraduate work: all these are the normal characteristics. They are normal, that is, in the military profession, but not in the Australian Public Service tradition. It is a striking fact that there is probably a much higher degree of international similarity (as measured by the officer production system) between military than there is between civilian public services. In this sense, we may say that a military career is more like a profession than is a civilian public career. Furthermore, there is no doubt that the Australian military has been consciously created on a basis of a general pro-fessional model rather than of local circumstances. Whether the international model can really work within the highly restricted Australian defence system is another matter.

Certainly the profession is quite different from the Common-wealth Public Service. The essential tradition of the Australian Commonwealth Public Service is to obscure the distinction between officers and other ranks in classification methods, and in confusion of the difference between promotion and advancement, particularly as this affects administrative careers. The Army not only maintains this distinction overall, but within the officer profession itself estab-lishes a perfectly proper difference between advancement (a fairly guaranteed degree of movement to the rank of major) and promo-tion (the riskier but more enticing business of ultimate promotion to general officer). In the Australian military forces, there is an im-pressive document[17] that lays down avenues of entry, conditions of appointment, selection procedure, promotion procedures, confiden-tial reports, and so forth, in regard to the officer's career. No such document could be prepared for the Commonwealth Public Service. The Commonwealth Public Service does not have planned careers and rotation; it does not lay down careful and different methods of appointment and promotion control for different levels. It is just beginning to use psychological tests for entry into clerical-ad-ministrative ranks, but they are not designed (as those for the A.R.A. officer are) to test officer potential.

The whole A.R.A. ethos is to develop the administrative general-ist; this is foreign to the Commonwealth Public Service tradition. The very careful relationship of promotion to particular career planning, examinations, and postgraduate training is a further dis-tinction. The Defence Act itself[18] provides that officers must qualify by a course of instruction before promotion to the substantive ranks of major and of lieutenant colonel. It would be a major revolution to introduce any such thing into the Public Service. The officer profession uses annual assessment reports very carefully designed and very carefully handled. These are absent from the Public Service as a whole and from almost all, though not quite all, its departments. Age-for-rank retirement is a further distinction. So is the careful maintenance of the career pyramid by controlling numbers of entry and numbers at each rank. For example, the number of R.M.C. graduates must not exceed 100 per annum, so that the prospect of promotion above major should never be worse than 1 : 3.[19] The officer is consciously prepared through education, training, and so forth for promotion to a rank two levels above that which he is normally holding.[20] Like the U.K. administrative class in Lord Bridges' portrayal of it, the officer profession is dominated by a single group with a strong *esprit de corps*: the R.M.C. graduates. There is no such elite domination, and so such single norm, in the Public Service. This is perhaps the major difference of all.

However, as we have said, the history of the officer profession in Australia has been very broken. Some of its features, such as career rotation, are achieved partly by accident. There are strong local influences: the distribution of levels of pay is much more equal than in other military services. In any case, it is not clear that the external prestige of the officer corps has been very highly established. In 1961 there were 100 vacancies at the R.M.C. The number of applicants suitable to go before the selection board was 118. Only 54 were selected. This left 46 vacancies. Second applications were called, but even after these were heard, there still remained 23 vacancies.[21]

Furthermore, the model being slavishly followed here has its own inherent problems: the image and its dilemma. The image sought after is a professional one, based on liberal education and technical training that will provide a basis for independence. This leads to the characteristic emphasis on early selection, training, postgraduate education, promotion tests, and so forth, and in general to a professional sense.[22] The *Report on the Production of Officers* apparently accepts the theories of military education of Huntington or Masland and Radway.[23] These are, centrally, that the significance of the military profession, the width of the factors determining its role, and the special difficulties that affect it provide very high requirements for entry and education. The standards are as demanding as those of a liberal profession; the implication, then, is that the military is indeed, at least in part, a profession. There is some truth but also some confusion in this. Independence may be in part created by technical expertise and this may be appropriate. But the independence that comes from a humane tradition (like the assumption of radical and rational methods) and a transferable vocation (governing itself with its own standards and providing easy movement from job to job) are not relevant to the military structure. In Australia the limitation of scale itself makes even the degree of technical expertise less effective or relevant. If the general military situation cannot fit into the full professional model, the Australian can do so even less.[24]

In general, we may say that the Australian system is seeking after an image that is inherently paradoxical and especially difficult for Australia to meet. For example, the idea of the officer as the generalist moving rapidly from job to job is all very well in organizations of vast size, where some officers can be generalists, some specialists, and all can be promoted to comparatively high posts. In Australia it means a frustration of the specialist and therefore a further reduction of the variety of participant influences and motivations. The R.A.A.F and the R.A.N. officer serving at headquarters has to feel (or at least pretend to feel) that he is uncomfortable and wishes only to be at sea or in the air or on a station. The military mind has also to be a managerial one, and so on. But these role tensions do not assist the effectiveness of the contribution. Furthermore, while Australia is following this particular doctrine, other influential military professions (as Janowitz has shown in his study of the military in the United States[25]) have been radically changing. The United States has been developing its specialists, its scientists, its engineers, and both the U.S. and the U.K. have been developing their Whitehall-type experts. It is in a way only the specialists like, say, General Gavin in the United States who have any degree of transferability and therefore real professional independence. It is precisely these that the A.R.A. must do without, especially at anything like a senior (brigadier or above) level. In Australia under present presuppositions (and virtually perforce within the local scale), it must be the generalists who get to the top, and as 'arts' men they are more dependent on the A.R.A.[26] A relatively isolated group is not the same as a relatively independent one. The military profession in Australia is unusual and is isolated within a settled policy. It is not, therefore, necessarily of very much help if there is a need for radical questions about the structure and dimensions of that policy.

CONCLUSIONS

Granted a dependent and restricted defence programme that is overwhelmingly determined by a rigid financial decision, do the organization of the Defence Departments, the military profession, and the processes of control provide ways of jolting this rigidity from time to time, or do the organization, the advisers, the controls simply reflect the existing established policy? Have we here another field of settled policy in fact? Ultimately this must depend on the total balance of military-civil relations: the civil role must primarily relate to financial control, the military role be relatively independent within narrow limits. These are the basic sources of conflict where objective control, in Huntington's sense, exists at all. Clearly however, the result that Huntington expects from his model can be threatened in different ways in different systems. In the Australian type, there is an inherent imbalance that inhibits it. In the first place, in Australia the problem may be that the field for independence granted to a professional adviser is simply altogether too small for any worthwhile influence at all. Hart has described the military role as defining the most profitable use of a given means or force towards some given end, object, or policy.[27] But if the means are too limited to achieve any worthwhile end or significant policy, independence in creating the definition is itself not very significant. The model may be very useful in certain circumstances—for example, in creating a new army for a new state, or in providing criticisms of the role given to a supreme commander of an allied force. But in the Australian type of situation, which may be an increasingly usual one, the restriction of expenditure might be so much the most important decision (in one sense, because of its importance, the only 'policy' decision) that, once taken, few other policy decisions are left to be influenced. In this case, perhaps the military must go beyond the lines laid down by Huntington, which are anyway substantially more generous within the limits of American expenditure. The Esher system, embodied in the U.K. Orders-in-Council about the Imperial General Staff, and highly influential in Australian defence organization, especially in the Army Department, might not be at all appropriate. An altogether more ambitious military spirit might be radically needed. But this is precisely what is unlikely to develop here. The military role is ineffectual within the too narrow confines of its independence.

A second fundamental is that the system has to buy overseas a good deal of what it needs, but it cannot buy quite enough: it cannot buy the sort of argument that tends to be absent from its own set-up. Quite particular agreements (e.g., about a U.S. naval radio communications centre at Exmouth Gulf) do not replace intrinsic debate. The embarrassing end of the Bluestreak co-operation was one case in point.[28] The equally embarrassing position of Australia in relation to the decision to reorganize the United Kingdom's command structure in Singapore is another. A third case is the clumsy artifices that have had to be used to transfer just one R.A.A.F. squadron from Malaya (there under one agreement nominally ruling out such movements) to Thailand (under another agreement), the whole move being sponsored by a third. The discontinuous hierarchies of the international agreements with which Australia is involved frequently fail to bring her in until too late, or without embarrassment, on matters that may be details for others but policy for her. When Australia was indeed simply one part of a single Commonwealth defence structure, this problem did not arise. If she is now more dependent on her own sources of argument, in her present situation only financial exigency prompts radical change and there is no guarantee at all that this is a sufficient incentive. If she is dependent on others, the system works very oddly.

Meanwhile, it is not possible to doubt the urgency of the requirement in defence policy for argument rather than its alternatives: either easy compromise or a single dominant influence, whether of the civilian financial controller or a single commander or a single strategic doctrine (like Sir Charles Harris in the wartime bombing case). After all, policy decisions, which are important and risky substantial commitments, always tend to be avoided in any field of governmental activity, so that the shape of activity expresses a certain degree of prejudice. This is both especially likely and especially dangerous in defence. It is especially dangerous because at certain times defence matters so much, and because on the other hand defence institutions can constitute a total waste. This at least could virtually never be the case in fields like social services, education, and health, where even a little activity must be better than none, and nothing is utterly beside the point.

The dependence of the Australian defence system, plus its narrow financial limitations, enhance rigidity. Wrong decisions are more likely to be taken and to be maintained, for it is only finance or discrete outside interventions that prompt them. Now this may be a matter of general importance, since it may illustrate the way in which several Western allies, particularly those outside NATO, have not been brought into the continuous strategic discourse. To find techniques of closer integration in some single defence alliance rather than limited and essentially occasional participation in several is a painful but probably a very necessary process for such systems. Meanwhile Australia may be getting the worst of all worlds; perhaps much less could be spent to achieve roughly the same degree of actual self-defence (now virtually nil); perhaps much greater expenditure must be provided before a minimum degree of defence is achieved; perhaps radical reallocations are necessary. All these policy decisions would be painful. They are more likely to come about through a different system of alliance, and also through internal organizational changes: a Cabinet Committee, defence advisers for Prime Minister and Cabinet independent of the Ministry of Defence, and a strengthening of the Chiefs of Staff Committee as against the Defence Committee and of the civilian contribution to the specialist service departments.

As the Jackson hearings have shown in the United States,[29] it is of the greatest difficulty to find in this policy field the correct balance between argument and agreement. What is clear is that at present the Australian system does not provide that balance from any of its most important or likeliest sources. The changes that would be required are peculiarly unpleasant ones but an avoidance of them is probably dangerous and certainly wasteful. This article has attempted to show, provisionally, how in a dependent and restricted situation some counters against rigidity tend to be absent. The implication is that changes in expenditure, alliance, and organization are probably required.

NOTES

1 *Parliamentary Debates, Australian House of Representatives*, November 26, 1959, and March 29, 1960.
2 *The Times* (London), July 18, 1961, 6.
3 See especially *Parl. Debs.*, H. of R., October 22, 1959.
4 The battalion-brigade division is to be replaced by a five-battle-group (pentropic division) system. Including the purely volunteer Citizen Military Force (C.M.F.) of (it is hoped) 30,000 men, there will be two pentropic divisions, one consisting of two Australian Regular Army (A.R.A.) battle groups, plus three C.M.F. battle groups, and the other of five C.M.F. battle groups. The A.R.A itself, therefore, provides two battle groups, a battalion in Malaya, the Pacific Islands Regiment, and certain additional and logistic support groups
5 Other instances can be seen in statements on re-equipment; e.g., *Parl. Debs.*, H. of R., June 29, 1961.
6 Australia Treaties, 1960, Mutual Weapons Defence Programme Agreement between Australia and the United States of America, Treaties Series, No. 11.
7 Capital equipment means net changes in total equipment due to policy decisions (as against the simplest maintenance of the stock of equipment).
8 Draft Estimates 1961-1962, Department of the Army, Explanatory Notes, Division 511, p. 2.
9 'The Strategic Basis of the Defence Programme' and 'The Composition of Forces'.
10 Clear instances of the operation of this factor can be seen in the ministerial statements of 1959, 1960, and 1961, particularly on the naval programme. It was quite clear at an early stage that the programme really needed nuclear submarines, and it became equally clear that

no one was prepared to fight for the considerable cost of getting them. Similarly, H.M.A.S. *Melbourne* has been retained, after many previous decisions to scrap it, partly for prestige and partly because it was much cheaper to achieve something by retaining the *Melbourne* and equipping it with helicopters than to scrap the *Melbourne* and move over to nuclear submarines. H.M.A.S. *Sydney* will come out of reserve as a transport, where an entirely new air transport command would have been preferable but also more expensive.

11   There was originally a Statutory Council for Defence, which was a ministerial body assisted by chiefs of staff in an advisory capacity. They had one department and particular boards (including the Civil Aviation Board, Munitions Board, and so forth) that were thrown off and became departments, like the Department of Supply in 1938. In 1939, under Menzies and with Shedden as the top civilian official, the Department of Defence Coordination became the Department of Defence. Under it developed the Joint Services Organization, the Chiefs of Staff Organization, the War Cabinet Secretariat, and so on. This Secretariat was serving the War Cabinet, which had replaced the lapsed Council of Defence. But the War Cabinet was simply the ordinary Cabinet for a few special purposes. The 1940 Advisory War Council replaced in Australia the actual coalition that emerged in the United Kingdom. In 1942 Treasury control was strengthened with the creation of its specialized Defence Division. By 1944 Shedden was considering postwar defence organization. He visited the United Kingdom and under Chifley in 1945 began to handle the move over to a peacetime organization. After 1945 the institution of a Chairman of the Chiefs of Staff Committee (Wells, Dowling, Scherger) appeared and the Statutory Council for Defence was revised, with its decisions carrying the authority of Cabinet decisions. But in 1949 a new Prime Minister and a new strategic philosophy meant the lapsing of the Council and its replacement by the Defence Preparations Committee. With the passing of this policy, that committee in turn lapsed. Menzies' division of the whole Cabinet into two—an inner Cabinet and the rest—meant, in conjunction with these changes, that no special Cabinet Defence Committee was revived or existed.

12   Public Accounts Committee, No. 50, 1960, Part III.

13   *cf.* Public Service Act, S. 25(2), and Naval Forces Regulations, Reg. 18.

14   This continuity is very impressive. There have been, for example, only three Secretaries of the Navy Department. The first was G. L. Macandie, who was clerk in the Queensland Navy Office in the 1890s, Senior Clerk when the Commonwealth Navy Office was established and, from July 12, 1915, when the Department was created, the first Secretary, in which capacity he continued to serve until the 1940s. (G. L. Macandie, *The Genesis of the Royal Australian Navy*, Melbourne 1949.) His successor, A. R. Nankervis, was on the Navy Board in the 1930s as Financial and Civil Member, and served as Secretary from 1939 to 1950, when he was succeeded by the present Secretary, T. J. Hawkins, who had entered the Department himself when it was set up in 1915. This is an astonishing record of continuity; whether it is a proper one is another matter.

15   *Report on the Production of Officers for the Australian Regular Army*, April 6, 1959, 20.

16   This contrasts with the United States, where under the Officer Grade Limitation Act there is one brigadier or general to 1,835 men.

17 Military Board Instructions, No. 124.
18 Sections 21A (i) and (ii).
19 *Report on Production of Officers*, 31.
20 *Ibid.*, 27.
21 R.M.C. Annual Report, 1960, 3.
22 'Portsea,' Adjutant-General Publications, No. 28/60, 19.
23 *Report on Production of Officers*, 25-26. *cf.* J. W. Masland and L. I. Radway, *Soldiers and Scholars* (Princeton 1957); S. P. Huntington, *The Soldier and the State* (Cambridge, Mass., 1957).
24 Yet it is in the Australian situation that very large claims are made; 'Duntroon', Adjutant-General Publications, No. 27/60, 5. The officer will be 'an ambassador at large ... [who] must take great public responsibilities and not only in the purely military sphere'.
25 Morris Janowitz, *The Professional Soldier: A Social and Political Portrait* (Glencoe, Ill., 1960).
26 *Report on Production of Officers*, 39; '... bearing in mind that most of the higher commanders would probably come from cadets doing the R.M.C. arts course'.
27 B. H. Liddell Hart, *Strategy* (New York 1955), p. 334.
28 *cf.* B. B. Schaffer, 'Military Affairs as a Field for Political Science in Australia,' *Australian Political Studies Association News* (Sydney), No. 2 (May 1961), 5.
29 U.S. Senate, Committee on Government Operations, Subcommittee on National Policy, Interim Report and Hearings, 'Organizing for National Security', 86th Congress, 2nd Session, Washington 1960; Senator Henry M. Jackson, 'Organizing for Survival', *Foreign Affairs*, Vol. 38 (April 1960), pp. 446-56.

10

DECISION-MAKING AND THE CIVIL-MILITARY EXPERIENCE

This chapter attempts to extract from a review of case-studies some conclusions about the special nature of civil-military relations, to categorize and explain them. It carries further the point about argument and disagreement in the preceding chapter and develops a theory of a natural selection of agenda. Organizations are seen institutionally, as non-instrumental; an alternative to either a Huntingtonian or servile model of civil-military relations is suggested; and certain general points about organizational decision-making are made, in particular the view of decision-making as a series, not a discrete moment: choices are always available. The nature and problems of case-studies were discussed in a separate paper, 'Leaders and Cases', published in Public Administration *(Sydney), Vol. XX, No. 3, September 1961.*

One indication of an increasing American emphasis on the political study of military affairs was the decision by the Twentieth Century Fund some years ago to launch a project on civil-military relations; though formerly it had almost exclusively assisted economic research. The project was inaugurated in 1953 under Harold Stein, already distinguished as director of the Inter-University Case Program from 1945 to 1953 and editor of *Public Administration and Policy Development*.[1] Not surprisingly, case studies were used, to begin with as a research tool. The first major publication was by Millis, Mansfield and Stein, *Arms and the State*.[2] The authors had available to them a series of cases, some of which have now been made generally available.[3]

The result is a large and impressive volume. Eleven cases, arranged more or less chronologically, cover a period from the 1931-32 Manchurian crisis, when Hoover was President and Stimson Secretary of State, to the 1949-51 period; the latter include the decision to re-arm Germany, bases in Spain, the rivalry of super-carriers and B36 bombers, and the Korean war.

Clearly, the cases vary in intrinsic importance from small dead issues like the 1937 decision to export helium, to issues that will never lose interest, like the Casablanca decisions about unconditional surrender. They vary in length from fifteen to over a hundred pages. Some of the best of the material, already used in the previous volume, has now lost some of its freshness. But not all the interest has gone by any means. There may be at least two reasons for this. One is somewhat odd. The documents for American civil-military relations are now very rich, including the material coming from civil participation in policy research and strategy,[4] studies of the sociology of the military establishment[5] and theories and cases on military politics.[6] We also have memoirs and other material for the Second World War, including the official series on the United States Army, edited by Greenfield, on the Navy, edited by Morison, and the Air Force, edited by Craven and Cate.

In contrast to all this vast documentation, the United States did not succeed in producing, as the United Kingdom under the editorship of Hancock did, an official history of the civil side. Plans were laid and much work done, notably under James Fesler in the War Production Board. But the whole of that side was killed, perhaps by overambitious overall planning, but especially by the hostility of Representative John Taber when he was Chairman of the House Appropriations Committee. What has come out has done so mainly under private auspices[7] save for the volume from the Bureau of the Budget,[8] one war production volume[9] and a *Short History of the Office of Price Administration.*[10] This has tended to concentrate too much attention on military actions and the military role in decision making, though in fact the material available in Congressional hearings would correct this imbalance for any serious student.

The second reason for a lively current interest is that the whole of this case volume is bound by a clear understanding of the sharp difficulties of civil-military relations where non-routine (non-programmed) decisions are involved.[11] These may involve 'control' relations as in the relationship between the President and military staff advisors or organizations. On the other hand, there may be no control relationship at all, as with many relations between personnel, between agencies, or between 'systems' as, for example, within a defence establishment or between a defence and a diplomatic establishment. It can be a relation built round particular controls, like finance, or services, like supply.

The relation may involve differences both on objectives and on methods. 'How should United States naval strength be allocated to protect American interests from foreign threats? Answers to this question had a double nature: on one hand, political; on the other, military. Had the two civil and military authorities been in agreement on both objectives and methods, there might not have been a situation of interest to a student of civil military relations. But civil and military authorities did not in fact agree.'[12] But it is not merely that the questions have a double nature (multiple, one might say, since different civil-military combinations are likely both on objectives and on methods) but also that the disputes that arise within the government machine are likely to be specially acrimonious, dangerous and complex. Why should this be so?

In the first place, in public administration, interests do not converge so as to achieve decision making, even in wartime, without extrinsic means, such as effective over-all directives. Understanding public administration is in part understanding the types of *disagreement* that may occur. This was the point of a model suggested by Thompson and Tuden.[13] Thompson and Tuden suggested that since disagreement can occur about (*a*) objectives, (*b*) cause-effect relations, there are four types of decision-making strategies, which they call *computational*, where there is agreement on both (*a*) and (*b*); *judgemental*, where (*a*) are agreed but (*b*) uncertain; *compromise*, where (*b*) are agreed but not (*a*); and *inspirational*, where there is agreement neither on objectives nor on cause-effect relations. To each correspond appropriate types of organization. The Weber model of a 'rational bureaucracy' corresponds only to the first. This is shown in other discussions by Dahl, Lindblom, Vieg and others.[14] Since non-routine civil-military relations often involve the other three types of situation, the bureaucratic-type organization is rarely appropriate.

In the civil-military situation we have two added difficulties. One is, that the civil-military division itself adds extra dimensions to the Thompson-Tuden model. The second point is that the civil-military field, while the one where the most complex conflicts are likely, is also the one in which it is assumed that there ought to be in fact less disagreement because of the presence of danger, patriotism, etc., as sanctions. This high moral premium on agreement leads to pressure for unification of organizations, that is, for a resort to rational-bureaucratic methods and hierarchy in organization. Not surprisingly, this volume gives example after example of how unification did not in fact achieve rational calculation but the opposite. The point is not that it is impossible to find the right sort of organization, but that this is less likely to happen in the civil-military than in other situations. There are more disagreements, accompanied by less recognition of their legitimacy and import.

Whose task is it to do anything about this? This is perhaps the second major problem indicated here: the inventing or the bringing into play of specific processes of decision-making from time to time. As Stein has also observed, public decision-making is not an act but a process[15] with special characteristics, including its primarily institutional character, the inter-play of the formal and informal, and the political setting and purpose. The formal setting of political and administrative institutions provides some degree of publicity, accountability, stability and evident lines of responsibility which may lead one to suppose that at any rate the processional route should be more or less inevitable, a given thing. But formal lines of responsibility are simpler in some machineries of government than others. They are, at least on the face of it, not simple in the United States.

In any case, however, this must be less true for civil-military situations than for any other, since the civil-military fact complicates lines of responsibility and this is very vividly illustrated in this book. In general, while disagreement is inevitable, the ways in which agreement will be found, including the formal rules themselves, will not be inevitable at all. At each stage the actual processes to be followed have to be to a surprising extent actually *invented*. An approach to administration as invention or innovation was long ago suggested by Graham Wallas.[16] More recently, a comparable approach has been adopted both by Selznick and by Simon.[17] Simon gives great emphasis to the necessity of searching for the alternatives, for the consequences and for the problems themselves. He also sees that the task of innovation includes the creation of the kind of organization in which problem-solving will occur. He gives less attention to such administrative tactics as convincing others that the processes to use and the problems, alternatives and consequences to be considered are those you have in fact already decided to use, those which in fact suit your interests.[18]

It follows that, if participation is challenging, so is judgment of the record. One cannot simply ask of the participants whether they were in fact abiding by the rules, that is, actually using the formal channels and nothing but those channels: the preparation of advice from experts to superiors reporting duly to responsible political chiefs, and so on. These rules evidently cover little of the ground. It may nevertheless be fair to ask to what extent there was present that sense of 'political evaluation' which Appleby[19] claimed ought to distinguish public administration from business administration: how far there was regard to a maximum widening of the scope and temporality of the interests considered, and how far this was a factor in the inventing of machinery of resolution from time to time.

Here are at least two dangers. One is that the fund of invention will be inadequate to the demands. Is it a tribute to a government or a criticism of it if it is seen to call into play many *ad hoc* supplements to its solution-finding equipment? The equipment used may not in fact act in the way in which Appleby suggests that public administration decision-making equipment ought to act. What one notes from the record presented here is that mere unification of overall organization was not necessarily at all an effective process either for simplifying civil-military decision making or in fact for enforcing responsibility. Secondly, one of the processes used was the actual avoidance of decisions; Roosevelt was especially adept at this. Thirdly, the decisional processes used in the civil-military field were often quite peculiarly better at maintaining arguments by protecting the interests involved than at securing solutions to problems.[20]

It is clear on this record that political evaluation is important. The notion that higher levels of decision making (e.g. top civil decisions as against secondary military ones) do have the distinguishing characteristics of much wider and long frames of reference, has some substance to it. The equipment invented ought to reflect this: the civil-military situation ought to be one in which the organization used for decision-making reflects this special 'political' demand. This may suggest that the answer to the question about the task of invention of processes is that this is a matter for civilian officials. If so, the demand is a peculiarly heavy one, because of the extra complexity of responsibility in the civil-military field, because the processes will be judged and tested by their political sensitivity and because this is not a 'neutral' or 'scientific' task at all. It is essentially a tactical one, in a field where everybody's tactical exercises will be especially suspect.

Processes have to be invented, then, and this is especially difficult in the civil-military field. The processes to be used ought to reflect the requirements of political evaluation and control. This may be very necessary in the civil-military field but may also be very difficult. In addition, the issues, the problems, the alternatives and the consequences themselves have to be discovered.

Part of the problem (and this is also a problem for case-study technique if the studies are to be fair accounts) is that it is for much of the time artificial to think of 'the' objective, 'the' issue, even 'the' dispute. There are two reasons for this, each related to the problems we have already discussed. The first is that, despite Eisenhower's efforts to achieve just this, we do not often see at work a simplifying hierarchial process of agreement, i.e. a gradual sifting out of the less from the more important, so that in the end there comes the agreed agenda and the final top decision on the programme, etc. On the contrary, from time to time there is either an accidental or a convenient emergence of an understanding that one particular thing had better be resolved on, one way or another.

This thing may be the point of the exercise, the policy itself, or equally a piece of machinery, e.g. that a particular paper be drafted.

The role of accident or convenience is so impressive, indeed, that one may be tempted to employ a recent suggestion to explain the process. Kaufman has proposed that we look at organizational survival (whatever the aids used) as a result not of rationality—'calculated strategies'—but of natural selection.[21] The evidence prompts a theory of a 'natural selection' of agenda: decisional survival, the emergence of one question rather than another as 'the thing to be settled'. In the civil-military field at least there is good reason for rejecting the alternative model, the notion of a rational sifting out of issues. If you regard the essential civilian role as top political control, then the line between the civil and the military becomes, as these cases show, a line between more complex and far-reaching issues, and simpler and more concentrated ones.

The second reason is that what is secondary for one is primary for another. It is a supreme political art to avoid commitment of major political strength as to what is primary as long as possible, and to make the commitment only when it is inescapable or probable of success. But at lower levels the ability to balance reserve against action is less likely to occur and the criteria more obscure. Each participant therefore is not merely, as we have observed, less likely to be supplied with an effective rule-book than one might think, he is not even sure what game he is playing. It is likely that he will look to us as though he is playing in a game with contestants who think they are playing a quite different game and may have good reasons for doing so.

It is pretty inadequate, therefore, to think merely of the difficulties of tactics in a decisional or even an argumentative process alone. Part of the thing is the ability not just to win, but first of all to convince others that the game is the one you want to play, involving your issues and your disputes rather than theirs. This is a very difficult sort of play, no doubt, and it is particularly likely to lead to bad temper and misjudgment. Lord Bridges elsewhere put this in a very cool fashion—the good administrator spots the old wolf in the new look sheep-skin. He gets others to agree that the real problems, dangers, issues, are the ones he is interested in, not the ones they may be concerned about. That is half the battle certainly. It is a battle of peculiar severity and frequency in the civil-military field. The battle is so many-sided and so complex that an organic theory may be a better explanation than one in terms of rational hierarchy.

Hence three great problems in non-routine decision-making are seen with special clarity and severity in the civil-military field.

There are patterns of disagreement both in terms of ends (or interests) and of means. Various organizational processes and decisional strategies are available, like incrementalism; a resort to unified hierarchy is only one. Secondly, when one thinks in terms of discovering of 'inventing' these processes, there is a double strain both of securing this fund of invention or discovery, and of political evaluation and control. Thirdly, in addition to discovering the tactics for solving arguments, there is the problem of 'discovering' the arguments, the issues themselves: the survival of agendas. Hence the acrimony of decision-making within a governmental system and hence its peculiar sharpness in civil-military relations. A quickened sense of this is likely to be a sufficient reason for reading these studies.

Among a rich wealth of material one may select the following for emphasis. Case after case has Roosevelt as hero, the hero who knows how to wait. As Stein says at one point[22] has 'hesitations, delays, reversals of policy ... fit within the framework of a comprehensible rationale'. He would wait till what essentially mattered to him, as Commander-in-Chief, in foreign policy, as President, etc., not to anyone else, was deeply involved. This is clear in the cases about the allocation of the fleet, or the occupation of Germany, where the case-author comments on his 'avoidance of premature commitment'. Again in the case about the rearmament of Germany, Marshall, in October 1951, proved himself a much better Defence Secretary than Louis Johnson (who frequently suffers in this volume) had been in June, precisely because he accepted that Allied agreements would take time. Delay and avoidance are not always the right answer. In the case of aid to Russia, Roosevelt committed himself immediately. The problem was precisely to overcome the delay which politics and administrative difficulties would themselves separately create.

Secondly, there is a great deal of material here to show how partial, 'biassed' and non-instrumental, organization and other apparently mechanical factors are. In the controversy about the export of helium to Germany, Congress had attempted to solve the situation by fixing precise functional assignments: the Department of Interior was to be responsible for price and an inter-departmental committee for export. But what determined the outcome was not these arrangements at all, but a very different point, that the Departments of War and Navy did not care and Ickes, head of the Department of Interior, did care very much indeed. Again, in the M-day plan, we see a series of conflicts about opinion and interest disguised as organizational choices. Basically in the 1920s responsibility for preparation for war could be a very specialized

CIVIL-MILITARY DECISION-MAKING

military question (at assistant secretary level, in fact) because it was of interest to so few and not to the general public at all. It is a problem for Huntington's theory of 'objective' civil-military relations that opinion about what the 'object' is changes so erratically. What Baruch thought of as his impartial expert advice about machinery, the President perceived as partial to its military and business sources and anti-Presidential. Baruch's complaints about 'professors on organization'[23] could not have been more beside the point. The interest of the President was to be the boss and it was this which should have been the starting point for any advice given to him.

In the Italian armistice case, the poor quality of Intelligence, the unreality of the Long Terms, the exaggerated hopes for benefits from the armistice itself, all were affected by the over-riding impact of what people wanted, including what they wanted to believe, e.g. that the government of Badoglio would possess real authority. The bias of intelligence services is seen again in the case of aid to Russia. The only acceptable expert advice to the army was such as showed that Russia would be defeated. Intelligence, like organization, was not a neutral fact. Stein makes just the same point about the new academic strategic analysis. 'It would be a sorry four or five-star general or admiral who could not find a scholar willing and able to construct an elegant model illustrating with precision the correctness of the officer's views on strategic bombing, guerilla warfare, or any other strategic matter of military concern.'[24] Crozier,[25] Goldstein,[26] perhaps Schilling and others,[27] would agree.

Thirdly, if interests, which are determinants, clash, so then do such objective factors as diplomacy and strategy, as in the case about the allocation of the American fleet between the Pacific and the Atlantic Oceans. These conflicts are indeed a special type of civil-military problem. The conflicting though equally objective (that is to say, expert and professional) advice of diplomats and naval officers is a further complication for the Huntington theory. This case illustrates very clearly that over and above disagreement about objectives or means there will be disagreement about which of the objects and the means are to be considered. Was the object in view to achieve war or peace, or delay, or to influence American opinion, or to influence American political leaders? Were the means to be considered the decision about allocation itself, or publicity about the decision or varying degrees of possible publicity from maximum secrecy to its opposite? At any rate, while it would be difficult to explain the role of many of the participants like Richardson, Kimmel, Stark or Stimson in objective civil-military terms, this would not apply to Marshall, who as Chief-of-Staff stuck to purely military points, e.g. if troops were to go to Iceland, they would have to have naval escort.

Some of the cases, then, give quite particularly useful information about aspects of general decision-making theory such as the role of delay and commitment, the lack of neutrality of apparently instrumental factors like organization and intelligence, the patterns of disagreement. On civil-military relations themselves, the cases make possible some tentative suggestions about a model which might fit the facts. At one extreme we may say that there can be no civil-military problem if prevailing values prevent any military role at all, e.g. in the 1931-32 Manchurian crisis American military force simply could not be used because domestic values prevented it. In other situations financial assumptions about military expenditure could have a similar effect. These cases indicate occasions when financial control in the American military establishment had dysfunctional effects, just as the over-use of financial control of a particular type as the essential civilian contribution has certainly prevented a proper civil-military balance of decision-making in the Australian system.[28]

The very notion of differences of interests, of objectives and of ideas about means may, however, give some hint of an acceptable model. If a simple 'objective' Huntington model cannot be used, neither can a 'servile' model, of the military simply as a servant of civilian policy. The military must make policy assumptions, at least the sort made both by Marshall and by Bradley.[29] Some indications of the answer have already been given. It is essentially that the civilian concern at the top is longer, more complex and more far-reaching than the military objectives. In the case of the Italian armistice Eisenhower wanted certain quite specific things whereas Roosevelt was pretty unsure what he wanted, and was partly bound by commitments, e.g. the dogma of unconditional surrender. This is not the same as saying that the military role is not political, because what Eisenhower wanted included political things too. In the aid to Russia case everything, including intelligence, was political but the civilian role of Roosevelt was more long-term in objectives or interests than that of any other participant.

An extreme example of this simplification-complication model is given in the case on the Washington controversy on directives for the occupation of Germany. In the original military assumptions (where, precisely opposite to the 1931-32 case, there was no civilian role at all) expressed in CCS551, April 1944, the occupation policy would, as always, be simply to prevent disease and unrest and otherwise use the existing governmental authorities. The move from this to the more acceptable JCS1067 lay through inter-allied organizations, cold war, intra-American arguments and arguments about the proper organization for developing a policy. It was essentially a move to a more complex position and to a more complex machinery for establishing it. This case is, in fact, continued in the one about the decision to rearm Germany. There again one sees the civilian role, this time of an agency, the Department of State, as against the military, the Department of Defence, as more complex, simply because State as a result of its responsibilities for allied relations had to take a longer-term view than did Defence.

If the extreme civil-military situation is war, is the model applicable then? The simplification of the military role may be thought to break down. If the model is to be used, then war is indeed too serious to be left to the generals. Military objectives even in war, then, should be limited, definite and immediate. The other objectives (e.g. in the Yalu case, the re-unification of North and South Korea) must be a civilian political activity, just as debate about them (e.g. about the original United Nations objective of maintaining the status quo in this case) must be kept in political, not military hands. The MacArthur case was not a straight military dispute, though. He was also in conflict with his military chiefs. In so far as he was left (we might think too much) alone, this was really an application of established American doctrine about the independence of the theatre commander. In the end civilian supremacy was demonstrated. It is a good civil-military case, showing the unfortunate results of the intervention of military simplification into civilian affairs, where specifically 'wide questions', issues the General was not interested in at all, in fact matter very much indeed. Another particularly interesting case is that about bases in Spain where, unusually, the presidential role was negative and Congress used military not civilian arguments without any military support save from admirals of the line. But this is a very complex case indeed and can hardly be summarized here, simply recommended as enlightening reading.

If the art of non-routine decision-making in the civil-military field is particularly complex, it provides interesting problems both of decision-making methods and of control. The problems are heightened in various ways. The interests in favour of simplification are always strong, and they have grown stronger from time to time, as a form of reaction. Further, the actual techniques available for programming decisions have obviously improved enormously. A search for ways in which the essential civilian contribution can be simplified equivalently inevitably occurs: sometimes this is purely political; sometimes it is a search for specific devices; obviously (as in the Eisenhower or Dulles-Humphrey-Wilson era) these can go together. The search is dangerous, though, and the traps many. For example, the case about super-carriers and B36 bombers shows very well that reliance on financial control in the form of fixed ceilings—a very simple device—is a defective civilian contribution. In the American case, it worsened the effects of outdated strategic thinking by making strategy more rigid and so effects of outdated political consequences, e.g. the military were preparing only for a full-scale Russian conflict. Yet the financial ceiling itself was, even as a financial control, always out of date, and unreal, as such controls always will be, in three different ways. The ceiling of the late 1940s-1950s was based on the assumption that $12\frac{1}{2}$ to 15 million dollars for defence expenditure could not be exceeded without national bankruptcy. Yet even in real terms that was less than 50 per cent of equivalent 1960 defence expenditure. Secondly, the ceiling frustrated the real opportunities for unification in favour of dysfunctional 'budgeteering'. Thirdly, it was based on a confused notion that 'good financial management' would itself lead to or indeed meant adequate defence services.[30] The case against financial ceilings, hitherto the basis of the unbalanced civilian role in Australian defence, should be more widely understood. An alternative is outlined by Stein:[31] large budgets; combined commands, functional development groups and joint staffs for strategic responsibilities (the attempt to establish roles and missions in terms of particular weapons has been largely abandoned); the use of individual services for training; fourthly, balanced defence; and finally a *dictat* by the Secretary of Defence in place of military discussion of financial questions.

Turning from control to method one notes that, despite the apparently revolutionary changes in the American civil-military situation in the period covered by this book and its predecessor, the effective decisions can be seen to have been incremental rather than radical. Despite calls for simplicity, for radical solutions, for complete breaks, for utopianism, in fact, and despite the increasing possibilities of calculation, optimal solutions have never been found. This is now a more acceptable fact than it once was. Further, the alternatives and consequences considered have been restricted and the solutions fitted to the currently available means without too many sudden changes. Consideration has been a relatively piecemeal and broken series. Unification has been a long, not a sudden story, for instance. The same applies to the co-ordination of strategic and diplomatic administration.

Incrementalism is not a panacea. Even piecemeal changes have unanticipated consequences, e.g. the benefits that have come to the Secretary of State from a stronger Secretary of Defence. Unified budgetary demands had particularly unexpected consequences. Stein indeed gives it as a lesson that, 'It is also true that when the budgetary requests use different channels, budgetary competition is avoided and co-operation encouraged: a single country mission budget enforces competition for limited funds'.[32] Nor does successful incrementalism mean simply following the past. Innovation is required. Thirdly, a number of piecemeal changes may still yield substantial results at the end of the series. This is seen in the way in which congressional pressure finally amounted to one big decision to have bases in Spain. It is also seen in the growth of significance of economic aid, and so of new questions like the economic-military balance.

Nevertheless, incrementalism is attractive. It steers quite clear from the limitations of the Weber or the Wilson models, or their over-use. It also avoids the present fashion for simplification, prompted by political desires or impatience, or, alternatively, by the use of apparently powerful devices or of objective techniques like the various methods of strategic analysis, beyond the range of their objectivity: it can employ them within that range. The occasional trend to despair of Kaufman, Simon, March, Cyert and others may yet be answered. This is the point to which Lindblom, having examined with Dahl previously the whole range of aids, has now come. Lindblom would specifically refute any universalistic claims for incrementalism. But it has many advantages, including that of being, in Lindblom's term, 'means-oriented', and serial. It does describe much that happens; it is an appealing device: a better description and also a better ideal.[33]

One general conclusion may be that the whole Wilsonian approach—the ideas of a clear dichotomy, a linear pattern, a servile relationship, secondly of a sifting out of issues rationally by a hierarchy, and thirdly of an absolute instrumentality of organization and processes, of means generally—is unacceptable yet persistent. That it is unacceptable is now established doctrine. That it is persistent is not, perhaps, as fully established. One potent example of its persistence is the frequent concern with what is called 'the blurred line' between civilian and military roles. On the whole, Stein and his authors are pretty sceptical about this, partly because it is not all that fresh, partly because in relation to the total society the actual influence of the military elite can easily be exaggerated[34] and partly because the actual scientific strength of some of the apparently impressive argumentative techniques now available to this elite from the social scientists (which is one of the aspects of the blurring of line which has concerned some commentators) can easily be exaggerated too.

This does not mean that there are not real problems here. A political involvement of the military, despite the American tradition, is not in fact at all new. One might think of the activities of retired generals, the necessity of political patronage for appointments to West Point, the intervention of commands in local politics and the relationship between staff chiefs and Washington politics. The depth and breadth of the involvement may be new, however. Furthermore, we note that after the frustrations of limited war (in Korea for example, as compared with the French in Algeria) American officers tended in some cases to follow the classic lines of searching for scapegoats and panaceas. A few entered into the radical right, a few were reported as mishandling the captive audiences which in that phase they tended to address, e.g. about the importance of brainwashing their recruits.

Perhaps what should be emphasised is not that this involvement was new but that the American system made it more difficult to handle than would a parliamentary system. Certainly it would be wrong not to see that a civil-military problem looks different in the parliamentary and the American presidential settings. Congress may well be anti-presidential and capable of establishing its own lines to the military, hence complicating or even breaking down such linear civilian controls as do exist. Congressional amendments to military appropriations are a good example. The material here however shows quite clearly that it is possible to over-rate the significance of this difference. In wartime Congressional control and intervention was certainly very limited. The role of the Truman Committee investigating economic mobilization is not without parallels in British parliamentary experience. In peacetime the basic determinations are almost always executive.

There may be more political difficulties between the President and Pentagon than between President and Congress in this field. There are exceptions, for instance the Congressional insistence on exemptions for farm workers, or the status of particular corps like the Marine Corps or the Corps of Engineers, but the exceptions are to be seen as such. The MacArthur hearings were a good demonstration of the genuine Congressional weakness in this field. The bulk of Congressional intervention furthermore is seen not on the central issues which involve the role of the President as Commander-in-Chief but on secondary questions like the National Guard or quasi-military questions such as economic as distinct from military aid. Perhaps the most real difference between the Presidential and the parliamentary systems is the difficulty about maintaining proper lines of secrecy and privacy, for example, about the H or the N bomb.[35]

In general it may be suggested that a concern with a blurring of civil-military lines is not so much a reflection of new developments or of greater weaknesses in the American than in the parliamentary system, as of a failure to understand civil-military relations themselves.

Altogether the problem does not seem to be nearly as significant as the problem of working out a balance of necessary contributions of strategy, diplomacy, and financial control, for instance, which these cases demonstrate time and again. The problem is not that one factor intervenes too much or too masterfully, but that the quantum varies from time to time, and the appropriate is barely evident. A diplomacy of containment will have very special military demands.[36] Though those demands were not in fact met in the pre-Korean situation, in that case at any rate military planning ought to have been the means and diplomacy the determinant of ends. That was not the situation with 'the New Look' Defence Secretary Charles Wilson's 'bigger bang for a buck'. The reduction of expenditure to a particular plateau led to a total reliance on nuclear arms, an unfortunate situation which Eisenhower and Dulles simply provided with a political rationale, like Dulles's notion of massive retaliation. State, Treasury and Defence were perhaps in agreement but it would be very difficult to say which was in the lead.

Kennedy's policy of balancing economic against military aid and his adoption of Taylor's notions of balanced strategy and defence forces were altogether a much more sensitive and sophisticated approach to the problem. This was a genuine advance in the civil-military field with which theory now has to deal. In any case in this volume's authors one finds few remnants of Wilsonianism, save for the inheritance of the notion of political studies, including those of civil-military relations, arising out of actual needs, and for the pardonable notion of the President as hero and Congress as mainly an excrescence. That sort of Wilsonianism, at any rate, is possibly an ineradicable part of the traditions of American political science.

The material available here does enable us to move forward to a more complex and acceptable theory of civil-military relations and some suggestions have been made about this. Bearing these suggestions in mind and moving from the civil-military field to public policy in general, a second general conclusion is possible. It is fairly well understood that decision-making is a process, but the implications of looking at the process as a series are not yet fully worked out. They need to be, for they are complex and exciting. In the first place, uniquely optimal decisions, either from a civilian or from a military viewpoint, are not made. We must surrender the notion of the optimum. What we perceive is a series of choices. The emergence of the choices is accidental. Having emerged, they may be decided more or less deliberately, though the techniques for programming or simplifying decision-making are in various ways suspect (partial or defective) and not relevant to the whole process, and deliberation is variable and not necessarily rational. The consequences will include significant commitments, some intended, some not. It is this notion of sometimes dangerous, always costly, commitments which is what perhaps we best mean by the term 'policy'.

The role of organization and procedures is to suit 'policy', to be appropriate to the choices and commitments. Since we are faced with a series of choices and commitments we can well assume that there will be no dramatic change in organization and procedures, unless there is some other determining drama such as total war or total disarmament. As Stein says, 'Save for massive disarmament or total war or a total shift in our position in the world, it can be said with assurance that there will be no dramatic reversal of present practices. The title of the Chairman of the Joint Chiefs can be changed, but there is no prospect for perhaps the next decade or even longer, that he or his equivalent will cease to have at least the position of *primus inter pares*. What is now the Agency for International Development may well have a new name; it may be officially closer to or farther from the State Department, but surely there will be an agency dealing with economic development constantly trying to juggle the balls of long-term and short-term interests, diplomacy, military means and desires, congressional preferences and presidential guidance.'[37] The field itself, the practices themselves, are already more sophisticated and it may be agreed that the notion of developing a satisfactory series rather than insisting on the unique optimum is currently accepted by Washington.

The encouraging side of the view of a system is that if there is a series, then some choices will always be available, always coming up, even in the apparent deadlock of a cold war, limited war, containment situation. This volume illustrates in fact very well the richness of the actual number and variety of choices available from time to time. The role of concepts or doctrines like containment is interesting in this respect. On the one hand it may have been a limiting factor, on the other hand it was invented, or at any rate best stated, by Kennan as essentially a method of providing a further alternative to moral outcry on one hand or all-out war on the other.

The discouraging side is that one must still postpone one's hopes for maximum rationality (especially perhaps about the emergence of the choices to be considered). This remains one of the most intractable of questions: to distinguish where simplification and programming can and cannot be employed, its limits and consequences. Further, it is inherent that any particular field of public policy is likely to have its own substantial strains, so that public decision-making, apart from the structural problems indicated here, is likely to be precarious and irritating. The substantial strains will increase from time to time and are likely to be more severe in some fields than in others, as in the civil-military-diplomatic field. Stein comments that 'the present stresses invite the revival of the Manichean heresy': [38] the idea, presumably, of an available choice between the one best and the one most evil decision. This doctrine would certainly be the worst of heresies from the point of view of contemporary decision-making theory for a non-programmed public field, and quite rightly so.

NOTES

1 New York, 1952.
2 Walter Millis and Harvey C. Mansfield and Harold Stein, *Arms and the State. Civil Military Relations in National Policy*. New York, 1958.
3 Harold Stein (ed.), *American Civil-Military Decisions—a Book of Case Studies*. A Twentieth Century Fund study, published in co-operation with the Inter-University Case Program. University of Alabama Press, 1963, pp. x + 705, $9.50. Referred to below as Stein.
4 A good summary of some of this is found in the *Times Literary Supplement* Nov. 14, 1963, pp. 917-918. This covers some of the recent productions of outstanding American workers like Kahn and Schelling, as well as some British and European contributors. See also a left-wing critique, unusually well-informed for contributions from that quarter: Walter Goldstein, 'Theories of Thermo-Nuclear Deterrence' in R. Miliband and J. Saville (eds.), *The Socialist Register*, London, 1964, at pp. 211-226.
5 The two best contributions are by Morris Janowitz, *The Professional Soldier*, Glencoe, 1960, and *Sociology and the Military Establishment*, New York, 1959.
6 See especially Samuel P. Huntington (ed.) *Changing Patterns of Military Politics*, Glencoe, 1962, especially at pp. 235 ff., for Huntington, 'Recent Writings in Military Politics—Foci and Corpora', a very useful bibliographical article.
7 E.g. H. M. Somers, *Presidential Agency: The Office of War Mobilization and Reconstruction*, Harvard, 1950.
8 *United States at War*, Government Printing Office, 1946.
9 *Industrial Mobilization for War*, Government Printing Office, 1947.
10 Government Printing Office, 1948.
11 J. G. March and H. A. Simon, *Organizations*, New York, 1958, *passim*, esp. ch. 7.

12   Robert J. Quinlan, in Stein, p. 156.
13   James B. Thompson and A. Tuden, 'Strategies, Structures and Processes of Organizational Decision' in J. D. Thompson *et al* (eds.) *Comparative Studies in Administration*, Pittsburgh, 1959, pp. 195-216. See also P. M. Blau and W. R. Scott, *Formal Organisations*, London, 1963, pp. 41-42.
14   R. A. Dahl and C. E. Lindblom, *Politics, Economics and Welfare*, New York, 1953. This is a stimulating discussion of available processes for calculating and controlling social actions, i.e. techniques available for relating means towards ends. Four central processes are discussed: the price system, hierarchy, polyarchy and bargaining. These relate to scheduling goals, rational calculations and so on and can be aided in various ways, especially by science, incrementalism, calculated risks and utopianism. Each of the four central processes is discussed in terms of its advantages and costs and its conditions. Once again we see that hierarchy has limiting costs and pre-requisites. There is a simpler but useful discussion along these lines by John A. Vieg, *Progress versus Utopia*, London, 1963.
15   E. A. Bock (ed.), *Essays on the Case Method*, New York, 1962: Harold Stein, 'On Public Administration Cases', pp. 5-7.
16   E.g. in his inaugural address to the Institute of Public Administration, 'Government', *Public Administration* (London), Jan. 1928; reprinted as 'The British Civil Service', in *Men and Ideas*, London, 1940.
17   See especially H. A. Simon, 'The Decision Maker as Innovator' in S. Mailick and E. H. Von Ness, etc. *Concepts and Issues in Administrative Behaviour*, Englewood Cliffs, N.J., 1962, pp. 66-69.
18   This aspect is better represented in the same volume by Norton E. Long, 'The Administrative Organization as a Political System', pp. 110-121.
19   In his *Policy and Administration*, Univ. of Alabama Press, 1949, and other works.
20   Compare M. Crozier, *The Bureaucratic Phenomenon*, 1964, for a general discussion on decision-making systems as protections in large-scale organizations against the dysfunctions of power.
21   'Organisation Theory and Political Theory', *American Political Science Review*, March 1964, at p. 13.
22   Stein, p. 201.
23   *Ibid.*, p. 89.
24   *Ibid.*, p. 13.
25   *op. cit.*
26   *op. cit.*
27   A. Warner, R. Schilling, Paul Y. Hammond and Glen H. Snyder, *Strategy, Politics and Defense Budget*, N.Y., 1962, esp. at p. vii.
28   B. B. Schaffer, *World Politics*, Vol. 15, No. 2, Jan. 1963, 'Policy and System in Defence: the Australian Case' at p. 236 *ff. cf.* B. D. Beddie, in *Australia's Defence and Foreign Policy*, Australian Institute of Political Science, 1964.
29   See Stein, p. 662, note 24. The United States 'must never have a foreign policy that sends our armed forces to world tasks beyond their capabilities', as Bradley is quoted as saying.
30   *cf.* Warner R. Schilling and others, *op. cit.*, for further budgetary studies of this period.
31   Stein, p. 567.
32   *Ibid.*, p. 11.

33 David Braybrooke and Charles E. Lindblom, *A Strategy of Decision: Policy Evaluation as a Social Process*, New York, 1963. Lindblom's term is 'disjointed incrementalism'.

34 The late Wright Mills was the best exponent of this. A good case-study of how military leaders can be repeatedly defeated is in J. W. Swomley, Jr., *The Military Establishment*, Boston, 1964, a study mainly about the campaign for universal military training.

35 *cf.* Edward Shils, *Torment of Secrecy*, 1956.

36 Maxwell D. Taylor, *The Uncertain Trumpet*, 1959, New York. Another good case would be the multi-lateral nuclear force, 1961 to date, in relation to the differences of civil and military sources, the place on the agenda, unanticipated consequences (especially for German attitudes), the weighing of civil against military arguments and the tactics of negotiation. The major point would be the demonstration of the impossibility of making either the civil or the military point predominant *a priori* at any stage.

37 Stein, p. 25.

38 *Ibid.*, p. 25.

11

THE CONCEPT OF PREPARATION

SOME QUESTIONS ABOUT THE
TRANSFER OF SYSTEMS OF GOVERNMENT

This paper, primarily based on work done at the Institute of Commonwealth Studies, London, examined the validity of the notion of a preparatory process as the explication of colonial policy in areas where the Durham report had not been felt to be applicable. It criticized the notion of stages and questioned the historical truth of the preparatory idea; and it discussed the nature of a bureaucratic colonial polity, the problems of gradualism, the transfer of institutions and the transfer of power, and it ends with some questions about inheritance and administrative styles.

TRANSFERRING CONCEPTS

A recent commentator has suggested that the value to political science of looking at new states is that 'one is forced to deal with the most basic questions of politics—the entire set of questions involved in the creation and maintenance of political societies.'[1] Certainly this appears to be true time and again. One is forced to look at the largest questions to the smallest, both because they are vivid and apparent, and because they are also urgent. The basic problem of obligation—why we do things we do not want to do, and allow unpleasant things to be done to us by political leaders, of why we accept the authority of power—is for us either a matter of analysis or of sociological inquiry. Clearly it is more than that in a new state. There the question is a living one, sometimes for a large minority, sometimes for many small sections or groups. The state and the nation are not, as yet, one. Rousseau or Hobbes have come to life.

Similarly, with questions of a different order, the concepts and controversies of Western political science take on a brighter colour. The debate between the Burkean theory of representation of interests and the Benthamite alternative is one example.[2] Dead debates come alive. Secondly, political forces—for example, strains on public service neutrality—are seen more starkly in a new setting. Without the sort of sociological scholarship of a Selznick, it may be difficult to detect the administrative ideologies at work in Western systems. They are seen very easily in dependent or new states because they exist in a franker or more extreme form, or because they are brought into the open by testing conditions or by debate itself. At one extreme, for example, administrative self-recruitment and the recruitment of an administration from a social elite have been undertaken more consciously and have been defended more openly for the U.K. colonial than for the home civil service.[3] There has been in home administration no ideology comparable, as a force, to indirect rule in African administration. Indirect rule may be termed an ideology insofar as its force derived not from conditions but from belief, and because when the ideology was not followed by action it was thought necessary to pretend that it was—'a ritual incantation', as Ralph Austen has called it.[4] It was unanalysed; that is to say, it was an emotive image, not a necessary prescription.

Thirdly, questions which for the West have become either purely mechanical or of secondary importance—like the drawing of electoral boundaries or the choice between plurality and proportional representation—may be passionate, violent, even bloody, in dependent territories and new states. Fourthly, one seems to be able to use in new societies some of the most familiar concepts of the West to enlighten some of the darkest problems. Thus the concept of totalitarian democracy seems to be at work in Kautsky's prognostications about elites and communication in new states[5] or in the local ideology as explained by Matossian.[6]

The very excitement of the situation ought to make us suspicious. Is it satisfactory to think of political development simply as a more than usually severe testing ground for our own agenda (for example, political obligation), our debates, our conception of political forces, our presuppositions and solutions? In particular, in the practice of the politics of the transition from dependence to new statehood, is it satisfactory to see the emerging states merely as more or less proximate to Western models? In his book *The Commonwealth*, Patrick Gordon Walker talks of Britain's being faced with her mirror image, and surrendering gracefully—an attractive notion: young bulls and old, the young learning their lessons well enough to fault their elders, and so forth.

In fact, however, one sees immediately that the very existence of emerging states changes the received notions of many parts of the discipline.[7] Furthermore, to apply any of our working concepts to the situation of emerging states can be dangerously misleading. Thus it is easy to talk of a Balkanization of Africa. Balkanization described Central and Eastern Europe after Versailles when a large empire was broken up, and when the only criterion for political boundaries was the self-determination of ethnic groups (which was necessary and sufficient too, since states appeared that were not viable in any other way). Although it is clearly tempting to use this concept to explain Africa now, it is wrong to do so. Not only are the new states not nation-states at all, but in fact they have been created in direct opposition to ethnic lines: the boundaries in West Africa run at right angles to the coast; the ethnic lines parallel.[8] The use here of the familiar Western concept, because of the apparent similarity of a part of the evidence, would blind us to the vital difference of another part.

There is a similar danger in using structural concepts like trade unions. In Africa, the term tends to refer to a centralized unit, built from the top down—an industrial wing of a party, not what we would have in mind at all.[9] Again, a technical ideological term like 'pluralism' in the evidence of the new states may refer to at least four different problems: multiracialism; the overlapping of state boundaries by ethnic loyalties and ties; the conflict between the rival, centripetal, and comprehensive demands of various types of small groups (extended family, clan, tribe, people) and those of the new central state itself; and the relations, generally characterized by intolerance, between majority and minority. In Western usage, pluralism is either a value (for example, as for the early Laski, Figgis, and others) or a description of ways in which loyalties can be shared between the state and other associations.

Finally, in analysing the practice of government in the new states, it is difficult but important to differentiate continuing problems on the one hand from rapid changes on the other. Within a year of Uganda's independence the balance of forces around three vital political issues (the position of Buganda, central-local relations, and the East African Federation) was altered altogether. It will not assist the detection of distinctions between the new states and the West to stress the continuities alone, or to ignore them either.

It is clearly not adequate to look at political development and government in new states exclusively in the concepts of Western political science, despite the apparently dramatic impact which the problems of such government have on the concepts themselves. Moreover, if it is inadequate to use these concepts to describe development, then how much more dangerous it is to suppose that development must actually be the more or less satisfactory working out of transferred Western models. To do so would be to adopt an extreme form of the 'gap' approach criticized by Ann Ruth Willner.[10]

Moving from the general to a more particular question, we can then look at the whole idea of preparation. Essentially, this is the notion of laying the foundations, before independence, for the working of a Western model (Westminster or whatever), which will then be transferred. The preparatory idea is an extreme instance of the assumption of the possibility and desirability of transferring Western political concepts—that is, of the political gap approach —not merely in analysis but actually in policy itself. How far does preparation theory explain the past and how far is it a sensible criterion for contemporary policy where, as for example in Papua-New Guinea, some sort of task along these lines still has to be done? This article is an attempt to raise some of the questions which have to be answered in assessing the idea of a policy of preparation—the notion that preparation in this sense explains what has happened and what ought to happen, what policy was like and what it ought to be. The implications of a negative result in assessing both the colonial record and contemporary policy would be considerable indeed.

PREPARATION THEORY

The standard United Kingdom picture of the preparatory process has been established with the very highest degree of scholarship and acumen by Wight and others.[11] It is customary in imperial historiography to distinguish between a first and a second colonial empire, though the number that can be distinguished in fact (whether from the point of view of acquisition, or chronology, or of policy) is as many as you like. It is clear that in the nineteenth century there was a definite conception of an imperialism for India, but a panoply of uncertainties about all the rest, though it may also be said that there resided in the Colonial Office a certain deposit of administrative notions—weights and measures ideas, as we might say—which it felt should be commonly applied. For our purposes it is important to distinguish two strands: those areas to which the Durham Report was felt to be applicable and, secondly, those to which it was not.[12]

It is true that the Durham Report did not conceive of an immediate self-government for Canada, but it did propound a system of political dualism, as a division of responsibility between the imperial and the domestic governments. Durham was quite clear about the essential equality of colonial and British-born and residing subjects. The 'constitutional assimilation' was accordingly to be definite and not without speed, and it was to proceed immediately beyond representative to responsible government. The executive council was to be responsible to the legislative council. 'I admit that the system which I propose would, in fact, place the internal government of the colony in the hands of the colonials themselves; and that we should thus leave them the execution of the laws, of which we have long entrusted the making solely to them.'[13] In the sort of colonial situation which Durham envisaged and where his ideas would apply, the case for an immediate self-government was already made by the situation itself. That was the essential point. Further, if there was a risk, it could in no wise be used as an argument against that immediate necessity for responsibility. There were several reasons for this, and the binding nature of liberty was one.[14] 'If the colonists make bad laws and select improper persons to conduct their affairs, they will generally be the only, always the greatest sufferers, and like the people of other countries, they must bear the ills which they bring upon themselves until they choose to apply the remedy.'[15]

Quite the other case was that where Durham did not apply, and where quite contrary ideas of trusteeship and preparation did. If Canada and Durham are basic for the one situation, then perhaps either Burke and India, or Ceylon and Donoughmore or Soulbury, might be basic for the other.[16] These were the colonies where the people were evidently not equal to the British. Accordingly, while existing state machinery would be used as much as possible (whereas in Canada it had from the first to be created), at the very same time neither the people nor the states could be very well trusted as ready for independence. Considerable delay, a fulfillment of conditions, and some relatively subtle and indirect processes of movement would be required, just as inherently the opposite were required in the Canadian situation or the Durham concept. The idea of trusteeship did imply that, eventually, there would be a change. The questions to be answered were 'how?' and 'when?' The process of preparation, the instrument of the vision of trusteeship, was meant to deal with the achievement of the change, the answers to these questions. It was the other side of the trusteeship coin.

It has been suggested that four essential stages can be distinguished in the whole preparation process.[17] The first consists of a division of legislative and executive councils and a nomination of unofficial members to the legislative council, leading to election of some unofficial members, as in Ceylon in 1910. In the second or 'representative' stage, the unofficial members are a majority, as in

Ceylon in the nineteen-twenties. This creates problems in the relation between the legislative and the executive councils. The third semi-responsible stage ensues when the majority of the executive council comes from or is related to the majority of the legislative council, as in Ceylon in 1931 as a result of the Donoughmore Report or in 1944 as a result of the Soulbury Report. In the fourth stage, nominated officials disappear from the legislative council, as in Ceylon in 1947.[18] This may be self-government, full self-government, independence; but perhaps a fifth stage should be distinguished to demarcate the actual transfer of power from the preparatory process. Furthermore, many complications, especially in types of ministerialization, will vary the pattern.[19]

Something like that is the preparatory pattern. Austin writes, 'The guiding principle behind the different stages in this advance —from an elementary form of Crown colony administration to a complete system of cabinet-responsible government—lies in the changing balance of power between British officials and representatives of the local community. By these means a colony is led to independence by a gradual process of emancipation through the careful training of the "unofficials" in the techniques of self-government.'[20] Austin adds the pregnant words, 'This at least is the theory.'[21] Such a theory of political development in the form of a preparatory process evidently has three essential and peculiar points, each concerned with political and administrative features rather than with modernizing, social, or cultural ones. The first point is that there are four stages of transition based on a transfer by training. The second point is that the pattern is primarily concerned with the legislative and executive councils. Thirdly, it assumes that progress is towards essentially one form of self-government: a slow but sure approximation of the Western parliamentary system and the Westminster form in absolute particular.[22]

Such was not the Durham idea. At some such stage as the third, when the legislature begins to acquire executive control, the pattern looks like the Durham situation. However, the beliefs of the colonial power itself establish a vital difference.[23] The theory of preparation implies certain specific presuppositions, each with severe difficulties.[24] The first is that while trusteeship might lead to independence, it is also supposed to do so very gradually indeed. The very nature of the process carries the possibility of a cut-off at any stage. It also carries the notion of tests or conditions for movement from each stage to the next. This means that trusteeship is interpreted as a preparation for efficiency or viability as much as for independence, and that the two ends can be contradictory. Hence efficiency may come to be seen, as Mboya pointed out later, as the last refuge of the imperialist.

Secondly, while in practice the only stage that mattered to the anticolonialist was the actual transfer of power, it was at that stage that institutions would and could be modelled on Westminster, if the people so chose (the idea of autochthony as Wheare, Robinson, and others discuss it).[25] In the ideology of preparation there is a fundamental distinction between the preparatory stages, which are concerned with the transfer of a system, and the process of transfer of power. Indeed this transfer is not an essential part of the preparatory process at all; it is a different sort of thing altogether. Preparation is concerned with the creation and translation of institutions (originally on certain conditions of viability), and transfer of power is concerned with independence. Preparation is essentially hierarchical, while transfer is a bargaining process. There is, however, always an attempt to graft the one category onto the other. For example, in the third and, especially, in the fourth stages, there could be a gradual reduction of the governor's and the imperial government's reserve powers. Thus transfer could be treated as simply an amendment of the fourth stage; of course, it is actually something else. In the end the nationalist and the colonialist might come to agree about the importance of the transfer of the Westminster model, but they would do so for quite different reasons: one as a culmination of training; the other as a symbol of liberation. If the theory of preparation differs from Durham it is also different from Lugard's 'Dual Mandate', and hence from the ideas of Goldie and, probably, Rhodes.[26] The theory is altogether different from what was present in the white-settler ideas of Lord Delamere.[27] For Delamere, the priority of economic development and the superiority and leadership of the white settlers were axiomatic; the long-term aim was concerned not with the movement of the indigenous people from one institutional stage to another, but with the creation of a European community which itself would deserve the Durham treatment. The axioms of the preparatory theory are quite different. Although many of those in charge never accepted them, nevertheless these axioms became very influential indeed in local opinion.

We can then distinguish between the idea of preparation and other notions of the colonial role. The idea of a preparatory process certainly (to say the least) has not had the field to itself. There have been many alternatives sought or found, and deep opposition. No one can pretend that preparation explains the actual process of acquisition, say, in Matabeleland and Mashonaland. However, by 1948, the Colonial Office would have wanted to claim that the preparatory process was not a method discerned only after the event but was a process always intended and foreseen.[28] This view of preparation implies a peculiarly Whiggish notion: a belief in a steady movement to better and better constitutional forms with the best form possible (a constitutional form, not necessarily independence) to be achieved at the end. The view is Marxian, too, in its socio-economic presuppositions that economic development comes before political development and as a condition for it. It is also very presumptuous in three ways. One is the ultimate assumption that the British form is the best, or, at any rate, that the British know best, as Macaulay had once believed. The second form of presumption is the conviction that the tests to be set could be determined by outside forces. Thirdly, in this view, the tests are presumed to be essential, however they extend the preparatory process—hence the reaction, in due course, of the United Nations General Assembly to any tests at all.

THE RECORD

There are then, it would seem, two distinct ways in which the preparatory ideas can be discussed. The first is essentially historical: Is the Whiggery true? Is it true, that is, that the whole plan of preparation was in mind from the beginning of each piece of Crown colony administration?

It is fairly clear that it was not, say, until 1948 and the Watson Report on the Gold Coast that the notion of using what in fact had happened in Ceylon as a model for Crown colonies generally emerged as a fully accepted official doctrine. The idea of preparation for the Westminster model itself—not merely of training, and a change of legislative and executive councils—was essentially a postwar idea.[29] That is the first point to emphasize about the record itself. The notion of preparation was essentially concerned with the creation of responsible institutions of a particular sort, although other opinion would have taken account of economic conditions, a desire for independence, nationhood, educational growth at postprimary levels, and so forth. Whatever the reasons for its emerging in this way, the idea was in fact convenient for three reasons. One was that it was a justification of the whole record, and of the British presence in postwar situations. The second was that it was a source of negotiation and of tactics of delay when delay may well, indeed, have been justifiable. (You would not seem to be delaying but only training and educating.) The third was that the theory in this form invited a concentration on just those purely institutional features which, it seemed, could most easily be debated, handled, and changed.

This version of preparation was a singularly brilliant sleight of hand. It is expressed in the 1948 claim that '... the central purpose of British colonial policy is simple. It is to guide the colonial territories to responsible government within the Commonwealth, in conditions that ensure to the people concerned both a fair standard of living and freedom from oppression from any quarter.'[30] Hence the tide of documents like *Origins and Purpose*, which as late as 1949 was both very cautious in terms, very conditional, and very limited in its view of preparation and of the move towards the end of trusteeship.[31] Hence also the enunciation of sets of conditions in case after case, especially in relation to the British West Indies Federation. However, in fact, these years were, inevitably, too late for preparation, save as a purely political, almost desperate effort to provide an ideology of delay. The times were too late, that is, for the provision of necessary nonpolitical conditions such as a higher secular educational structure and the garnering of its fruits. The first legislative council with an unofficial majority in the Gold Coast came in 1946; full internal self-government in 1954; independence in 1957. That was relatively much slower than was to be the case of the next batch in the later nineteen-fifties and early nineteen-sixties. Then the so-called preparatory steps trod hard on each other's heels. In Nyasaland steps were jumped. In Kenya it became obvious that the steps were mere negotiating points and did not represent either standards or education or conditions of viability. They did give a lot of work to the Colonial Office's legal department. The steps also had one singular disadvantage: they were so well known, in the end, on the other side of the table. So preparation became doctrine when it was just too late. Perhaps we should always be suspicious of any official statement that the central purpose of any policy is simple and that it has always been what it is then claimed to be. At any rate, if the theory emerged after the event in this way, it did so when it was too late to have substantial truth.

It might be argued that the whole theory of preparation was always a somewhat delayed ploy. Studies of particular colonial records show that it is very difficult to trace any continual preparatory process at work, or any signs of a preparatory policy, until after the war. The colonial polity was essentially bureaucratic. Colonial government was dominated by the secretariat.[32] Its aim was efficiency. The interesting prewar processes led to such things as the growth of technical departments, not to the growth of the roots of independence. Often, as in Uganda, the executive council until after the war was purely official in membership (although Kenya in 1938 and Nigeria in 1943 had unofficial members). More important, the legislative council was doubly subordinate both to the executive council and to the Colonial Office—a peculiar training for parliamentary government. It was not a matter of the legislative council's being controlled by the executive council but of its being simply the executive council plus a few unofficial members, meeting rarely (in Uganda in the nineteen-thirties, four to ten times a year), without parties, politicians, or an opposition, and certainly without either an alternative government or the possibility of understanding such a thing—again a peculiar training for parliamentary government.

This pattern was generally true for the legislative council form. 'A council such as this differs from the parliament of a self-governing dominion in the essential particular that the members comprising it are not divided into two parties—a government and an opposition', as Sir Hugh Clifford said in Nigeria.[33] But that was not the only problem even when war instigated changes. The 1940 Colonial Development and Welfare Act did not lessen the emphasis on administration and efficiency as against the legislative council and self-government. The 'member system'—that is, the system of bringing unofficial members into the executive council—introduced in Northern Rhodesia, Kenya, and Tanganyika, was rooted in responsibility to the governor, not to the legislative council. In Kenya and Tanganyika, when formerly unofficial members of the legislative council were appointed they had to become civil servants. The member system simply was not ministerial at all, however late in preparation the device appears. The Africans were scarcely participating anyway.[34] Furthermore, even in the policy of Creech Jones, the Labour Colonial Minister, the member system was to lead to ministerialization only very slowly: first, executive council members were to be responsible for branches of central government; then indigenous people outside the civil service were to be members; then members were to be renamed ministers; at last ministers were to be responsible to the legislative council.

Nor was this the whole of the limitation. Not everyone wanted to see a parliamentary development of the legislative council: Governor Hall, in Uganda, did not, nor did, perhaps, Lord Hailey.[35] As late as 1950, in Uganda, when only eight of thirty-two members were African, and only five were elected and those indirectly, Governor Hall said, 'All I ask of all African members of the Council is that they will take the pains to acquaint themselves with the facts and will make it their business to pass on the facts in simple terms to as many as possible of their fellow Africans outside the Council chamber.'[36] This was in 1950. It was much what Sir Hugh Clifton had said in Nigeria in 1923; and it was clear that the function of the legislative council was not at all to represent the people to the government, still less to make the government responsible to the people, but instead to act as a spokesman for the administration to the people. Not surprisingly, when ministers came, the concept of official and unofficial ministers was used.[37] The ministers were responsible to the government and the administration, not to the legislative council. In Uganda, changes in policy were made public before they were announced—much less debated—in the legislative council.

At the very time the preparatory process was, so late, at last consciously begun, there also began an emphasis on local government. There was no clarity about whether this was meant as a training for parliamentary self-government, and for the Westminster model in particular, or as an alternative to it.[38] Creech Jones seemed to mean local government development for economic development, for electoral colleges, and for political education. These were three very different and to some extent contradictory purposes.[39] Certainly there was a new concern with democracy, or, as it was later put, with 'representative forms'.[40] Hailey, however, spoke of a '... federation which would in time take over the legislative and executive functions of the present government. The value which the scheme possesses as a method of attaining self-government otherwise than through the development of parliamentary institutions of the normal type is an aspect which is clearly of great importance.' The whole structure of councils was thus set up, but the administration was strongly opposed to direct elections, precisely because they wanted a check upon 'the would-be professional' politician.'[41] Even if in the later nineteen-fifties there was a more specific emphasis on local government for political education and recruitment, it is very doubtful, because of its failure in the key urban areas and because of the rise of new parties and leaders, how far this worked at all.[42] Significantly, it worked best when it did not follow British models, and was freed of the weakness of local town clerks, relying on district commissioners and acting as the agents for central departments.

Not surprisingly, Kaunda criticized the whole emphasis on local government in this era as a colonialist diversion of political attention away from central government.[43] There were difficulties about whether or not the local government policy was meant as an alternative to Westminster (and clearly not all those responsible saw it as an alternative) and even about whether the policy was as tied to the British model as the whole preparatory process was supposed to make it. The Wallis Report said, for example, that past errors had been committed.[44] Local government had been led to think of itself as a source of future native states; back, then, to the essential preparatory process. According to the report, there was no point in the question whether or not 'British principles were suitable for export to Africa.' Again, 'There is no space here to argue the merits of the British, French, American, Irish, or other kinds of local government. I must content myself with the practical argument that no principles other than British principles can be imported into Uganda by an administration composed of British officials.' Possibly; but could British officials carry out these principles, did they want to, did they know British local government? In Uganda, at any rate, Buganda remained a peculiar factor. Domination by the district commissioner meant that the local government was very little like the British system, and the district commissioners knew little of that system anyway. As one district commissioner said, 'I, for one, must admit that until I had spoken to him [Wallis], I was not at all sure what constituted the essential difference between the two systems [the British and the European].'[45]

BUREAUCRACY

If preparation occurred, then, it did so very late in the day, not in wartime, nor even immediately postwar. Some of the apparently preparatory institutions, like the legislative council, did not seem to be effective. Those officials responsible were often opposed either to the preparatory process or to the institutions being used, and sought alternatives; the particular pieces of the United Kingdom model used—like local government—were fraught with difficulties and were not always either fully understood or fully British. Essential features of the Westminster model were lacking. A knowledge of the model was often lacking, too. The operative values were bureaucratic.

This was utterly true of all other parts of colonial government, at any rate until the end of the war. One might look at such a major innovation as the unification of the colonial service.[46] Even apart from Furse's deliberate hostility to examinations rather than interviews for recruitment, and his deliberate preference for those who were 'chiefs in their own country', unification meant precisely a step away from local recruitment. The old empire had used local recruitment much more. Reforms meant a concentration on British university qualifications, which made indigenous recruitment much more difficult. In forestry, British degrees plus a qualification from the Oxford Imperial Forestry School were required; in veterinary science, the qualification of the Royal College of Veterinary Science, and so forth. 'Standards' were all-important; standards meant

British, not even American or Indian, qualifications; localization could proceed only via scholarships to the United Kingdom, and scholarships were limited by the educational system which relied so heavily on primary mission schools. Caution in favour of standards was all-important as late as 1955. 'We made it clear from the beginning that we had no intention of pressing for the appointment of Africans to the higher posts merely because they were Africans, but we wanted to be satisfied, first, that if fully qualified Africans were available there was a place for them in the higher ranks of the civil service.'[47] This attitude was buttressed by the domination of the administrator over the rest of the colonial services, and by recruitment from Oxford and Cambridge over all others, and by the maintenance of that recruitment in the hard days of the nineteen-thirties when the other services were actually being retrenched.[48]

A second example of the gap between preparatory theory and practice was indirect rule. In all its ramifications, from administrative convenience to ideological pretence, indirect rule was not intended to be a preparation for independence on Westminster lines. All nationalists, including relatively evolved ones like Chief Awolowo, were hostile to it.[49] And there was never any ground for supposing that indirect rule was itself a more appropriate piece of machinery than any other. It is true, as Perham says, that 'the expedient by which a conquering people makes use of the institutions of the conquered is as old as history'.[50] In its application in the particular sense defined by L. P. Mair,[51] it was full of problems and pretence; of difficulties in definition and recognition; of limits of authority; of movement from an administrative device to a political doctrine to an almost religious dogma; of acephalous societies and useless chiefs; of the conversion of traditional leadership to merely appointed chiefs; of native treasuries and native administration funds. By its application, two problems were put. The first was the role conflict discussed by Lloyd Fallers in his classic work *Bantu Bureaucracy*,[52] and by A. Southall, who wrote, 'It is still, after nearly forty years of European rule, not possible to be true to Alur and European values at one and the same time. Administrators are compelled on the logic of the situation to view the chief's loyalty to them as right, and to consider the disloyalty to his people and their values, in which support of the British government involves him, as a stand for enlightenment. But they cannot force his subjects to view it so. There will always be moments of critical decision in which what is officially required of the chief will be seen as treachery by many of his subjects.'[53] The second problem was discussed both by Mair and by Hailey. Indirect rule naturally meant the creation of chiefs where there was no tradition. Chiefs were then petty officials, with an extended and, above all, an unencumbered (since nontraditional) authoritarianism.

What one sees at work in both the unification of the public service and the doctrine of indirect rule is what one saw in relation to the legislative council: the predominance of bureaucratic values over other considerations. These bureaucratic values were themselves excessively narrow. Thus the colonial administration opposed the Creech Jones policy of ministerialization, bureaucratic as that itself was, because it would upset the existing system of secretariat and of indirect rule.[54] The narrowness of this peculiar bureaucratic philosophy was effective and dangerous; preparation was probably ineffective and not nearly as dangerous as people like Hall supposed. The danger lay in the creation of inappropriate values. As Sir Christopher Cox pointed out, 'Projects for developing trade schools and training artisans have not won general support if they are suspected of being the policy of the ruling power more concerned with the supply of hewers of wood and drawers of water than with programmes of advancement.'[55]

Oddly enough, the actual importance of the bureaucracy for preparation was not a part of the preparatory theory. Yet Hailey himself commented that localization was more significant to the indigenous people than advance in the legislative council itself.[56] This was a serious comment on the theory of preparation as a whole, and reflected two weaknesses. One related to the gap between the theory (concerned as it was with the legislative and executive councils) and the actual colonial experience. It was not a part of the theory at all to acknowledge that indigenous people (and therefore the nationalist movement) would know more, from their experience of life, of the colonial administrator than of the legislative or the executive council. Secondly, the Westminster model fundamentally requires a public service prepared to operate a ministerial system. A transfer would require an indigenous public service of this type. Yet localization at an early stage and preparation for a ministerial public service were not made an inherent part of the preparatory process at all. The actual colonial government (so different from Westminster anyway) delayed localization very much indeed. Further, the power of the specific bureaucracy prevented the possibility of any discussion of alternatives to the one administrative system.[57] This could, of course, be treated as fidelity to a preparation for Westminster; but the colonial administrative system, whatever its virtues, was not at all like Westminster's. Whether localization and the ministerial public service were actually possible was, of course, another matter.

It is certainly one aspect of the limitations of the theory of preparation that not only did the actual process of preparation begin very late indeed, but that also it was all along rivalled and hindered by other values, which were predominantly bureaucratic. That was perhaps inevitable in a colonial situation. The colonial situation frequently looks more like a special sort of bureaucratic haven than an education for democracy, and Westminster democracy at that. The limitation of the legislative council as a parliamentary form is an example. To some extent the limitation was benevolent, as in the search for indigenous authority, or for public service unification. To some extent it was narrow, even dangerous, as with the adoption of a particular ideology of the superiority of a particular sort of recruitment.

The triumph of the bureaucratic position is seen very fully in, say, the Ceylon Civil Service before independence.[58] A description of such a service would be rather like an elaboration of a high-prestige bureaucracy of the Weber type or, as Mason said, of Plato's itself. That was certainly so in its training, pay, and position, its domination of central government (in departments like the Colonial Secretary's or the Colonial Treasurer's), and in provincial administration. It was a superbly rewarded and regarded service, especially after the Stanley reform of 1844. There was a superiority of the executive over legislative or judicial forms of government. There was a domination of the legislative and judicial institutions by administrators on the legislative council, and also by district judges and magistrates until the nineteen-thirties. All executive and administrative forms were dominated by the one type: the Ceylon Civil Service. Meanwhile, actual minutes, which, for example, forbade to expatriate civil servants the ownership of property, and equally real social norms dominated the service itself. The service was heavily committed not merely to its norms and its status but to its own goals also, even to the extent of opposing (effectively) governor after governor. The esprit had nothing to do with a Westminster preparation; it had to do with the rule of law and a sort of economic development. The commitment has been explained more crudely in African district administration, 'Ask different officials, "What is administration?" and you will get divergent answers. . . . The general idea will be that it is to hear cases and get revenue for the government.'[59]

Such a clear past and such firm norms had their advantages and their disadvantages. The structure was not conducive to political education. 'This training also did not provide for any sympathy with local aspirations, particularly political aspirations. The civil servant was only trained in "good government" as the service knew it and training the ruled in self-government was unnecessary.'[60] The system was very slow. It could conceivably adapt to the great changes only if they were slow also, as they were in Ceylon but not in Africa.[61] It created a virtuous but not a brilliant service.[62] It had little to do with developing the political responsibility of the Westminster system. We may say that transfer was too rapid in Africa for the possibilities either of indirect rule as an alternative or of the translation of the bureaucracy; it was too slow in both Ceylon and India either for the nationalist movement or for the hardening arteries of the civil service. Though very splendid indeed in many other ways, the record was not convincing in either case as preparation.

INHERITANCE AND COMPARTMENTALISM

The theory of preparation propounds that the new states within the Commonwealth are examples of a deliberate process of preparation, by training and institutional change, for a very special form—that is, for Westminster. It has implications about gradualism and conditions. The theory is interesting, too, in relation to the distinction between the transfer of institutions and the transfer of power: the assumption by one side that the first process could assimilate the second; the assumption by the other that the second process required the first as a necessary, if passing, symbol. Historically, the theory seems to encounter at least two grave difficulties. One is that preparation actually has looked more like a tactic of negotiation than a permanent policy. The second difficulty is that in practice the dominant operative values were not preparatory but bureaucratic in a quite particular sense. Perhaps this was inevitable in colonial government. It had a good deal to do with what the legislative council was like, with the nature of the colonial civil service created by Furse and others, with the doctrine of indirect rule, and so forth. Thus preparation was in a double sense too late—and was both too rapid and too delayed, in the different sectors of the colonial empire.

Other values had generally been preferred by colonial government: first, law and revenue, then development and efficiency, and so on to particular measures like public service unification. There is rich evidence of hostility to the domestic model and ignorance of it by those in charge. There is also evidence in authoritative statements of a search for alternatives, especially in relation to the very un-Westminster problem of communal representation. The search was expressed early in the Morley reforms or the Montagu-Chelmsford Report,[63] later in the Simon Report,[64] or even, as here, by Donoughmore itself: 'It must be our aim not slavishly to follow the forms and practices of the British model, which was not designed to meet conditions similar to those obtaining in Ceylon, but to devise a scheme in consonance with local circumstance, a scheme which will be concerned not to reflect an alien philosophy but to give free play to the peculiar genius of the Ceylonese themselves.' This attitude was also expressed by expert voices like those of Lugard[65] or Hailey.[66] Sometimes this was ignorance, sometimes opposition, sometimes actually an awareness of the complex conditions of Westminster and of local circumstances, sometimes a preference for alternatives in organization, public service, local government, and so forth.

Insofar as there was preparation for Westminster it came very late and was enforced. On the one hand (in Wallis's terms), no alternative seemed to be available. On the other hand, preparation was either a convenient tactic or a necessary though transient symbol for the transfer of power, although this was the one stage with which the preparatory theory was not designed to deal. A Westminster model became merely a tactic of negotiation on the one hand, or a symbol of independence, even of autochthony, on the other. In particular, some, like Jennings, saw the necessity of local adaptation yet clung to the notion that preparation could assimilate the problems of independence. Their idea was that the final Westminster-model constitution in full could be a useful and comparatively permanent guiding line for the new states. This notion was clearly faulty. For one thing, bills of rights, public service commissions, judicial service commissions, and so forth are unknown to the original. Further, the constitutional document was itself the most impermanent of things: a tactic, or a slogan on a banner.

Such a conclusion for preparation was a paradox, but not the only one. It was odd to expect bureaucrats to prepare responsible government; odd to educate through missions, schools, and a legislative council an elite that was always excluded either before or immediately after independence. Only one member of the 1951 Gold Coast Assembly government party had been 'prepared'.[67] After Simon, Donoughmore, and the rest had given so much attention to communal and minority problems, it was odd to use a model which is so much more than any other system open to unrestricted cabinet, party, and majority domination. It is not that the people were not good enough for Westminster; Westminster was, after all, a faulty model—an empty vessel, as it were, which could be filled with many different spirits.

It has already been suggested that the theory is a combination of Marx and Whigs. The Marxian side was given up: nonpolitical conditions for the stages of transfer were surrendered. The Whiggery cannot be sustained against either the actual early history or the very last stages of the later days. One may go beyond historical record in assessing the whole theory of preparation as the gradual, staged transfer of a model of government. Whether or not preparation had been adopted as a policy, one might consider how far it would even be valid as a theory of what might or should have occurred or now occur. This is in a way a more general question.

Five questions have to be put about the assumptions of the training or learning part of the theory. One is that it is precisely unlearning rather than learning that seems to be required. That has already been stressed in relation to the legislative council as a training ground for parliamentary government. It may have been a fault in a particular colonial record; more likely it is an inevitable fault in any preparatory process. The problem is not (as is often said) that people fail to learn the lesson, but on the contrary that the wrong lesson has been taught and then learned very well.[68] Secondly, the notion of learning is, anyway, much too simple a model for the process of culture contact involved in a valid preparatory situation. Many other responses than imitation or incorporation (themselves alternatives) are possible: rejection, transformation, retreat, manifesto, trance, and so forth.[69] Thirdly, the learning almost inevitably involves the wrong people: a selected, not an evolved, elite, who will be rejected by the leadership turnover of the independence process.[70] Fourthly, the learning process is very partial: one thinks in the British experience especially of the neglect of localization and the limited use of native authorities.[71] Fifthly, learning clearly does not at all describe the process of preparation in its culminating—tactical and autochthonous—stages. What is involved then is not a matter of embryology but of tactics plus a national restatement. When such embryology has been successful in the earliest colonies, it was not as a result of learning or deliberate transfer at all, as Madden has reminded us, but of the political desires of the British colonialists themselves.[72] Even there a thorough transfer was never achieved.

Preparation for a particular model had to be tied to a specific constitution, yet the original itself is highly contingent. It is certainly not necessary to stress that in general. Yet one or two aspects do need emphasis. The faults of the U.K. constitutional system itself are just those which were likely to be exacerbated by transfer. One could scarcely think of a less transferable system in one sense, or a more transferable system in the sense that quite other essences of government could be fitted into it. Jennings said, 'The process of adaptation to local circumstances is essential.'[73] No doubt. But the adaptation was not to be guided by those in charge of preparation. That was not what preparation came to mean, though the effort towards adaptation was made, in a very un-Westminster way, with judicial service commissions and the like. The local adaptations were likely to be peculiar. If, then, preparation did not really appear until very late in the day, it may also be said that it did not really occur then either. Transfer came to mean something quite different from a culmination of preparation for Westminster. Yet a consideration of the possible employment of any alternatives before transfer, including alternatives in organizational forms, was prevented. Now these may appear as the flaws of a particular record. The alternative is to regard them as almost inevitable concomitants of any such process. A consideration of the problem of administrative style would suggest that this is indeed the case.

The problem of bureaucracy needs as much emphasis as anything in the process of preparation and transfer. It receives the least, partly because of the concentration of the preparatory theory on constitutional points. Yet a special sort of bureaucracy is part of the contingency of the constitutional form. The creation of such a bureaucracy (itself a highly contingent thing) is inevitably difficult since it requires two different solutions. One is the creation by a nonministerial bureaucracy of a public service loyal to ministerial forms. The other is localization by an expatriate public service when localization challenges both the personal ambition and the public identifications of the expatriate bureaucracy—its standards, goals, tasks.

Other factors may worsen the problem: a late start, for example. The bureaucratic legacy of the British process had many features which aggravated the problem of a successful transfer: the social privilege of the service and especially of the administrator; his role in policy; his discretion; his relations with ministers, and his inexperience of neutrality or anonymity (the essential conditions for a ministerial public service of the Westminster type); his deep commitment to his own ideology,[74] an ideology quite unlike that proposed by a Bridges or a Bagehot; the salary gap; the place of the specialist. Such was the tradition which the people knew. Very late in the day, indeed, an attempt was made to impose quite a different model, though it was administration rather than constitutional forms which seemed to be continuous. Not surprisingly, the Tanganyika government quickly rejected the attempt to impose a delayed impartiality on the public service. There was no executive public service commission before 1962.[75] Such a commission was foreign to Westminster; it was not like the local tradition, nor probably was what was required or possible. The whole problem was exacerbated by the delayed and exaggerated form of Westminster bureaucracy which there was an attempt finally and probably unnecessarily to impose.[76]

Whatever the record, however, the bureaucratic problem must be profound. Further, there seems to be one inherent problem in the situation which makes Western bureaucracy an inappropriate model. It is not that the preparatory theory and the transfer and emergence processes are not of interest to Western public administration. They are of the greatest interest in relation to a whole series of questions, though great care is needed in comparisons, as in any discussion of corruption in the public service. What basically makes the model inappropriate is the necessary assumption for Western methods of what we might call 'compartmentalism'.

There are two central points about Western administration. One is that for the most part political responsibility can be total, though control is necessarily limited, because the bulk of administrative questions will have very limited ramifications, and a limited or a negative political significance. When questions do have such significance they will be referred up. The second is that administrative questions can be considered in a more or less rational way because all possible alternatives and consequences do not have to be considered, but only a few, only some: the rule of *ceteris paribus* is one of the greatest help and importance. Thus, both the responsibility and rationality of Western administration depend on the assumption that most questions have a limited significance and that where the limitations lie will be fairly obvious too. School building relates mainly to education and building, and so on. The nature of the assumption is essentially that the simulation involved in administrative decision-making—the metaphor used for the actual field—can be a process of simplification and elimination of a fairly radical kind. The condition of such simulation is extremely important and peculiar. It consists of a high degree of social stability, of a specialization of roles, and of a universalization of standards. Building a school will not revolutionize a community; the administrator is accepted as an administrator, whomsoever he is related to, wherever he lives, and so on; he is expected to act according to certain depersonalized universalistic or bureaucratic standards. These are the assumptions, and they are more or less valid. The assumptions can be relied on for the most part and most of the time without distress or disaster.

This can be put in other ways. For example, Dror has suggested (and Lindblom has accepted) that the notion that public decision-making can well proceed by a merely incremental process depends on conditions of social stability.[77] He specifies new states as an instance of the sort of situation where that sort of administration will not work. Incremental decision-making is an aspect of compartmentalized administrative behaviour and it is ruled out in certain conditions.

Indeed the whole point about the situation of administration in the new states is that total compartmentalism is not workable there. The British Guiana police administration may lay down the rule that five feet, eight inches, should be the minimum height for recruits; the question is not compartmentalized, however, because the rule either is or appears to be a way of recruiting Africans but not Indians. What is true of apparent administrative rules for police recruitment is clearly true of question after question in administration in such conditions. The presuppositions on which compartmentalism can operate—stability, specialization, and universalization—simply do not exist. Indeed we might go further and say that these presuppositions would be resisted; they would not be acceptable. There are requirements other than efficiency, or efficiency is suspect, just as there are demands other than incorruptibility. This was, perhaps, obvious to colonial administration itself, which did not compartmentalize questions (and could get away with not doing so, as a result of the discretion and prestige of the colonial administrator).

What follows? A depoliticized public service cannot be created. It is almost certainly the wrong model to use. Other problems in the concept of preparation as a transfer of a model have been indicated and are familiar. The particular problem of compartmentalism has been almost totally neglected.[78] Its implications are considerable. What is very likely is that to neglect and go against this difficulty will in the end lead either to a rejection of the Western method altogether or to an actual breakdown of the system. Yet at the very same time it has also to be recognized that to ask the West consciously to prepare not a neutral but a highly politicized public service may be to ask almost the impossible. We have not been good even at providing a consideration of alternative organizational forms to the hierarchy with which we are familiar. How then can we invent a sort of public service which will be relatively efficient and responsible and yet not compartmentalized at all? Yet if we cannot do just that, we cannot claim to be able to provide an effective preparatory process. This is a major, perhaps the major, conundrum of preparation.

Previous preparatory theory tended to misrepresent the British colonial record and to mislead us about what a preparatory process could be like. Alternative ideas may be worked out giving attention to matters ignored in the older theory. A great task for such a theory would be to answer this final conundrum. It will not be answered if it is ignored and goes unheard. An answer may depend on finding quite different conditions for relatively rational administration than those assumed by the compartmental style. The answer may depend on finding more appropriate models than those of the highly controlled bureaucracy of the settled societies. We need not assume that an answer will not be found. Indeed it may well be that in searching for the answer to this particular question we shall manage to escape at least in part from the pathology of the gap approach itself.

NOTES

1 Sidney Verba, reviewing Clifford Geertz, ed., *Old Societies and New States: A Quest for Modernity in Asia and Africa*, in *American Political Science Review*, LVIII (March 1964), 110. *cf.* Manfred Halpern, 'Toward Further Modernization of the Study of New Nations', *World Politics*, XVII (October 1964), 161.

2 Thomas Hodgkin, *Nationalism in Colonial Africa* (London 1936), 44.

3 Philip Mason, *The Men Who Ruled India* (London 1953, 1954); Sir Ralph Furse, *Aucuparius* (London 1962); Robert Heussler, *Yesterday's Rulers* (Syracuse 1963).

4 *The Official Mind of Indirect Rule: Tanganyika 1924-1939*, Institute of Commonwealth Studies (London 1964).

5 J. H. Kautsky, ed., *Political Change in Underdeveloped Countries* (New York 1962), 113; 'In this fashion, the industrialization sponsored by the totalitarianism of the intellectuals may yet, in the future, convert that system into one in which most of the groups of the new society have access to representation in the governmental decision-making process. . . .'

6 Mary Matossian, 'Ideologies of Delayed Industrialization', in Kautsky, 264: 'Democracy must be introduced into a country in two stages. In the first stage, a single "all-people's" party of the most "enlightened" and "progressive" elements of a nation takes over the government and acts as a faculty for educating the masses in democratic ways. At some time in the indefinite future, the masses will be ready for direct self-government and the "all-people's" party will "wither away" '—a nice combination of Marxism and attitudes borrowed from the colonial administration.

7 See Thomas Hovet, Jr., *Africa and the United Nations* (London 1963), and Conor Cruise O'Brien, 'Africa and the United Nations', *Voice of Africa*, III (12 December 1963), 13-16, for the impact on theories of international relations.

8 Brian Crozier, *The Morning After: A Study of Independence* (London 1963).

9 Elliot J. Berg, 'French West Africa', in W. Galenson, ed., *Labor and Economic Development* (New York 1959); D. I. Davies, 'The Politics of the T.U.C.'s Colonial Policy', *Policy Quarterly*, XXXV (January-

March 1964), 23-24; *cf.* also the comments on the inappropriateness of a Western concept like elites in P. Morton-Williams, 'A Discussion of the Theory of Elites in a West African (Yoruba) Context', West African Institute of Social and Economic Research, *Fourth Annual Conference, Proceedings* (Ibadan 1956), 25-32.

10 'The Underdeveloped Study of Political Development', *World Politics*, XVI (April 1964), 480-82.

11 Martin Wight, *British Colonial Constitutions* (Oxford 1952); Dennis Austin, *West Africa and the Commonwealth* (London 1957); A. J. Hanna, *European Rule in Africa* (London 1961); W. J. M. Mackenzie and K. E. Robinson, eds., *Five Elections in Africa* (Oxford 1960).

12 Representative government was conferred by the British government on Upper and Lower Canada in 1791. Imperial control was, however, firmly maintained. The result was fifty years of strife between the executive and the legislature. The rebellion of 1837 led to the sending out of Lord Durham as Governor-General, the radical Whig magnate. His report of 1839 is held to be the source of British responsible government overseas. A convenient abridged edition with notes, etc., is Reginald Coupland, *The Durham Report* (Oxford 1945).

13 W. Houston, ed., *Constitutional Documents of Canada* (Toronto 1891), 296.

14 Coupland, *Durham Report*.

15 Houston, 297.

16 Austin; Ceylon, *Report of the Special Commission on the Constitution* (Chairman: Lord Donoughmore), Cmd. 3131 (London 1928); Ceylon, *Report of the Commission on Constitutional Reform* (Chairman: Lord Soulbury), Cmd. 6677 (London 1945).

17 Austin; Wight.

18 See also *Report of the Commission of Enquiry into Disturbances in the Gold Coast, 1948* (Chairman: A. Watson), Colonial No. 231 (London 1948); *Report to the Governor by the Committee on Constitutional Reform, 1949* (Chairman: J. H. Coussey), Colonial No. 248 (London 1949).

19 S. A. de Smith, *The New Commonwealth and Its Constitutions* (London 1964); see also Wight.

20 'Institutional History of the Gold Coast-Ghana', in *What Are the Problems of Parliamentary Government in West Africa?*, Hansard Society (London 1958), 7.

21 See Wight; see also the Perham Series on Colonial Legislatures by Joan Wheare, Wight, and others.

22 de Smith, 'Westminster's Export Models: The Legal Framework of Responsible Government', *Journal of Commonwealth Political Studies*, 1 (November 1961), 2; H. V. Wiseman, *The Cabinet and the Commonwealth* (London 1958), 15; Uganda, *Report of the Constitutional Committee, 1959* (Chairman: J. V. Wild), (Entebbe 1959), 33; W. Ivor Jennings, *Democracy in Africa* (London 1963), chap. 3, esp. p. 33, for a short statement on the Westminster model.

23 *Origins and Purpose*, Central Office of Information for the Commonwealth Relations Office and the Colonial Office (London 1949), 146: 'Trusteeship has given place to Junior Partnership. But much remains to be done before the peoples of the colonies, now in different stages of political and economic development, are ready to take their places as citizens of mature, self-governing nations and our objective—co-partnership between equals—is attained. For many years to come the

peoples of the colonies must rely, to a greater or lesser degree, on outside help. It is our duty to see that this help is forthcoming.'

24 Mason: Furse; Jack Simmons, ed., *From Empire to Commonwealth* (London 1949).

25 K. C. Wheare, *Constitutional Structure of the Commonwealth* (Oxford 1960), chap. 4; K. E. Robinson, 'Constitutional Autochthony in Ghana', *Journal of Commonwealth Political Studies*, 1 (November 1961), 41; Sir Kenneth Roberts-Wray, 'The Authority of the United Kingdom in Dependent Territories', in J. M. D. Anderson, ed., *Changing Law in Developing Countries* (London 1963), 60-62; de Smith, 'Westminster's Export Models', 55 *ff*.

26 Lord Lugard, *The Dual Mandate in British Tropical Africa* (London 1922 and 1965), 26; cf. Mason, *The Birth of a Dilemma* (London 1958), 125. Sir George Goldie, with Sir William Mackinnon, was responsible for reviving the old system of Chartered Companies as a device for colonial development. His Royal Niger Company was chartered in July 1886.

27 Elspeth Huxley, *White Man's Country: Lord Delamere and the Making of Kenya*, 2 vols. (London 1935; new ed. 1953).

28 Sir Charles Jeffries, *The Colonial Office* (London 1956), 38.

29 Robinson, 'Colonial Issues and Policies with Special Reference to Tropical Africa', *The Annals*, vol. 298 (March 1955), 84.

30 Jeffries, quoting Cmd. 7433 (1948).

31 *Origins and Purpose*, 22 n.

32 Sir A. Bertram, *The Colonial Civil Service* (London 1930), 34.

33 Joan Wheare, *The Nigerian Legislative Council* (London 1950), 42.

34 Austin, 'Institutional History', esp. 9-10.

35 Lord Hailey, *Native Administration and Political Development in British Tropical Africa* (London 1942).

36 *Legislative Council Proceedings*, 6 December 1950, 1st meeting, 30th session, p. 7. cf. Sir Hugh Clifford in 1923 in Joan Wheare, *Nigerian Council*.

37 *Uganda Protectorate: Buganda*, Cmd. 9320 (London 1954).

38 The postwar emphasis on local government as the key to political development began with Creech Jones' February despatch: *Despatch to Governors of African Territories, 25 February 1947*. Was this an alternative to Westminster or a step forward from indirect rule? See R. E. Robinson, 'Why "Indirect Rule" has been replaced by "Local Government" in the nomenclature of British Native Administration', *Journal of African Administration*, 11 (July 1950), 12-15.

39 Reports on African local government produced by the African Studies Branch of the Colonial Office, *Journal of African Administration*, the Advisory Panel on Local Government in Africa, and special committees come very fast between 1949 and 1953, and cover especially the Gold Coast, Uganda, Tanganyika, Sierra Leone, Nigeria, East Africa, and East Nigeria.

40 David Apter, 'Some Problems of Local Government in Uganda', *Journal of African Administration*, XI (January 1959), 236 n. For early statements see Donald C. Cameron, *My Tanganyika Service and Some Nigeria* (London 1939), esp. 114-16; Margery Perham, *Summer School on Colonial Administration* (Oxford 1938), 105-6.

41 C. J. Bryant, *Some Problems of Public Administration in Uganda*, unpublished Ph.D. thesis, University of London (July 1963), 202.

42 Lucy P. Mair, 'Representative Local Government as a Problem of

Social Change', *Journal of African Administration*, x (January 1958), 1-24; Mackenzie and Robinson, *passim*.

43   Kenneth Kaunda, *Zambia Shall Be Free* (London 1962), 20-21.
44   C. A. G. Wallis, Colonial Office, African Studies Branch, *Report of an Inquiry into African Local Government in the Protectorate of Uganda* (Entebbe 1953), 15. On Buganda, see D. A. Low and R. C. Pratt, *Buganda and British Overrule* (London 1960).
45   Bryant, 210.
46   Furse, 233-44; Jeffries, 63.
47   *Final Report of the Standing Committee on the Recruitment, Training and Promotion of Africans for Admission to the Higher Posts in the Civil Service* (Entebbe 1955), 4.
48   Harold J. Laski, 'The Colonial Civil Service', *Political Quarterly*, x (October-December 1958), 543.
49   Obafemi Awolowo, *The Path to Nigerian Freedom* (London 1947).
50   Perham, 'A Restatement of Indirect Rule', *Africa*, vii (July 1934), 21.
51   *Native Policies in Africa* (London 1936), 12-13: 'The element in the indirect rule policy from which it takes its name is the maintenance in their position of the authorities recognised by the native population, as the basis of development of native administration fitted to perform the functions of a modern government.'
52   (Cambridge 1936).
53   *Alur Society* (London 1956), 307. See also A. I. Richards, ed., *East African Chiefs* (London 1960).
54   Wiseman, 79.
55   'The Impact of British Education on the Indigenous Peoples of Overseas Territories', *Colonial Review* (December 1956), 232.
56   *An African Survey* (London 1956), 359.
57   'Administrative and Departmental Staff—Coordination of Works', *Journal of African Administration*, vii (April 1955), 75.
58   W. Ivor Jennings and H. W. Tambiah, *Development of the Laws and Constitution of Ceylon* (London 1952); Lennox Mills, *Ceylon Under British Rule* (London 1933); Leonard Woolf, *Diaries in Ceylon 1908-11* (London 1963), esp. the introduction by Saparamadu and Mervyn de Silva.
59   C. H. Stigand, *Administration in Tropical Africa up to 1914* (London 1914), 60; Woolf, xxii.
60   *Ibid.*, xix.
61   *Ibid.*, xxii.
62   *Ibid.*; N. Mansergh, *The Commonwealth and the Nations* (London 1948).
63   *Report on Indian Constitutional Reforms*, Cd. 9109 (London 1918).
64   *Report of the Indian Statutory Commission*, Cmd. 3569 (London 1930).
65   Huxley and Perham, *Race and Politics* (London 1956), 10-11. One must temper one's judgment of F. D. Lugard. He surrendered the notion of administrative separation for Kenya by the 1940s (p. 12). Further, on returning to Nigeria in 1912 he had been upset by and was opposed to the extent to which indirect rule had spread in North Nigeria in 1906-11. He was in favour of more direct ruling', despite his fiscal memorandum and his dual mandate'. He was in favour also, for example, of direct taxation. See M. Bull in K. E. Robinson and F. Madden, eds., *Essays in Imperial Government* (Oxford 1963), 47.
66   *An African Survey*.
67   Austin, 'Institutional History', 81.

68 G. F. Engholm, *The Uganda National Assembly*, Institute of Commonwealth Studies (London, November 1963).

69 Margaret Mead, *New Lives for Old* (London 1956), 16.

70 Perham, *The Colonial Reckoning* (London 1962); K. Nkrumah, *The Autobiography of Kwame Nkrumah* (Edinburgh 1957).

71 Hailey, *Native Administration in the British African Territories*, IV (London 1951), 29 *ff*.

72 Madden in Robinson and Madden, *Essays*, 20: 'The superficial acceptance of the notion of the common form of government which developed in royal proprietary and corporate colonies is therefore misleading if it comes to the conclusion that it derived from any desire to export the Westminster model. The instruments of government which were devised by the Crown and its advisers were based on feudal and mercantile origins in palatinate or corporation. Perhaps it has relevance to the experience of parliamentary democracy among non-British people, to emphasise that it was the political ethos of Britons in exile which moulded the makeshift institutions they received into a likeness to the British. But there was no exact identity.'

73 Jennings and Tambiah, *op. cit.*, p. 42.

74 Hailey, *Native Administration and Political Development*, 44: 'The experience elsewhere shows the strength of the influence which a conception of this character can exercise in the day to day policy of administration. It tends almost insensibly to shape its institutions to conform with the final development indicated, even though it may at the moment appear to represent an ideal whose fulfilment must be left for the distant future.'

75 *Proposals for the Tanganyika Government for a Republic*, Government Paper No. 1 (Dar es Salaam 1962); J. Nyerere, Tanganyika African National Conference, 14 January 1963, in *African Digest* (April 1963), 161.

76 Robinson, reported in *What Are the Problems of Parliamentary Government?*, 95.

77 Y. Dror, 'Muddling Through—"Science" or Inertia', *Public Administration Review*, xxiv (September 1964), 154; C. Lindblom, 'Contexts for Change and Strategy: A Reply', *ibid.*, 157.

78 Two brief discussions might be referred to, both noted after the material of this article was first presented. R. A. Packenham, in 'Approaches to the Study of Political Development', *World Politics*, xvii (October 1964), 115, has suggested that the relationships in developing societies (so different from those assumed by F. W. Taylor and described here as the conditions of compartmentalism) may be studied by organization theorists to discover what sort of contribution they can make to organizational effectiveness. Secondly, V. A. Thompson, in 'Objectives for Development Administration', *Administrative Science Quarterly*, ix (July 1964), 108, has written about the limiting conditions and irrelevance for new states of what he calls 'control-oriented administration' in a way very similar to what has been said here about compartmentalism, and has indicated the outlines of a possible alternative, most helpfully.

12

ADVISING ABOUT DEVELOPMENT

THE EXAMPLE OF THE WORLD BANK REPORT
ON PAPUA AND NEW GUINEA

In 1964 the International Bank for Reconstruction and Development reported on the economic development of Papua and New Guinea. Save for the mandatory reports of the missions of the Trusteeship Council on New Guinea, the World Bank report was one of the first major international incursions into this enclave of Australian colonial policy; an extreme example of the bureaucratic colonial polity. It was also an example of the visiting mission, that major instrument of development policies through this decade. The confrontation of the mission and the polity provided an intriguing occasion. The paper suggests that the politics of the situation made the mission a defective factor.

It has been suggested that Papua-New Guinea is especially interesting for development economics.[1] Certainly there are striking features. One example is the dominant role of public expenditure: gross domestic product in 1962-3 was probably £A55 million; export income £A16 million; public expenditure £A35 million, more than two thirds of it an Australian Government subsidy (71 per cent in fact). A further peculiarity may be mentioned. Until about 1962 Australian policy for the territory was explicitly committed to the notion of 'equal development'. That meant three things: spreading development equally but slowly, as against concentrating on rapid development of a few peaks; emphasizing the infrastructure (primary education, local councils, agriculture) rather than national political centres; and an attempt to exclude world influences. Since then policy has changed.

One sign of the change was the new House of Assembly, elected in 1964. Another sign was the invitation to the International Bank for Reconstruction and Development to report. The Bank's team finished their work in September 1964; the Report was released in December of that year. It contains a great weight of detail which, it is not unfair to say, is either description of the situation as it is already changing or application of a general attitude. The general attitude may be indicated by the major conclusions and recommendations. These are:

1. The Report believed that the major obstacle facing the Territory was a shortage of skilled manpower, and that that shortage could best be met by migration from Australia.
2. Government policy should concentrate on stimulating cash production for export in crops, livestock and forestry, livestock being a quite new field. That would mean relying on Australian plantations in copra, coffee, cocoa, and rubber; new crops like tea and pyrethrum; a new export meat industry from Australian management of breeding herds; and big new leasings of forestry to overseas interests (which has already occurred).
3. Indigenous advance would mean more participation in production and education; in particular, primary educational expansion would mean 'making the full course available in existing schools rather than ... broadening the base by the establishment of new schools'.
4. The role of the Administration in industrial expansion was to be the formulation of policies conducive to investment and to ... providing information for investors'.
5. Tourism should be promoted.
6. A development finance corporation should be set up as an autonomous government institution.
7. There should be some major changes in the pattern of government expenditure: e.g. less for housing and curative health programmes.
8. Australian government financial assistance shou'd continue and grow. Roughly we might say that without the Report, and increasing at its usual rate, this assistance would have averaged, 1964-9, £A46 million per annum, and on the Report's programme £A50 to 52 million.
9. Changes in policy as a whole should be based on certain principles of concentration, appropriate standards, and reducing paternalism.

The Report[2] is of general interest in a number of ways. It is the first major outside investigation of this exceptional territory. It represents a characteristic exercise in an exclusively technical enquiry which, though predominantly economic, would, in so far as its recommendations are influential, affect policy as a whole. A study of the implementation of the Report, though not the main concern of this article, would nevertheless show the peculiar susceptibility of this sort of Administration to this sort of document. In any case the Report is in general an example of the big outside enquiry as a device in policy-making. In particular it is an example of the 'economistic' approach to development and as such is of prime interest to this article and relevant to problems of policy making in developing societies.[3] One aim of the article is therefore to see the results of that sort of device in general and its particular consequences in this instance. A second aim is to say something about the implications of the critique.

The approach adopted by the Report accentuates the characteristics of the outside and ostensibly economic consideration of development as a basis for policy. This raises three problems: the question of strategy, or terms of reference; the tendency to use statements of preference as general principles; and the disguise of particular doctrines as objective wisdom so as to ignore either the political effects of recommendations or the political presuppositions on which specific recommendations are in fact based.

First as to strategy: the principle difficulty here was the contrast between the need to be inclusive and sensitive, and the actual situation of the World Bank team, which was not provided with clear terms of reference by the Australian Government and was committed to a specific approach by its own background, predilections, and membership (dominated by its trans-Atlantic, economist, and Bank staff members). There were several possible terms of reference: e.g., to increase the standard of living; to achieve an economy which could 'stand on its own feet' as a condition for self-government, or for other reasons, and/or to do so as soon as possible; to achieve a more rapid rate of economic growth; to lay down a five-year plan; to achieve economic viability, apart from any term of time, independence, or standard of living; or, possibly, modernization itself. Two things actually happened. The report never makes it clear that the possible considerations were different and in many cases opposed. For example, economic viability is not necessarily a pre-condition for independence and in any case, as the report admits,[4] not a possible fact for Papua even by the 1980s. The report submerges the problem of choice and the choices it is making. Specifically, the demand for viability and the demand for speedier growth are precisely opposite, since more speed means more dependence.

The report mentions a variety of considerations. 'The basic objective of the Mission' was 'to make recommendations to assist the Australian Government in planning a development programme designed to expand and stimulate the economy and *thereby raise the standard of living of the people*'.[5] Further, when self-government is achieved, which, it is assumed, should be as soon as possible, the Territory should 'to the greatest extent feasible, be able to stand on its own feet economically'.[6] Nevertheless the report actually commits itself to one particular aim, different from these: over a five year period, and assuming Australian government assistance growing at 10 per cent per annum, to increase the rapidity of what has been, recently, an already rapid rate of economic growth.

Having then made, though as obscurely as possible, that determination of objectives (in the circumstances a striking and peculiar one), the Report goes on to develop the strategy in terms of 'principles' and 'conditions', or guidelines and types of action. The principles are, firstly,[7] a concentration of effort: 'To obtain the maximum benefit from the development effort, expenditures and manpower should be concentrated in areas and on activities where the prospective return is highest.' The idea of concentration is applied particularly to agricultural development, especially in terms of areas; to health, especially in terms of a cutback in hospital-building and curative work; to general administration; and to education, especially in relation to primary education. Secondly, at any rate one of the consequences of dependence on external government assistance as the major developmental factor is to be eradicated as far as possible: 'The standards of administration services and facilities should be related to Territory conditions.' The idea of using standards appropriate to the Territory is applied particularly to salaries, public works, and questions of design and materials. Thirdly, there should be a fostering of responsibility. Here again we are to see an effort to eradicate the consequences of a reliance on external governmental assistance and the local administration. There is to be a move away from 'benevolent paternalism'. What we should see 'as a modern economy emerges and as increasing numbers of indigenous people acquire education and a greater understanding of the modern world' is 'a shift in emphasis towards policies giving greater responsibilities to the people'.

The problem of the use of general principles can be looked at in any of these instances. Thus, the notion of fostering responsibility and moving away from benevolent paternalism obviously has a lot to recommend it. The only way of breaking paternalism altogether is, of course, to move to self-government and, indeed, independence. If the achievement of self-government is the only way by which in fact a fostering of responsibility can be secured, and as long as that achievement is delayed, there will be conflicts between a fostering of responsibility and other types of policy which will in the meantime be pursued. Such conflicts are to be seen very clearly in a whole series of Report recommendations.

Furthermore, there is more than one way of interpreting the notion of a fostering of responsibility and a movement away from benevolent paternalism. For example, the encouragement the Report gives to native local government councils and to a movement towards payment in full by cash wages is welcome. Each may have a relationship to responsibility, but in different spheres and very different senses: political and individual. The Report is deeply committed to the doctrine of economic charges for services in place of subsidized or free services. This may also be called anti-paternalistic, but again in quite another sense.

Where the Report recommends the implementation of the latter doctrine in detail, it is not necessary to assume that the recommendations are progressive. A movement away from free or subsidized services in the medical field, for example, is not necessarily modernization at all. It is characteristic of welfare policies in developed states that they have attempted to secure, precisely, on the one hand income guarantees and on the other hand free or subsidized services in kind in a range of social fields, particularly health services. The notions of external economies and diseconomies, the economies of scale and of social costs and profits, have long been the basis of theories of welfare economics. This has developed from its early eloquent statement by the Fabians—like Bernard Shaw in his *Common Sense of Municipal Trading* at the beginning of the century—on to the very advanced notions of cost-benefit ratios in present planning techniques. The Report tends either to ignore this or to give a very simple discussion indeed of social costs.[8]

Then there is a severe contradiction between the demands of responsibility and the type of role which the Report feels itself bound to give the European, and particularly the European settler, as a factor in rapid economic development towards economic viability. At this point we see a basic flaw in the Report's methods: it appears to deduce economic recommendations from acceptable principles when it is actually stating dogmas of economic policy which in any case cannot be considered outside of their socio-political implications; the problem of choice and conflict is avoided. This can be seen clearly in three fields. On the basis of certain criteria of land and markets, the Report argues for an expansion of cocoa, rubber, and copra and possibly for tea and pyrethrum, an expansion in forestry and the build-up of a beef cattle industry. In most of these cases, the role of European enterprise is to be exclusive or predominant. There are, then, to be more European settlers, more European agriculture, more European farmers, in the interests of expansion in general, especially in fields like cattle and tea, and for demonstration. The administration is to continue to lease land to Europeans; Europeans should also be able to lease land directly[9]—a recommendation which could well lead to chaos and is typical of what can only be called a sociological brashness.

Here clearly we see a complete contradiction with the notion of fostering local responsibility, and here also we see the influence of the notion of economic growth as a thorough contrast with notions which would be suggested if there was a greater emphasis on political development itself. Papua-New Guinea is up to this point a territory with a relatively restricted number of settlers and therefore a relatively restricted settler problem. There is no doubt that in general the presence of settlers has created about the most severe, and in some ways the most heart-rending, of all problems in those phases of political development up to the achievement of independence.[10]

The Report's terms of reference lead consistently to an over-emphasis on the European role. One of the bases for this is seen very clearly early in the Report: 'The mobilization of unskilled indigenous labour for development should not be difficult; ... the *mobilization* of capital and managerial, administrative, professional and technical skills', which will come from the Europeans, 'will be much more difficult.'[11] Admittedly the Report says it will come in a gradually decreasing scale. But it is quite clear from the figures the Report gives that the emphasis on economic viability will prevent any diminishing, at any rate for several years, and as long as its particular strategy is followed. Now, apart from our questioning of the strategy itself, we may say at once that the notion that the mobilization of indigenous labour is not difficult would only be true on a purely economic and statistical valuation. The recruitment of indigenous labour has technical difficulties and political-social implications. Furthermore, the presentation of the problem in this way enables one to assume that all European recruitment and all the European role is of skill and capital, and that, as the Report elsewhere admits, is by no means the case.

There are other confusions embedded in the Report's evaluation of the European role. The Report says that the education and training of indigenous people to take over a top role 'cannot be accomplished in just a few years'. In fact it must be. In any case it is very important to make a distinction between the several types of European contribution which the Report tends to confuse and identify. A need for a European farmer for demonstration purposes is not the same as a need for a European farmer for other purposes, and the needs, in any case, for these types of skill are not the same as the needs for other types of European contribution. Not merely are the needs distinct, the political and social implications in each case are also distinct. It is only by distinguishing them that we can evaluate each and decide how much of each we can in fact, politically and socially speaking, afford.

Again, the Report argues that the Administration is to provide a policy framework within which a European contribution can continue to occur. It gives nothing like a clear analysis and evaluation of the different sectors of policy. We may distingush at least between:

(a) fiscal, taxation and budgetary policies;
(b) positive assistance;
(c) internal administration; and
(d) national security.

As far as the first is concerned, the Report indicates that it would support types of fiscal policy which would continue to encourage European enterprise: particularly maintaining a very low rate of income tax on the European sector. It also applies to the development of a tariff policy, at least up to that point at which it would be a challenge to the Australian economy and therefore to Australian domestic politics themselves. As far as the second point is concerned, we may distinguish between Australian assistance for Territory development in general, government provision of funds as a sort of guarantee to European investment, and direct assistance to Europeans as in the ex-servicemen's credit scheme in the past. Thirdly, different patterns of internal administration are likely either to act as an incentive or a disincentive to European participation. Thus the development of directly elected urban local governments on a universal suffrage could be interpreted as a potential disincentive. Finally, the Australian commitment to defend Papua-New Guinea as a whole is, of course, a necessary pre-condition for the European presence.

Now some of these policies would be required in any case, and some of them in fact can work directly in favour both of the European presence and of indigenous development. A good example would be such defence expenditure as assists both security and economic development, like road-building. However, at many points any assessment of policy must differ according to preferences for an encouragement, a stabilization, or a reduction of European participation.

Lessons from elsewhere would suggest that the question ought to be treated as of severe importance. It cannot, however, be quite as important as the whole question of indigenous response and participation. The apparently straightforward attitude of the Report is that participation and responsibility ought to be encouraged right across the board. But in fact it is not the same thing to recommend greater functions for native local government councils, cash wages, economic charges for services and indigenous participation in credit, and so forth. These may be good and necessary. The difficulty is partly that some of them will conflict with other requirements of the Report, and some of them may be either less necessary or more complicated than the Report seems to indicate. What ought to be treated as an extraordinarily complicated and sensitive matter is treated as though it was relatively straightforward, to be handled with simple techniques and structural recommendations.

The fact is that the implementation of the Report's recommendations, taken as a whole, will make an enormous difference to the social stratification of New Guinea society. There will be an increased number of cash farmers, subject to a great variety of land systems. Some will be smallholders in peasant, family-based farming; others may themselves be employers. There will be some development of industrial work. There will be a development of urban services. There will be office employment at clerical, administrative, technical, and professional levels. There will be indigenous people using credit as entrepreneurs. Some of the credit may come on a long-term basis, or as special risk money from the Development Finance Company, and some in other ways.

These changes will be provoked particularly by education, by the introduction of cash wages and by changes in land tenure systems. They are themselves going to provoke the appearance of new types of social structures like labour organizations. They will demand an acceptance of role differentiation and specialization on the one hand, and of universalistic and rational standards of performance and role fulfilment on the other hand. One conclusion about the methods of this sort of Report is that it fails to consider such questions as the implications of enhancing the European role in the private sector, and that it does to some extent confuse the assessment of policy. A second conclusion is that the dimensions of the indigenous response are not considered at all.

The third field in which political implications may be considered is that of planning and public enterprise. The Report gives[12] a succinct description of the existing arrangements and asks for a commitment to five-year development plans, the appointment of an economic adviser and a staff of (apparently) two other persons, an amendment of the Central Planning Committee, and certain other developments. The techniques are to be simple. A distinction is to be made between the long and the short views.

What is implied here? Apparently we have a modest but firm and clear-headed recommendation for planning arrangements. It is, of course, obvious—though perhaps not fair to say—that much more detail is really required. It is all very well, for example, to

recommend that 'the planning committee should prepare a statement of development criteria',[13] but what ought those criteria to
be? Little guidance is given. It is not clear whether the Report
perceives the enormous significance which the introduction of an
effective planning arrangement is likely to have for the society but
wishes to disguise or diminish it; or whether, on the other hand,
it does not itself realize how significant it will be. Let us, for
example, suppose that the Report, if implemented, is successful
in achieving what it wishes to achieve, namely, a rapid expansion
in the scale of the New Guinea economy and the private sector
within that economy. As the private sector grows, it will presumably
be insufficient for the planning arrangements to abide simply by
'guides' for the private sector if the plan is to be sure of achievement. Nothing about the controls to secure the achievement of
the plan is, however, discussed.

There are, fairly obviously, a large number of sheer organizational questions to be discussed here. The Report is specific about
some of them. Where it is much less helpful is in assessing the
political and administrative implications for Papua-New Guinea of
its general commitment to planning and of the lessons of that sort
of commitment in other developing societies. Suppose, for example,
that the starting point for the quinquennial plan is the desire to
achieve a faster approach towards the take-off point. The marginal
rate of saving may have to go up to 15, 25 or even 40 per cent.
It is quite obvious that whatever plan is drawn on the basis of
that sort of rate, it will fall by the wayside unless the strains of
securing such a rate can be met. These may involve strains for
political democracy. They may involve the temporary maintenance
of standards of poverty and inequality which would be difficult
to accept. They may also involve enormously increased rates of
external assistance. The problems will initiate tremendous internal
pressures. The actual techniques of information, priority, and delegation are by no means simple to achieve. Uncertainty will always
remain. The planning mechanism will certainly not succeed without quite exceptional measures of political support, based on
political strength.[14]

In the case of the European role, the indigenous response, and
the introduction of planning, the fault of the method may be to
obscure the implications which need to be assessed in the context
of the very recommendations themselves. In the case of the introduction of economic charging, the fault is slightly different: it
may be the disguise of a preferred dogma as a technical deduction.
The presence of such disguised preferences is to be seen also, and
significantly, in the attitude of this Report to public enterprise.

Public enterprise is apparently to play no role in meeting the problem of industrialization. The role of government will be restricted to information and to policies which will help the private sector in taxation, tariff, land, and credit and in the provision of an infrastructure, as far as possible at economic rates. New experiments, like the Department of Transport, are specifically not to be operational. Though the market for forestry is good and forest land amply available, though the major problem[15] in developing this industry is in fact industrial organization, and though the only type of indigenous participation actually to occur is to be cash wage employment, nevertheless here, too, there is to be no expansion of public enterprise. Yet forestry is, after all, a peculiarly suitable field. Again, though the first priority in transport is to be given to the Development of Coastal Shipping, there is to be no public role there either.[16] Even in relation to the recommended Development Finance Company there is a vagueness about whether the status is to be private or governmental.

When we come to questions of administration and organization we see a rather different sort of problem, not the disguise of preferences and only in part the blindness to other demands and implications, but something else. In general one can, presumably, infer a support for localization of personnel, but there is no sense of immediacy about this and little is said. The Report supports what is being done in the Administrative College, but it does not—as we have already commented—perceive the urgency of high level localization. Certainly the Report does not quite understand how radical some of its recommendations would appear to be in an administration based on Australian practices, as when it says of the Department of Agriculture, 'The existing structure does not differentiate sufficiently between professional, sub-professional, intermediary, and support categories'.

The major problem is endemic to the big outside enquiry: No one could fail to give a welcome to recommendations asking for more authority for districts, decentralization, co-ordination, and closer relationship between extension and research. Here, however, the vital details are missing. The Report is at times, in its discussion of administration, rather like the presidential candidate who said he was standing against sin. This is quite especially true in relation to urgent problems like the role of the districts in planning and the relationship between agricultural research and agricultural extension. It would be impossible to extract from the Report any details about how these two long-sought ends are to be achieved. There is a sense in which the Report is blind to implications here, too.

Characteristically of its type of approach, its perceptions fail in three ways. In the first place, the Report has nothing at all to say about the problem of 'dispersal'. In any national organization, whatever pattern of subdivision is used, there is a problem of communication. As Robb and Riggs have pointed out:[17] 'This problem is particularly marked when functional differentiation is combined with a high degree of centralization in the organization responsible for each function and a considerable subdivision of each functional organization on a geographical basis without any real delegation of authority'. This could be an explicit description of the pattern in Papua-New Guinea. The problem, according to Riggs, is 'an inherent weakness' of administration in Industria—that is in modern industrial type society. Indeed, he describes it as 'the critical political and administrative problem' of such a system. It is unfortunate to find the problems of industrialization in such a particularly agrarian society: that is the worst of both worlds. Yet it is evident that there is such a problem.

Second, the Report does not go out of its way to anticipate or make recommendations about the administrative problems which we can be sure are about to emerge from its own recommendations: particularly, the control of public corporations, the relationship between central departments and developing local authorities, and the relationship between *ad hoc* authorities, like an urban housing authority, and local government, like urban local government councils. Nor does the Report in fact go out of its way at all to recommend any experiment with organizational forms. In fact some public corporations will appear, like the Harbours Board; others could appear, like the Development Finance Company and the Housing Authority. Many authorities have commented on the difficulty of the question of public corporations in economic development.[18] The Report has nothing to say about that or about the overall problems of the machinery of government. The machinery of government is indubitably about to become much more sophisticated. That can very clearly be seen in the planning function, with relationships between the staff, committee, and political levels, and between the planning, budgetary, statistical, and departmental statistical functions. Planning has to be planned and the government has to be organized. This is certainly a continuing, not an occasional, function, and disaster is likely to face Papua-New Guinea unless the problem is tackled. The fact that localization is to occur, and at a rapid rate, makes the problem all the more urgent. Similarly, what it has to say about local government councils is either generalized and benevolent on the one hand, or particular and occasional on the other, and the Report does not seem to be aware of the total impact of its recommendations when they are brought together.

In the third place, the major weakness of the Report here is its total failure to consider the need for new types of administrative technique for undertaking development in dependent societies. Hitherto we have tended to proceed on the assumption that the domestic model should either be transferred holus-bolus to the dependent society, or should at any rate be used as a guide for it. Now that, of course, has been subject to severe criticism. For one thing it is based on the notion that there is a gap to be filled between the good (that is to say, the domestic model) and the deficient (that is to say, the local). That has been criticised as a pathological approach.[19] Secondly, it is obvious that any particular model is socially contingent and it is simple-minded to assume that it can be transferred. Thirdly, the model itself might not be liked either by local administrators or by local people. It might not be understood and it might be deficient in itself.[20]

Over and above these problems, the methods of Western administration are based on a set of assumptions which can be called 'compartmentalism'.[21] Administrative questions can be handled in developed and relatively stable societies on the assumption that they are pretty separate from other questions and that the political implications, when they have any, will be fairly easily apparent. They can be handled, that is to say, in a discrete and therefore in a more or less rational fashion. But, it can be argued, the conditions for compartmentalism are exclusive and not present in the developing society. A question of building a school, say, or altering the standards for police recruitment, cannot be abstracted in developing as they can in stable conditions.

We therefore need a different model and a different style from the Western guides which are normally employed. As Thompson argues, 'Control-oriented administration assumes stability-fixed conditions, goals, and resources. The administrative problem appears as the maximum allocation of these extra resources. This model is a poor analogue for development administration'. It is not from the normal but from the crisis situations that we can draw lessons, if from anywhere in the West, for development administration. There will be ambiguity of authority, status, and jurisdiction. Personnel assignments will be somewhat indefinite; communications uncontrolled; groups will take decisions. Morale and excitement may be high and the administration will be oriented towards particular schemes rather than general programmes or normal allocations. This is the situation in a crisis; control comes later.[22] Yet, at the same time, in developing societies, the very shortage of resources makes any lack of control actually all the more dangerous. Thus what may be required is a doubly new approach. For example, we could consider replacing the settled department and the separation of politics and administration with politically highly sensitive project units. In any case it is vividly clear that problem after problem central to the actual matter of the Report—the relation of planning to action, or the district to the centre—or participation, information, and consensus, or hierarchy and professionalism—can only be solved if we can find a fresh approach to development administration: if we can escape from the compartmental model without falling into chaos. About all this the Report seems totally unaware. At any rate there is a severe problem here. It is a problem to which the Report gives absolutely no attention.

In many ways the problem is not how far the Report goes but its apparent unawareness or pretence about where it is going. This is true within its economic recommendations themselves. They are dependent in the first place on a maximum use of European settlers. Second there is to be a large indigenous movement from subsistence to a small-holding peasant economy in tropical cash products. What is noticeable is the Report's restriction of recommendations about subsistence improvement to secondary measures; its failure to recognize the dangers of relying on tropical commodities as the exclusive basis for development; its failure to deal with the need for some industrialization; its somewhat pathetic emphasis on tourism. Tourism for most countries is an exaggerated factor. Where it is a large factor, it is a multilateral rather than nett unit. Of itself, it has extremely sensitive political and social consequences which it would be a criminal folly to ignore when a radical development is recommended. It may be the cautious attitude of the Report to public enterprise and to pricing policy which leads to this caution about industrialization as a whole. Yet surely it is, to say the least, regrettable. This is particularly true when one perceives that the Report admits severe agricultural problems: the need for an improvement in subsistence agriculture; the structural weaknesses of the indigenous Highland coffee industry; the world market problems for most tropical products; and the exclusion, or virtual exclusion of products where the Territory would be competitive with Australia, like sugar and peanuts.

Thus the economic policy is incomplete as economics and unwise as politics: the methods of the Report reflect a bias (e.g. about the European private enterprise role), a blindness about implications, and a caution about following arguments through. Thus the problems of the co-operative movement are largely ignored, important as they are to indigenous development. The argument about tariff policy is left short.

In the discussion of education, too, the flaws are clear. Recommendations become questionable as soon as political and social criteria are applied to them. This is especially the case with the plan in which all future primary teachers are likely to be indigenous and for some time all secondary teachers European,[23] and in which, for the time being at any rate, the only universal education to be attempted will be primary.[24] The notion of concentrating rather than continuing to spread primary education, provided it went with a radical, ambitious, and even risk-taking series of measures to build up secondary and higher education, would be sensible.[25] Here the Report seems to be arguing something that is politically well advised. But it only argues part of it and does not seem to be aware of the significance of what it is saying. It has recently been demonstrated by Austin[26] that it is in educational policy especially that we have to look for the reasons for the failure of the particularly well-prepared and hopeful Gold Coast experiment. Up to the 1948 riots in the Gold Coast, it would have been looked to as the most promising example of the preparatory process in the British colonial experience. Then came the 1948 riots; the speedy growth of the radical nationalist Convention People's Party after 1949; the failure of the two-party system after 1954; and the events since 1960. How did such a preparation fail so abysmally? The answer lies in the peculiar nationalism of what Austin refers to as the rise of the elementary school leavers. By 1948 about half the children of primary school age were at school in what was then the Gold Coast. The education was, however, severely limited. Qualifications gained by primary school leavers were minimal. The class differentiation that occurred was severe and pathological. The attitude of commoners and 'youngmen' to the native authorities and to the leadership of earlier and moderate political forces was irate in the extreme. The fact is that if we compare what were the Gold Coast educational figures, or pyramid, with those applying to Papua-New Guinea now, we see a very close approximation:

GOLD COAST, December 1948

Infant junior, standards 1-3	237,026
Senior primary standards 4-7	49,662
Total	286,688
Secondary	6,490
Teacher training	457

PAPUA-NEW GUINEA, 1963

Preparatory first and second primary grades	106,740
Primary grades 3-6	43,612
Secondary	3,800

While the higher primary figures are better in percentage terms in Papua-New Guinea than they were in the Gold Coast, the secondary figures are worse, particularly since they are concentrated in the lower secondary classes. In secondary sixth grade, the number was 14, fifth grade 5, and fourth grade 77.[27] The secondary growth has been very recent indeed and it consists of many varied patterns in six year schools, three to four year schools up to intermediate level, technical schools and a secondary agricultural school. The Report goes so far as to desire a concentration rather than a further spread of the primary effort: this is meant as an example of its principle of concentration. What it does not perceive is the necessity for a rather different policy. If we are to gain any lessons from the Ghana experience, what we need is a great variety of quite radical measures to push the maximum number of existing primary children through secondary education.

The methods used by the Report are defective, for example in ignoring the indigenous response. This is easy to demonstrate; difficult to remedy. If recent work on development amounts to anything it ought to help in providing some better alternative. Deutsch's work may be a starting point.[28] Doubtless it is very difficult to develop projections. As we have indicated, the merely pathological gap or requisites approach, the mere use of Western models and comparisons as guidelines, is likely to be inadequate at the best, and severely misleading at the worst. Even non-Western comparisons are difficult to apply.[29] Nevertheless we may well try to develop projections along Deutsch's lines. That is, economic change must mean exposure to machinery, buildings, consumer goods, mass media, residential changes, urbanization, change in occupation, growth in literacy, growth in per capita income.[30] Accordingly, social mobilization is likely to occur. By social mobilization Deutsch means 'the process in which major clusters of old social, economic and psychological commitments are eroded and broken and people become available for new patterns of socialization and behaviour'. Accordingly one hypothesis will be that developmental policy ought to consider the sorts of mobilization which are in fact likely.

Further, the actual difficulty of comparisons is no reason either for ignoring the criterion or for replacing it by a reliance on *a priori* preferences for concentration, appropriate standards, or responsibility, interpreted as you will. To take some key recommendations in this Report purporting to embody respectively the principle of standards and the principle of concentration: all comparative experience would suggest that a division of teachers into primary indigenous and secondary European groups, or a maintenance of the division between five-year trained assistant medical officers on the one hand and European doctors on the other is likely in the end to be politically difficult and troublesome. The Congolese experience is certainly a good case in point. It is all very well to concentrate agricultural development on what is called the most promising and developed areas,[31] but what, apart from the question of acceptability, is going to be the criterion of most promising? 'Most promising' and 'most developed' are not necessarily at all the same thing. This depends entirely on the details of response and on ways of anticipating response. This applies also to such recommended measures as maintaining a light European load in income tax, while developing graduated personal and council taxes along the African model.[32]

In any case there are general hypotheses (e.g. about the limitations of a tropical peasant economy) which ought to be applied to specific recommendations. Thirdly, where development advice touches on non-economic processes, like administration, it needs to consider them fully, not tangentially. Fourthly, the inevitability of implications and the likelihood of non-technical preferences in any economic recommendation must both be recognized. Partly, then, we are faced with a team problem: the sort of expertnesses required; and partly with a problem of responsibility.

Taking the problem of development advice as a whole we may say that in the first place it faces us with paradox: e.g. that comparative lessons are warnings rather than invitations; or that 'purely economic' advice is dangerous precisely because the prestige of the purely economic tends to usher in highly specific political preferences. Secondly, the actual implications will concern cultural, structural, and institutional categories. As Eisenstadt puts it,[33] there will be demands in three sectors. These are:

(1) an ideological transformation;
(2) an initiation of a modern political framework; and
(3) specific systems of social stratification.

Without meeting these demands, even if emphasis is to be given to purely economic criteria like the development of economic viability or even a higher standard of living, growth will not occur, save, if at all, at severe costs for social and civil life.

There will be variation as to where the pressure is felt. In some instances, the key demand will be for suffrage, for independence, for a secularization of culture; in others, the economic question or the organizational question may be dominant. During the process conflict is inevitable. The key question is to know how it will be contained. The problem is to develop in institutional, elite, and ideological sectors appropriate forces for containing the types of conflict which will constitute a good deal of the indigenous response. This is the way in which there can be a successful move from the precontractual situations, or the situations of primitive societies in which there is typically a mixture of precontractual and contractual relationship, to the contractual mechanisms of modern society.[34]

In particular, what we must expect to see is, in the first place, a development not of a single elite but of several, so that there will be questions of relationship between the elite groups, between these groups and the other types of social stratification that will be developing, and between these elites and the developing institutions. The elitist problems are likely to show three factors. One is the modernization of the elites themselves: the degree, for example, to which they accept universalistic standards or can operate a centralized governmental and administrative structure. The second is the harmony or dissociation between professional, technical, and administrative elites, and older leading groups. The third is the flexibility and openness of the new elites and how far they can continue to change and recruit fresh members.

This article is not an argument for pessimism. We would, however, be foolish to underrate the dimensions of what is going to occur, or, along the lines of the Report, to ignore them altogether. A recent discussion,[35] deeply concerned with the defence of Western values, has given us sufficient warning. Following precisely the Eisenstadt approach—that is, of an analysis of demands relating to elites, ideology, and organization—Sinai severely criticises the actual achievement of more or less democratic efforts in Africa and Asia. Secondly, he criticises the attempt to employ Western models. The actual demands of urbanization, industrialization, capital growth, and public expenditure impose tremendous strains on a society. Communist forces have built-in advantages along precisely these lines of leadership, value change, and organization. In particular, they give priority to and have some solution for the problem of the provision of a new sort of state bureaucracy.

One part of the argument therefore is about the problem of what may be called 'the team': a demand for an inclusive strategy, for the analysis of the situation, for the development of policy and for the anticipation of results. Of course, a purely political or institutional type of preparatory strategy which concentrated simply on legal, political, administrative and formal institutions would itself be inadequate, but the purely economic strategy is inadequate also. We need to employ strategies considering also administration, social systems, and political culture. The administrative strategy will attempt to solve the problem of administrative style. A solution may be found along the line suggested in my previous paper and by the discussion by Victor Thompson. A social systems strategy will consider the development of social communication, the problem of group relations and group participation, and so forth.[36] Finally, the strategy will have to include references to the development of political culture : Packenham has defined this as 'the set of attitudes and personality characteristics that enables the members of the political system both to accept the privileges and to bear the responsibilities of the democratic political process'.[37]

It may be unfair to suggest that the World Bank Report ought to have developed strategies quite as embracing as these demands. No doubt, ideally, a good deal more research needs to be done into Papua-New Guinea before such strategies could be developed. The tragic fact of the matter, however, is that we simply cannot wait. Meanwhile nothing other than the government itself has the responsibility of developing the strategy used : That is the second part of the argument. Even if the research had been done, such a study must be political simply because it is inclusive. The major danger of the Report may well be that precisely in situations where research and data are most lacking government is most susceptible to the prestige of that sort of inquiry. For example, the governments of dependent territories may or may not be anxious to transfer authority; they may well be ready to adopt the prestige of bodies like the World Bank for their policies. Further, it is in developing societies that data for decision-making about development is most likely to be absent but most required. Any apparently authoritative report can easily carry a weight that is heavy but dangerous. There is in fact no real alternative to the improvement of the local administration and the acceptance of local responsibility.

NOTES

1   E. K. Fisk, 'The Economy', in D. G. Bettison *et al., The Independence of Papua-New Guinea* (Sydney, 1962), 25-7.
2   *The Economic Development of the Territory of Papua and New Guinea* (Baltimore: The Johns Hopkins Press for the International Bank for Reconstruction and Development; London: Oxford University Press; 1965, 68s.). Hereafter referred to as 'Report'.
3   Since this article was first written the general problem has been brilliantly discussed by P. Nettl and R. Robertson in *Industrialisation, Development or Modernisation?* (University of Manchester, Centre for Development Studies, Conference on Political Development, 1965).
4   *Report*, 31 and 60-2.
5   *Ibid.*, vii (italics added).
6   *Ibid.*, 31.

7   *Ibid.*, 35.
8   *Ibid.*, 239, on transport services, e.g.
9   *Ibid.*, 39 *ff.*
10 M. Perham, *The Colonial Reckoning* (London, 1963 edn.), *passim*; 59-66 esp.
11 *Report*, 40.
12 *Ibid.*, 407 *ff.*
13 *Ibid.*, 411.
14 A very good discussion of planning in practice in a developing situation is Mahbub Ul Haq, *The Strategy of Economic Planning: A Case Study of Pakistan* (London, 1963). A parallel study concentrating on organization is A. Waterson, *Planning in Pakistan: Organisation and Implementation* (Oxford, 1965). For a general discussion, see A. H. Hanson, *Public Enterprise and Economic Development* (London, 1959), 106-114 esp.; *U. N. Analyses and Projections of Economic Development* (New York, 1955).
15 *Report*, 158.
16 *Ibid.*, 238-9, 247-9.
17 H. Zink *et al., Decentralisation in New Zealand Government Administration* (Wellington, 1961), 47; and F. W. Riggs, 'Agraria and Industria in W. J. Siffen (ed.), *Toward the Comparative Study of Public Administration* (Bloomington, 1959), 93-4.
18 A. H. Hanson, *op. cit.*, 342 *ff.*; A. D. Gorwala, *Report on the Efficient Conduct of State Enterprises* (New Delhi, 1951).
19 For a discussion of the pathological or requisites approach, see A. R. Willner, 'The Under-developed Study of Political Development', 16 *World Politics* (1964), esp. at 480-2.
20 'In other words, if Braibanti is correct, as he certainly seems to me to be, in asserting that the bureaucracy is necessarily a reflection of the larger social environment of which it is a part, it would appear somewhat irrational to superimpose on any other developing nations the principles and organisational characteristics of public administration that have evolved in the United States. Indeed, the irony in much of this is that the principles we try to export do not even operate in the United States.' J. La Palombara (ed.), *Bureaucracy and Political Development* (Princeton, 1963), 20; the reference is to R. Braibanti's contribution to the volume, 'Public Bureaucracy and Judiciary in Pakistan', 360-440.
21 *cf.* Chapter 15 above, and V. Thompson, 'Objectives for Development Administration', 9 *Administrative Science Quarterly* (1964), 91-108; Y. Dror, 'Muddling Through—Science or Inertia?', 24 *Public Administration Review* (1964), 154: 'The three conditions essential to the validity of the 'muddling through' thesis are most likely to prevail where there is a high degree of social stability. Under conditions of stability, routine is often the best policy, and, change being at a slow rate, incremental policy change is often optimal'. Lindblom has also accepted that his analysis for an incremental style in administration applies only to 'stable, well established, deeply rooted democracies'. See 'Policy Analysis', 48 *American Economic Review* (1958), and *Public Administration Review, loc. cit.*, 154 note and 157.
22 W. J. M. Mackenzie has recently suggested some of the possible content of development administration: *Theories of Administration Development* (University of Manchester, 1965), at 7 esp.
23 *Report*, 302 and 313.

low, Spitz and Weidner and Hart and Meadows, which appeared between 1961 and 1963. There was a sufficient feeling of agreement, newness and promise to lead Hart and Meadows, in their volume on *Directed Social Change*, which was an attempt to produce both a reader and an annotated bibliography, to refer explicitly to development administration as 'the fascinating though capricious new field of entrepreneurial thought'.

The field has, indeed, been capricious, not to say disappointing, partly because of the contrast between the hopes with which it was taken up and the results so far, and partly in a closely related, indeed explanatory way because the motivations, concerns and initial points of agreement were more scattered than was at first clear.

I think it is worth distinguishing at least three separate strands of concern and then two, or perhaps three, separate strands of work. For example, one of the very first articles actually to use the phrase Development Administration, (Goswami, *The Structure of Development Administration* in the Indian Journal of Public Administration, 1955), explicitly meant that development administration was simply the administration of community development programmes and in that case, because of the 1952 regulations, that it should be separated from regular district administration concerned with regulations and revenue matters. But that was a more particular type of concern than was being expressed at the same time, for example, by F. W. Riggs, in his 1956 article, *Public Administration, a Neglected Factor in Economic Development*, or than was implied by the Hart and Meadows definition of 1961, the Meadows definition of 1963, ('Public management of economics and social change in terms of deliberate social policy'), or by Richard Gable in his *Plan for research and publications in public administration*, which was in fact a letter to the Chief of Public Administration Division of I.C.A., the predecessor for the U.S.A.I.D., ('development administration is the process of formulating policies necessary to achieve development goals and the mobilizing, organizing and managing all necessary and available resources to implement these policies').

It was the emphasis on the wide scope of the changes with which development administration would be concerned and its relationship to political mobilization on the one hand and the sense of some calculus of resources and obstacles on the other, which was perhaps most important in these new sorts of definitions. But there was also a third sense of concern to be expressed before the whole agenda could be present. That was argued most explicitly by Ed. Weidner in his 1963 volume *Technical assistance for public administration overseas: the case for development administration.* The essence of Weidner's argument was that technical assistance had been disappointing, not so much because it had neglected public administration as because on the one hand its organization of a public administration content had been ill-designed and, on the other hand, precisely because the administrative content had been inappropriate. It had, to use the most convenient and succinct piece of jargon, precisely been involved in public, where it should have been involved in something new and different to be called development administration. Weidner illustrated his argument in terms of the sorts of experts employed, the sorts of things they were concerned with and prescribed and, as in the case of the 1951 and 1961 United Nations handbooks, the sorts of things they summarized and wrote about: what he called the triad of improvement or prescription peculiarly in O & M, in fiscal management and in personnel management. His argument could also have been illustrated from the great mass of case material about technical assistance records which was beginning to be available and some of which had indeed already been collected in volumes life Teaf and Franck, *Hands Across Frontiers*, as early as 1955.

It is evident that the roots of concern with aspects like community development, induced change and technical assistance lay partly in sheer experience and partly also in the research and field results and perceptions of the social sciences, perhaps particularly social anthropology, and in the contemporary application of the rapidly changing field of comparative politics to development. A great mass of field results as well as the actual methods of social anthropology seemed to be extremely relevant, and much of it was being collected in convenient form, (e.g. E. H. Spicer *Human Problems in Technological Change*, 1952). The interest in social systems theories and in theories of development and change inevitably led to a sharper reassessment of the relevance of Western administrative theories and methods, as expressed, for example by Victor Thompson in his well-known article *Administrative Objectives for Development Administration*, (1964 Administrative Science Quarterly, p. 91). 'Control oriented administration assumes stability—fixed conditions, goals and resources. The administrative problem appears as the maximal allocation of these fixed resources. This model is a poor analogue for Development Administration.'

In addition to the contingency and costs of Western methods, three other things were particularly stressed by these new perceptions. The first was the communications gap between administrators and communities. The second was the significance of what F. W. Riggs himself wanted to call the ecology of public administration, that is to say, the whole social situation in which the administration found itself. That went along with a sense of the weakness of the available political controls over the administration. The emphasis was derived from the application of systems theory to administration. It followed that effective processes of research and of aid possessed different demands from what would otherwise be taken into account. In general, research should be a condition of development policies. In particular, in the arguments of people like Binder, Riggs, Foltz and Pye, and the case studies of say Goodnow on Pakistan, or Tilman on Malaysia, there was an emphasis on the weakness of the political institutions available to control the administration. Hence extrinsic intervention, like technical assistance for public administration, came to be looked at from that point of view very critically and even unsympathetically. That tended to reinforce the different and more applied criticisms of people like Weidner.

A third perception came from a sharper and sometimes a more experienced and therefore perhaps sadder understanding of yet another factor. That had to do with actual demands and outcomes of development planning. The administration and implementation of development plans showed up clearly the costs, the uncertainties and the obstacles to public action in the conditions of less developed countries.

Now clearly, part of the sense which motivated the development administration movement, if we can call it that, was a combination either of assumptions or alternatively of observations about the actual importance and degree of reliance on administration for the purpose of nation building in the newly independent and the less developed political systems, with the actual inadequacy of the administrative system, as they faced the first post-localization or post-independence experience and new demands. But I think it is important to see that what was special about the development administration movement was certainly quite usually an involvement in processes of technical assistance, development planning, programme implementation, community development and so forth, but also a growing sense of criticism, disappointment or uncertainty about these processes. That is perhaps particularly important in Weidner's book; hence if we look at the writing or research side of the movement I think we need to distinguish quite clearly between three types of activity. First of all, we might think of something which could be called administrative development rather than, say, development administration, as the actual improvement of administrations or public services themselves. Once problems of communications, of implementation or of the gap, and once the problem of the imbalance between political and bureaucratic levels, are perceived, it could no longer be supposed that administrative development and development administration were synonymous.

Secondly technical assistance was no doubt more or less of an intended or unintended factor in the administrative situation in the less developed countries. Again, however, it was no longer possible after the work of the early 1960s to take technical assistance for public administration as synonymous with the needs of development administration itself; setting up for example, an O & M unit may have been right or wrong. The calculation was actually one sort of problem; the needs of development administration may have been another matter.

Thirdly, there was a lot of work being done about the general description or analysis of the situation for administration in the less developed countries. The best known example is F. W. Riggs's own work, *Administration in Developing Countries* but this work did not, for the most part, provide prescriptions about what development administration would require or would be like. Indeed, as far as Riggs's own work was concerned, in effect, it gave warnings that assistance for administration in the less developed countries could be negatively effective.

We may make the following summary points:

(a) There is a recognizable set of concerns of the last decade or so in development studies and policy which may be called the development administration movement.

(b) Certain distinct influences seem to have been at work in this movement. The influences include the perceptions, motivations and experiences of community development; the application of systems theory to the comparative politics of the developing areas; experience of the implementation problems of planning and of field projects; and technical assistance, particularly as far as it has been concerned with administrative improvements. The influences have come to affect the way in which certain policy issues are looked at. These include the recognized need for administrative improvement and development for technical assistance for administration and for the role of administration in the implementation of public decisions. In particular, the movement distinguishes more or less sharply between the following agendas: descriptive or generalizing work about administration in the less developed countries; technical assistance for administration, including administrative development which may be looked at as the strengthening of existing agencies of public services; the community development movement; and development administration itself.

(c) Accordingly, we might say that the concept of development administration represents a fairly distinct agenda of concern about conditions, demands and ends. What is less clear is the actual content of development administration, that is to say precisely how those concerns are to be met. However, it is clear that the movement wishes to distinguish between development administration on the one hand, and on the other, public administration, administrative development, including some technical assistance processes, the actual situation of administration in the less developed countries and possibly community development also.

(d) If one can recognize that the development administration movement has a record of concern and debate rather than conclusions and if one recognizes, as one must, that the movement is partly esoteric, it follows that it is not likely to be easy to relate the record to clear policy recommendations for a technical assistance agency. However, it may be worth seeing tentatively where the movement might take one.

The following points could be made:

(1) It does seem well worth while distinguishing between public administration and development administration. That is after all the major issue which the movement has been concerned to work out. Public administration may be taken as referring to the content of the Western experience of administration and to Western ideas. For various reasons that has come to mean in such advisory processes as technical assistance, an emphasis on particular techniques of change, like O & M work and on particular notions of desirable changes, especially in fiscal and in personnel management. Development administration needs a completely different definition. If we can put together the definitions of Gable, of Hart and Meadows and of Weidner, we might say that development administration is about development programmes, policies and projects in those conditions in which there are unusually wide and new demands and in which there are peculiarly low capacities and severe obstacles to meeting them.

Development administration may well then need amongst other things administrative development, but that will be only one requirement. Furthermore, the concerns and perceptions which have given rise to the development administration movement show that public administration itself may not give the correct or the complete prescription for how administration ought to be developed, and also that efforts to improve it may have surprising and not always welcome consequences.

(2) Those distinctions between public administration, development administration and administrative development may have important implications for technical assistance agencies. That applies to at least three points. The first is that the content and sources of advice and help should not only, by any means, be concerned with aspects like O & M or orthodox Western processes for the improvement of personnel and fiscal management or indeed primarily with such questions at all. The second point which follows from the first is that the agencies might need to rethink their policies about the sorts of experts whom they employ. Irrespective of the questions which they might well think ought to be handled, their recruitment policies might actually be determining the questions which are in fact handled and the ways in which they are handled. If public and development administration ought to be distinguished, it follows that assistance to what could be called public administration is not necessarily synonymous with assistance for development administration. Present technical assistance recruitment policies might not be at all helpful in implementing that distinction.

A third point, with which Weidner and others have been particularly concerned, is the problem of the actual location as well as the recruitment of administration experts. On the one hand that might be regarded as a fairly safe question. For example, should administrative experts be located in headquarters or research positions or, say, in area divisions or even in country or field project teams? On the other hand, the implications might also be regarded as going rather far, even too far. As many commentators have pointed out, technical assistance for administration is a peculiarly sensitive question. A greater or even merely an apparent stress on ideas about administrative change as part and parcel of technical assistance at the recipient end could be inconvenient. Any relocation of administrative expertise in technical assistance ought to be looked at with this problem in mind.

(3) It is inconvenient that the development administration movement has been evidently more successful in its critical than in its prescriptive work. That is at the heart of the present United States debate about the legitimacy and the strategies of technical assistance for administration. A hard reassessment and re-evaluation of development administration and technical assistance strategies does now seem to be very urgent indeed. That seems to need, apart from anything else, a consideration of the actual difficulties of evaluation in technical assistance. Nevertheless more self conscious experiment to be followed by

evaluation should be employed, for example experiments with alternative strategies of persuasion, advice, demonstration, direct action, leverage and conditions, with devices like servicios and with participant and third party training.

(4) We are suggesting, then, that the whole field of technical assistance might be reassessed from the development administration point of view. But, technical assistance for administration and quite especially technical assistance for development administration is likely to be peculiarly sensitive and difficult. However, there is no first reason why such technical assistance as is concerned with development administration should begin by assuming that it must employ training as its only means, even training in all its many possible senses, and certainly not training narrowly interpreted. Nevertheless it is true that assistance for education and training in administration in less developed countries does seem to be intimately connected with the implications of the development administration movement. The experience and perceptions which have gone into the movement should now make it more possible to understand the setting of administration and the implications of change and accordingly, the implications of any training experience. The sharp difference, for example, between a training institute and a rural development academy becomes clear. While they may both be said to be concerned with training there is all the difference in the world between training mid-grade officials in office processes and using training as a means of communication between field officials and village community leaders.

Some other points about training should be considered. For example, the priority for overseas top level and public administration training could be replaced by local, less institutionalized and field official training. Secondly, training should perhaps only be considered in terms either of requests received, rather than what happens to be available, or alternatively, in terms of actual ongoing programmes and field projects so that training would become an integral part of project implementation. That would mean a redefinition of what is conceived of as training, possibly much less emphasis on institutionalized training, great changes for the training officer career and a consideration of the problem of a scatter of occasional, discrete, applied and quite small pieces of training experience. In the end it might carry rather far reaching implications for the whole relationship of the meaning of administration to the meaning of training.

Technical assistance for development administration should

not necessarily be identified with training, but it may well be, not simply that training needs reinterpretation along those lines, but also that training may be the most acceptable, and for development administration in particular.

(5) As we have noted, even when it is admitted that the content of development administration has its own peculiar dimensions of concern, it is not easy, particularly from the West, to provide the content itself. For example, in a comparatively recent discussion, the Director of the South and South East Asia programme of the Ford Foundation, (George F. Gant, *A Note on Applications of Development Administration* in Public Policy 1966) sees clearly enough that development administration is about the focus on achieving change in situations where change is difficult, and seeks for something more than the existing restriction to reforms and improvements in internal administration. As he says, 'failures in the execution of development programmes persist' despite a high degree of such attention. What, however, he finds difficult is a recommendation for anything other than more management analysis, more competent management in nation building departments and more managers for local enterprise. Unless one is prepared to take the implications very far indeed beyond what Mr. Gant himself talks about, certainly for at least two of these three topics, his recommendations do not seem to be adequate.

If for the moment one can put aside the questions raised about technical assistance strategies, and if one seeks to go beyond Mr. Gant's recommendations, for example, and beyond what has been suggested here about a reinterpretation of training, one might ask what the actual content of development administration could be as distinct, say, from implementation of national planning on the one hand and community development on the other. In general, considering the definition we have given, one would say that development administration, in comparison with public administration, requires a new approach to institution building and to information and communication processes and a more continuing emphasis on evaluation, implementation and innovation in public action.

Meeting those requirements clearly requires more field work and research than has yet been done. From the agenda of concern indicated by the development administration movement, a whole series of research questions could be indicated. For example,

(1) designing organizational structures which, unlike administrative or centrally dominated departmental or secretariat forms, emphasize field, project, executive, specialist or area elements.

(2) New ways of organizing for representation, participation or conflict.
(3) Alternative public service career structures to give greater expression to the prestige of the field and the project.
(4) Alternative forms of district organization and of organizing the relations between market towns and rural areas.
(5) Alternative to heirarchical or pyramidal organizational structures.
(6) New forms of consultancy processes.
(7) Inherent rather than extrinsic, occasional or devised forms of control or evaluation.
(8) Ways of employing destabilizing and anti-institutionalization processes.
(9) The implications of seeing administrative action and especially the relations between administrative organizations and clients as inherently an educational and training process.

That is a purely indicative and general list. It is not a budget of possible field research projects. It does not deal with the great variation of conditions in less developed countries. It does not solve the problems of technical assistance policy. However, it does seem to follow that a technical assistance agency should in general be conscious of the local administrative effects of its programmes and open to research and experiment about those effects. Further, that sort of consciousness might at least have a negative effect. For example, some technical assistance for administration might get less support or even disappear. Some elements, like overseas or participant training might be altered. Some elements might be seen in a different way: for example, the use of OSAS insofar as it might be considered as tending to reinforce rather than to alter existing public service structures.

14

PUBLIC EMPLOYMENT, POLITICAL RIGHTS
AND POLITICAL DEVELOPMENT

As dependent territories move through preparatory pro-
cesses towards self government and independence there is
experienced a whole series of questions about the transfer
of institutions and the development of acceptable con-
ventions. These phases of political development are made
no easier by the imitation of models, like Westminster, or
frequently by their misunderstanding by many, like some
administrative officials. The general record of these prob-
lems in the British colonial experience was discussed in a
previous paper. Here there is an examination of one parti-
cularly difficult problem which came to the fore in Papua
and New Guinea: the relations between leading expatriate
officials and indigenous members of the elected legislative
body; and the doctrines to be employed in formulating the
political rights of indigenous members of the public services.
The problem is made more difficult partly because of peculi-
arities of Westminster doctrines about the separation of
politics and administration which may not be transferable
and partly because of the exceptional importance of educated
officials in a very much less developed society, where there
are as yet, for example, almost no non-official professional
resources. What sort of elites are going to be encouraged?

'That the People will ever suspect the remedies for the diseases
of the State where they are wholly excluded from seeing how
they are prepared.'—Halifax, *Maxims of State*, 26 (Miscel-
lanies, 1700).

A number of issues in the current development of public service
policies in Papua and New Guinea indicates the sensitivity of
public employment in dependent territories in a phase of 'preparation'[1]: viz, moving through institutional changes towards self
government, transfer of power and independence. There seem to
be immediate concerns about the relations between members of the
House of Assembly and senior officials, and with the Common-

wealth government, rights of debate, comment and reply and the status of officials.[2] Can, for example, an official as an official comment in public on public statements of members of the House of Assembly which may be relevant to the performance of the official; on the other hand, can an official but not as an official comment in public on public affairs generally when those affairs may not be relevant to his official performance? Behind these questions there lie connections with training policy and other matters. Several positions have been taken up, explicitly or implicitly, on discrete issues here or on questions of this sort. The concern of this note is not to deal with the particular issues but to elucidate some of their implications.

In the first place, a unique, unambiguous and non-controversial meaning for public employment (in the sense of the status of an official, a public or civil servant or a bureaucrat) is, as this list of terms at once suggests,[3] unlikely. If an agreed meaning has ever been present it has been peculiar, local and contingent. There is not, and never has been, some single, inevitable or essential concept of public employment from which, in any circumstances, unarguable rules about rights and obligations or about public service policies can be deduced. What, for example, seems to be in the minds of some of the present protagonists is, broadly, the sort of rules which some of them, at any rate, believe apply to public servants in the Australian (or civil servants in the British) types of parliamentary systems. Leaving aside for the moment the radical differences between those systems and their relevance to the situation in Papua and New Guinea, one sees that the rules do produce one clear but quite unusual advantage: there is barely any difficulty in seeing who is a politician and who is a public servant. That is what the present controversies are about.

But the advantage is so unusual as to suggest doubt: is it real; is it not costly; for whom is it most advantageous? Many other systems neither recognize the distinction, at least in this way, nor apparently suffer any indubitable net loss because of its absence; they may, of course, have their particular problems, costs and limitations, but so, perhaps, does this system too. Certainly, we had better remember that it took a long and complicated route to establish it: the steady flow of 'place-men' bills, for example, in the English parliaments from 1690s onwards; and the gradual development, over nearly a century, from 1780 to 1870, of the conditions for this quite special interpretation of public employment.

Now the recent Fulton Report may assume that the United Kingdom civil service is still, essentially, a product of those developments or, at least, of one of its features, the Trevelyan-Northcote

Report.[4] But the Australian public services have, in many ways, been very different from that; so, more radically and more relevantly to the present controversies, have many, indeed most, other modern public services and their reform movements. Above all, the possibility of achieving a clear political-official distinction by a reform of recruitment was, in fact, dependent, not only on a very long process of change but also on some quite peculiar conditions and, as it were, a highly complicated bargain. Mean-time, recruitment is seen to have a quite different role in public service policies.

It is those peculiar conditions and bargains, on which above all that apparently so advantageous distinction depends, which need to be understood and costed. It may be very nice to have a system in which you do not seem to have to worry about who are your officials, whom you merely have to appoint, rely on and keep silent, as distinct from your politicians, whom you must elect or reject. But it is peculiar; it became possible because of some convenient Victorian inventions like central ministerial departments.[5] It operates, we see, within severe limits; and there is this bargain. There was a time and there are places where the political system needs the public service for jobs: patronage and support. When that need lessens and a need for proficiency increases, it becomes possible to make a bargain about proficiency: for example, proficiency in return for permanence. But politics may have other needs, for example elections, responsibility and a changeover between governmental and opposition groups from time to time. Then, it seems, the reliable and proficient public service must either surrender its permanence or accept other conditions, especially its more evident reduction to instrumentalization (or bureaucratization) in the particular guise of anonymity: unheard it may be treated as neutral. It so happened that there was once a coincidence of the conditions of just that sort of responsible government (party organized elections, and so forth) with that sort of public service bargain: anonymity, some sacrifice of political rights and proficient performance in return for prominent careers, honours and a six-hour working day, when the middle classes wanted just that, and neutrality was possible, credible and inexpensive.

One only has to recall the coincidence to see how peculiar it is, and the more one thinks of its conditions the more striking this becomes: the electorate, the parties and the parliament accept the minister as the answerable and liable symbol for the host of officials; the other ministers will stick by him because their party will support them, and the party will do that because the ministers will. But that is the full rigour of the system. What we know is that ministers shuffle out of their part of the bargain, the demands of proficiency increase and even British civil servants no longer get their old guaranteed ration of honours. Yet this anonymity and permanence seems to last and the anonymity at least—public silence and no politics—seems to be thought a proper, indeed an emphasized, part of New Guinea 'preparation'.

It lasts, to return to our questions, because this de-politicization of the public service is somewhat unreal, has only hidden, distant and delayed costs and is very advantageous for some. The unreality at least, or, rather, the limitations of the de-politicization were, of course, a familiar theme in the critique of liberal democracy in the 1930s: the bureaucratic instrument would be neutral between policies, parties or governmental alternatives because the alternatives were not, in fact, very far apart. One sees, then, why at moments of more radical change, like transfers of power, indeed, the de-politicization is less viable or less credible, just as one may also see that, on the record, the critique was unfair; or another may say that it was, after all, an anticipation of the now familiar Marcusian criticism of a related feature of liberal democracy: tolerance. But, then, Marcuse is a man of the 1930s, is he not?

There are more important questions about the reality of the de-politicization of the public service. It posits an unacceptable view of the policy making process: one group of politicians, called, in this sort of system, ministers, are supposed to make policy decisions; and other sorts of people, called officials, are supposed to carry them out. I suppose that no one now believes in or is even prepared to state this notion of a distinction between policy and execution; what, then, becomes of the dependent distinction between responsible politicians and instrumental officials? Secondly, the system may be all very well if ministers are responsible, that is can indeed be held accountable and subject to sanctions like discharge.[6] But, beyond the provisional worries about how the system actually works which we have already raised, we know that in some instances, particularly as it happens, in the Australian experience, ministers may become very long term, and the important devices of responsibility, like parliamentary questions, are very poorly developed and employed indeed; and, on the other hand, the system, sensibly, is being amended by inquisitorial committees and by ombudsmen so that anonymity itself must be incomplete if the amendments are to function. At that point, we shall see, some very difficult questions about de-politicization begin to arise.

The reality is limited, then; and it is changing. At one stage it seemed the most important and perturbing aspect of the change would be a demand for much more than mere neutrality, with its apparently concomitant condition of anonymity, from the public service: there would have to be an acceptance on the part of the service of a further, new condition to a bargain—an investigation, precisely, of privacy to test for conditions, not only of loyalty (to country and regime but not to government, presumably) but of security, too.[7] Perhaps this is not now the aspect we have to worry about; perhaps it is. In any case, the other side of the bargain—how the ministers behave—is changing too. In the British (the paradigm?) case, we have to learn that collective responsibility is not what we thought it. On the one hand, the condition of responsibility, power, may move from the cabinet: 'power can very easily pass not merely from Cabinet to one or two ministers but effectively to sources quite outside the political control altogether', as Mr. George Brown, explaining his resignation, said to the House of Commons. On the other hand, we have been recently and authoritatively told that a minister in the cabinet who does not like the way decisions are going will use the 'unattributable leak': he will let the press know that he differs from his friends.[8] Now, many of these features —committees, security checks, the relevance of the cabinet and press leaks—are old and familiar features of the American presidential systems. But it is precisely that system which has never accepted, employed, or propagated a non-political public service, in decision-making or in appointment. So, if the conditions of the bargain are to become so different, and unreal, should we not wonder about the bargain itself?

The bargain is costly too. Perhaps that was the point which the older critics had tried to make. You could have a neutral service if it did not do too much. But the costs are showing themselves in other ways now. Let us give three examples. Let us suppose as we have suggested that the weaknesses, changes or peculiarities of the ministerial system (which happen, in fact, to be a feature of the sort of preparatory situation in which Papua and New Guinea now is) do indeed suggest its emendation by the addition of inquisitorial committees: some more leisurely, more probing and more instructed investigation of that mysterious policy-making process is required than the old bargain seems to provide or to need. But then the bargain exerts its price: officials may, indeed, appear; but they will clutch the last, convenient vestiges of the garb of anonymity around themselves. Terms of reference will then be cut; questions will not be answered; or the answers will lack meaning. The bargain must be altered or the amendments frustrated.

The second example relates to precisely those sorts of changes in governmental policy and decision-making which planning, interventionist government and developmental regimes most require: that is, which territories like Papua and New Guinea have all elsewhere come to experiment with. Two instances may be mentioned. The first is what is generally called the public expenditure survey: that is, there is a standing survey and calculation of the details and totals of public spending plans over a phased period ahead, perhaps three years in detail and a further two in less detail. It is recognized, that is to say, that, irrespective of the use or non-use of medium-term overall planning, an annual budgetary process cannot alter significantly public spending and activity plans. The second instance is the adoption, beyond increasingly sophisticated cost benefit studies, decision matrices and network analyses, of PPBS. Now one of the key elements in PPBS is the rejection of the assumption that the value of public activity and achievement, sector by sector, is equivalent to the measurable costs of the inputs in that sector, in favour of the use of defined, if complicated and 'intermediate' networks of objectives or, perhaps, rather more something like the programme yardsticks.[9] Both instances indicate the way in which developmental government means the employment of devices of systems management. It follows, not merely that the simple policy-administration dichotomy is irrelevant, but also that some hallowed principles of responsibility, like annual finance debates, are fairly deficient too. Either the public will be kept still more remote from the arena of effective decision-making, or on the contrary, more open government, all the more illuminated by the clearer light on policy choices, could now be available. But appeals to the old rules of a silent service are demands, really, for the closed not for the open arena.

It has been said that the use of PPBS could be 'a harbinger of a more confident and candid professionalism in government, replacing the old secretive amateurism'.[10] Now, without adopting too simple a distinction between professionalism and amateurism in government[11] one would agree that PPBS and similar devices do allow government to publish meaningful statements about the dimensions of policy choices; but one must also see that this sort of professionalism creates problems for the old bargain and its rules. This has, for example, been seen in public enquiries and inspections into particular planning decisions or proposals, as in town and country planning: precisely where the planning has become most professional. The professional official is called as a witness; does he give his evidence, so to speak, as a professional or as a neutral instrument of his political masters, irrespective of their use, pro or contra of his professional advice. To put it more briefly; intervention needs these professional developments; professionalism can provide more open government; openness will mean a change in the rules; the only alternative is a far greater public remoteness from policy making and a much less real responsibility. The bargain will be quite unfair.

There is a third example of the costs which the bargain may now impose. It is familiar that the old system of responsibility and anonymity meant a firm employment of the golden rule for defensible administration and accordingly the adoption of severe bureaucratized rules for relations between public administration and its clients.[12] It is also relatively familiar that this was viable in particular social conditions for particular services or within severe limits but that it is hopeless for the conditions of a developmental administration and indeed that this is central in the problems precisely of that sort of change. Of course, one may well say that it was well understood by colonial or dependent administration that the district administrator was both on his own and should be well known. How odd, then, if precisely in days of localization and of a movement from good government to development and of dependence to independence these exotic rules of silence, anonymity and reduced discretion should now at last be imposed.[13]

Of course, the bargain was not highly relevant to conditions of dependent government and administration: on the one hand the system was not one of responsibility and on the other hand the officials while powerful were also separated from the society in which their power was exercised.[14] In the phase of preparation when responsibility is not yet fully established but when we are moving away from the full condition of dependence and separation and are at the same time moving towards a more developmental administration and interventionist policies, should one be seeking for the nineteenth century myth, the silent service and the ancient bargains or that system. It is not, of course, peculiar to this particular bargain if only one side of it operates but it becomes very convenient indeed for some of the parties. When we do not have responsibility but we do have silence and anonymity the situation is certainly highly convenient to some: to distant ministers, to irresponsible politicians and to dominant but permanent officials. But the point of depoliticization was as we have indicated a balanced bargain, not just a one-sided advantage. In any case, a biased silence might not in the end prove to be as convenient as in the short run it appears. 'Men are so proud of princes secrets that they will not see the danger of them.'

It may not then be difficult to understand why despite its contingency this peculiar depoliticized and dichotomous system has lasted but may yet have to undergo changes. Change is, after all, somewhat less peculiar in political history and surely what we should be looking for in Papua and New Guinea. Indeed, change in just this direction of participation, communication and publicity is what can be most easily exemplified. There are those who now, apparently, oppose publicity for administration and decision-making, and debate by public servants. Socrates once opposed the adoption of writing: 'For this invention of yours will produce for-getfulness—neglected memory—with written discourses you could fancy they speak as though they were possessed of sense' and it was once thought we should remember that publicity for the very debates in parliament itself was improper, offensive and dangerous. The predecessors of Hansard were once sub rosa until people understood that 'the time is now come in which every Englishman expects to be informed of the national affairs, and in which he has the right to have that expectation gratified.... Whatever may be urged by ministers, or those who in vanity or interest make followers of ministers, concerning the necessity of confidence in our governors, and the presumption of prying with profane eyes into the recesses of policy.'[15] So the flow of changes about public employment and its rights and conditions goes on. In most public service systems, for instance, as in the American, a participation in strikes is illegal but now by the force of convention possible and indeed frequent.[16] We have recently seen in the United Kingdom the unbearable spectacle of the very top officials having a public meeting and debate about the government's refusal to implement what they regarded as the specific conditions of their pay award. As long ago as 1949 the Masterman Report recommended the revision of the rules about silence, anonymity and political participation for public servants in the United Kingdom, broadly along a line of distinction between senior policy participating officials and others. More recently we have seen a significant debate and publicity about the growth of a convention of some considerable complexity which shows how inadequate is the picture of a system of silent but neutral official instruments on the one hand and equal but rival politicians on the other. Briefly, before a coming general election in which, as is always possible in responsible (though not in dependent) systems, the government in power may be changed in favour of the opposition, senior officials will have consultations with the leaders of the opposition so as to assist continuity itself. This is to maintain continuity rather than change in the machinery of government. These delicate relations are conducted within the rules and conventions of the public service and they are consultations which distinguish precisely some more leading politicians from others who may be merely on the backbenches. Furthermore, it is the civil servants who will decide what papers affecting a previous government the members of a now incoming government may be allowed to see.[17] Similarly, and quite unsurprisingly, in the phase of preparation for which the institutions of Papua and New Guinea are now going, we can see instance after instance in which the precise conditions in which a depoliticized public service was established now have to be amended, as with the Administrator's announcement by name of the members of his executive council who will serve on its estimates committee.

The peculiar and delicate conditions which, then, had permitted the creation of that sort of depoliticized public service with which Australian and British administrators and politicians have been familiar in their metropolitan politics, have been and are being subject to as much change as other political contingencies. Those conditions of party, parliament and ministerialization, of electoral organization and choice, of devices, of responsibility, limitation and departmentalization, were never present in colonial and dependent systems. The convenience of silent instruments biased as it has been is, of course, appealing to those who would seem to enjoy or hope for the possession of the advantages and not the limitations or the costs or the disadvantages of a one-sided bargain, but the important thing for preparation in Papua and New Guinea is surely to cost the bargain and to estimate its present relevance, to think about what the future needs of institutional politics and administration are going to be and to debate and choose between the many alternative routes ahead. There is nothing at all in the history of responsible government, the contemporary experience of independence and of development or the immediate situation to suggest that a replication of isolated elements of any one other system such as Australian or British parliamentary government must be the correct and only guide to change. That is surely all the more so when it seems that some of those elements are imperfectly understood by their components dependent on now disappearing variables one-sided in their operation and subject to investigation, debate and alteration in their parent circumstances.

There seems to be two aspects which should be examined with particular care when we ask ourselves what sort of instrumental public service should be developed in situations like Papua and New Guinea. We can have little doubt from comparisons alone that the scale of public employment is going to be heavy and its role significant for political and for economic development. But it is another matter to see clearly what sort of instrument in detail public employment is going to be and to see secondly what sort of balance can be established between instrumentality and political development. We have no special reason to assume that a quite particular nineteenth-century bargain will provide the details for this new sort of balance. There are, however, certain points which can now be made on the side of instrumentality and administration. As it happens, even the bureaucratic model itself did not particularly emphasize anonymity and silence. On the contrary the characteristics which Weber emphasized were rather those of expertness on the part of the officials and known rights of appeal on the part of the clients and the community. If one was to examine how these requirements would work out in conditions of underdevelopment then one sees that it is not an anonymous and silent public service which is required. The official expertness which we must now have in mind is clearly quite different from that either of colonial traditions, of nineteenth century government or of Weberian bureaucracy. That is familiar. Equally, what was once seen as a needed right of appeal, now has to be met rather by systems of decentralization, of co-option and of access. The Masterman line of distinction is obviously irrelevant in development administration. Local community leadership and initiative has to be brought into administration itself. The relations between communities and clients on the one hand and administrative services on the other hand which we call the problem of access have to be dealt with in quite new fashions. There have been many lines of experiment here: administration as education for local level leadership; administration as applied research, and administration indeed as political leadership.

One is not saying here what the particular answers for Papua and New Guinea are going to be. What one can see, however, is broadly the impossibility of attempting to build for a changing and developing system some model of official arrangements which would consist of a handful of central departmental masters and a mass of silent and invisible employees. The impossibility is clear, in fact, whatever starting point one takes: the future needs of political leadership; the professionalization of administration for development; problems of implementation, or the relations between officials communities and clients. At any rate, we are faced with a need for invention not for invocation.

We have to assume then that the place of public employment is going to change. It has all too often been emphasized from many different premises, those of Riggs or of Fanon, of Dumont or of Huntington (and one could scarcely imagine four more different points of view) that it is easier to build the appearance of development than a whole political system. If we simply emphasize administrative development, that is to say, the improvement of the conditions of public employment itself, we may by no means be securing the conditions of systematic change. Public employment in underdeveloped and changing societies, is not only a function of its instrumentality, that is of its manifest programmes, important as those programmes, the expenditures and the costs and the whole public sector tend to be. But if one looks at the population structures and their peculiarly youthful shape, at the educational pyramid and what they are built to serve, and at the resources and ambitions, (the culture, as it were) of the elite, one sees how closely related these three phenomena tend to be and the quite peculiar role which public employment in these societies has for them. Comparative experience suggests that in the latest stages of preparation and the earliest phases after the transfer of power and of independence, the occupation of roles of political leadership in societies of such erstwhile discontinuity and the imprint of high infantile mortality rates, is explicable by combined accidents of contact, patronage and age survival itself. The succeeding generation of elite recruitment, however, is explained in quite other ways. The intimate relations between public employment and educational success then tend to play a very important part indeed. Hence if we invest resources of personnel, of goods and of political leadership in building up a youthful, intelligent and trained public service of which we then demand silence, de-politicization and alienation, we are doing something more perhaps than merely following an outworn and irrelevant model, appealing as that might be to some interests. We are also setting out on a dangerous and probably impossible preparatory route and picturing a society in which dominant elements of the most active, most intelligent and best educated sections of the second generation of the leadership are instructed that authority expects of them a public morality of silence. That may not at all be a sensible, viable or necessary nexus to expend such resources on attempting to build, between authority and elite cadres.

The importance of the public sector in processes of preparation and development, and at the same time the domination of public employment for a youthful population, for education and for emerging elites, both demand the working out of new rules for instrumentality and political rights in the public service. Why should that not be expected of developing societies as it is happening in other societies too? If preparation is not a pretence, it should be precisely an opportunity to work out such solutions and to anticipate what would happen from attempting to follow such inappropriate models as elements of established Western bureaucracies. We can certainly now see elsewhere how such models have provided havens for some but very little either of development or responsibility. In particular we have to see that in working out the relationships between public employment, political rights and instrumentality in conditions of political development, we simply cannot escape a series of severe problems by hankering after the delightful simplicities which other conditions once permitted. The first set of these problems is concerned with elite emergence. There are two opposing attitudes here. On the one hand there were those who sought for a possible route to development without the dangers and difficulties of elite recruitment and change at all. The supposition was that there could be a gradual establishment of conditions for political development by preceding economic, educational and other development. It is a notion which has had already perhaps too much debate and familiarity in Papua and New Guinea. The other and opposed attitude is now receiving more attention here and is in any case more immediately relevant to the problems of public service policy. This is the notion precisely of the investment of heavy resources in the rather rapid recruitment of a fresh elite as the pre-condition for independence. It is a theory with several difficulties revealed by experience elsewhere. Some of the difficulties have to do with the separation of the elite. Its coincidence precisely with those gaps and discontinuities which scar developing societies. The elites tend to employ the resources invested in their emergence in building an arena within which there are factions connected with wider social arenas only by ideology and patronage. The other problem is indeed the way in which the new elite emerges through Westernized institutions of education and public employment. What we have seen time and again in other developing societies is the way in which the symbols of these institutions, the 'Sandhurst' tradition, public service training itself, the language of scientific management or of planning have severally been employed. The 'guardians' of army, police or civil service have used their arbitral roles in coups leadership. That may be regarded as exceptional or pathological but the technologizing language of public administration and so forth has been employed not objectively or instrumentally at all but as a sort of ritual resource for institutionalization, elite career management, extraction, separation, legitimation and the pleasantries of the life of aid, technical assistance and international relations.

One does not at all mean to agree with extraordinary arguments about non-political pre-conditions for political independence. Nor does one mean to deny that political independence and development must mean a change from one sort of political elite to another. Quite the contrary. What one does mean is that the existing model of extreme inequality and the inevitably irresponsible administration in territory conditions becomes very dangerous for the future. It is combined with an emphasis on mere success in the acquisition of the trickings out of management (or other technologizings) in training or other approved situations. What has to be taken care about is what sort of inequalities and discontinuities are institutionalized and what sort of rites are established for satisfying the gatekeepers to the favoured arenas. Development, for example, does need an administration which is effective but humble, educated but open, instructed but objective, organized but not necessarily so hierarchical in pay or in status as we may assume.

The problems of elite change, then, take us back to problems of public service policies, but we have to see how fresh and how wideranging the implications of decisions about these policies are. Let us suppose, first, that we are facing problems about recruitment, training and localization. These are partly quantitative matters in education and manpower planning, of course. We had certainly better begin by getting our sums right. But then we have to see that what we do about these matters amounts also to what we are doing consciously or not about establishing a new sort of elite. Is a silent hierarchy of non-political technicians quite what we want? But, secondly, then, if we think it is something else that should be sought for, we do have to recognize that the relationships between political development, development administration and an improved public service, are very difficult indeed. It did once seem that silence and anonymity, that depoliticization gave one a neutral but proficient instrument. But it was the proficiency and the controllability of administration that was the sought end, silence and anonymity were the instruments. We still want those ends but their content and conditions have utterly changed. The problem, then, is to understand that and find the new instruments, not to ache for the past instruments of other conditions. Working that out will be, we see, partly a quantitative task. It will also be in part, a task of methods and procedures for control as for access, co-option and decentralization. But, thirdly, it will be a matter of criteria too. Papua and New Guinea will still need responsibility and proficiency in its public service. The methods, however, may have to alter.

NOTES

1 Preparation is discussed in relation to the idea of inheritance in Peter Nettl, 'Political Mobilization', London, 1967. See also B. B. Schaffer, 'The Concept of Preparation', Institute of Commonwealth Studies, London, 1965.
2 Some of the exchanges reported in the *Post Courier*, 19th March, 1970, are particularly relevant.
3 Variations in the descriptions of personnel in public employment are both complicated and significant. Braibanti, (ed.) *Asian Bureaucratic Systems Emergent from the British Imperial Tradition*, Durham, 1966,

is a treasure-house for the student in this matter as in others.

4 See Report on the Civil Service, Command Paper 3638, 1968.

5 It is often forgotten how difficult an invention the ministerial department was. De Tocqueville in his 'Journey to England', 1835, writes
'administrative action by the government is scarcely found in any
detail in England.

'Almost all the public services are in the hands of small deliberative
bodies, called trustees or commissioners, created from time to time by
Parliament which, at the time of their creation, appoints their members
by name.'

6 Accountability and liability was the succinct definition of responsibility by Jeremy Bentham. Professor S. E. Finer and others have
reminded us how rarely the sanctions operate.

7 E. A. Shils, *Torment of Secrecy*, London, 1956.

8 Patrick Gordon Walker, *The Cabinet*, London, 1970.

9 A good description of the planning, programming, budgeting system is
in *Department of Education and Science, Output budgeting for the
Department of Education and Science*, HMSO, London, 1970.

10 *The Times*, London, 22nd April, 1970.

11 For a discussion and comparative study of the more meaningful
aspects of this distinction, see the papers edited by F. F. Ridley (ed.)
Specialists and Generalists, London, 1968.

12 B. B. Schaffer, 'The Deadlock in Development Administration' in C. T.
Leys (ed.) *Politics and Change in Developing Countries*, Cambridge,
1969, pp. 177-212.

13 J. M. Lee, *Colonial Development and Good Government*, Oxford, 1967.

14 Leonard Woolf, *Diaries in Ceylon*, London 1963.

15 Samuel Johnson, *Observations on the state of affairs in 1956 in Works*,
edited Murphy, London, 1823, Vol. XII, p. 34.

16 The specific legislation in the United States to take one example is
United States Code, title V, Section 7311, with penalties detailed in
title XVIII, Section 1918. Despite the explicitness of these titles, there
has, of course, recently been a strike of approximately a third of the
postal workers in the United States, a number in total 740,000.

17 There have recently been interesting and enlightening exchanges on the
conventions in this matter in the United Kingdom Parliament. See
Hansard for April 21st, 1970.

15

COMPARISONS, ADMINISTRATION AND
DEVELOPMENT

The protagonists in the development administration move-
ment of the 1960s were very much brought together in one
particular organization: the Comparative Administration
Group of the American Society of Public Administration.
The CAG operated from 1963-1971 with the advantage of
two grants from the Ford Foundation and the leadership of
F. W. Riggs. The ending of the grants and the change of
chairmanship in 1971 made it possible to look back over the
work that had been done. It was the more timely to do so
partly because of the publication of many of the remaining
CAG papers in the series edited for Duke by Ralph Braibanti
and partly because of the change in mood in development
studies, including development administration, at just this
time.

When Alfred Diamant visited the PSA at Oxford in 1967, 20 persons attended his meeting; he did not, apparently, meet all the
people he had hoped.[1] His was a limited rather than a plenipotenti-
ary embassy from the Comparative Administration Group of the
American Society of Public Administration and the impact of the
CAG has been much greater than that occasion might have suggested. The Group is now at a moment of change. Its first three-
year Ford grant went to 1966; its second five-year grant is now
coming to an end. A last conference will be held at Syracuse in
April 1971. Other signs of change have already been apparent. The
famous grey-coated CAG occasional papers no longer appear. Instead, we look to the new journal.[2] Over 100 such papers were
issued during what can be called the forward years of the CAG.
Many have already been brought together in book form.[3] Most of
those remaining will now appear in the CAG Series published by
Duke and edited by Ralph Braibanti.[4]

The most important thing, however, will without doubt be the
ending of the Chairmanship of the Group by Fred Riggs from
February 1971 when Professor Richard Gable of Davis will take
over from the man who has been chairman throughout its history,

who has written, edited or initiated most of the Group's output and whose beliefs and style explain so much of the nature and extent of the Group's interests. With that Chairman, it was no accident that the characteristic activities were seminar papers and newsletters nor that a mission (the word is deliberate) for comparative administration became all but indistinguishable from development administration.

But what was interesting, considering the parentage of the Group (by Ford out of ASPA), was that the concern was always primarily with the setting or environment: the 'ecology' (as Riggs insisted, after John Gaus's earlier teaching, on calling it) rather than the hard details of administrative practice. So while 'encouragement of better communication between scholars and practitioners concerned with development administration' was intended to be at least its third 'mode of operation', its success has surely been least noticeable there.

The CAG has not been only Fred Riggs. Nor has it only been the occasional papers. There have been extremely useful bibliographies.[5] Each of us may feel his own particular indebtedness apart from Riggs's own work: for example to Bertram Gross's volume on planning, say, or to that splendid paper by Henry Hart, The Village and Development Administration.[6] But the resignation of Riggs coming with the end of what may be seen as the first decade of an explicitly named and defined concern with development administration and the publication of these two further volumes in the Duke series, is a moment for reviewing what the CAG has been.[7]

The position which the Comparative Administration Group came to stand for can be seen clearly in the memoranda which it submitted for its November 1963 meetings with the Ford Foundation.[8] It included contributions by people like Riggs himself, William Siffin and Edward Weidner. Some of its proposals like an international centre for development administration did not go forward. What did continue were the conceptual points. In particular, two things stand out. The first was an interest in the relations between public administration and politics, expressed on the premise that 'a live and vital public administration' was a necessary instrument of government and politics seen as a comparatively beneficent source for welfare. The second point was that there could and should be a new version of that instrument, to be called development administration: development administration was, perhaps, public administration when it became an instrument in the hands of governments 'everywhere' who were 'struggling to improve the lot of man'.

At the same time, development administration itself had to be established. One of the factors in its growth was to be 'a group of scholars that is development minded both in theoretical and especially applied research and teaching'. So the leaders of the CAG had written the label (as they themselves called it) and they had written their own programme. What they were now to do in particular was to establish that group of scholars. About the other conditions of development administration (a group of public officials and an exchange between officials and scholars) they came to be much less effective, or, perhaps, concerned. An early survey by the CAG showed that at that time few scholars acknowledged or saw themselves as teaching development administration: only 10 courses under that rubric as against 50 on comparative administration. Perhaps the most significant thing about the CAG was precisely to create the group, to increase enormously the number of courses and in the end in a strange way almost to remove the distinction between 'comparative' and 'development': if you were doing a comparative study you were likely to think of yourself as contributing to development; if you were interested in development you might assume that you had to make comparative statements or, in particular, statements about comparative methodology. This was a very Riggsian contribution.[9]

By 1964 and the second year of the Ford grant, some of the names, featured activities and what remains as the most important output of the CAG were already becoming familiar. The distribution of papers in the mimeograph series anticipated volumes like that by Montgomery and Siffin and, in a second series, the papers on planning edited by Bertram Gross. Despite its parentage, interests and concerns, the CAG was already dominated by seminars, papers and volumes of publications. It was, in fact, a much more thorough-going academic establishment than its parent body the American Society for Public Administration. It was also admirably and remarkably busy with its pamphlets, its newsletters, its rapidly expanding membership and contacts and its re-publications.[10]

Its second annual report said, 'interest in the Comparative Administration Group has extended overseas': the device of corresponding members was already well used. It had a panoply of associations with other bodies like the International Institute of Administrative Sciences and EROPA, and its own committees, like the Latin American Committee (LADAC), were already being established. 'Everyone', one felt was in touch. Bernard Cohn and T. V. Sathyamurthy, for example, were working on a bibliography on Indian administrative history; Peter Savage joined the staff in May of 1964 to plan for the 1966 terminal conference for the end of this first three-year grant.

Once it seemed to have been accepted that the new label of development administration was worthwhile, that the CAG could do something with it, that what it could do was primarily building a group of scholars and that that was a legitimate and worthwhile implementation of its role, it was astonishing how rapidly the activities multiplied and bore fruit. They constituted a range from bibliographical to highly theoretical work.[11] By 1965 it was clear that Ford would give a renewal grant if at a reduced level and that seminars and papers would continue to be the core of activity: 1966 at Hawaii, 1967 at North Carolina and so on. CAG was the vehicle through which one got the news of other ramifications in the rapidly emerging development administration business, like the Ford $400,000 three-year grant for studies of institution-building under Milton Esman. But it was CAG itself which was the most impressive: in 1965 350 members; three or four newsletters; and a rapidly increasing number of committees, including a European committee under the leadership of people like Diamant and then James Fesler.

If one looks at the picture by the end of that year, one can now see that things were already at a sort of peak: two books, six pamphlets, numbers of occasional papers, two reprints, five miscellaneous papers and so forth. Bertram Gross was working on the editing of the July 1964 Minnowbrook seminar: one would have to acknowledge that the CAG was very early with the criticism of formal or documentary planning and the change of interest to plan implementation. Its reprint of a key paper by Waterston[12] adds to that claim. Secondly, and in some ways more important, an energetic reader of its flow of occasional and of some of its miscellaneous papers, would have detected an emerging debate of great complexity and importance between scholars like Ralph Braibanti and David Brown on the one hand and Riggs himself and others. In one sense this was a debate about what you could do with, and how you should organize, technical assistance for public administration. The answer to that question constituted the whole agenda of development administration for a writer like Weidner. But the debate was also about ecology, balance and change: what did it mean for the politics of a society if through technical assistance (for ministries, institutions, and personnel, for example) there was imbalanced development? There is perhaps a less than wholly fair sense in which one could say that as a result of this debate the leader of the CAG came to seem to be a spokesman against technical assistance for public administration. That position was, after all, quite distinct from a demand for radical changes in such assistance.[13]

At the same time, other papers continued to come out. Some of them were the by-products of other work.[14] Some of the most interesting covered specific areas of concern: rural development, educational administration, particular geographical areas or the problems of the military.[15] There was a constant flow of theoretical discussion and model building;[16] there were important studies designed to help with empirical research projects, particularly the papers by Lynton Caldwell, and the extremely influential paper by Wallace Sayre and Herbert Kaufman.[17]

By 1965, we were also to see the important study of the JCRR model of rural improvement and political development in Taiwan. There had been the conference on temporal aspects of development administration at the Maxwell School whose papers have now been edited in the volume by Dwight Waldo before us. The great debate on imbalance and development administration would continue in the paper by Joe LaPalombara.[18] Ford produced their five-year grant which is now at its end. The 'areas' of development administration were being clearly demarcated: agriculture, public health, education and public enterprise. The personal bent of Riggs (for example, in Tom Carney's classical, historical and content analysis studies) acted as an excitement and a factor of innovation.

If the development administration label had been captured by the CAG for one sort of comparative political science at any rate its members were aware of a certain lack of multi-disciplinary discussion and were trying to do something about it as at the Washington conference. So after that College Park conference in 1966, there was a flood of comments for improvement. A selection can be read in the June 1967 newsletter.[19] Milton Esman wrote that what was now needed was 'a much larger, more complex and more diffuse operation'. But the contacts of the CAG with over 300 members in the United States and over 100 overseas were impressive; its output was well planned: there were good reasons why so many people were anxious to be in touch with the Group. There were available the papers of the Hawaii conference on development administration in Asia, now edited by Weidner, and many other interesting things: there was, for example, the brilliant contribution by Ferrel Heady to the technical assistance debate.[20]

However, there were also certain continuing problems. In the first place, the overall model which the CAG took to justify its position was a simple piece of positivism. On the one hand, there were specific needs, those 'operational needs of practitioners', of the 'classroom' and, thirdly, of 'career development training'. These were to be met by a sort of provision of ideas and the ideas would come from specific hypotheses to be tested in field research. The functions of the conferences and papers were then a matter of formulation merely. But in practice, the members of the Group saw well enough that something or other consistently prevented them from being sufficiently 'action oriented'. To put it another and harsher way, they had their conferences and wrote their papers, but the practitioners did not seem to take much notice and changes in developing countries did not seem to be directly affected.

There was surely a second feature which may also have been a problem, but was certainly remarkable. The CAG members could scarcely have asked for more institutional development contacts and activity, as long as that was academic. There were by now under the CAG, for example, something like twelve committees: on Africa, Asia, comparative education, comparative urban studies, Credga, Europe, international administration, Latin American Development, Middle East, national planning research, systems and theory of organization with a highly distinguished list of chairmen (Burke, Weidner, Siffin, Cleaveland, Heady, Fesler, Weidner, Thurber, Crow, Gross, Kateen and Landau respectively). This CAG complex of institutionalization was interwoven in many instances with committees and groups growing up from other sources: the CAG Asia Committee, for example, with the South East Asian Development Advisory Group and with EROPA. In that sort of way, complicated joint research projects like the 'self-anchoring scale' on Asian officials (designed by Gable, Abueva, Inayatullah and Paige) were prepared. And further conferences were held like that at the Villa Serbelloni for July 1967. This institutional complex not merely brought Americans into contact with overseas, and particularly South East Asian scholars. It also affected new sorts of academic careers in those countries. When one thinks of the significance both of the intelligentsia and of the career concept in the development process, one sees that this spin-off was not the least important development effect of the CAG, in fact.

The highly academic membership of the CAG (80 per cent gave research or teaching as their predominant activity as against 12 per cent who gave administration), may not then have been as important a feature as its wide spread, the career influence it had for some, and the Group's acting as a forcing ground at least for talking about the terminology of development administration. As contrasted with the situation in 1962, in July 1967 over 25 per cent of the membership heavily stressed their development administration teaching. Meanwhile, the occasional papers kept coming out by new figures from overseas like Inayatullah from West Pakistan or Nguyen-Duy Xuan from Vietnam or older figures now in touch with the group like Emmette Redford. Fresh steps (like the journal) were already being considered. One sees the point of the occasional critics. Diamant, for example, was doubtful about the need for the new journal. Siffin quoted George Grant appositely, 'Well with all this theorizing and all this study,—what are you going to do about it? How are you going to get ideas into action?' But a certain sort of activity was remarkable and surely admirable; the effects not wholly predictable, but generally very enjoyable for the scholars. The measure of academic success in quantitative terms was always striking: the number of members, the number of correspondents, the depository libraries, the American Society for Public Administration allowing not one panel on comparative administration, but a full set by 1968, and the American Political Science Association not smuggling in comparative administration under the heading of comparative politics or public administration, but allowing again by 1968 a full set of panels.

Now there is clearly a problem of judgment on this record. Just what sort of 'action' in fact was this? At the same time, for those at the centre of the Group, there was the problem of keeping it going and of implementing its promises and its intentions. The Ford grant was going to come to an end in 1970. But the Journal of Comparative Administration Studies was already being planned so as to be interstitial with the Journal of Comparative Political Studies (which would, in fact, in that July, be devoted to comparative administration). Riggs and Braibanti working together had already got the new CAG series planned through Duke University Press. Complicated but generous arrangements continued to keep overseas members in touch. The Group was now evidently drawing to a moment of pause, pending its change of chairmanship, Duke's printers' preparation of the CAG series, and the work by Peter Savage and Bill Siffin on what became known as 'the grand central project'. That project was to be aimed, not surprisingly, at involving younger members of the Group, and substantively 'to relate administration, as both independent and dependent variable, to the processes of revolutionary political and social change'. The parenthesis on variables summarized succinctly the debate throughout the CAG which had sometimes become explicit (as about technical assistance) and sometimes not.

Certain things stand out clearly as one looks back over the near decade of CAG activities through the 1960s. The first is the way in which a nominal concern with comparative problems became almost submerged in a more complicated and oblique concern with development. For example, one of the earliest papers by the CAG was Dwight Waldo's 'Comparative Public Administration: Prologue, problems, and promise'.[21] As we would expect of its author, the paper is remarkably tidy, for instance in its summary of the position which Riggs was then occupying. But now, after that 'development decade' of the CAG, it looks, if not outdated, a little beside the point. Only at page 28 of its 30 pages does it indeed get to development as an interest. Then it was prescient, since it explicitly relied[22] on two remarkable papers. The first was E. Weidner's,[23] the second was by Edgar Shur.[24] Those papers began from slightly different positions, and Weidner's, which is now enshrined in a full length study[25] has been seminal. So in 1962 Waldo was able to conclude his paper by writing that 'development administration is becoming a focus of interest among students of Comparative Public Administration': by 1971, one would say that it has been simply 'the' focus of interest for the CAG.

There are more doubtful matters: how that came about, what was meant by development, and therefore in particular by development administration, what its peculiar model of science and utility was and how successful the Group's mode of operation was in some directions ('the encouragement of better communication between scholars and practitioners' as against 'support for research, seminars and conferences, the improvement of teaching materials and approaches'). Certainly the Group did not consistently pursue (as why should it?) the substantive content of administration for development distinguished from the conditions of development administration, the problems of administrative development and the ecology of administration in poor (not necessarily changing) societies. Its early membership figures were not, in fact, dominated by a developmental concern. As late as 1966, the Group found it worthwhile to re-publish those remarkable 1953 papers of the Sayre-Kaufman outline, which were, after all, a research design for a pilot study in comparative but not in development administration.

On the other hand, when in 1966 Milton Esman wrote his reflective essay on the first two years of the CAG[26] it was clear that for him there the problems of development and the instrumentality of administration and of the Group were the key to the matter. He began with an excellently imagined typical failure of an instrument in a developing country: in that case a United Nations Advisory Plan. For Esman, the CAG's agenda was to be about the politics of development administration, the process of development planning and the performance of administrative systems in developing countries, together with his own particular interests in institution-building: an agenda that one could summarize as Riggs plus Gross plus Esman. Development administration was the thing for the CAG but in certain particular fashions. For Riggs, for example, the peculiar problems were the political ecology of administrative instruments as wholly dependent variable, and the dangers and problems of alternative approaches. The brilliance and fecundity of Riggs's work does not need any more words of praise. Its difficulties were that it was not in the end centrally concerned with administration; that it had a sort of incipient fatalism, hostility and determinism, and that combined with other influences it could all too easily suggest that development administration was a sort of definitionally insoluble problem. But that was vastly to be preferred to the blithe social engineering that assumed that development administration might be about games with formal organization charts,[27] the introduction of sophisticated and exotic gimmicks, or ritualistic planning and other documentary exercises.

The problem for development administration is to avoid certain traps and to take certain things into account: the cultural considerations which Riggs reminds us of; the costs of the sort of public administration devices which Weidner showed as dominating technical assistance; the paper formalities of medium-term national planning; the long history of empirical failure which Esman's story indicated; the failures in other areas like training; the confusion of ideologies in community development. But development administration is not only the study of the conditions of public administration in developing countries, either empirically or conceptually handled. It is not only an enunciation of the dangers of administrative development. It is not only the negative lessons and the institutional costs of technical assistance for public administration. It is also the business of working out what can be expected of administration for development in peculiarly difficult circumstances. The interesting questions about the CAG are how as a group it emerged over this past decade at just that time to meet just those challenges, and how far it has at all succeeded in doing so.

Colin Leys has already discussed how behavioural studies, politics and the problem of the developing countries came together in certain sorts of work.[28] Leys's essay also indicates what development may be taken to be about for political scientists with that sort of orientation at that time and interested in those problems (or cases): 'A very definite, if infinitely, complex, fact of life; a compound of private and collective actions and their intended and unintended consequences, through which the society moves from one state of organization and one system of beliefs and ideas and stocks of equipment to another, in the context (more or less dimly perceived) of others which have followed or are following a similar, though far from identical, route, with similar, though also differing, hopes and fears.'[29] The problem is that a special focus on administration easily confuses that sort of admirable perception. That is partly because we may be even less sure or have even less agreement about what administration is (a field, a sub-system, a method, a number of people, a discipline, an instrument, a procedure, a style of behaviour, a function) than politics. It is partly because students of administration, unlike 'other' students of politics, may occasionally be supposed to be asked to be or claim to be 'useful', like some economists. It is partly because, at the very same time, a prescriptive position for them is peculiarly difficult.

It was then striking and courageous of the core of the CAG to set out to do what it did. It was certainly very timely for the study of public administration itself, which was then going through a bad time. Because of its close association with the substance of Leys's essay it was not surprising that the CAG has had relatively so little to do with other things that have happened to administration and administrative studies over this period: the training movement and the debate between business schools and management training; or the aftermath of Herbert Simon's work and the whole of decision theory.[30] Some of us would indeed think that the application of decision theory to organizational studies and public policy making might be peculiarly fruitful for development administration, but the CAG has done little about that. So, on the whole, despite Gross's work on national planning and some work in agricultural administration by people like Luykx, there has been strikingly and disappointingly little contact with the development economists.[31] Perhaps this is why one is doubtful about the impact of CAG on practitioners, or in fact on training: if few of its home members were in 'administration' and more of them in 'research, teaching and training', few of them, in fact, were in training itself. On the other hand, a glance at its overseas membership, its conferences and its seminars will show, as we have indicated, its vast impact on one particular and very practical direction; people in developing countries moving between academic, administrative and training careers.

The CAG came, then, to face the problems which it did because of certain features of behaviouralism, political studies, development studies. In particular, there were the ways in which technical assistance programmes were working out as a linkage between the United States and the developing countries. One might say in the end that the peculiar features of the American university contract system as a vehicle for technical assistance explains much of the CAG. It does not, of course, explain it all. Its ecological, methodological and theorizing bent have to be explained in other ways. And there is the irony that what had so affected it (technical assistance) was what it had to be so critical of. But however it came to face such challenges, what it did, apart from the help it gave to many overseas people, in the end has to be judged by what it produced on paper. Hence the interest of the two volumes before us.

To take Waldo's volume[32] first: the problem suggested by the title is certainly important, practical and on the whole avoided. If one takes what Redford calls micro-politics or micro-decisions,[33] or the relations between bureaucratic organizations and their clients,[34] one can see that this is a distinctive and neglected problem in administrative study. It is likely for a host of reasons to work out with peculiar difficulty, constraints and uncertainty in typical situations of development.[35] Some of these points are made in passing by Berton Kaplan in the special number he edited for Administrative Science Quarterly in 1968.[36] It is interesting that his background in the sociology of mental health organizations is precisely one of the areas which the CAG has not much drawn from.

Quite apart from ideology, plan, programmes, institutions, careers and so forth, development administration has to mean successful service relationships with clients and recipients in exceptional and difficult circumstances. The difficulties include the perceived significance of the service and its felt lack of continuity. In particular, there is likely to be an incoherence between the bureaucratized rank and file and the clients or recipients because they differ fundamentally about the ways in which they see, value and make calculations about time. Hence the service situation is likely to move over to riots or raids on the one hand, or camping out and other alternatives (like brokerage systems, exchange and group relationships) on the other.

Is it this sort of question which the essays have in mind? They admittedly are for the most part highly academic and in any case somewhat old papers written for a 1965 seminar. They present an excellent cross section of the CAG, with older figures like the editor and Diamant, and figures like Sherwood and Bock and younger people, Ilchmann, Savage, Gunnell and Jowitt. They also include the highly experienced Hahn-Been Lee, the essence of whose work here is already familiar.[37]

Our references on the time perspective are all post-1965 and these papers written presumably in the early part of that year, do, therefore, mark an early discussion. What a pity the volume did not come out then. For example, Savage takes a large bag: administrator's 'rational' time and environmental, political and cultural time. But he does see that the development drama includes different senses of time. On the other hand, Gunnell's and Diamant's essays now seem less useful from that point of view. Gunnell's is clearly an important and profound but somewhat remote effort. His discussion of time, change and development surveys many problems of social science but not many of administration. If we may quote Waldo's own 1962 paper on comparative public administration, then Gunnell's essay does not 'lower' comparative public administration. Similarly, Diamant is at one remove. His concern is with theories of administration and organization not with theorizing about let alone describing the administrative situation. Nor is his criticism of theories of mobilization systems (that is, political mobilization) as helpful now as when it was written. The papers by Ilchman and by Lee are both in their separate ways more interesting. Ilchman's is a cultural anthropology of time as a sort of ideology: a metaphor for simplifying and codifying reality for action. Western time is therefore one sort of metaphor. This explains gaps in developing countries between national elites and ancient cultures and resultant problems in management and productivity. His paper can in some ways be associated with Lee's essay, written with a combined insider's and social scientist's view of the incidence of the various sorts of time orientations (metaphors in Ilchman's sense) among elite groups.

Sherwood's essay is more empirical. It is about a comparative American-Brazilian study of the use of time by administrative leaders and it is very interesting indeed about time technologies and concepts. Does the editor imply a criticism in suggesting that it has 'faint echoes of early time and motion studies'? If so, that seems unfair. This remains a good study of the transferability of a particular technological reform.

Jowitt's is a sort of meta-narrative on Time and Development under Communism: the USSR case. He uses elite theory, Wilbert Moore's triad and Selznick's distinctions (from his Leadership in Administration). Bock's essay now reads like a reflection on American power to shape the future as a sort of benevolent colonialism. The editor himself contributes a brief conclusion and a kindly introduction. Some of the papers do indeed read as though they were written (as they were) six years ago. Some of them are exercises in social science meta-theorization and there is little empiricism through many of these pages. Savage and particularly Ilchman and Sherwood are obvious exceptions to that. Nor is one giving here a fair review of the papers from the point of view of their authors as they were written in 1965. What one is arguing is that if the CAG is still about communication between scholars and practitioners, and if it is concerned to do something about administration for development, then some of these papers are now much less helpful than others. The CAG (or its publishers) claims with absolute justification a great deal for itself, in particular that 'these papers represent what is undoubtedly the most exciting, provocative and imaginative research published in administration in the past century'. Without accepting the superlative, one does accept that many of the 100 papers as they came out did excite and provoke remarkably. In their handsome but not inexpensive republication in Professor Braibanti's series, one tends inevitably to subject the papers to tests which are different from those one put as they first appeared.

Weidner's volume is bigger, based on later papers (the 1966 Hawaii seminar) more scattered and in some ways more interesting. As we have suggested, the editor is in some ways a key figure for the whole movement. The authors of the papers include six Americans and six Asians. The papers in the volume fall into two categories. First, there are general essays by the editor, Riggs, and Martin Landau. Secondly, there are a number of case studies: Hahn-Been Lee again on the time orientation of members of the Korean higher civil service; Abueva on the Filipino civil service; Bernard Silberman on Japanese prefects and B. F. Khanna on the Indian civil service. There are two papers on Pakistan by Harry Friedman and by Inayatullah and one by Norman Meller on the Micronesian Congress. Then there are two quite uncritical pieces on technical assistance, one by Shou-Sheng Hsueh on EROPA, and another by Nguyen-Duy Xuan on the National Institute of Administration in Vietnam. The volume concludes with a fresh essay by Weidner to which we shall refer later.

Weidner's opening essay on 'The Elements of Development Administration' is highly organized. Apart from its presentation two things stand out. The first is that it is, in the CAG sense and context, very Riggsian and ecological: certain stated conditions will lead to development, other stated conditions will lead to a 'static society'. Carefully handled, that is no doubt a sensible starting point. The difficulty is that it is unclear what can then be done with separate studies of administration. Weidner himself seems to realize this towards the conclusion of his essay. The second thing is that it anticipates some points on innovation which Weidner takes up in his concluding essay. That makes the whole volume read in a tighter and tidier way than Waldo's. His propositions about innovation are indeed highly applied and empirical. However tentative his conclusions, they do lead anyone interested, particularly in technical assistance, to sit back and think. For example, 'perhaps if Vietnam had had a personal system based on civil service classes together with personnel rotation, as do India and Pakistan, the budget reforms would have been far more difficult to consummate'.[38] One knows that Americans did not like what they found about generalist administration in South Asia any more than the Fulton Committee did in Britain. One recalls Malcolm Parson's satirical piece about 'performance budgeting in the Philippines'.[39] But still one sees the point of Weidner's question.

Riggs's essay on 'The Idea of Development Administration' is as thoughtful as usual. On this occasion, development is taken to mean 'increase in the level of discretion of the social system' so that development administration is about the increase of discretion. But there is a difficulty. Is development administration in fact an instrument for increasing discretion, a discretion factor as it were, or is it merely the implementation of decisions which are themselves increasingly discretionary? Landau's essay, on the other hand, is very important in two ways. In the first place, it is one of the very few examples in the whole CAG opus where decision theory is explicitly recruited to the assistance of development theory. In consequence, he is able to make more interesting comments on spatial metaphors, time metaphors and cognitive maps as distinguishing social situations, than was the case in several of the papers in Waldo's volume. Indeed, Landau's paper acts as a most useful bridge between the two books. He acts as a bridge to other things also like Hall's work,[40] or the James Thompson-Tuden matrix, which has certainly been inadequately employed,[41] and he has a leavening degree of humour. It is only a pity that, save for a few references, as to La Palombara,[42] Landau was not able to bring his paper up to date with the tremendous strides in relevant work in decision theory since the material by Simon, Thompson, Tuden and others on which he is relying here. That does not blunt the point of the second main thing in Landau's work—his perception that development means an increased reliance on a factual basis for decision-making.

There are various good things in the case studies. Abueva's excellent and now well-known paper tells us for once something about medium-level civil servants in a developing country. And it is also an explicit attempt to see how far administrative development (professional standards and cultural change) is a condition for development administration. The papers by Khanna and Silberman are unexceptionable. The one is a summary of familiar material about selection and recruitment at the central and state levels in India, the other about the continuing achievement orientation of Japanese provincial governors, between 1868-99 and 1940-45. Harry Friedman argues, from Pakistani material, that programme changes will lead to more local participation, so to changes in administrative roles and so to a new sort of bureaucracy. After 1969-70 and the various crises in and about the CSP, this looks a much less acceptable piece of empiricism. So, too, Inayatullah's otherwise invaluable piece on the basic democracies now cries out for the sort of revision which its author could so well perform; or perhaps there is a case for leaving this paper as it stands for the sake of its material and as an exemplar of the opinion of that moment. It might be a pity to spoil its last footnote. 'This essay was written prior to the resignation of Ayub Khan in 1969. No change in the text has been made to reflect this development'.

This is nothing that is not admirable in Meller's 'Indigenous Leadership in the Trust Territory'. It might encourage some people to go on to read his full study on 'Congress of Micronesia',[43] or to look forward to the forthcoming volume in the CAG series to be edited by Kornberg and Musolf.[44] But it does stand by itself here, both because of its area and its problem, which is about small semi-colonial legislatures.

The two papers by Hsueh and Xuan also stand by themselves not so much because or their areas as because they are both essentially straight descriptive pieces. That is not to say they are not useful. For anyone interested in the CAG itself, it becomes very important to look at technical assistance and co-operation and its institutionalization. EROPA is an outstanding case. Similarly, the National Institute of Administration in Vietnam provides an excellent example of the work of one of the US university contracts, in this case Michigan State. Indeed, one might say that both these papers should be read by anyone fresh to the CAG before reading anything else at all. The way in which Xuan carefully relates points in his paper to other papers, in this volume particularly, adds to its usefulness in that sense. One is otherwise left to draw relationships, as between Khanna and Silberman, for oneself.

Khanna's conclusion asks for fresh thinking about 'the organization and ethos of civil services'.[45] Silberman's Japanese material provides it explicitly. 'Recent investigation and observation, however, have indicated that at certain stages of economic, political and social development, a civil bureaucracy need not exhibit all of the characteristics of Weber's legal rational bureaucratic type to be successful in development policy making and administration'.[46] Administrative development may be a condition for development administration; technical assistance might help. The problem is certainly to find alternatives to bureaucratic administration. Some of these papers get much nearer to that central problem than others in the whole CAG output have done.

How much further does Weidner's concluding essay take us on these points? It is certainly a good thing to try to give some specific and operational meaning to innovation. On the whole we have used this loosely and as though it were much the same thing as adaptation.[47] Probably Weidner is right to attempt to distinguish specific innovating roles which can then be more or less recognized in the field situation. Whether his particular list (inventors, borrowers, culture transmitters, advocate-leaders, detailers, change agents) is quite the most useful for administrative situations is perhaps to be doubted, as again is his use (as with so many of the authors here) of 'bureaucracy' to mean indifferently both a public service and a specific way of doing administration. In the light of Khanna's conclusion and of Weidner's concern to distinguish innovating roles for administrative systems in the fields he is interested in, that seems an unnecessary confusion. On the other hand, Weidner attaches to his list of roles some typically realistic examples. So when he gets to the end of his list, with 'the target group', he is able to provide both a recognizable picture of a likely situation and to ask some good questions about it.

Much more could be done both through role and through decision theory to distinguish innovators[48] and to see what that would mean for policy making and for administrative systems. If we can distinguish between adaptation and innovation, we could also distinguish between the critical and the crucial and between policy and political aspects. But the point is that Weidner is doing something about what the CAG was supposed to be concerned with. At this moment a new chairman of the CAG is taking over. With his bibliography[49] and his work for AID,[50] Gable ranks as one of the first figures in the movement; 1961 was very early for anyone to distinguish so clearly and explicitly between development planning, development assistance and development administration. Some people will be looking forward to the further volumes in the CAG series. Others, partly because they feel that they have already read many of these papers, may be more interested in what the CAG can now do under this new chairman to establish administration as another sort of consultative discipline for development. As we have indicated, development administration itself presents one sort of a checklist on the problems: broadly, what administrative behaviour for development in those sort of conditions would be like.[51] But the problems the CAG set itself were not merely to get answers to those questions; it was also to do something about it: a daunting task.

NOTES

1 Newsletter, Comparative Administration Group, Vol. V, No. 2, 1967, p. 41.

2   Peter Savage (ed.) *Journal of Comparative Administration* (Sage Publications).
3   See especially J. D. Montgomery and W. J. Siffin (eds.), *Approaches to Development: Politics, Administration and Change*, (McGraw-Hill, 1966); Bertram M. Gross, *Action Under Planning: The Guidance of Economic Development* (McGraw-Hill, 1967); Robert T. Daland (ed.), *Comparative Urban Research: the Administration and Politics of Cities* (Sage Publications, 1969).
4   Braibanti has already edited *Political and Administrative Development* (Duke, 1969). Forthcoming are: Fred Riggs (ed.), *Frontiers of Development Administration*; James Heaphey (ed.), *Spatial Dimensions of Development Administration*; A. Kornberg and Lloyd Musolf (eds.), *Legislatures in Developmental Perspective*; and more distantly, perhaps, Martin Landau (ed.), *Organisation Theory and Comparative Analysis*; Fred Riggs (ed.), *Comparative Bureaucracy*; C. Thurber (ed.), *Development Administration in Latin America*; Ed Bock and Brian Chapman eds.), *Comparative European Bureaucratic Development*.
5   E.g. W. Bicker, D. Brown, H. Malakoff, and W. J. Gore (eds.), *Comparative Urban Development: an Annotated Bibliography* (CAG, Special Series, No. 5, January 1965); T. E. Menge, *Government Administration in South Asia: a Bibliography* (CAG, Special Series, No. 9, December 1968).
6   CAG, 1965. This will be republished in the volume edited by Heaphey.
7   Dwight Waldo (ed.), *Temporal Dimensions of Development Administration* (Duke University Press, 1970), pp. XI + 312, 10$; Edward W. Weidner (ed.), *Development Administration in Asia* (Duke University Press, 1970), pp. XXIII + 431, 12$.
8   'Strengthening Development Administration', memoranda submitted by the Comparative Administration Group for a meeting jointly sponsored by the Ford Foundation and the Comparative Administration Group (New York, November 15/16 1963).
9   See the CAG newsletter Vol. I, No. III, May 1964, p. 24, for the survey of courses in 1964.
10 A nearly and excellent example, F. Heady and S. Stokes, (eds.), *Papers on Comparative Public Administration* (University of Michigan, Institute of Public Administration, 1963).
11 For example, William Gore, *Comparative Urban Development: An Annotated Bibliography*. CAG pamphlet series, 1965. That was published coincidentally with a remarkable work in high theory, Glenn Paige, *Proposition Building in the Study of Comparative Administration*, 1965.
12 Albert Waterston, *Administrative Obstacles to Planning*. Reprint from Economia Latino-Americana, Vol. I, no. 3, July 1964.
13 See especially the paper by Braibanti, 'Trans-national inducement of Administrative Reform; a Survey of Scope and Critique of Assumptions', now in the volume edited by Montgomery and Siffin.
14 For example, Garth Jones and Robert Giorvano, *Planned Organisational Change: a Working Bibliography*.
15 Nicolaas Luykx, *The Role of Rural Government in Agricultural Development*; Adam Curle, *Education, Administration and Development*; George Grassmuck, *Poverty, Bureaucracy and Interest Groups in the Near East and North Africa*; Jess P. Unger, *The Military Role in the Goals of National Building and Economic Development*.

16 S. N. Eisenstadt, *Continuity of Modernisation and Development of Administration.*

17 Lynton K. Caldwell, *Documentary Sources for the Comparative Study of Development Administration*; Wallace S. Sayre and Herbert Kaufman, *Outline of a Suggested Method Study of Comparative Administration.*

18 J. LaPalombara, *Strategies for Developing Administrative Capabilities in Emerging Nations.*

19 CAG Newsletter, Vol. V, No. 2, p. 12 and following.

20 Bureaucracies in Developing Countries: Internal roles and external assistance.

21 CAG, Papers in Comparative Public Administration, Special Series, No. 2. Published February, 1964, prepared for symposium April 1963 at the GSBA, Harvard, and presumably written between 1962 and 1963.

22 See Footnote 60 of the paper.

23 Edward Weidner, *Development Administration: A New Focus for Research* in Heady and Stokes, pp. 97-115.

24 Edgar L. Shur, 'Comparative Administration; Static Study Versus Dynamic Reform', *Public Administration Review* September 1962, pp. 158-164.

25 *Technical Assistance for Public Administration Overseas; The Case for Development Administration* (New York, 1963).

26 Milton J. Esman, *The CAG and The Study of Public Administration: a Mid-term Appraisal.*

27 G. E. Caiden, 'Development Administration and Administrative Reform', *International Social Science Journal*, Vol. 21, No. 1, 1967, pp. 9-22. The work of Victor Thompson is a remarkable exception, see for example, his 'Administrative Objectives for Development Administration', *Administrative Science Quarterly*, June 1964.

28 Colin Leys, Introduction, especially p. 4, in the volume edited by him, *Politics and Change in Developing Countries* (Cambridge, 1969).

29 Leys, pp. 11, 12.

30 With a few exceptions, notably Landau.

31 The sort of work which might have been but has not been done by the CAG in these directions is brilliantly indicated in the article by A. O. Hirschman and C. E. Lindblom, 'Economic Development, Research and Development Policy Making: Some Converging Views', *Behavioural Science*, Vol. VII, 1962, pp. 211-22.

32 *Temporal Dimensions and Development Administration.*

33 E. S. Redford, *Democracy in the Administrative State* (New York, 1969), pp. 94-5.

34 Mark Lefton and William R. Rosengren, 'Organisation and Clients: Lateral and Longitudinal Dimensions', *Americal Sociological Review*, December, 1966, pp. 802-10.

35 See Chapter 16 below.

36 Special Issue on Organizations and Social Development, December, 1968.

37 *Korea: Time, Change and Administration*, 1968.

38 p. 17.

39 *Public Administration Review*, Vol. 17, 1957, p. 173.

40 E. T. Hall, *The Silent Language*, (New York, 1959), in Landau, footnote 12, p. 80.

41 See Landau at p. 88, footnote 44.

42 Joseph LaPalombara, 'Theory and Practice in Development Administra-

tion', CAG papers, 1967 and one or two other publications.
43 Hawaii, 1969.
44 The papers in that volume were originally presented in a conference in New York in December, 1967.
45 p. 250.
46 p. 188.
47 There are important exceptions like the work of Jason Finkle.
48 See B. B. Schaffer, 'Deadlock in Development Administration', in C. T. Leys (ed.), *Politics and Change in Developing Countries*, p. 211, footnote 2 especially.
49 'Development Administration and Assistance: an Annotated Biblio-Bibliography' (Washington, 1961).
50 'Plan for research and publication in public administration' (Washington, 1961).
51 See definition in Weidner, page 393, footnote 42.

16

'EASINESS OF ACCESS'

A Concept of Queues

This chapter is concerned to distinguish a particular level of politics: the access by clients to the services or resources allocated by organizations. The notion of such a level is therefore associated with a particular view of organization. The paper argues that the problems of the acces relationship have been solved bureaucratically by arrangements whose peculiarities are best symbolized in the queue. Queuing, however, has certain limits and conditions. Outside those contingencies it can vary, break down or simply be unavailable. The problems and limits of queuing coincide with certain forms of integration and certain aspects of socio-political development.*

ORGANIZATIONAL CONNECTION

Students of comparative social change are inevitably attracted by dichotomous arrangements of types of societies. A common tendency is to think of some societies where men are self-sufficient or at least enjoy relationships which are simple, limited, near at hand, constant and familiar, in contrast with others where they are deeply involved in and dependent on relations with large but constantly changing numbers in specifically enacted situations. But men's lives are not often like Robinson Crusoe's. Thus, to take two extremely different examples, Burridge in his studies of Melanesia sees that men's lives develop meaning through organization. 'A man becomes a man within the terms of activity that are organized.'[1] The French novelist de Montherlant allows his introverted protagonist in 'The Bachelors' to become aware that all around him people are seeking connections and having difficulty in finding them, and that his peculiar vulnerability is precisely that has attempted to escape from that by relying on 'the family'.

* The ideas in this chapter have been helped by discussions with several friends and colleagues including Raymond Apthorpe, Douglas Ashford, John Ballard, Jeremy Boissevain, John Dearlove, Bruce Graham, Colin Leys, Theo Mars and Rita O'Brien.

The helpful thing is not to ask whether man needs organization or not but to see the intensity and variety of the need for connections, their rates of change and the ease or difficulty of securing them. In relatively small and stable social situations, the connections may obviously be more easily made, though other difficulties can intrude.[2] Similarly in 'total institutions', like prisons or hospitals, connections are again easier. As we move away from either of these situations, the difficulties of connections increase. Hence, if we conceive of organization as those arrangements in social situations which make connections more or less possible, we can say that the characteristics of organization in various societies follow the peculiar strains, the varying degrees of intensities, mixtures and change which these difficulties present. In adaptive societies, we try to create situations which can meet those complexities of intense, mixed and changing needs for connection. We then have to try to make the arranged connections (the complex organizations) more easily recognizable : with specific buildings and titles, for example; and with quite specialized roles to be performed (like leadership, maintenance, rank and file and customers) including the role of attempting to maintain some degree of stability, continuity and those recognizable features. Maintenance men allow rootless people and changing fashions to meet.

It is not easy either to handle the conflict of maintenance with the instabilities which called for the complex organization in the first place or the necessary communication between roles. To understand 'modern societies', how societies change and become more adaptive, evidently we have to understand this organizational syntax. It may be an instrument for explaining organization, for comparing more or less integration and different sorts of disintegration. One step towards this is to see that organizations are situations where many different connections, otherwise difficult, are made more possible. The adaptive situation makes connection difficult but vital. More organization becomes worthwhile. Hence, the artifice of formality obtrudes. To make it easier to get a taxi at London airport, 'a new independent board under the general authority of the Greater London Council' becomes necessary.[3]

So in the organized parts of complex societies, the varied demands of value affirmation, institutional management and career patterns are regulated to the level of programme. Many distinct though syntactically related activities will be at once going on : statements about objectives and programmes by some people; others trying to prevent too much change; others, again, struggling for better returns in careers or wages. But there will be others who are interested only in the occasional marginal connections for the bits of service, or allocations of resources, which made the whole arrangement necessary in the first, frequently all too distant, place. These are the interstitial activities, where demands and expectations are conditional, specific and short-term; patterns of service instead of programme. Organizations are situations where there are ideological, administrative or maintenance, and career or incentive activities going on: big programmes being announced and perhaps produced. But they are also situations where some people want and others are there to give small bits of service. The organization may be a major department of state seen by its leaders as a political resource and therefore to provide a great programme to make the resource worthwhile. It may be seen by others in other ways. Some people would not want the 'programme' but only a piece of it: a service; not a national pension scheme, or a change, or a career in running it, but merely a particular pension payment. This distinction between programme and service is what we are concerned with here. It has elsewhere been called a distinction between micropolitics on the one hand and sub-system or intermediary politics and macropolitics on the other.[4] It is also a difference between political levels or domains. Access and service across a divide is one sort of political exchange with its own stresses, characteristics and more or less unstable solutions. It is distinct from but related to political functions at other levels.[5]

The function of service means some potential recipients with access to other people providing the service, or allocating it at that point of access. The service, the point of access and the people have to be more or less visible. Hence the badges of recognition. For example, there may be a programme for agrarian reform by distribution of improved or 'miracle' seeds. Amongst other things, that has meant individuals wanting them, a place to get them and people to hand them out. In the Punjab, PV18 high-yielding wheat variety can be bought by farmers from agrarian universities. The farmers need to know about that and other services like getting machinery from similar sources to help them. There have to be such sources relatively available. That is the service relationship, obviously important and difficult, and equally obviously not a complete description of any of 'the organisations' involved: either the village, where the farmer who may be clever at knowing about the seeds and machinery himself came from; or the agricultural university too.

The service relationship, then, is one important but difficult part of organizational experience. In the first place, some people are often unexpectedly better at it than others:

' "but Sadhu is a clever man. Look how he brings all these machines from the university to do his work."

"Yes, times have changed. Now cleverness is almost as important on a farm as hard work." '[6]

Secondly, its difficulties can have unexpected but important consequences. A young child may be kept waiting an inevitably but unlooked-for length of time for a specific hospital treatment, the service which he needs. Meanwhile, he will become tense, insecure and aggressive. Attempts at solving or improving the organizational service connection can become very sophisticated (as in the Beeching recommendation for a complete distinction in the legal system between waiting for criminal and for a civil jurisdiction). The actual structures of the service relationship are likely, then, to vary between social situations in interesting ways.

Service is, then, only one of several relationships in organizational situations. It is relatively marginal and occasional for some, at least, of those involved. Hence, it is rather different from much more involving organizational relationships like leadership or maintenance. Yet save in situations of extraordinary abundance (like William Morris's News from Nowhere) it is nevertheless highly demanding. Most often, it demands knowledge and waiting. For example, a youngish member of the usually employed mass of Casablanca wishing to migrate to France needs a passport; to get it needs further papers; to get the papers needs a long visit to his native, long forgotten village, a resuscitation of family and friendship ties, patience, suffering and insults. It is not surprising that the decision to enter into a service relationship is regarded as at least a cost, at the most a veto, and whether this is with a hospital or government credit. The interest is that it is a peculiar, difficult but marginal relationship, varying between social situations, and likely to have unexpected consequences. As social situations get more adaptive or fluid, the service connection becomes more familiar: agricultural extension and the green revolution provide instance after instance. So how it is handled becomes our focus. Specifically, what we are doing here is to distinguish service or micro-politics from other organizational relationships, such as those between bureaux and interest groups, major political relationships and so on. These service relationships are characterized by what Redford calls micro-decisions, by a narrow or marginal involvement in the decisional process and by a sort of dyadic or mutual non-interference.[7] There is a growing literature on the relations between clients and formal organizations.[8] We wish to use the term 'applicant' to distinguish patronage situations, to indicate that the applicant has special needs,[9] is not a 'judgmental dope',[10] and that how these problems are handled is a 'critical determinant' in organization and an example of the significance of 'the routine grounds of everyday life'.[11]

In looking at how the service relationship is handled, we are going to use the model of the queue, of people waiting or standing in line at the point at which they have access to the service. For the management of a whole programme and organization, a problem is presented by arrivals and departures in any sub-system, like a service point. For orthodox queue theory the problem was the probable waiting times with a variable flow of arrivals at a service point and random intervals of time between arrivals and random servicing time. This can cause queuing. 'With a mean arrival rate (number of arrivals per unit of time) somewhat less than the maximum service rate, a fairly long waiting time, fluctuating in length, will occasionally form. This is called "queuing". At other times, the service facility will be idle, waiting for an arrival.'[12]

Queues are, then, a way of handling a situation in which service, or the resource to be allocated, is scarce and the applicants are to be treated as equally as possible; they will be distinguished only according to the amount of time they have waited and when they started to do so. Queuing will occur between the limits to permissible applicant inconvenience and the maximizing of costs by providing excess service. It is one sort of problem to calculate what the amount of queuing will likely be; it is another to work out the costs, when other management criteria will be set and when the limits will break down.[13]

As Hough says, 'A queue is only of interest when it imposes a recognizable cost.' But the mathematics and the management are only parts of this: they are about questions like what percentage of time a servicing channel will be idle; and how wide a span a manager, regarded as a servicing channel, can handle.[14] There are other ways of looking at the concepts here, and other aspects to them: the service, the applicant, the limits for him and the limits for the service. Queuing is a way of mechanizing the service relationship in organizational situations when there is less than excess capacity.[15] It is, in fact, a familiar example of the experience of this sort of organizational relationship and all the more familiar as situations become more modern and adaptive and organizations more bureaucratic. Queues are, too, rather easily researched, perceived and compared.

Queues are more familiar to some than to others. We know that their use may lead to a wide range of unanticipated consequences, sometimes with severe dysfunctions like the child waiting for hospital treatment. Even queuing at counters between applicants and those who are controlling the actual allocation of service can be highly sophisticated, depending on the types of system control which are, in fact, being used.[16] The queue structure for programming micro-decisions may be qualified by the intervention of associations, influence or politics; it may have heavy costs and it may break down. 'In spite of the devices for eliminating or minimizing micro-politics, access to administrative agencies making micro-decisions will still be unequal. All the formal arrangements may still not prevent the police from dealing more sympathetically with the sons of the rich and powerful than with the sons of the poor. The devices we have mentioned do not guarantee access to all. Costs of effective access may be too high.'[17] If we can get an operational definition of the queue as a structure for the service function of organization, we may be able to get some interesting comparisons. We may, since the comparisons will be about different social situations, even see the points of discontinuity; some sorts of dichotomies, then, for example, between those situations where queues will more or less work and those where they will not at all. We are likely to see the comparisons as those between situations and changes from one to another, as queues become more familiar, as in more adaptive societies. That is to say we do know that queuing as waiting in line is a familar experience in certain types of societies with various consequences and considerations. In others it does not seem to happen like that.

Now that is not simply looking at queue behaviour. It is concerned with trying to see the use of the queue as one sort of organizational structure for one sort of organizational function. It is not concerned simply with seeing that some people are standing in a line and these people may be a group with observable relations between them.[18] It is one thing to look at the queue as an almost self-sufficient social system of the queuers themselves, partly but inadequately explicable by environmental phenomena like publicity or the cultural values of the larger society. It is another thing to see the queue as a device or structure explicable as one of several organizational means which then needs situational study.

QUEUING

The queue is not simply a group situation which happens to appear, but a necessary element of certain situations produced by the structures of bureaucratized organizational connection. Queuing is a difficult and therefore revealing situation. It is a competition for definition, for the terms of understanding, of cognition, between people on either side of the counter.[19] It is also a competition of a different sort, amongst the applicants themselves, and between ego as applicant and in other roles. Behind the counter the service relationship is likely to be affected by other dimensions of organizational politics. Yet the queue is the bureaucratic solution to the organizational function of service. Bureaucracy turns 'clients' into 'applicants' waiting in a line, and some of the rank and file or employees into the 'men behind the grille' at the point of contact for service. The queue is about equality and orderliness in the specialized sense of bureaucratic depersonalization both of the applicant and of the man behind the grille. Thus, access for service becomes sharply distinguished from other organizational functions which other organizational members may be interested in; service is what the customer is interested in. He gains access to service from bureaucratic organization by accepting its conditions: the depersonalization of being nothing more or less than a cardinal position in the line. Queuing of some sort does and can of course occur in non-bureaucratic situations but it is bureaucracy which uses queues for its openness, publicity, equality and simplification: just join the line. In so far as other organizations in other situations use some sort of queuing to solve their problems of access, some degree of bureaucratization is emerging.

There are three special features of queues looked at as bureaucratic structures. Firstly, they become interesting not so much as groups or masses but as face to face and calculating dyadic situations between the man waiting for service and the man giving it.[20] Secondly, there is ample evidence of the rich symbolic significance of the queue, not only for 'order and equality', but rather for 'cleanliness or anticorruption'. Queues are not explicable by egalitarianism alone but they might be a limited and chosen symbol for it within notional groups. Queues are a bureaucratic structure, but they are also sometimes a symbol for the avoidance of its pejorative or ideological connotation.

Take two contrasting situations. Firstly, a British sporting journalist reports on ways in which the Firestone Country Club Golf course operates, 'They run it this way: any of Firestone's 9,000 workers providing they live within 50 miles of the course can apply for family membership at 180 dollars a year. There is no waiting list queue jumping by executives. Kimball Firestone is said to have waited two years to get in, and even those workers who are not in can play if they pay.'[21]

Firestone has clearly seen it as worthwhile to invest money in a demonstration of fairness. But the fairness is limited (a) to their own workers, (b) to workers within an area, and (c) to workers who pay an entrance fee. Secondly, there is an explicit contrast: 'queuing' equals 'good' and 'queue jumping' equals 'bad'. Within the group there is equality but equality only extends to the group as carefully defined. Thirdly, certain symbols are developed like the term queue jumping for the evil to be avoided and the two year wait by Kimball Firestone as the myth or story. Yet actually queue jumping is perfectly possible pragmatically since anyone can 'play if they pay'.

Now take a strikingly opposite case. In a London Times report on the 'objectives' (that is to say the ideological statements about policy) or the radical reforming group in Libya led by Colonel Al Kaddafi, it was explained that the group was highly concerned with the whole problem of corruption. 'Oil company representatives secretly had to bribe minor officials just for the right of seeing the official they wanted to negotiate with.' Here was a clear identification of queue jumping with corruption of another sort. There were two different sorts of corruption being discussed. In the report on the revolutionary command council (RCC) anti-graft programme, the first thing mentioned is that 'the principle of the queue has been instated in government offices, from the Ministry of Petroleum (sic) to the Ministry of Transport'. The queue is referred to as a 'principle', and indeed the first principle. At the same time it is contrasted with 'paper work', 'obstructing bureaucrats' and so forth. It is not, then, that the 'principle' of the queue is seen as an instrument of bureaucracy with inevitable paper work but precisely as its opposite. The symbol of the queue is powerful in two quite different situations, Firestone and Libya. It is a fairly complex symbol. Much more than equality, and not necessarily orderliness at all, are symbolized: fairness, notional group solidarity, reform, etc.

Thirdly, the history of the queue not as a symbol but as an actual structure shows just how it was the specialized bureaucratic answer to a preceding problem of access. Access is one of the oldest and most interesting of organizational problems. It implies more than service and its distinction in organizational situations. Boswell quoted a report about Lord Chesterfield's 'general affability and easiness of access',[22] but Boswell's readers know that that could go wrong quite dramatically where access was about a relationship between a client and a patron. If queueing is a solution to problems of access, it must have something to do with the solution to the problems of clientele, that is, a depersonalization or precisely a bureaucratization of service. The Lord Chesterfield or patronage type of service institutionalized queue jumping by providing for corruption, random selection, ambiguous or unstable criteria and back door entry. Hence the necessity for various multiplex reinforcements of client/patron relations either by brokers or by compadres. But it was the queue which really provided 'easiness of access'.

Access implies a means of entrance; an action of admission, and a criterion of admissibility. Like accession, it means some change for the applicant, but only as a limited or incremental improvement, by a piece or item of service received. Its problems are ancient, but the sort of freedom from patronage implied in the Firestone or Libyan symbol was provided by queuing. Bureaucracy apparently came into the English language in the 1820s and 1830s.[23] Queues in our sense of people waiting in line came into the English language precisely in 1837. There was, then, always a problem of access; there were only queues (as a matter of usage) when bureaucratic organization emerged to do something about that problem.

We can now then define the queue situation more. We see a queue situation when there are people who are in some sense in line and waiting. They are expending specific resources of time and evidently accepting certain rules about their ordinal position rather than anything else as giving them access to service, in the sense of their being ready to meet the criterion of admissibility. One would not tend to talk about a queue if the line were endless or if the members were 'bunched' as a group (a club, association etc.). The queue is linear because its members are merely positionally adjacent and not in any other relationship and because the two points (actual access to service and the end of the line) are not incalculably distant. Nor, for queues to work, need the line be physically present. It is the business and the acceptance of the criterion of waiting which makes the queue. It is most easily seen and most obviously experienced in a physical line. When other communication can function, that is not the necessary as it is not only condition, like waiting to get your house or your operation.

It is not, then, merely the individuals in a line which tells us what a queue is. It is also something about their resources, their calculations and expenditure of them, where by no means the only but the most immediately significant resource demanded is time: how long to the counter of service point. This is the other sense of access: the action of admission to service. And then it is something about the head of the line at the point of access; the man behind the grille and his relations with the man at the head of the line. The queue as a solution to the problem of access for service is a relationship between the applicant as the bureaucratized client and certain individuals in the bureaucratized rank and file. The ideal type queue has, then, two elements; individuals who have made certain calculations and perceptions about meeting the conditions of access; and then the actual point of access (like the counter or grille) and what happens there, when the relationship between the queuer and the rank and file servant behind the grille occurs. 'In the firm it isn't the manager who represents God for me, it's the cashier in his iron cage; deaf, dumb, blind—God personified.'[24] The queue is a structure for competition between applicants for a scarce allocation, who want it, know about its conditions and will meet them, as long as there is a limit to the number who will do that and the conditions (like waiting) which they will meet. It is also a structure for reconciling the interests and cognitions of the applicants and the allocators in touch; some of all the potential consumers and some of all the organizational members; the rank and file, the men behind the counter. No one else and nothing else is present in the encounter, and there is no change: it is too momentary. It can be varied, modified and qualified, by making the conditions of access easier or 'better'; but access might also be more confusing, and reconciliation riskier and less likely. At certain points, the structures will collapse; in some situations they are unnecessary or impossible.

THE STRUCTURE

The attraction of the queue is the degree to which it simplifies problems, like responsibility in public bureaucracy; in other situations it provides a simplification for all organizational members. Generally, bureaucracy means pyramidal supervision. That demands adequate lower level expertise or knowledge of the rules about allocation. For such decisional functions the queue was the optimal answer because it provided a single but sufficient and extrinsically available tool. It reduced the burden of politicization or responsibility in public bureaucracies and in pyramidal supervision generally by an utter simplification of the criterion for allocation down to a patent positional test amongst those who had been waiting (in one sense or another). Queuing suits bureaucratic organization because it helps to maintain and simplify exchanges at the level of service; perhaps it suits applicants, too, to limit the degree to which organization and programme intervene in their lives. That depends on how easy it is for them to make a deal about the conditions of access, like the timetables of hospital patient and physician,[25] on how many separate presentations the applicant has to make before he has put together the whole service he wants[26] and how effective various symbols are (like the waiting line as fairness).[27]

But queues have two problematic aspects. The first concerns the distinction, of interests and position, between the rank and file servant and the queuing applicant: how it is established and how nevertheless the relationship is managed and the interests reconciled. The second aspect is concerned with the problems of the conditions of access. Let us look first at the applicants and the rank and file. If we think of the rank and file as the men in contact with the queue at the service point we are using one distinction about organizational employees that can be made. In some situations and from some points of view the dominant theme seems to be the problem of morale. In another sort of situation where he is 'on his own', the problem may be role confusion; is this man, say, a rank and file servant or a chief or an uninterested passing urbanite lost in his country's service; is the function one of service at all? If we look at the applicants in the queue, again we get rapidly to a sense of the differences between one queuing situation and another and to its limits.

The basic problem of the rank and file position in the large, complex and formal public organization of the developed society, is morale.

> 'Your leading article recognized that the problems confronting the civil service are by no means concentrated at the higher level. There is a danger in discussing the civil service of concentrating on the policy makers at the top. It is true that their work is crucial to the task of government and senior civil servants have felt the strain in recent years. But the reputation of the civil servant with the public depends almost entirely upon the performance of the middle and lower grades. These civil servants often have to discharge unpopular duties, but despite music-hall portrayals, they have obtained public confidence.
> It is in this large area of the civil service that morale matters most.'[28]

In a less developed country the dominant rank and file problem may be different. Think of the replacement of sheiks for administration of a new irrigation service by appointed officials. Here one is not so much exchanging confusion for specialization or vice versa, or extortion and tyranny for corruption, lack of interest and knowledge, as one is exchanging one sort of confusion for another.[29]

With the applicants in the queue, we will see their problems altering in varied situations too. We can give three immediate examples: the first shows that a queue-type simplification may be imposed which will have very different connotations from the applicant's point of view. For example, there is an attempt to introduce a better queuing system into the allocation of local authorities' housing in Northern Ireland. This is to be done by a reduction of discretion and a greater reliance on an objective points system: that is, a queue type system. An obvious criterion for points would be family size but that would act so as to appear to favour Catholic rather than Protestant families; and it therefore appears as both a radical and a sectarian change. Some potential queuers would be bound to see it in that way.

Take a second example, of unanticipated gaps or discontinuities between applicants and rank and file. Here the situation was that the rank and file employee was a taxi driver who was a recent urban migrant. Coming from a distant rural area, he held in contempt the relative readiness with which people formed queues to wait for taxis. In consequence he tended to delight in attempting to break the queue in the way in which he allocated his service. Here, then, from one point of view the applicants were seen as only too ready to queue.

A third case is one where potential applicants need to but are apparently incapable of forming a queue, as in one of the FAO's 'permanent disaster' areas in North East Brazil (Ceara State). Here the military regime set up 'organized' food depots and provided 'emergency' jobs for an estimated 165,000 peasants. The emergency figured as a result of regular features like unemployment at the end of the cotton picking season; an exceptional drought, and actual food raids. Food depots, as a service for which peasants should queue, were set up as a response to macro-political exchanges like raids and presidential visits. The results, however, were not the formation of a successful queuing situation. Raids continued. If they stopped at all it was because of army supervision.

There were doubtless several factors preventing the formation of a queue rather than riots. The applicants had inadequate economic resources. Even with an emergency job the wage (2 cruzeiros a day) did not buy a ration. Nor did the peasants have adequate communication resources. They were put in camps, that is they were grouped. According to the bishop, they 'had not the courage' to speak to authorities, a different sort of courage, presumably, from raiding. Equally, local officials simply said that the peasants were 'accustomed to misery'.

There are various ways of trying to deal with the strains which enter the relationship between the servant and the applicant. One is by advertising and publicity for the service. Another is law, points and the ration book. Reduction of the information available to applicants may be another means. Applicants may not be allowed to know how reduced and simplified their rights are.

'You'll have to wait,' said a Russian in a Leningrad restaurant queue when two drunken men tried to push in front of him. 'It's the same in America or England, everyone queues to get in a restaurant.'

If such a belief is widespread here, it may help to explain the resignation with which Russians tolerate this persistent and unattractive institution. From student canteens to the best restaurants the infuriatingly slow queue is commonplace.[30]

Big international hotels seem to be an exception, since misinformation and therefore acceptance cannot be enforced there, and it seems to be accepted that foreigners may anyway be exempted from or 'allowed to jump' the queue. The extent of queue institutionalization can indeed go very far. If it becomes accepted that queues are a simple way of getting access to a scarce service, then despite the necessity of calculation and the conflict of interest at the point of service, the very presence of a queue may be taken to imply that something worthwhile is being allocated. A queue creates queuing because of what it symbolizes. 'A large jostling queue formed in lunchtime Oxford Street. With no means of knowing what was at the other end, shoppers joined it just because it was there. Massive ladies emerged from the scrummage triumphantly clutching three signed copies of selected poems which they reckoned would make lovely Christmas presents.'[31]

There were three aspects of that queue for Mrs. Wilson's book. The queuers could not calculate the time invested against the value of the resource since they had 'no means of knowing' what it was. The queuers accepted the queue as a symbol of fairness and of a worthwhile resource. The queuers wished to compensate either for the investment or for what they found to be an error by purchasing three copies rather than one, for the explanation of the value was clearly a rationalization. One would not argue that Russian cities, Oxford Street and wartime Britain are identical social situations. What is interesting is that each can variously accept queuing with different solutions to its problems of reconciliation and of access; other situations, like the Brazilian northeast, cannot do so at all.

The reconciliation of the distinct positions of different members is a general concern of organizational studies. The difference of position between applicant and servant is clear. The way in which the queue simplifies the breakdown of service into discrete elements may not cohere with the needs of programme, institution or ideology; it certainly does not cohere with the applicant's needs. The ideal type servant assumes that the only criterion he need regard is queue leadership. If he is removed from that utter simplification he will wish to fall back on similar simplifications which convert the client into the case as in a queue plus points system. The applicant, having fulfilled the minimum requirement by his calculations and time investment, will wish to make the best not the least use of his position.[32] That is the essence of the problem of positional reconciliation in queuing.

There is also the problem of the conditions of access, of getting in the queue. This is a competition of a different sort; not for definition but for allocation. Queuing does not necessarily mean actually standing in line. In any case not everyone can stand in line or gain admission in physical terms. Here the law again can be resorted to, but a problem of enforcement will remain.[33] Sometimes it is the access not the service which is the whole problem, like queuing at a gate to have a railway ticket clipped when the train itself has a surplus of seats. Access also makes demands on recipients' knowledge. Potential recipients cannot gain access to the pleasures of remote beaches unless they have and can use road maps. Few do, so queues do not actually form. If access conditions are eased by road improvements queues will form.

'The basic trouble is people. More than five hundred thousand live within an hours drive of Pembrey. More than one and a half million live within two hours drive. Access difficulties make it look splendidly remote but it isn't. The pressures will build up as roads improve.'[34]

In a sophisticated society the problems of access can be affected by legislation and its enforcement or by a balance between less common resources like map knowledge and more common like a readiness to drive (or in fact to queue) on better but crowded roads. Such a society can tolerate complicated access systems, as during the second world war in Britain, when queuing for limited public transport was statutorily enforced but so also was priority for pregnant mothers.

If we turn to South Asian situations we see that the demands of access are less easily met. We can take three instances of this: queuing at government shops, selling a limited but distinct number of consumer foods at subsidized prices from aid programmes; family planning clinics; and income taxation offices. In the food shops queuing for one food does not provide a perception by the queuers of the situation for other foods. Coming to the head of one queue gives no right in any of the others. The applicant's problem is to know where to turn next. To solve this, brokers begin to appear, but they may be by no means efficient or disinterested.

The queues then tend to disintegrate either into an exchange situation or into an opting out; the applicants 'camp out', a heavy, scarcely calculable investment of time, not so much to succeed in as simply to avoid the queue, and hope for some other solution.

In the family planning clinics, problems of access are reinforced by the problems of reconciliation. The applicant is unsure of his status between beneficiary or sufferer.[35] Is this resource something wanted or something enforced? It is unfamiliar and open ended, the very opposite of the certain and discrete elements of service in the ideal queue. At the same time, the servant sees himself and is equipped to be merely the gateway or means of access, while the applicant needs from the servant much more than that: reassurance, advice and respect. Hence it is not surprising that a survey showed that queuing at clinics worked badly in family programmes.

In queuing the applicant has to remain that and nothing else; the servant has to remain a bureaucratic rank and file member; and no one else can be present in the situation. But in a South Asian taxation office almost anyone who at one moment may be applicant may calculate, time being plentiful and the role undesirable, that it would be worth moving into a brokerage or advisory relationship for someone else in the queue. That is not 'corruption' but a constant positional fluidity. Queuing is a simplification partly because it reduces the service situation to two specialized, distinct and stable roles. That is exactly what is so difficult to achieve in the tax office. On the servant's side defences are then set up. He may reinforce his position by dysfunctional enthusiasm, by a refusal to look at the papers sufficiently carefully (over-simplification) or by a sort of desimplification which treats all data and papers coming before him equally but non-functionally (over-expenditure of time).[36]

DIFFICULTIES AND CONDITIONS

Situations which lead to queue variation are not necessarily the same as those which exacerbate the difficulties of queuing. Thus several factors in the blood transfusion service operated by the Birmingham Regional Hospital Board make it attractive and possible to avoid the apparent or nominal use of queuing. 'There can be no assembly line treatment of blood donors.'[37] The voluntary status of the donor, the difference between a donor and an applicant and technical reasons for individualization demand expensive qualification of queuing. Computer identification makes the elaborate disguise possible. This is not the same as disintegration.

That is not to say that queuing always works well and easily, if with sophistication, in relations between individuals and bureaucratic organizations in developed societies. The model is for applicants to be treated individually in queuing, as distinct from the articulation of group interests in quite other ways.[38] In fact, the opposite can sometimes happen. It may be the group which is excluded and the individual who is co-opted. The group cannot queue as an alternative and the co-opted applicant has no need to do so. An example is a group like an amenity society. Despite its formal rights under the Town and Country Planning Act 1968 and the Civic Amenities Act 1967 it may be excluded from co-option in the authoritative decision-making process while the authorities (here the local government council) co-opt a particular individual recipient. 'Councils and developers acting together make more than a match for any number of amenity societies.'[39]

Yet if we take either the applicant/servant relationship or the problems of access we do see some social situations which make the structures more tolerable and others where that is not so. 'There is nothing that is not based on misunderstanding,' but in some situations queuing may make misunderstanding between an individual and an organization tolerable, insignificant or even functional. Queuing is meant to make access to and allocation of service simple. Its advantages remain where the servant does not use other criteria, only simple impositions of the queue, and where the conditions and necessary calculations remain patent and do not become complicated or forbidding.

Queuing suits those situations where the imprudence and risks of human contact can be reduced without preventing and sometimes assisting the degree of contact necessary for service. That may be why the Englishman is rather good at and ready to accept the queue. Much becomes irrelevant and therefore hidden. As the Egyptian proverb has it, 'Hide your life as the cat hides its excrement.' The German playright contemporary of Weber, Carl Sternheim wrote about the advantages that this indifference and depersonalization provided for the rank and file bureaucrat. His public role could not be simpler or less significant. What might his private life and dreams then be?

But in other social situations than English society, or the German society of Weber and Sternheim, things may work out much less satisfactorily for any and in the end every participant in this attenuated relationship. One may think of the 'administrative enthusiasm' of the Russian 19th century rank and file official: the railway ticket clerk or the church verger.[40] ' "I doubt whether you know what administrative enthusiasm means in practice and what sort of thing it is.'

'Administrative enthusiasm? I have no idea.'

'I mean—vous savez chez nous—en un mot—appoint some miserable nonentity to sell some absurd railway tickets, and this nonentity will immediately imagine that he has the right to look down upon you as if he were a Jupiter himself, when you got to take a ticket, pour vous montrer son pouvoir. "You wait", he says to himself. "I'll show you my power", and in them this sort of thing reaches the point of administrative enthusiasm.' "

The official used the relationship not to simplify but dysfunctionally to enhance his role. That puts the applicant to some risk beyond his calculations. The risk may indeed become severe simply because of the inadequacy of the decisional resources which the rank and file official can bring to bear even on his simplified role in such underdeveloped societies, apparently.[41] In 1847, for example, Alexander Herzen had at last gained the passport which would enable him and his immediate family to leave Tsarist Russia. He gets to the border; the Prussian gendarmes receive him: a very simple queue situation; the difficult queuing should, by then, have been over. But two things still go wrong. The rank and file bureaucrat, in this case the gendarme, insists on reading out, as Herzen puts it, all 'that was unnecessary': all the purely formal descriptions in the papers. The passports had been signed by a Russian general and the gendarme read 'three times in three passports all the decorations of General Perovsky including his buckle for an unblemished record'. The second thing to go wrong was that Herzen's own passport seemed to be missing; here the farce of the first situation could have been absolute tragedy through the same inadequacy. The passport was in fact found, at the last moment, by the official. Herzen asks him, 'Where did you find it?' 'Look,' he said, 'Your Russian sergeant folded them one inside the other: who could tell it was there? I never thought of unfolding them.'

In some situations, then, queuing may become qualified and a less easily calculable and acceptable relationship. In other situations, it may disintegrate and become impossible. That is so when the potential applicant cannot see the bureaucratic rank and file servant as such at all, rather than as a potential factional ally, a resource or prize to be captured or lost, as a potential patron, or someone who, like the gentry in Southern Italy, has to be approached only with tribute in one's hands.[42] In faction-ridden village situations the official is an intervenor not a servant: just like the landlord for the share cropping peasant or the shopkeeper or money lender in the mercantile domain.

That is all the more likely where the low level functions of the officials have been related to censuses, law and taxation. But the reductionism of queuing is no easier where the official takes on interventionist functions, like extension. Community development is a catalogue of the difficulties or establishing and reconciling the applicant/servant relationship. In the Philippines the applicant wants to establish his complicated concepts of gratitude and payment (which do not necessarily prevent his cheating). They are not eased by the youth, eliteness, sometimes the sex, the language and the different types of knowledge which the servant (the rural reconstruction worker) brings into the relationship. An apparently easy reconciliation through an adoption of the role of compadre has extreme costs and dangers. The calculations of time and distance on either side of the relationship are quite distinct.[43]

Herzen's memoirs indicate risk to the applicant. Flavier's study indicates risk to the rank and file official when queue reduction does not operate at all. 'In one barrio a young rural reconstruction worker made the breakthrough when ten families agreed to plant onions as a secondary crop. Before the end of the season, he was threatened with bodily harm because the onions were not forming bulbs. He knew they would bulb as he had tried that variety in another part of the province. But then who could foretell. The people were about ready to lynch the worker when the onions decided to bulb. The villain became the hero overnight.'[44] The recent legislation in India removing the recognition of India's hereditary aristocracy took pains to abolish privileges in queuing explicitly.[45]

Disintegration is not surprising since both aspects of the queue, the access arrangements and the reconciliation of the applicant and the servant, make their demands. If we look at it from the point of view of the bureaucratic applicant we see that the queue can function on three conditions. He must be able to make calculation of his investments of resources, primarily time. He needs certain other resources, for example, knowledge about mapping, special arrangements or form-filling. Certain accidental difficulties of access must be evened out in the society so that equalization, in that sense, does prevail. Yet at the point of access to service, he then will wish to distinguish himself. From this point of view, the queue is a condition or test. Having fulfilled it, he will wish to be treated specially rather than indifferently. The position of the bureaucratic rank and file official servant is precisely the opposite. The calculations, resource demands, and access problems for the recipient are totally irrelevant for him. At the point of service, he wishes to routinize, simplify and depersonalize the applicant's service relationship as far as possible. Reconciliation is possible 'when the behaviour of the official however it may conflict with the client's interests and perceptions, is at least comprehensible to him'.[46] The 'disregards' and the false attentions, the hidden stigmas and the precedence of case just balance out.

The strains can, we have seen, be affected by institutionalizing the value of the queue itself; by raising the value of the allocated service, as by advertising; or by a reduction of the recipient's comparative knowledge as in the Soviet restaurant queue. More generally, the relationship is most tolerable in those sorts of situation where the recipient has empathy for the official. 'The client, though irritated, will remember that he too understands the distinction between home and office, between the lay and the specialized and between duty and will. He is a member of an adaptive society in which he himself is not always a client.'[47] He has or hopes for a career too.

The most obvious demands of the queue system and the most general conditions of reconciliation are precisely a description of one sort of society, and the opposite of another: the encapsulated village situation, for example, where officials have to be seen as prebends, intruders or prizes, where the service is incomprehensible, unwanted, of no significance, and, above all, the gap between the applicant and the official very severe indeed. The applicant does not, in fact, move in his life, through a career, out of the encapsulation. Inter-level discontinuities make it impossible for the villager to distinguish the position of the official or, say, between a bureaucrat and a party functionary.[48]

Similar discontinuities may prevent queuing arrangements (like the allocation of public housing by points systems) from operating in developed and adaptive societies. For example, 'a considerable over-representation of Commonwealth immigrant families among London official homeless,' indicates such a breakdown. The service is too scarce, the resources of applicants too low, their demands too severe. Reconciliation and access cannot function.[49] Queuing disintegrates and is non-functional. The applicant is seen explicitly not as an individual but as a member of a group. The bureaucratic organization can then defend itself by calling on a political evaluation theme like 'problem or pathological families'.

Clausewitz said that in war even the simple is difficult. In a queue, even its simplifications are very complicated. An applicant may wish to be re-personalized at the moment of service. The official must retain the depersonalization when he has been asked not to, and yet must not resort to 'prejudiced' perception, as in housing allocation. It is not surprising, then, that queuing is a delicate structure easily altered and sometimes breaking down in any situation at all. For example, the member of a potentially prejudged group or equally an individual suffering from a peculiar rather than a group stigma may hope that the very reduction of the relationships in the queue is a solution to the problem of 'passing'.[50] That is, of getting by and of getting what you want without showing too much of who you are or your whole self. Hence embarrassment and potential breakdown when the very getting in the queue constitutes a display, the opposite of passing, and turns both the servant and standers-by into an audience. Such are the problems in UK schools of administering exemptions from payment for school meals for underprivileged children without showing them as such; and hence the extraordinary contortions which the authorities have suggested in desperate attempts at solving this problem.

In any case, the irony of queuing is that it is the very need of the member of the potentially suffering group for the item of service, like housing, which may force or tempt the bureaucratic servant to call on irrelevant prejudice to simplify his severe problem in allocating this over-demanded and under supplied service. Similarly, it is the very participation in the mere impersonalities of queuing which can, at the moment of service, of contact between applicant and servant, break down the apparent advantages of passing for the person suffering from stigma. 'But he who passes finds unanticipated needs to disclose discreditable information about himself, as when the wife of a mental patient tries to collect her husband's employment insurance or a "married homosexual" tries to insure his house and finds he must try to explain his peculiar choice of beneficiary.'[51] The stigmatized individual has moved out of forbidden and 'back places' into the civil world.

It is not merely the conditions of access and the problems of reconciliation and tolerance in the applicant/servant relationship which have to be met, but certain calculations beforehand also. It is not surprising, then, that change, disintegration, or even sheer unavailability, is the fate of queuing in some situations. From the point of view of the applicant, for example, in some societies there is a host of reasons why the queue may not form and become something else, like the exchange situation in Indian government food offices. Disintegration into a riot, on the one hand, or camping out on the other may occur.

There are two particular demands made on the applicant which he is unlikely to be able to meet in poor and discontinuous societies. One is the cultural resource of knowing how to handle the problems of access: at its simplest, which line to join. The second condition is that time must be a calculable and relatively valuable resource for him.

He will queue but not indefinitely. That, in its turn, assumes that time is a categorically similar concept for him and the official. The second condition demands also that he sees the service as significant but not overwhelmingly so, and available in a fairly continuous stream. He can then make choices about when it might be more sensible for him to join the queue. These will be meaningful and functional choices available to him because of his previous experience or other learning. He is then calculating, rational and adaptive. But in many societies none of these conditions can operate. Time is not shared, the service is not of limited significance, he cannot make choices on the assumption of continuity. The continuities and breaks in the service provided by the organization through the rank and file may make no sense to him at all. That is a common and important characteristic of administration in developing societies.[52] In the analysis of these conditions we have some of the explanations of the difficulties of service, the problems of access and the vulnerability of queuing in many situations.

The significance of queuing is seen partly in its symbolic role, as in Libya, in the Firestone Country Club or with Indian princes. Its significance is seen too in the emotion of language around it. Opting out is spoken of as 'corruption' or 'queue jumping', or 'private affluence'.[53] Its significance is also seen in its vulnerability and the severity of its demands, as in the ease with which dysfunctions and disintegration (or 'corruption') occur, even in Soviet life:

'When the sought-after items appear, they may sell out in a few frantic hours. Women rush to telephone their relatives or queue resolutely to buy for their friends as well as themselves.'
'It is no use blaming under the counter dealings, the police also tour the shops and regularly find the recipients holding back scarce goods for their own use or to sell to anyone who offers a bribe. Such abuses are a function of shortages not their cause.'[54]

This is disintegration. The queuers become group members buying for their friends as well as themselves. The servant becomes also an applicant. The assistants hold back scarce goods for their own use. The mere rule of waiting in line is confused by economic exchange or bargaining (or 'bribes').

Further, there are significant differences in queuing and reactions to it. There does seem to be a difference between opting out, reconciliation and qualification on the one hand, and grouping, riot, camping out or role exchange as disintegrations on the other. The group life of the Japanese apparently makes him wish to take all his leisure activities, even his travelling, not merely in groups but in the same group as that in which he will undertake his other activities. One has at that point moved away from the dysfunctions and qualifications of individual queuing altogether.[55]

Similarly, there is a distinction between a situation where there is a legal entitlement to a service but the supply is so low that the bureaucratic organization falls back on irrelevant defences, prejudice or political themes, and another situation when any legal entitlement itself is simply not available. Here the problems are inherently insoluble, because the applicants are simply not going to get any service at all. Such may be the case with immigration.

Again, the actual conditions of access by queuing may become intolerable. Waiting is one thing, running is another. One thinks of Tolstoy's story, 'How much land does a man need.' The devil, disguised as the chief of a Bashkiri land-owning tribe, with a great surplus of land, says that the potential recipient will gain as much land as he can run round in a day. The devil knows full well that the test of 'greed' will always prevent the recipient from fulfilling the condition. He will try to run round so much that he will die before the end of the day. Similarly, Perlov's description of a queue running for herrings in wartime Turkmenistan is a case of intolerable queuing.[56] On the other hand, queues become something else again, when they are institutionalized so as to become ends in themselves as in the example studied by Mann or as in situations of social disintegration when they are the only places where people have something to do and an opportunity to meet. Such a situation is described by Paustovsky in Odessa after 1917.[57]

These are general or social breakdowns. They are distinct from purely individual instances as for the stigmatized person or for other types who cannot maintain the necessary disassociation.[58] In almost any social situation queuing can be interrupted. The more the discontinuities or gaps of empathy between the categories from which the officials the applicants come, the likelier the breakdowns are. Blau has shown the susceptibility of queuing in public agencies to irrelevant criteria. They emerged as an unanticipated consequence of statistical controls where there was such a gap.[59] Not surprisingly, then, arrangements by the United States Federal Government for poverty programmes often break down at the point of queuing. That was so initially with the arrangements for the Federal food stamp plan.

Similarly, queue arrangements constantly break down in the UK in arrangements for service to applicants coming from categories which are seen as specially separated groups, like immigrants' relations with housing and with police authorities, or gypsies' and 'travellers' arrangements with local authorities who are supposed to provide permanent sites and facilities.

The difficulty arises because the empathy of 'disregards' is meant to provide an easy flow of information: a non-strenuous communication between applicants and the rank and file members of the service organization. That is, the organization has imposed a self-denying ordinance on itself about the range of data it will require from applicants for its services, and the ordinance is actually accepted in the way in which the rank and file servants go about their work. The applicants, at the same time, can see, then, that there are things which they are not going to be asked about, which they can continue to possess, which will be an area of privacy. But these communications of 'minimal' information, as in art, are quite demanding. That condition of queuing often breaks down even in relatively rich societies, for some individuals, for categories who can all too easily be segregated as groups, and in emergencies.[60] So it is not surprising but revealing to see where the conditions of queuing cannot be provided in other situations, typically with encapsulated villages, suspicious peasants, and societies with interlevel problems of communication, where the possibility of setting up the minimal qualifying signals of queuing systems are too much for the communication pattern.

That will certainly be true in emergencies. The attempt to distribute food and water through a queue in Amman in September 1970 broke down completely. Jordanian army officers called on women and children in Amman streets to 'queue up for water being distributed from a water tanker while armed soldiers looked on'. But the queue did not form. Distribution was at its best wasteful and irrational.

'Army lorries arrived from time to time to distribute flour and were mobbed by famished townspeople.

'These distributions turned into near riots and most of the people who tried to get flour finished up with their hands and faces dusted white. The Bedouin soldiers in charge of the distribution used their gun belts freely and when that failed started shooting into the air.

'Armed troop carriers and armed cars were also shooting into the air to clear a way through the crowds.'[61]

Queuing structures change and break down, then, relatively easily but significantly. If we see what the minimum conditions of a queuing system are, then a failure to meet the minimum conditions is likely to be revealing about social discontinuities. One condition is that the queue servant and the queuing applicant have and maintain distinct interests. They can only be reconciled without surrendering that distinction (which would mean a cessation of the queue) if each has some though not too ready a possibility of imagining himself in the other's situation. There also has to be a presumption about the relative continuity of service. The service has to be wanted but not overwhelmingly. Temporal calculations on either side of the counter have to be compatible. Alternatives (exchanges, grouping, camping out and riots) are always easily available. Hence the symbolic strength of the queue and the rich and fanciful variety of emotive descriptions of breakdowns and for defending the service.

Queue disintegration is familiar but revealing, for example, about cultural differences. The bureaucratic servant may like regularity and simplification in measurement; the applicant may positively dislike it. Karen Blixen makes just that point in describing the operation of her Kenya farm clinic as an out-patient department.[62] She learned about the people, 'their deep dislike of regularity, of any repeated treatment or the systemization of the whole'. It was not a lack of courage, it was a fear of 'pedantry'. The patients waited well enough. What they would not do was form a queue.

Again, a lack of queuing or an acceptance of a poor service when a much better seems almost equally available, may reveal another sort of gap. What the bureaucrats know is not what the recipients know. Recent discussions of poverty and migration in the United States have indicated that 'a poor family of four in Alabama or Mississippi can count itself lucky if it is given 50 dollars a month by a grudging state officialdom. If the same family moves to New York City and goes about things the right way, it can receive as much as 5,000 dollars a year from the welfare bureaucracy.' But the family has, of course, to know how to go about things 'the right way'. What seems to the bureaucracy to be a simple calculation, may not seem so simple on the other side of the counter. Hence benefits may not be taken up, exemptions may not be claimed, treatment may not be asked for: family income supplements, school meals and psychiatric services in Aberfan all provide recent U.K. examples.

Being able to conceive of the counter is a further minimum condition. That means knowing where the counter is and what it is; knowing about and understanding the separation of house from office and knowing where the several offices which may be necessary to the completion of one bit of business (one case) are. Bureaucracy demands such separation but it has not always been achieved. Leonard Woolf, with his experience of Ceylon administration and life, commented on the open nature of South Asian houses and offices.[63]

It is indeed a characteristic of administration in poor societies that institutionalization of organizational bureaux becomes very complete; communication between them, and knowledge about each other becomes extraordinarily low. If that is true of the bureaucrats, how much worse the situation must be there for the potential applicants.[64] Attempting to complete an essentially simple transaction the applicant finds that his wants have been broken up quite incomprehensibly to him, though not at all vindictively on the part of the officials. The discreteness is too much.

BREAKDOWNS AND POSSIBILITIES

Queuing is two things: a solution to competition about the allocation of administered services by applicants meeting certain conditions of access, and a reconciliation at the point of service, of the competition about cognition, between the applicant and the rank and file servant. In the pure queuing situation access will mean waiting within limits by a limited number of people; and reconciliation is possible because no one and nothing else is present: the interaction and decisions are simple because the roles and interests have been reduced. Access can be made easier: by points systems, priorities, advertising and strategies of diffusion. Reconciliation can also be made easier by rules for disregards which assist the applicant to 'pass', and by the applicant's empathy, from his own experience, for the position of the man behind the grille.

Qualifications can make access and reconciliation more difficult: an institutionalization of the queue, its seeming to have benefits in itself, can make access too long and too slow a process. In desperate situations (as in Paustovsky's description, or in reports from Bengal refugee camps) people join queues to have something to do, somewhere to meet; it is, in a horribly attenuated sense, at least a sort of action. Reconciliation becomes more difficult if the disregards do not suit the applicant or he feels on display.

Qualifications in access or reconciliation can mean that the queue will break down. The access conditions (like running for the herrings) cannot be met or are not accepted; the officials are simply too remote; and elbowing is not queuing. Reconciliation is unlikely when other people and other data are present. The rank and file servant of the Supplementary Benefits Commission is asked to allocate to applicants more than his own salary; he becomes a rival, a competitor, not a bureaucratic allocator.[65] Or the service is itself stigmatized: an employment exchange manager in Birmingham is reported as saying that 'many people regard walking into an exchange as an admission of defeat. He says *the stigma attaches not so much to being without a job as to having one found for you*'[66] (my italics). Prejudice and pride make reconciliation unlikely. Ambiguities begin to enter: between passing and display, servant and competitor; the service may seem penal, the beneficiary a sufferer, the servant a master. The demand may change radically: something quite different is wanted. There may be no demand at all: the service is not taken up. Queuing cannot of itself provide salvation in disaster.

There must be types of social situation in which the structure is impossible: the access conditions can simply not be met, the reconciliation is impossible; the resources (like some degree of information) and role specialization (like the total absence of faction, ties or patronage) unavailable. Where queuing is impossible, there will be alternative structures. An individual may opt out altogether, or attempt to use a middle-man, brokerage, patron or corruption. Numbers may camp out patiently; others may form groups and riot: This may vary from small group raids and hold-ups, to larger, much less organized riots, or highly organized seiges.[67] The 'armed criminals' of West Africa are a special sort of applicant, not at all content to queue.

Apparent rioters, like people seizing land on the site of pueblos jovenes which ring Lima, may seem to the authorities to be 'invaders' led by 'professional troublemakers'; the more important point is that their needs for minimal housing are great, the conditions of access too demanding (not only to register and to queue, but also to pay back a state credit, to meet the cost of the plot and to do all the labouring) the numbers too many, the supply of service too little. Yet as one report from Lima appositely said, 'This impulse to seize land seemed to me to have behind it the hardly revolutionary urge to save and build a home.

'The Man from the Pru might almost have gone straight to work, seeing the squatters' signs saying: "We don't want to be given land gratis. We want to join a building co-operative." '[68]

That is the whole political significance of the relationships around access to service, where a structure like a queue might operate, or where it breaks down, is rejected or is impossible. These sorts of political outcome are one sort of alternative structure, where queuing cannot operate within its necessary limits. There is a breakthrough to other political domains. But a second limit is that queuing is meant to be occasional and marginal as well as relatively short-run. What happens when the applicant and his family has need after need, the most urgent, for administered services? He is then part of a special dependency group and is likely to be demoralized: his fear is, precisely, the ending of the queue relation; the outcome is a feeling and a perception of incompetence.[69] Thirdly, there are some groups who do have specific recognized needs which organization does not seem able to allocate them; hence a sort of duality, a 'broken back' in society between those who become applicants and those who consistently seem unable to do so. There is a withdrawal and a growth of apathy, a persistence of an existence discontinuity. Thus queuing difficulties coincide with three sorts of social discontinuities: the outsiders, the 'armed criminals' and the special dependency groups (who queue too much, so that what they are becomes what they queue for).

There are some situations where queuing is unnecessary. The crowd strolling through a park with many flower beds may see them in any order. There is no need for any member of the crowd to see one flower display before another. Hence there is a scene of agreeable drift rather than queuing. There are other situations where everything is done by queuing all too easily, as in a totally controlled institution like a prison camp in a terrorizing, totalitarian society. There the sanctions against 'queue jumping' are so overwhelming that there can be nothing but waiting and moving in line. This is the situation described by Solzhenitsyn in *A Day in the Life of Ivan Denisovitch*. What interests us are situations which lie between these two points. That is where queuing would be useful but does not seem to be very easy.

These situations are interesting because of what queuing is and what it demands. It is not just waiting and moving in line. That might also be a march, a demonstration or a ceremony. Indeed, people in societies who are used to and good at ceremonies may be particularly bad at queuing. Nor is queuing interesting because it indicates necessarily full rationality. It does not do so. It was not rational to queue for extermination in a Nazi camp but people did so. Queuing is more easily accepted where information is falsified. Queuing is interesting because of what its breakdown reveals about an individual, like stigma, or about a society, like discontinuities. It is interesting to see when queuing is impossible and how it gradually becomes more possible.

It was clearly not possible in, for example, the gaucho society of nineteenth-century Argentine described by Sarmiento: the barbaric, self-sufficient pastoral society where civic intervention through justice and taxation so rarely succeeded and so frequently failed, and where the only form of connection which men were used to or felt in need of was for drink, gambling and competitive fighting.[70]

Where there is a settled (like an arable) society, where there is a beginning of a feeling of a need for the services provided by the civil organization, where other forms of gathering become habitual, and there is a growing experience of access as with the party, the district administration, the big farm or the market town, then queuing begins to become possible. These are the most interesting situations after all. Queuing is not impossible but qualification, disintegration or breakdown is always likely. Here we see the symbolic appeal and the language of corruption. Here the comparative experience and variety of the life of queuing is likely to be revealing indeed.

Two broad conclusions emerge: the first is about the variety of ways in which the peculiar differences of applicants and rank and file servants can be reconciled and this sort of access arranged. The applicant might feel an actual but less than overwhelming requirement for the item of service. There must be some degree of correspondence between the perceptions on either side of the counter. That means some premises of continuity so that the applicant can exercise choice about when to turn up. On the other side of the counter the relations between the rank and file and the administrative maintenance men must not be upset by too constant a possibility of critical change or unanticipated dysfunctions of controls.

Getting to the head of the queue means a handling by the applicant of appropriate resources of time and understanding. At that moment of access other difficulties intervene. The disregards the applicant wishes to enjoy may be quite different from those which the rank and file servant must maintain. The career or adaptive society provides sufficient empathy to overcome this testing moment. To quote Baudclaire again, 'It might be pleasant to be alternatively a victim and an executioner.' But the discontinuities of under-development mean that some people are always victims and cannot imagine themselves on the other side at all. Nor can the rank and file easily manage either the disguised attentions and pseudo-actions of bureaucratic officials in some situations, or the balance of empathy with disregard of others: just sufficient understanding from just sufficient data. They are more likely to move uneasily behind the defences of complete formality since they must know all too well the risks of patronage, kinship and other ties that will threaten them as soon as they move outside.

The second conclusion is that just where queues can operate is a measure of a certain sort of continuity and civility in society. That is so for three evident reasons. The first reason is some correspondence about service between the politics and programmes and the particular items actually provided, between what people want and what they are given and between what they expect and what happens. So it is a matter of actual experience of stability and continuity also.

The second reason is a degree of objectivication and demystification of roles and their relationships. People can see and measure their own behaviour and that of others with whom they are involved in important but passing contacts. They will neither avoid nor miss nor fear the possibility of contact, nor be too submissive or too aggressive. It is altogether a matter of a capacity for measurement. Queuing means premises about continuity of service and then about an acceptance of a sort of civil order, but it should be tolerable and acceptable only as a relatively short-term experience and sacrifice. Where it is intolerably long, civil relationships have broken down.[71]

Thirdly, queuing means a tolerable balance of empathy and impersonality in the interactions of access, disregards and attention.

These may not be the most attractive aspects of order. They are the Spenlow-Jorkins ploys of civility. 'I should be happy myself to propose two months ... but I have a partner Mr. Jorkins.'[72] But it is surely preferable to those discontinuities which happen when the Indians of Brazil's north-east riot, or when in Britain a local authority actually spends public money in 'muck shifting exercises' to block exits and entrances to open land rather than exercise their statutory duties for travellers,[73] or when New Zealand manages to insult single women from Samoa queuing for immigration entry permits.[74] It is significant that these breakdowns in communication, about what sort of conditions can be regarded as objective or tolerable for access to a service, or about time and other resources, occur at such moments. That is when applicants can be regarded or feel themselves to be a group, exotic and possibly hostile, rather than a temporary category of individuals organized merely and for the nonce as a queue: people who simply want homes, or whatever.

A study of queuing seen as measurable but discrete relationships between applicants and rank and file officials at points of access to service, can provide an insight into certain aspects of integration in social situations, like changing agreements about time and other resources and widening experience of jobs, careers and organization. One can see queue relationships spreading and increasing. One can see them being qualified and improved as in a blood transfusion service. One can also see them breaking down, as in some societies which are discontinuous because of extreme wealth inequalities or in other ways. There some people can opt out of public services altogether while others can scarcely reach them, like private cars combined with hopeless public transport.

Queuing is the imposition and acceptance of reasonable conditions for access to a service by certain sorts of tolerable relationships between clients as applicants and officials as servants. It represents a rationalization of the distributive policy arena or the micro-decisions of a polity, the increase of mutuality or mutual non-interference in a society. It is a structure whose conditions, functions and occurrence can be researched.

NOTES

1 K. Burridge, *Mambu*, 1960, p. 260.
2 That is not to argue that in poor societies organization is easier: E. C. Banfield, *The Moral Basis of a Backward Society*, 1958, has exploded that myth.
3 Report of the departmental committee on the London taxicab trade, HMSO, October 1970.
4 E. S. Redford, *American Government and the Economy*, New York, 1965, pp. 58 following.
5 B. M. Villanueva, *The Barrio and Self-Government*, Manila, 1968, illustrates the distinction between the two domains: the politics of participating in 'barrio decision-making' and service relations, like access to and reception of services, payment of taxes, etc.; but clearly there are relations. Variations in barrio accessibility, or isolation, are related to voting turn-out: pp. 109-10.
6 Richard Critchfield, *Sketches of the Green Revolution*, Alicia Patterson Fund, 1970, p. 29.
7 Compare T. J. Lowi, 'American Business, Public Policy, Case Studies and Political Theory', *World Politics*, July 1964, pp. 673-715. The idea of the service relationship is like Lowi's 'distributive' policy arena as distinct from the regulatory and redistributive.
8 See P. M. Blau and W. R. Scott, *Formal Organisations*, London 1963, p. 77, Charles Perrow in J. G. March, *Handbook of Organisations*, N.Y. 1965, pp. 650-77. A. Etzioni, *Modern Organisations*, NY 1964, p. 94. I am grateful to John Ballard for the reference to the extremely enlightening cases in D. J. Murray, *The Work of the Administration in Nigeria*, Ife, and Murray's edition, *Nigerian Administration*. Berton Kaplan's special number of the Administrative Science Quarterly, Dec. 1968 is also useful. There are useful hints in Erving Goffman, *The Presentation of Self in Everyday Life*, NY, 1959.
9 E. Katz and B. Danet, *Petitions and Persuasive Appeals: A Study of Official-Client Relations*, 31 American Sociological Review, 1966 at p. 811 *ff*.
10 One of the many points in H. Garfinkle, *Studies of the Routine Grounds of Everyday Life, 11 Social Forces*, 1964, p. 225 *ff*.

11 Garfinkle. See also the work of Alfred Schutz, C. Kadushin, *Social Distance between Client and Professional*, American Journal of Sociology, 67, 1962, p. 517 *ff.* is interesting and is a way of relating this work to Simmel. M. Lefton and W. R. Rosengren, 'Organisations and Clients: Lateral and Longitudinal Dimensions', *American Sociological Review*, 31, 1966, p. 802 *ff.*, is an attempt at using time and space measurements, for a typology. Martin Landau's chapter in Dwight Waldo, ed., *Temporal Dimensions of Development Administration*, Duke, 1970, at pp. 80, 82 esp., is helpful.

12 L. Hough, *Modern Research for Administrative Decisions*, Englewood Cliffs NJ, 1970, p. 329.

13 See Hough, p. 331, on alternatives.

14 L. S. Hill, 'The Application of Queuing Theory to Span of Control', *Journal of Academy of Management*, 6, 1963, p. 58 *ff.*

15 I am grateful to Professor Ashford for referring me to the relevance of the discussions of excess political capacity by Eisenstadt, Simon, and others.

16 S. Eilon, 'Relationships between Controllers of the System', *Nature*, 18th July, 1970, pp. 233-238, for distinction of three types of system control affecting relationships at the point of access.

17 E. S. Redford, *Democracy in the Administrative State*, New York, 1969, pp. 94-5.

18 Leon Mann, 'Queue Culture: the Waiting Line as a Social System', *American Journal of Sociology*, Vol. 75, No. 3, November 1969, pp. 340-354. This is an excellent and welcome study which is limited from our point of view (a) because the material is explicitly about an exceptional, that is peculiarly long term institutionalized and publicized queue group, and (b) because it is not concerned with the queue as access, but with the queue as a group of waiting people. It is interesting that Mann sees that egalitarianism is an inadequate explanation for queue behaviour and that there are problems with other explanations by E. T. Hall, *The Silent Language*, New York, 1959, and *The Hidden Dimension*, New York, 1964 (as with a cultural value of orderliness).

19 I am grateful to Professor Graham for a reference to Charles O. Frake, 'The Ethnographic Study of Cognitive Systems', in Stephen A. Tyler, *Cognitive Anthropology*, NY, 1969, p. 28 *ff.*

20 Two papers by Professor Jeremy Boissevain are interesting in this respect (1) 'Patrons as Brokers', Dutch Sociological Association 6th/7th June, 1969, and (2) 'Networks, Brokers and Quasi-groups; Some Thoughts on the Place of Non-Groups in the Social Sciences'. In this respect, the queue dyad may be seen as that where the patron and broker become unnecessary as the client becomes the mere applicant.

21 Dudley Doust, *Sunday Times*, 13th September, 1970.

22 *Life of Samuel Johnson*, Everyman Edition, 1906, v. 1, p. 158.

23 Compare M. Albrow, *Bureaucracy*, 1970. *The Letters of Queen Victoria*, edited Benson and Esher, London, 1908, Vol. 1, pp. 106-108, provide an example in 1838. The young Queen Victoria, conscientiously reading the despatches from her (then admittedly on our modern lines limited number of) embassies, new to the throne and barely 18 had received from her ambassador to Prussia, a despatch containing the troubling word. It was her Foreign Secretary, Viscount Palmerston, who explained what it meant, in letter 25th Feb. 1838. It was something which would come (we see from his account) with irresponsibility, an increase in scale and particularly in impersonality in the conduct of

business and permanence of office. Some of this was paradoxical, since we would say that bureaucracy has increased precisely as a condition of responsibility, but his explanation was perceptive. The 1837 occurrence of queues is therefore remarkable.

24 H. de Motherlant, *The Girls*, Penguin Books, 1968, p. 160.

25 Julius A. Roth, *Timetables*, NY, 1963, pp. 48-53.

26 Anselm Strauss and others, *Psychiatric Ideologies and Institutions*, NY, 1964, esp. pp. 373-6 and p. 174.

27 Lefton and Rosengren, p. 803. Strauss, Goffman, Roth, as well as work by Gouldner and Glaser, are relevant here. See Glaser and Strauss, *Awareness of Dying*, Chicago, 1965.

28 *The Times*, London, 3rd September 1970, Leslie Williams, Secretary General Civil Service, National Council Staff Side. See also the study by Nigel Walker and the more recent studies conducted for the Fulton Committee.

29 W. Thesiger, *The Marsh Arabs*, Penguin 1967, p. 134.

30 *The Times*, London, 5th August 1970.

31 *Ibid.*, 22nd September, 1970. Colin Leys has suggested the comparison with Solzhenitsyn, Cancer Ward, II, where the hero, having his day after discharge, wanders into the store to find people queuing for something, but what? (see p. 531 of 1971 Penguin ed.). This was nearer to a camp or a riot than a queue; a 'flood', as it is called, where quite other factors than waiting time operated and where the limits had been exceeded. There was a much stricter queue at the railway station (p. 559). It was sophisticated, like the UK wartime bus queues, since it allows exceptions; but, like most queues, dehumanised and mechanical: the initial sympathy for the invalid is soon exhausted.

32 See B. B. Schaffer, 'Deadlock in Development Administration' in C. T. Leys, ed. *Politics and Change in Developing Countries*, Cambridge, 1969, p. 193.

33 *The Times*, 23rd September, 1970.

34 *Ibid.*, 7th September, 1970.

35 For a discussion of such uncertainties see Anselm Strauss, *Mirrors and Masks: a Search for Identity*, 1959.

36 *cf.* The sergeant cond. Herzen's passport, p. 13, n. 2.

37 Statement by the Board, *The Times*, 21st September 1970.

38 See Philip Selznick's discussion of co-optation in *TVA and the Grass Roots*, Berkeley, 1949.

39 *The Times*, 23rd September, 1970.

40 Dostoevsky, *The Devils*, part 1, p. 70, Penguin Books, 1953.

41 Alexander Herzen, *Memoirs*, edited London 1924, Vol. 3, pp. 2-4.

42 Weber, *Theory of Social and Economic Organisation*, New York, 1947, pp. 378-381. See Weber's Comparisons also between bureaucratic situations as in Egypt, Babylon and China with non-bureaucratic situations using prophecy, hierocracy and therefore ethical relationships and sanctions. *Ancient Judaism*, 1955, pp. 252-5 and 259.

43 See, for example, J. M. Flavier, *Doctor to the Barrios*, New Day Publishers, Quezon City, 1970.

44 Flavier, p. 101.

45 Ironically, this was first seen the mid-term poll in the southern and previously communist-dominated state of Kerala where the family of the former Maharaja of Cochin lost the use of special booths and had to queue like everyone else.

46 Schaffer, 'Deadlock in Development Administration', in C. T. Leys,

(ed.) *Politics and Change in Developing Societies*, 1969, p. 195.

47 *Ibid.*, p. 195-6.

48 Colin Leys, *Politics and Policies: An Essay on Politics in Acholi, Uganda 1962-1965*, Nairobi, 1967. Compare, Martin Staniland, Single Party Regimes and Political Change, in Colin Leys (ed.) *op. cit.*, p. 169.

49 Unpublished paper by K. Lambert and C. Filkin, Centre for Urban and Regional Studies, Birmingham University, Joint Conference, Institute of Race Relations, Royal Anthropological Institute, British Sociological Association, London, 1970.

50 E. Goffman, *Stigma*, Penguin Books, 1968.

51 Goffman, p. 195.

52 For the problems of time see Dwight Waldo (ed.), *Temporal Dimensions of Development Administration*, Duke University, 1970, particularly the essay by W. F. Ilchman, 'New Time in Old Clocks: Productivity Development and Comparative Public Administration', p. 135 and following. See also Ilchman and Uphoff on 'The Aggregate Propensity to Use Violence', for the tendency to riot (as against camping out) as alternative to queueing: Ilchman and N. T. Uphoff, *The Political Economy of Change*, 1969 p. 118. E. T. Hall's work is the most important.

53 Compare the sentiment of Arnold Toynbee's arguments about abolishing the use of private cars from 'the world city' and maximizing the use of queuing for public transport. *Cities on the Move*, Oxford 1970.

54 *The Times*, 27th August, 1970.

55 Chie Nakane, *Japanese Society*, Weidenfeld and Nicolson, London, 1970.

56 *The Adventures of Ytzchok Perlov*, New York, 1967.

57 K. Paustovsky, *Years of Hope*, pp. 39-40.

58 See de Montherlant's description of his protagonist's surrender of his queueing in the War Pensioners' Review Board offices in *The Girls*, Penguin Books, pp. 59-63.

59 P. M. Blau, *The Dynamics of Bureaucracy*, Chicago, 1955.

60 See Accident Services Review Committee, Great Britain and Ireland, Report of Working Party, Pilot Study, October, 1970. For a typical but fatal instance of breakdown at that point see report in *The Times*, London, September 28th, 1970.

61 *The Times*, 29th September, 1970.

62 *Out of Africa*, Penguin Books, 1954, pp. 31-2.

63 Leonard Woolf, *Downhill All The Way*, 1967, p. 23. The problem is two-fold: both being able to accept the separation and then being able to accept the necessity of moving between the several counters which then become necessary.

64. *Cf.* a recent novel by Ousmane Simbene *Le Mandat*: a study of the difficulties of the poor urban migrant in a French West African town, in finding his way from counter to counter or queue to queue.

65 Child Poverty Action Group evidence by Peter Adams to committee on Abuse of Supplementary Benefits, 1971.

66 *The Times*, 20th April, 1970.

67 There is a very large relevant literature. See esp., T. R. Gurr, *The Conditions of Civil Violence: First Tests of a Causal Model*, Center for International Studies, Princeton, 1967; H. Eckstein, ed., *Internal War*, NY, 1964: Douglas Ashford, 'Politics and Violence in Morocco', *Middle East Journal*, 13, 1959, Ilchman and Uphoff, *supra*.

68 *The Times*, 19th May, 1971.

69 *cf.* the relations between Apache Indians and the Bureau of Indian Affairs.
70 D. F. Sarmiento, *Life in the Argentine Republic in the Days of the Tyrants,* ed. New York, 1961, chapters II and III especially.
71 As indeed in a headline like '20,000 Kenya Asians queue for entry', *The Times,* December, 1970.
72 Charles Dickens, *David Copperfield,* p. 23.
73 The reference is to some experiences under the British Caravan Sites Act, April, 1970.
74 The condition was to undergo pregnancy tests. The National Council of Women, Western Samoa, wrote to the New Zealand Government protesting: 'They asked whether Samoan women should be tattooed on the forehead with the brand "tested" '. *The Times,* 29th September, 1970.

INDEX

INDEX